Sophia Studies in Cross-cultural Philosophy of Traditions and Cultures

Volume 11

The Sophia Studies in Cross-cultural Philosophy of Traditions and Cultures fosters critical and constructive engagement of the intellectual and philosophical dimensions—broadly construed—of religious and cultural traditions around the globe. The series invites innovative scholarship, including feminist, postmodern, and postcolonial approaches.

More information about the series at http://www.springer.com/series/8880

Sharad Deshpande

Editor

Philosophy in Colonial India

Editor
Sharad Deshpande
Indian Institute of Advanced Study
Shimla
India

ISSN 2211-1107   ISSN 2211-1115   (electronic)
Sophia Studies in Cross-cultural Philosophy of Traditions and Cultures
ISBN 978-81-322-2222-4   ISBN 978-81-322-2223-1   (eBook)
DOI 10.1007/978-81-322-2223-1

Library of Congress Control Number: 2015930505

Springer New Delhi Heidelberg New York Dordrecht London

Printed on acid-free paper

Springer (India) Pvt. Ltd. is part of Springer Science+Business Media
(www.springer.com)

To
The first generation modern Indian
philosophers on whose shoulders we stand

Foreword

Philosophy in Modern India

It is a challenging endeavour, by any measure, to try and delineate the defining yet changing characteristics of a particular field of knowledge. When such knowledge is crafted through hesitant transactions between unmistakably divergent world-views, the task of tracing its evolutionary trajectory becomes especially complicated. Ideas and concepts are fluid. They blend with each other and are, thereafter, often assimilated into a larger way of thinking. Even acts of resistance—by simply recognizing and engaging with incompatible viewpoints—create a space for interaction. Philosophical contestations are rarely conclusive, and the space thus created by indecisive disputation becomes home to future possibilities.

Not all ideas enter such conversations as equals. Earlier disagreements between diverse pre-colonial philosophies, too, occurred amidst unequal access to power and legitimacy. Colonial rule, however, initiated an altogether different kind of cultural interface. It posited western philosophy against a range of counter-positioned ideologies that came to be seen collectively as 'Indian' philosophy. It is possible to compare and contrast the two positions. But it appears rather unlikely that these completely divergent world-views permeated or agreed with each other in truly fundamental ways. While modern Indian philosophy responded to the challenge presented by western thought processes—and even assimilated several of the new ideas—its foundational principles remained rooted in older indigenous traditions. The rejoinder offered by Indian philosophers under colonial rule (both by those in academia and above all by those outside) grew out of a deeper exploration of their own situation: one wherein new doctrines from the west had begun to challenge the essentials of the Indian way of thinking and to propose new perspectives on prevailing human values.

Powerful ideological cross-currents sweeping across colonial India created fissures in the common ground occupied by Indian thinkers of all description. Intellectuals trained in modern educational methods became part of a relatively small group that attempted to engage seriously with western philosophy. On the other hand, an entire world of traditional Sanskritic scholarship chose to turn its back to the altered realities being forcefully fashioned by colonial rule. Not surprisingly, the latter's insularity practically ensured its marginalization from crucial new developments influencing thinking in India. Unfortunately, however, even the westernized Indian scholars failed to gain appropriate recognition amongst western philosophers. Why did this happen? Were they not creative and self-reflexive enough? Was their subordinate position a reason for the insensitivity with which their work was treated? Did the apparent alienation from their roots make their endeavour a soulless enterprise? These essays which were originally presented at a study week held at the Indian Institute of Advanced Study, Shimla, seek to address these and other similar questions.

Professor Sharad Deshpande has very diligently edited this volume. On behalf of the Institute, I wish to acknowledge with gratitude the debt that is owed to him on this account. To use his words, it is hoped that these essays will 'initiate a critical engagement' with the work of the leading modern Indian philosophers who responded to western ideas, and that it would help recover several of the 'insights that may have gone unnoticed.' If this does indeed happen, the Indian Institute of Advanced Study, in publishing these essays, would have made an important contribution and taken yet another step towards justifying the rationale for which it was established.

Chetan Singh
Director
Indian Institute of Advanced Study

Shimla

Acknowledgments

This anthology has its impetus in the study week held at the Indian Institute of Advanced Study, Shimla in October 2009. Professor Peter Ronald DeSouza, the then Director, IIAS, Shimla, facilitated this project and provided generous assistance at its early stage. Professor Chetan Singh, the present Director, extended the same attention to the demands of this project to see the light of the day. But for their nurturance and patience, this project would not have culminated into its present form. Thanking them formally would fall much short of the deep sense of gratitude.

The administrative staff of IIAS, particularly Dr. Prem Chand, Mr. Shashank Thakur and Dr. Debarshi Sen, need special mention for their diligent cooperation at various stages of publication of this volume.

Last but not the least, thanks to the contributors of this volume for lending credibility to this volume by their erudite and insightful contributions.

Shimla   Sharad Deshpande

Contents

Contributors

Tathagata Biswas School of Education, Azim Premji University, Bengaluru, India

Nirmalya Narayan Chakraborty Department of Philosophy, Rabindra Bharati University, Kolkata, India

Amita Chatterjee Jadavpur University, Kolkata, India

Sharad Deshpande Indian Institute of Advanced Study, Shimla, India

P.G. Jung Department of Humanities and Social Sciences, Indian Institute of Technology Bombay, Mumbai, India

Mangesh Kulkarni Department of Politics and Public Administration, Savitribai Phule Pune University, Pune, India

S.G. Kulkarni Department of Philosophy, Central University of Hyderabad, Hyderabad, India

Kanchana Mahadevan Department of Philosophy, Mumbai University, Mumbai, India

Shefali Moitra Formerly Department of Philosophy, Jadavpur University, Kolkata, India

Mohini Mullick Formerly Department of Humanities and Social Sciences, Indian Institute of Technology Kanpur, Kanpur, India

V. Sanil Department of Humanities and Social Sciences, Indian Institute of Technology Delhi, Delhi, India

Proyash Sarkar Department of Philosophy, Jadavpur University, Kolkata, India

Chapter 1
Introduction—Modern Indian Philosophy:
From Colonialism to Cosmopolitanism

Sharad Deshpande

The issue of colonialism and the emergence of new identities in traditional Indian society have engaged the critical attention of scholars from diverse fields of inquiry such as history, sociology, politics, as well as religious and subaltern studies. However, to a considerable extent, the emergence of 'modern' Indian philosophy—sometimes characterized as "Anglophone Indian philosophy"[1]—situating it in a certain historical context, in contrast to the so-called traditional Indian philosophy under the rubric of *darśana-śāstra* or *adhyātma-vidyā* remains an unexplored area of critical inquiry. This anthology intends to fill the lacuna, at least to some extent, by addressing the intricate relationship between history, freedom and thought in the shadow of colonialism by focusing on the writings of modern Indian philosophers during the colonial period, specifically from the late 19th century through the middle of the 20th century. It examines the emergence and the consequent role that academic philosophy played in the development of cross-cultural philosophy and the cosmopolitan consciousness in colonial India. Some of the essays included in this anthology revisit the first generation modern Indian academic philosophers such as Brajendra Nath Seal (1864–1938), Hiralal Haldar (1865–1942), Krishna Chandra Bhattacharyya (1875–1949), Ghanshamdas Ratanmal Malkani (1892–1977), Rasvihary Das (1894–1973), and Ghanshyam Nevandram Mathrani (1914–1994) as well as the so-called non-academic philosophers such as Bankimchandra Chattopadhyaya (1838–1894), Rabindranath Tagore (1861–1941), and Shankar Ramachandra Rajwade (1879–1952) by undertaking a first-hand reading of some of their writings. This list is representative and not

---

[1] The expression 'Anglophone Indian philosophy' refers to the philosophical writings of Indian philosophers of the late 19th and early 20th century in colonial India who used English as the chief medium of expression. But this characterization need not be taken as a necessary condition for Indian philosophy being 'modern.'

S. Deshpande (✉)
Indian Institute of Advanced Study, Shimla, India
e-mail: sharad.unipune@gmail.com

© Indian Institute of Advanced Study 2015   1
S. Deshpande (ed.), *Philosophy in Colonial India*, Sophia Studies in Cross-cultural
Philosophy of Traditions and Cultures 11, DOI 10.1007/978-81-322-2223-1_1

exhaustive.[2] But as the contributors to this volume suggest, the writings of these philosophers not only reveal their thorough acquaintance with the world of ideas of the West but also the preparedness to take philosophical positions and participate in philosophical debates that were current particularly in Anglo-German philosophy of the West during the latter part of the 19th century. However, this participation is not without struggle when it comes to assimilate the distinctively Western concepts and world-views into their own as is evident in the writings of most of these philosophers.

1.1 Towards Interculturality

The Indian reception of the West not only marks the adoption and assimilation of the European philosophical tradition comprising various concepts, doctrines, and ways of thinking but also, and perhaps more importantly, the reinterpretation of indigenous concepts and ways of thinking in the light of what was so assimilated. To understand the nature of this reinterpretation, the contributors to this volume seek to strike a balance between (a) the narrative content, needed to form an adequate perspective on the life and works of modern Indian philosophers; (b) theoretical issues involved in comprehending the multifaceted phenomenon of colonialism; and (c) the specific philosophical issues that engaged modern Indian philosophers during the colonial period. Some of these essays highlight the specific issues raised by the professional and the so-called non-academic philosophers. These issues concern the search for identity through education and response to the science–culture of the West; local and global identities; the possibility of doing intercultural philosophy, for instance, by appropriating Mill's utilitarian doctrine with its notions of utility and justice for the reconstruction of Hindu ethics; the assimilation and also the overcoming of Hegelian and Kantian idealism and the initial impact of utilitarianism; attempts at the synthesis with classical Vedāntic doctrines of self, freedom, and the non-dual nature of ultimate reality; and the significance of modern Indian philosophers' engagement with the nature of self for contemporary debates in the philosophy of mind. Some of the core disciplinary issues that are raised in these essays include the appropriate mode of doing comparative philosophy. Some of these essays highlight yet another set of theoretical issues such as the structure of thought, context, and history, the interaction between the traditional system of knowledge and the one introduced by the colonial rulers, and the Indian response to modern science and technology and through it to colonialism itself as structured in three principle reactions to modern science ranging from its unqualified to qualified acceptance and rejection.

It needs to be acknowledged right at the outset that nomenclatures such as 'Indian philosophy' and 'modern Indian philosophy' gesture towards the subtext underlying

---

[2] Some omissions—to mention a few, Sri Aurobindo (1872–1950), Muhammad Iqbal (1877–1938), R.D. Ranade (1886–1957), and S. Radhakrishnan (1888–1975) can only be regretted.

the introduction of modern Western education as also a much wider, complex, and two-way traffic between India and Europe in terms of their respective *life-worlds* from the 16th century onwards. The subtext invites "the hermeneutical task of understanding the past in terms of the present, of translating from one age to another, and of the impingement of one tradition upon another" (Mehta 1974: 59–60). The term 'colonial period' with its political connotation refers to the two phases of a historical period from 1601 to 1857, i.e. the period when East India Company began gaining political control through trade and conquest in different parts of Indian subcontinent till the first war of Indian Independence in 1857 and from 1858 to 1947, i.e. the period in which the British Crown took complete political control of India from the East India Company, and thus, India officially becoming a British Colony till 1947 when India achieved full political freedom.[3] However, the mutual exposure between India and the West that inaugurated Indian modernity dates back to the 16th century and even earlier, and cover such diverse fields as philosophy, religion, art, architecture, science, and technology. This two-way reception was initially facilitated by the writings of the Christian missionaries of the 17th and 18th centuries and later by the scholarly work of Orientalists and Indologists. In these writings, what is conveniently labelled as 'Indian philosophy' turns out to be a generic term that clubbed together six major and some minor *darśanas*, often translated as 'schools' or 'systems' of the speculative thought of the Hindus, Buddhists, Jainas, and even the Heretics. The nomenclature 'Indian philosophy' in effect, replaces the plurality of *darśanas* that embodied the diverse views on the nature of ultimate reality. Significantly, the prefix 'Indian' in the nomenclature 'Indian philosophy' is not a simple geographical marker. It illustrates, in part, the way Europeans have received Indian thought by way of translation, codification, and interpretation of various Hindu, Buddhist, or the Jaina metaphysico-religious texts. For missionaries such as Roberto Nobili (1577–1656), the translation and the hermeneutic understanding of Hindu religious texts were essential prerequisite for "possibility of understanding and being understood" while spreading the Christian faith among the Hindus (Halbfass 1990: 43). This was to be done by highlighting the ideas and ideals which are supposedly shared by Christianity and Hinduism. For the Orientalists and Indologists, on the other hand, understanding Indian thought was essential for the scientific exploration and objectification of India's past. Thus, for the missionaries and indologists, the term 'Indian philosophy' refers primarily to the philosophical content expressed through various concepts, doctrines, and world-views found in religious and other texts in Indian tradition. Max Müller's 50-volume *The Sacred Books of the East* (Müller 1879) proved to be a major source for several Western thinkers and philosophers of the colonial period to explore the sacred texts of Hinduism including the Upaniṣadas, Buddhism, Jainism, and also Taoism, Zoroastrianism, Confucianism, and Islam. Besides Max Müller, there are a number of European Indologists and Orientalists who have created a massive body of scholarly works by

---

[3] It was only in terms of its political context that this reception was subjected to such binaries as east–west, traditional–modern, religious–secular, rational–spiritual, scientific–occult, and colonial–national.

translating important texts from Indian tradition. The translations of Bhartṛhari's *Śatakas* and *Ritusamhāra* by Peter von Bohlen in 1835 and 1840, *The Laws of Manu* by Otto von Böhtlingk in 1886, *Śukranitisāra* and *Vāgvaijayantikośa* by Gustav Oppert in 1882 and 1893, *Panchatantra* by Johannes Hertel in 1912, Paul Duessen's translation of 60 *Upaniṣadas* in 1897 and of *Śaṃkara*'s *Brahmasūtrabhāṣya* in 1883, and *Amarkośa* by Henry Thomas Colebrooke in 1808 are some of the well-known examples.

1.2 The Politics of Nomenclature

The nomenclature 'Indian philosophy' is not politically neutral. The term 'Indian'—or for that matter 'African' or 'Chinese'—prefixed to 'philosophy' is usually taken to be a qualifier for philosophies that have flourished outside Europe. However, for the philosophical thought that flourished in Greece, from which the European philosophers and their philosophies claim ancestry, no such qualifier is thought to be necessary by the European historians of philosophy. European philosophy is, by definition, a philosophy 'proper', whereas philosophies that flourished outside Europe are demarcated with some qualifications that draw a boundary between European philosophies and those of the rest of the world. Thus, within the colonial context, such qualifiers express a doubt as to whether non-European civilizations have or can have, even in principle, a concept of philosophy comparable to the one that the European civilization claims to be its own. Indeed, this was a matter of doubt for the European historians of philosophy in the 19th and the early 20th century. It was believed that the non-European civilizations have formed their conception of philosophy by adopting the one that was distinctly European. In fact, it was in this adoption that the non-European civilizations could meaningfully reinterpret their own ways of thinking *as* philosophy. Such beliefs, *inter alia*, have given rise to the problem of equivalence—whether philological, semantic, and conceptual—between the Western conception of philosophy as *logos* and Indian conceptions of *ānvīkṣikī* (review or critical examination), *darśana* (derived from the root '*dṛś*', etymologically 'to see', a visual perception, but is taken in this context as a 'standpoint', or the 'synoptic or spiritual vision or experience', or 'seeing within' or 'direct realization of truth'), and *dharma* (as connected with the means for realizing the ultimate goals of human life as conceived by different *darśanas*).[4] It was one of the major preoccupations of indological scholarship to find out the equivalence between the Western; more specifically, the Greek conception of philosophy as *logos*, i.e. a reasoned discourse; or more generally, as autonomous rational inquiry on the one hand, and the Indian conceptions of *ānvīkṣikī*, *darśana*, and *dharma* on the other. Some, like Jakobi, find the

---

[4] Reference to *dharma* opens up the issue of the relationship between four *pūrūṣārthas* (goals of human life) and *darśana*. It is stated that '*Artha* and *Kāma* do not fall under the field of philosophy' (Bhattacharyya 1982: 226).

term *ānvīkṣikī* as used by Kautilya in his *Arthaśāstra*, to be equivalent to the Western concept of philosophy, i.e. *logos*, which is essentially analytical, discursive, and objective. But some like Paul Hacker repudiate this view saying that Indians might have had the concept of philosophy, but they did not have a corresponding *word* which could express that concept fully and exclusively (Halbfass 1990: 285). This amounts to saying that philosophy 'proper' is possible only with "a certain level of reflexivity and of explicit self-positing" (Halbfass 1990). Hacker's statement implies that Indians could engage themselves in philosophical reflections without reflexivity; without linguistic or conceptual self-awareness.[5] Such readings can be linked to the deep-rooted bias in the thinking of the modern West. Recent critics of modern Western thinking argue that it introduces 'a system of visible and invisible distinctions'—the latter being established 'through radical lines' that divide social reality into two realms, the realm of 'this side of the line' and the realm of "the other side of the line" (de Sousa Santos 2007: 45). The division is a result of the abyssal thinking of the West which treats the non-Western forms of thinking in an abyssal way. It is further argued that

> In the field of knowledge, abyssal thinking consists in granting to modern science the monopoly of the universal distinction between true and false, to the detriment of two alternative bodies of knowledge: philosophy and theology. The exclusionary character of this monopoly is at the core of modern epistemological disputes between the scientific and the non-scientific forms of truth (de Sousa Santos 2007: 47).

In the context of the European encounter with the Orient, particularly with India, the realm of 'this side of line' will be the realm of the 'subject', i.e. the knowledge of Westerners—Indologists and Orientalists—and 'the other side of the line' will be the realm of the 'object', i.e. indigenous traditions of thought.

In the Indian context, the exclusion of the so-called non-scientific from the 'scientific' can be seen as operating in the ways in which the study of Sanskrit as the medium of knowledge was reformed on the ideals of Western critical thinking. The study of Sanskrit as the medium of knowledge became historical, comparative, and philological. The study of Sanskrit did not decline under colonial rule but the type of study undertaken by pandit was devalued (Seth 2008: 175). This devaluation resulted into the change of focus of governmental patronage to the study of Sanskrit. It was initially an encouragement to preserve both the ancient language and the knowledge it preserved, but under the new dispensation, the learning of Sanskrit was made possible through the medium of Western methods of research and in relation to modern ideas. The new class of Indologists, as opposed to the traditional *paṇḍits*, was an outcome of this transition. Sir Ramakrishna Gopal Bhandarkar (1837–1925) the foremost pioneer of scientific Orientology in India[6] was the first 'modern' Indian professor of Sanskrit,

---

[5] Halbfass accepts that Indians had philosophy which is comparable to the philosophy in the West. But he does not explicitly admit that Indian concept of *ānvīkṣikī* is a conceptual equivalent of Western concept of *philosophy*.

[6] The Bhandarkar Oriental Research Institute was founded in his honour in Pune, India. The Institute was munificently aided by Sir Ratan and Sir Dorabji Tata and was inaugurated by Lord Willingdon, the Governor of Bombay on 6th July 1917.

who was not trained as a *paṇḍit* but was graduated from Bombay university and taught Sanskrit in Deccan College in Poona which were by all standards institutions modelled on the system of Western education. In his presidential address to the first All India Oriental Conference held in November 1919, Bhandarkar refers to the body of Orientalists which consists of "those educated as *Paṇḍits* of the old school" and those "who have been studying the literature of the country and the inscriptions and the antiquities which are found scattered in the different provinces by the application of critical and comparative method" (Bhandarkar 1920: 13). As regards the class of *paṇḍits*, he mentions the traditional manner in which Vyākaraṇa and Nyāya are studied and argues that the "whole learning has become extremely artificial" (Bhandarkar 1920: 13). As regards the critical and comparative method, which is primarily of European origin, he insists that "Our aim, therefore, should be to closely observe the manner in which the study is carried on by European scholars and adopt such of their methods as recommend themselves to our awakened intellect" (Bhandarkar 1920: 15–16).[7] The consequence of this insistence on the critical and comparative approach to the study of ancient Indian intellectual traditions and the antiquities turned out to be paradoxical. "Indology advanced in direct proportion to the slow demise of once-living Sanskrit intellectual tradition" (Seth 2008: 176).

1.3 The Orientalist Bias

The Orientalist bias against the non-Western forms of knowledge and rationality resulted in the neglect of vibrant traditions of philosophical reflections in diverse fields of human experience, which existed in India before and even during the colonial period. Consequently, the practicing grammarians, logicians, and metaphysicians were treated as mere narrators of classical texts, as 'local informants', while the vibrant conceptual schemes, still alive all over the country, were treated as if they were dead. The vibrant philosophical engagement among the *Naiyāyikas* and the *Vedāntins* or among the *Mimāṃsakas* was seen as part of Hindu religious discourse. This identification of philosophical schools and the philosophical discourse with religious discourse is to be seen on the background of their separation that took place in Renaissance and the post-Renaissance Europe. In India, the separation between the philosophical and the religious might have existed in the Upaniṣadic or in the classical period as is evident in the manner in which the Upaniṣadas and the classical *darśanas* conduct inquiries into metaphysical questions. But in the later period, this distinction must have got blurred due to the

---

[7] Thus, by following the critical and comparative method, Bhandarkar was able to compare the Sāṃkhya idealism of Kapilamūni with that of Fichte, a German Idealist (1762–1814) in terms of subjectivity and consciousness. But as far as the critical aspect goes, Bhandarkar also highlights the difference between Kapilamūni and Fichte saying that the former was concerned with liberation of soul from its fetters, while the latter was concerned with the explanation of the world. (Bhandarkar 1919: 71).

emergence and spread of pan-Indian devotional Bhakti movement from the 7th century till the 15th century and also due to the impact of Sufism.[8] The erasure of the boundary between philosophy and religion through Bhakti movement gave rise to a unique category, i.e. 'saint–philosopher' and to the subsequent ongoing debate whether saints such as Jñāneśwara and Tukāram are philosophers.

The view that philosophy in India was part of religious discourse found its legitimation in Max Müller's view, which Bal Gangadhar Tilak approvingly quotes in the editorial, titled '*Moksha Müller Bhaṭṭānchā Vedānta*' (Max Müller's Vedānta) that "Whether religion leads to philosophy or philosophy to religion, in India the two are inseparable" (Tilak 1894).[9] Müller's repeated assertions that philosophy and religion are not separable from one another can be traced back to his commitment to a Christian standpoint throughout his life, and though in his later career, he became more receptive towards Vedānta, his idea of Vedānta, in effect, remained that of a "Christian Vedānta" (Halbfass 1990: 82). The Orientalist discourse thus turned the rigorous philosophical inquiry undertaken by the indigenous *darśana* tradition into religious and philological. On the other hand, Indologists like Friedrich Creuzer (1771–1858) saw Indian civilization as 'archaic' expressing its "religious knowledge in 'symbolic' and 'mythic' rather than rational and discursive forms" (Inden 1986: 431).

The above-mentioned issue of the equivalence between Indian and Western conceptions of philosophy is rooted in such biases. However, it is doubtful whether the notion of strict equivalence is available in discourses other than logic and mathematics. The strict equivalence holds between two concepts which can be substituted for one another without the loss of meaning as in the case of 'brother' and 'male sibling.' But there cannot be a strict equivalence between any two concepts in cultural or religious domains, either within the same culture or across cultures. This being the case, what needs to be distinguished is the *difference* between two concepts being held as equivalent to one another; as in the case of expressions in mathematics or logic, and two concepts being held as rough or tentative approximations of one another; as in the case of concepts rooted in different cultural and religious settings such as 'religion' and '*dharma*' or between the Greek *Eudaimonia* and Indian *Pūrūṣārtha*. In such cases, translating the meaning of one concept into the other is always a rough approximation. In rough approximations, as in the case of comparing different hues

---

[8] It is commonly accepted that individualism and nationalism are the two 'modern' values the traditional Indian society was exposed to after coming into contact with Europeans. But the contribution of the Bhakti movement to the emergence of the value of individualism in terms of equality among men and even women is significant, since it acted as a 'great leveler on the spiritual plane' (Patankar 2014: 183). The assimilation of individualism as a social value also led to the emergence of social movements.

[9] The editorial appeared on 4 September 1894 in *Kesari*, the newspaper Tilak used to edit and publish from Pune. Tilak's mention of Max Müller as 'Moksha Müller Bhaṭṭa' is in line with Radhakant Deb (the compiler of *Śabdakalpadruma*) who too mentions Max Müller as 'German Bhaṭṭa', elevating him from being a *mlenchha* (an uncivilized outsider) to the status of a venerated Brahmin because of Max Müller's six-volume critical edition of the *Ṛgveda* with Sāyana's commentary.

of a particular colour, one side of the proposed equivalence cannot be held as immutable and the other as changeable. Given the distinction between the strict equivalence and loose or tentative approximation, the question is not "whether the Indian tradition possessed a concept identical with the Western concept of philosophy. The question is whether the Indian tradition has a concept which closely approximates to the Western concept of philosophy" (Gokhale 2012: 151–160). There is no specific word in Sanskrit which is an exact equivalent of the Greek *logos*. Similarly, Arabic too does not have an exact equivalent, and "owing to the influence of Greek civilization, the Greek ... 'philosophia' is now an Arabic term" (Murti 1965: 132). Similarly, and equally importantly, the concept of philosophy itself has undergone radical changes in the history of Western philosophy. So the issue of equivalence between the Western and the Indian conceptions of philosophy is either false or methodologically misconceived since there is no fixed concept of philosophy on either side. More importantly, the issue at stake is about the ideal of rationality as conceived from within and from outside the cultural setting of any society and this issue cannot be relegated to the relativism debate. The ideal of rationality as conceived from *within* the socio-cultural-religious framework of any given society has its own method of validation which is internally available to the members of that society. Judged from the outside, the validity of this ideal of rationality will always lack the internal ground available to the members of that society whose ideal of rationality is being critiqued. Explorations into these deeper issues expose the myth; or a set of myths, concerning the so-called equivalence between conceptions of philosophy across the cultures, and especially so in the colonial context, as also the myth about any particular conception of philosophy as privileged *vis-à-vis* the others.

1.4 Tradition and Transformation

Whereas 'Indian philosophy' is a generic term, a colonial construct, what is labelled as "'modern' Indian philosophy", registers a variety of Indian responses with their distinctive cultural background to Western philosophical traditions and the world-views they express. The prefix 'modern' in this nomenclature suggests the element of 'newness' which is not present in the traditional cast of ideas. But how is the 'newness' of modernity related to tradition? If modernity is judged essentially in terms of newness of ideas or doctrines or world-views, then it completely denounces the traditional set of ideas, doctrines, and world-views. Early 17th century European philosophy is supposed to have experienced this kind of modernity, i.e. something which was claimed to be is absolutely new in virtue of a total rejection of the past as in the works of Francis Bacon and René Descartes. But this standard picture, as Ganeri argues, "... radically simplifies the complex ways in which the moderns drew upon the ancients" (Ganeri 2014: 2). This standard picture was not a true picture because the history of ideas, whether of Western or of Indian origin, is always a stream of discontinuous continuities. What appears to be discontinuous with tradition is in fact its reconfiguration and transformation. Thus, the emergence of modernity is to be seen in relation to the tradition itself, i.e. modernity as critical reflection over the past but at the same time taking the past as a source of insight for the pursuit of truth. In this sense, both in Europe and in India, there have been modern philosophers whose 'new' philosophy drew significantly from their own traditions.[10] But if we pursue this line of argument, then the historical question—i.e. *when* a given tradition become 'modern', or more specifically, *when* Indian philosophy began experiencing modernity—loses much of its significance since in an important sense, as this argument suggests that modernity is always continuous with tradition.

However, the question persists, especially when it is raised in the context of India's coming into contact with the West. The received opinion is that modernity entered in the Indian way of life and intellectual traditions when India encountered the West exclusively under colonial condition. More specifically, it marks the response of the English-educated intellectuals—the anglophone Indian philosophers—of the 19th and early 20th centuries.[11] However, this response has its own history. It was first materialized in the form of translations of English texts, both literary and philosophical, in Sanskrit and later in regional languages. This is because Sanskrit was still the main language of expression of literary and cognitive enterprise. Some of the earliest translations and independent treatises in Sanskrit cited by Hiralal Shukla include Vinayak Bhaṭṭ's history of England written in Sanskrit and titled *Āngleya-Chandrikā* and *Ītihāsatamomani* written in 1891 and 1813, respectively, and published from Madras. Shrishaila Dikshit translated Shakespeare's *Comedy of Errors* as *Bhrāntivilāsam*, and P.K. Kalyana Rama Shastri's translated Shakespeare's *The Rape of Lucrece* as *Kanakalatā*. Madhusudan Tarkālankār translated M.W. Wollaston's *Principles of English Grammar for the use of Natives of India* as *Inglandiya Vyākaraṇasāra* in 1835. A similar book on English grammar appeared from Varanasi in 1847 under the title *Inglandiya Vyākaraṇam*. But more interesting are the Sanskrit translations of Hutton's *A Course of Mathematics* under the title *Kshetra-tatva-dipikā* by E. Ramaswamy in 1823 and published from Bangalore and Francis Bacon's *Novum Organum* as *Baconiyasūtra Vyākhyānam* by Pandit Vitthal of Varanasi in 1852. During the same period, Berkeley's *Principles of Human Knowledge* was translated under the title *Jñāna-Siddhānta-Chandrikā*, and Locke's *Essay Concerning Human Understanding* was translated under the title *Mānaviya-jñānavishayak-shastra*.[12] (Shukla 1989: 20–21, 33). Around 1860, Krishnashastri Chiplonkar wrote Socrates's biography in Marathi.

Assimilating European ways of thinking in terms of a new set of philosophical concepts and doctrines, this response sought to reinterpret indigenous concepts and

---

[10] In Indian context, Ganeri documents the works of several philosophers and argues that indigenous early modernity in *navya-nyāya* and other schools of Indian philosophy was taking place from the 13th century till the end of the 18th century (Ganeri 2014: 4–5).

[11] But referring to the travel accounts of François Bernier, a French philosopher and a court physician of Dārā Shukoh and Aurangzeb, Jonardon Ganeri argues that the Varanasi *paṇḍits* in the early 1660s were aware of the works of Descartes, a key figure in early Enlightenment, through Persian translations (Ganeri 2014: 13–14).

[12] Contrary to the general impression that the tradition of learning in Sanskrit had become stale and was not open to new ideas, these and other translations indicate that the tradition of learning in Sanskrit was in fact receptive to new ideas coming from the West. Hiralal Shukla describes this period as *Anūvāda Yuga*, 'the age of translation' (Shukla 1989: 69).

ways of thinking in the light of what was assimilated.[13] Given the historical conditions which governed the Indian response to European modernity and its technological and scientific culture, modern Indian philosophy as a response was bound to be
uneven; ranging from outright rejection and indifference to the whole-hearted
acceptance of the Western modes of thinking and practice. Going beyond the academia, this response came from religious, social, and political reformers who were,
to use a popular phrase, 'makers of modern India': Ram Mohan Roy (1772–1833),
Ishwar Chandra Vidyasagar (1820–1891), Dayananda Saraswati (1824–1883),
Keshab Chandra Sen (1838–1884), Bankimchandra Chattopadhyaya (1838–1894),
Mahatma Jotiba Phule (1827–1890), Mahadev Govind Ranade (1842–1901), Bal
Gangadhar Tilak (1856–1920), Gopal Ganesh Agarkar (1856–1895), Rabindranath
Tagore (1861–1941), Gopal Krishna Gokhale (1866–1915), Swami Vivekananda
(1863–1902), and others. These makers of modern India were primarily religious
and social reformers engaged actively in various reform movements, and being so,
they were not so much interested in the pursuit of philosophy per se or with philosophy as academic discipline. They were more attracted to philosophical doctrines,
views, and ideas which they thought were needed to bring about the desired reforms
in political, social, and religious spheres. Therefore, what appealed them were the
philosophies of Auguste Comte, Herbert Spencer, John Locke, John Stuart Mill, and
Thomas Reid. It is through them that they were attracted to a new set of values of
liberty, individual freedom, women's rights, value of education, and rational attitude.
The influences of these philosophers were mixed and of varied combinations of utilitarianism, agnosticism, and evolutionism.

Though these makers of modern India accepted "the broad framework of ancient
Indian thought as articulated mainly in the Upaniṣadas, and Gītā, they did not allow
themselves to be restricted to the groove of accepted doctrine" (Deshpande 1997: xv).
Their encounter, as also of those such as Jotiba Phule who denounced the Vedic tradition, "with the Western ideas and ideals was essentially in terms of their own exposition
of the traditional texts and of the tradition itself. The way they apprehended their own
tradition became the basis of their life's mission" (Deshpande 1997: ibid). Thus, the term
'modern Indian philosophy' acquires a much wider and richer meaning in such nomenclatures as 'modern Indian thought', or even 'contemporary Indian philosophy.' These
latter nomenclatures are operative more in the wider public domains than the restricted
academic one. These nomenclatures are often used to refer to what is called the Indian
Renaissance. In fact, the above-mentioned reformers, visionaries, and national founding
figures were depicted as 'philosophers' and philosophy itself was projected as a 'vehicle
of national self-affirmation' during the colonial period (Halbfass 1990: 262).

As the term 'modern Indian philosophy' acquires wider meaning, it also, in a
restrictive sense, records the way English-educated professional Indian philosophers

---

[13] In this understanding, especially in the context of philosophy, the concept of *darśana* serves
as 'a terminological device' to appropriate the Western concept of philosophy and its discursive
and objective spirit of inquiry but at the same time asserting the uniqueness of the *darśana* conception of Indian philosophy as a way of life, as an intuitive realization of the highest reality
(Halbfass 1990: 263).

of the late 19th and early 20th centuries responded to their European counterparts in terms of assimilating various philosophical concepts and world-views offered by Western philosophers. The nature of this assimilation and the efforts to negotiate with these concepts and the world-views in terms of the indigenous ones is an extremely complex phenomenon which is yet to be scrutinized with historical understanding and hermeneutic sensitivity. The term 'modern Indian philosophy' in its wider as well as restrictive sense therefore stands for a two-way hermeneutic exercise of understanding the 'other' and by implication, one's own self-understanding. In this hermeneutic exercise, modern Indian philosophers sought to reinvent Indian philosophy in relation to (a) science and utilitarianism, which was distinctly Western, and (b) spiritualism and mysticism, which was distinctly Indian. The focus of this reinvention, in between these two strands, was the nature of self in terms of self as worldly agency and self as freedom.

1.5 Philosophy in the Academia

As the term 'modern Indian philosophy' poses the problem of tradition and modernity, the terms 'Indian philosopher' or 'modern Indian philosopher' pose a much deeper problem of identity than that of identification. The issue at stake is whether a person of Indian origin engaged exclusively with Indian philosophy; i.e. the *Vedas*, the *Upaniṣadas*, or the *Darśanas*, i.e. six classical systems, or a person of Indian origin engaged with philosophy *qua* philosophy irrespective of its geographical and cultural markers is called an Indian philosopher. This indeed is a political issue. But since any philosophical activity would normally be grounded in some tradition or the other, the 'modern Indian philosopher'; by virtue of his being an Indian, will be expected to do philosophy in the setting of the traditions available to him. On this assumption, one would think that "the philosophizing of a modern Indian will not be really Indian unless it is of a piece with some classical Indian Tradition or traditions…" (Prasad 1983: 293). Kalidas Bhattacharyya, in his Editorial Note to *Recent Indian Philosophy*, which is a collection of 'a fairly good number of excellent papers' from the proceedings of the first decade of Indian Philosophical Congress (1925–1934), in fact goes on to say that

> It is unfortunate that though the thinkers whose papers are published in this volume are all Indian and though for that reason we ought to have called their thinking *Indian Philosophy* we cannot do that … because … the living continuity of their philosophical thinking with the old philosophical traditions was snapped and … it has not been completely restored even today. (Bhattacharyya 1963: viii)

But the obligation to engage only with Indian philosophy if one is an Indian by origin is to be weighed against the alleged *Indianness* of Indian philosophy by raising such questions as what is Indian *about* Indian Philosophy? (Bowes 1982; Rao 1982) This question suggests that if philosophy is a reflection on human condition, then such reflection will be a characteristic feature common to peoples of different times and cultures, and to diverse people in the same cultural and historical setting. This openness enables a modern Indian philosopher engage freely and without being apologetic with Western philosophical reflections on human condition as well as with his own philosophical tradition.

But was the philosophizing of a modern Indian philosopher really grounded in Indian tradition? Was that tradition available to him the way it was available to the slowly disappearing class of *śāstries* and *paṇḍits* who were its natural inheritors? In the colonial milieu, the modern Indian philosophers' philosophizing was rooted in a cosmopolitan tradition which could not have been purely Indian or Western, and hence, the activity of philosophizing that emerged during this period was bound to assume a different role that was, so to say, determined by the historical condition in which these philosophers were placed. The tradition either purely Indian or Western that they could claim as theirs was in fact not theirs. Being philosophers in the colonial era, they were exposed to the major Western philosophers belonging to the Greek and the European traditions and as professionals they were connected in some way or the other to modern educational Institutions such as universities and colleges. And being Indians, these philosophers were also expected to be acquainted with the traditional systems of classical Indian philosophy. However, what was thus expected could not become a defining attribute, i.e. acquaintance with classical Indian philosophy was not a sufficient condition for them to be designated as Indian philosophers. This was due to the fact that exposure to Indian philosophy was not integrated into the philosophy syllabus in Indian universities.[14] Datta (1956: 195) reveals that it was through the private study that

---

[14] One of the most widespread beliefs that was generated in the colonial period by the Indologists and the Orientalists was that classical Indian philosophy deserved to be studied only historically; it could not enter into the contemporary consciousness of modern Indians. There was an essential distance between the classical *Darśanas* and the newly acquired concerns of the English-educated Indian philosophers of the colonial period. The distance was mainly due to the very structuring of the syllabus that was taught in Indian universities established at Calcutta, Madras, and Bombay in which students were exposed only to western philosophy, logic, and ethics. The only institutions where Indian philosophy, i.e. the traditional *darśanaśāstra*, was taught were Sanskrit *pāṭhśālās* which too was fast disappearing. But more importantly, and as a result of the total absence of Indian philosophy in the university system introduced by the British, philosophy graduates in this system identified themselves with Western philosophy as if it was their own. Due to this distancing, the entire corpus of knowledge and various world-views which were distinctly indigenous, ceased to be living and relevant for the westernized Indian mind. A vital link with the issues around, which the everyday life as well as the intellectual life of the colonized Indians was historically organized, was lost. The ideal form of knowledge now was the western rationality, science, and scientific method. This view of the ideal form of knowledge along with its continued influence made the indigenous traditions irrelevant for the colonial forms of life.

To overcome this distance was a historical challenge for the modern Indian philosophers in the colonial context and they had to take it up not by subverting their new acquisition; namely, the world-views which the Western philosophers have offered, but by using *that very* acquisition to express themselves adequately vis-à-vis their European audience. In this process, acquaintance with Sanskrit became a marginal issue, at least for some, as per the D.M. Datta account cited above. At this juncture, the issue of assimilation of ideas became important, not only in the case of those which were held to be alien, but also with regard to those which were held to be one's own. It became more and more a matter of sentiment to hold that the classical systems of Indian philosophy were still a part of the colonial consciousness of modern Indian philosophers. In reality, they seemed as alien to the modern Indian philosophers as were the ideas coming from the West. Modern Indian philosophers had to fuse the alien past with the alien present.

S. Radhakrishnan, S.N. Dasgupta, K.C. Bhattacharyya, R.D. Ranade, and other modern Indian philosophers came to acquire both exposure and scholarship in Indian philosophy. Indian philosophy was as alien to these modern Indian philosophers as was Western philosophy. There was thus a dual estrangement—of the tradition from the intellectually inclined and of individuals from the issues and problems with which the Indian tradition was engaged. The history of modern Indian philosophy beginning practically from the first decade of 19th century could have been a history of authentic dialogue, a real exchange of concepts than their superficial comparison between the Western and the classical Indian philosophies. But it resulted only in "parallel maintaining a good distance from each other" (Bhattacharyya 1963: iii).

Reception of Western philosophical thought and the establishment of separate departments of philosophy to study philosophy as an academic discipline are different though inter-related phenomena. The 19th century religious and social movements that constituted what is usually labelled as Indian Renaissance were centred on the former, whereas the latter was a result of British education policy.[15] A new class of college and university teachers called 'lecturers' and 'professors' had begun to emerge in these establishments, slowly replacing the traditional class of teachers who were titled *āchāryas*, *paṇḍits*, and *śāstries*. As the ideal form of knowledge was now Western rationality, the ideal institutional form meant for imparting knowledge was the system introduced by the colonial government as well as by individual Englishmen. Governor General Warren Hastings established the Calcutta and *Madrasas* in 1780, and in 1791 Jonathon Duncan established the Benaras Sanskrit College, which along with similar colleges in Calcutta and Poona, was subsequently patronized by the British government. These establishments displayed 'self-interested calculations' which prompted the colonial patronage of oriental knowledge and triggered the interest of European scholars such as William Jones in Sanskrit in the light of the discovery that Sanskrit, Latin, and Greek share the same common root. Although these establishments employed *paṇḍits* to read Sanskrit texts to impart traditional knowledge,[16] what was

---

[15] The Poona College (1921), which was later reconstituted as Deccan College in 1864, is one of the oldest institutes modelled on the British system of education. But the year 1857 proved to be a benchmark year for the university system in India as the three major universities were established in the same year in Calcutta, Madras, and Bombay. The philosophy department was established in the University of Calcutta in 1913.

[16] The term traditional knowledge refers to two streams of learning—Vedas and Śāstras. One becomes a *vaidika* by virtue of mastering any one of the four Vedas. Mastery over the Vedas was aimed primarily at preservation rather than understanding their meaning of the original Vedas as they were recited with particular pronunciation, intonation, and accent. Therefore, "When the new elite in Maharashtra such as M.G. Ranade and M.M. Kunte made an attempt to revive the ancient Indian tradition in the second half of the 19th century, they emphasized the revival of the Vedas with their meaning" (Patankar 2014: 142). But besides keeping intact the oral tradition of preserving the Vedas, the *vaidikas* served as qualified priests to perform religious rites.

happening as a matter of fact was a replacement of the traditional system of education[17] by a new one in which the traditional *guru-śiṣya paramparā* (teacher-disciple lineage) was completely altered. In this alteration, the roles and relationship between the *guru* and *śiṣya* were completely changed. Teachers began to receive their monthly salaries by virtue of which they became professionals. Pupils began getting scholarships and stipends for being full-time students and prizes for their performance at regularly conducted examinations. The relationship between the *guru* and the *śiṣya* became incidental to the system of annual examinations. With these alterations, the basic structure of the traditional system which was based on the inseparable relation between the form and content of knowledge acquisition was mutilated. Whereas the traditional system stressed knowledge acquisition based on the informal relation between the teacher and the taught, the modern education system converted the informal relationship into a formal one, thereby separating the form of knowledge from its content. This separation was reflected in the restructuring of Sanskrit colleges established at Poona, Calcutta, and Banaras. In this reformation, the learning of Sanskrit was supplemented by learning of English, and the underlying sentiment was that the addition of English would mitigate the 'undue encouragement' given to learning Sanskrit which served only to cultivate a dead language and the study of obsolete knowledge. It was also hoped that introduction of English into the curriculum would support Sanskrit for philological purposes (Seth 2008: 172).

As the terms 'modern Indian philosophy' and 'modern Indian philosopher' are open to critical investigation, so is the distinction between the 'academic' and 'non-academic' (or 'professional') philosophers. Although there were formal systems such as the *pāthaśālā* (school)[18] and the famous *guru-śiṣya paramparā* (teacher-disciple lineage) for imparting knowledge, the distinction between the so-called academic and non-academic, with a subtle glorification of the former, never existed in India. It is a peculiar colonial importation. Although there were learned

---

[17] The traditional system of education and the imparting of traditional knowledge are to be understood in a wider context of socio-economic and political conditions prevailing in the pre-British period. It was the 'military prowess and its fruits in the form of revenue assignments', not the academic scholarship, that was the 'most coveted status symbol' (Patankar 2014: 140). But the military training and academic scholarship in the study of Vedas and Śāstras under the British became redundant and government service became the chief avenue to secure livelihood. 'Education through books thus became the chief way to reach the new goal' (Patankar 2014: 141).

[18] The institution of the *pāthaśālā* exhibits a peculiar mix of formal and informal aspects. This institution invariably depended on patronage. Āchārya-Kula, a *pāthaśālā* in Pune, had the support of the Thackersey family, whereas Shambhurao Karandikar built a fairly spacious house for the famous Prājña Pāthaśālā at Wai, District Satara in Maharashtra (Patankar 2014: 142). But usually, many *pāthaśālās* were situated at the guru's house in which disciples stayed and the guru looked after them along with his own family by performing *pravachana* and *keertan*, i.e. religio-ethical discourse at public places, mainly at temples. Those who used to teach at *pāthaśālās* conducted by institutions received Rs. 5 per month as their remuneration. (Patankar 2014, quoting from Nurullah and Naik 1933) Because of its informal character, there was no uniform pattern of examination and the examinations were mainly oral, conducted by the learned *paṇḍits* from places such as Varanasi or Paithan. Patankar gives some details of the syllabus to

people with such titles as *āchārya*, *śāstri*, and *paṇḍits* whose job was to impart knowledge of *śāstras* and, if required, engage in *śāstrārtha* (a debate over the correct meaning of concepts and doctrines in the *śāstras*), they did not form the class of professional academicians in the modern sense of the term. Similarly, given the *darśana* conception of philosophy, the age-old seer and the saint tradition of India would always confront the dichotomy between academic and non-academic philosophers, so would the spiritualists such as Ramaṇa Maharshi, Aurobindo, Jiddu Krishnamurti or social, religious; political leaders such as Tilak, Gandhi, and Vivekananda and poets such as Tagore in contemporary times.

The chasm between academic and non-academic philosophers in the Indian milieu can be traced back, both historically and conceptually, to the emergence of the modern state and its necessity for 'more exact knowledge' and also in the gradual separation of science and philosophy in 15th to 18th century modern Europe. It is in this context, the institution of the university "was revived in the late 18th and early 19th centuries as the principal institutional locus for the creation of knowledge" (Wallerstein 1997: 6). The institutional structure of the university required the "disciplinarization" and "professionalization" of knowledge by "the creation of permanent institutional structures designed both to produce new knowledge and to reproduce the producers of knowledge" (Wallerstein 1997: 7). In the process of departmentalization of knowledge, the gradual demarcation of various faculties from one another was inevitable. The demarcation among faculties of knowledge and the subsequent emergence of multiple disciplines was based on the assumption that "systematic research required skilled concentration on the multiple separate arenas of reality, which was partitioned rationally into distinct groupings of knowledge" (Wallerstein 1997: 6). Not only did this separation of disciplines drastically revise the traditional, i.e. the Platonic conception of philosophy as a synoptic vision of reality and its role in society, but as a result, it also created a rift between the academic and non-academic philosophers. However, academic philosophers were part and parcel of the institutional set-up of the university system despite the fact that the status of 'departments' of philosophy remained ambiguous as compared to those in the faculties of natural and social sciences, since each department of specialized knowledge claimed to have its own philosophy. But in traditional Indian society, this rift never existed because philosophies,

---

Footnote 18 (continued)

be studied during the period of 6 years at Prājña Pāthaśālā for the qualifying test to become a *paṇḍit*. For example, the study of Nyāya comprised the reading of *Muktāvali* (6 months), *Tattvacintāmani* (2 years), Gadādhara (*Siddhāntavyāpti*, *Paksatā*, *Avayava*, *Sāmānya Nirukti*, *SavyabhicāraSāmānya*, *Satpratipakṣa*, (3 years), and *Goutama-Kaṇāda Sūtra* with commentaries (6 months). Likewise, there were six-year courses in each of these branches of knowledge—Veda, Vyākaraṇa, Dharmaśāstra, and Vedānta. However, the Prājña Pāthaśālā, most probably unlike many other *pāthaśālās*, seems to have been receptive to modernity as it also incorporated in its syllabus English language and literature, physics, and chemistry with a view that a *paṇḍit* trained in the Vedas and Śāstras should also be acquainted with the modern world (Patankar 1999: 129). In contrast to the traditional pattern of oral examination, Prājña Pāthaśālā adopted the method of continuous internal assessment followed by surprise weekly tests (Patankar 1999: 130–1).

i.e. *darśanas* were never treated as specialized fields of knowledge in the modern sense of the term. The study of *darśanas* was a part of the comprehensive scheme of knowledge, i.e. *ānvīkṣikī*, *trayi*, *vārtā*, and *daṇḍanīti*.

The introduction of the Western educational system not only engulfed the learning of Sanskrit and the acquisition of ancient knowledge, it also redefined the concerns, modes of engagement, and pursuits of both the 'traditional' *paṇḍits* and the 'modern' *lecturers* and *professors* and underlined the total separation of concerns and a rift between academic and non-academic philosophers. As the newly emerged class of academic philosophers was interested in presenting Indian philosophical thought to the West, the traditional *paṇḍits* and *śāstries* were not. In fact, the traditional system of learning under the tutelage of *āchāryas*, and *śāstries* stood completely insulated from the impact of the West. But for the English-educated professional philosophers, it certainly was a historical necessity to write in English and present Indian philosophy to the English-educated populace in India and to the Western audience. In this process, some of them chose to present Western thought, especially the philosophies of Plato, Kant, and Hegel to the English-educated Indian audience. This two-way presentation is exemplified by some of the best representative writings of modern Indian philosophers such as B.N. Seal, Hiralal Haldar, R.D. Ranade, Rasvihary Das, K.C. Bhattacharyya, G.R. Malkani, M. Hiriyanna, P.T. Raju, S.K. Maitra, D.M. Datta, and is evident in such anthologies as *Contemporary Indian Philosophy* (Radhakrishnan and Muirhead 1936, 1952), *Radhakrishnan: Comparative Studies in Philosophy Presented in Honour of his Sixtieth Birthday* (Inge et al. 1951), *Krishna Chandra Bhattacharyya Memorial Volume* (Maitra et al. 1958), *Recent Indian Philosophy: Papers Selected from the Proceedings of Indian Philosophical Congress, Volume One, 1925–1934* (Bhattacharyya 1963), *Facets of Recent Indian Philosophy (four volumes)* (S.P. Dubey 1994–1998) and some recent ones such as *Indian Philosophy in English: From Renaissance to Independence* (Bhushan and Garfield 2011).[19] As a part of the newly emerging professional activity of publication of research, a large quantum of the philosophical literature comprising research papers, monographs, discussion notes, comments, etc., used to be regularly published in *The Philosophical Quarterly* and a bilingual, *Tattvajñāna Mandir* (Hindi and Marathi)[20]—the two quarterly

---

[19] There are a few other anthologies of the writings of modern Indian philosophers such as *Current Trends in Indian Philosophy* (Murty and Rao 1972) and *Indian Philosophy Today* (N.K. Devraja 1975). But these include the writings of Indian philosophers of post-colonial decades as well.

[20] But even before this journal, the Institute seems to have brought out a journal titled *Journal of Indian Institute of Philosophy* in January 1918 under the editorial committee consisting of S.K. Maitra (as President), Pt. Shripad Shastri, G.R. Malkani, N.C. Ghosh, and J. Masuda. However, no record of its continuation is available. Most probably, it was renamed as *The Philosophical Quarterly* and its first issue seems to have appeared in April 1925 under the editorship of M.N. Tolani and G.R. Malkani. This journal was an official publication of Indian Institute of Philosophy and the Indian Philosophical Congress. The first nine volumes were published from Amalner and volumes 10 to 19 were brought out from Calcutta. The remaining volumes from 21 to 38 were again published from Amalner. After the publication of volume 38 in 1966, the journal ceased to exist. The first issue of *Tattvajñāna Mandir* appeared in July 1919 under the

journals of The Indian Institute of Philosophy at Amalner.[21] By these stipulations, all those who contributed to such professional publications were modern Indian philosophers. They were well exposed to the writings of ancient Greek philosophers such as Socrates, Plato, Aristotle, and also to modern Western philosophers including Descartes, Spinoza, Leibniz, Kant and Hegel, Locke, Berkeley, and Hume. They were also trying to present their own traditional Indian thought to the West. On the other hand, historians of Indian philosophy such as Surendra Nath Dasgupta (1887–1952) wrote a comprehensive history of Indian philosophy,[22] while Brajendra Nath Seal prepared the first-ever syllabus of Indian philosophy in 1924. In 1925, the Indian Philosophical Congress was established with the initiative of Rabindranath Tagore and Sarvepalli Radhakrishnan as a national forum for modern Indian philosophers to engage in purely professional activities such as presenting research papers, participating in symposia, and delivering endowment lectures.

1.6 Dilemmas of Intercultural Philosophy

Although the modern Indian academic philosophers swiftly adopted these new modes of expressing their research and erudition, their engagement with Western philosophy and by implication with Indian philosophy is not without problems. This dual engagement was prompted, at least partly, by one of the most widespread beliefs generated by the Indologists and Orientalists that classical Indian philosophy should be studied as part of a distant historical past that could not enter into the contemporary consciousness of modern Indian philosophers. The gap between their 'philosophical past' and the 'colonial present' was due to the very structuring of the syllabus that was taught in the modern Indian universities established at Calcutta, Madras, and Bombay where students were exposed only to Western philosophy, logic, and ethics. As a result of the total absence of Indian philosophy in the university curriculum, philosophy graduates in this system identified themselves with Western philosophy and its concerns as if they were their

---

Footnote 20 (continued)

editorship of Mr. M.R. Oak. These journals used to be the only Indian journals devoted solely to research in academic philosophy. From 1926 onwards, G.R. Malkani remained as the editor of *The Philosophical Quarterly* till its closure. Interestingly, the Scott Philosophical Club and the University of St. Andrews in England began publishing a journal with the same title from 1950.

[21] The Indian Institute of Philosophy at Amalner in East Khandesh region of the erstwhile Bombay Presidency (now the State of Maharashtra) was founded in July 1916 by two individuals, Pratap Sheth, a textile mill owner and Sheth Vallabhadas, a cotton merchant. From 1920 to 1950, this Institute was the only center of philosophical research in India. It attracted many distinguished professional philosophers of the time as fellows and lecturers including K.C. Bhattacharyya as its first Director for a brief period and G.R. Malkani who succeeded him in 1935 until the Institute was formally closed in 1966.

[22] The first volume of Dasgupta's *History of Indian Philosophy* appeared in 1922 and the fifth and the last in 1955.

own. In this context, Datta's (1956: 195) admission that Indian philosophy became progressively alien to Indian philosophers is very illuminating. Due to this distancing, the entire corpus of knowledge and various world-views, which were distinctly indigenous, ceased to be living resources accessible to the Westernized Indian mind. The indigenous systems of thought and practices lost their cognitive worth and efficacy and could not contribute to the emerging praxis of colonial Indian society. All this resulted in losing the vital link with the issues around which the everyday social existence and intellectual life of the colonized Indians was historically organized. All these facts determined the nature of the modern Indian philosophers' preoccupation with and the importance they attached to issues faced by the British idealists, i.e. the nature of the absolute, the knowledge of the self, and the reality of the transcendental.

These facts have been acknowledged by P.T. Raju, S.K. Maitra, and many other contributors to the 1936 Radhakrishnan-Muirhead volume. P.T. Raju explicitly states that most of them were exposed to Western philosophy, particularly of Kant and Hegel, mainly through the secondary literature comprising of commentaries and interpretations by J.H. Sterling, T.H. Green, John Caird, Edward Caird, F.H. Bradley, R.B. Halden, and G.S. Morris. Modern Indian academic philosophers were exposed to Hegel through these sources. But to assess Hegel's influence in India, particularly in the context of neo-Hegelianism, it is necessary to have an adequate historical background of Hegel's philosophy as it was received in 19th century England. In the absence of such a background, it will not be clear how Hegel, the ardent rationalist, was accepted by the predominantly empiricist and intuitionist English philosophers in the early part of the 19th century. It is interesting to find that J.S. Mill, one of the most powerful exponents of empiricist philosophy, did not think that 'the study of Hegel would have a salutary effect on the immature minds of university students' and refused to support the candidature of J.H. Sterling—one of the chief exponents of Hegel in England—for the chair of Moral Philosophy in Edinburgh University in 1868 (Haldar 1927: 4). The question as to why some British philosophers were drawn to Hegel also becomes pertinent. One finds Immanuel Kant, the predecessor of Hegel, echoing David Hume's distinction between two types of knowledge, the one based on matters of fact and the other on relations of ideas when he distinguishes between analytic and synthetic propositions. T.H. Green, Edward Caird, and F.H. Bradley were called British idealists precisely because they were opposed to metaphysical theories of materialism and naturalism, to the standard empiricist view of consciousness as nothing more than sensations, and knowledge as nothing else but association of ideas. During the early 19th century, the Victorian age was facing a formidable challenge of reconciliation of the two opposite world-views, the one generated by the new science and the other by Christianity. The reconciliation of these world-views had to be 'scientifically tenable' and also 'religiously satisfying' (Haldar 1927: 3). What was needed was a comprehensive metaphysics of reconciliation between science and religion that would enable one "to comprehend the true nature of the universe we live into justify the stand point of religion without neglecting the conclusions of science" (Haldar 1927: 3). It was on this background that British philosophers such as James Hutchison Sterling and Sir William Hamilton found not only Hegel but also Schelling and Victor Cousin as the "most illustrious representatives of the doctrine that the mind and matter are only phenomenal appearances of the same substance" (Haldar 1927: 4). For Sterling and Hamilton, the acceptance of Hegel was a step beyond Kant's synthesis of the 'inner' and the 'outer', i.e. a synthesis between the categories of understanding which belong to the realm of the 'inner', i.e. the mind and the sense data supplied by the outer world. Hegel's dialectical moment introduced the notion of a synthesis of a *higher* order in which the so-called opposite principles of mind and matter stand synthesized. Kantian subjective idealism is thus sublated into absolute idealism. The philosophical world of England is exposed to Hegel through absolute idealism, the term which was made popular by the British admirers of Hegel. For them, Kant's critical philosophy "finds its culmination in the philosophy of Hegel" (Haldar 1927: 10). It is true that British idealists had appropriated Hegel within the framework of the idealistic doctrine, but not completely. Modern Indian academic philosophers took this selective reading of Hegel as authentic. It was this Hegelian legacy of absolute idealism that appealed to modern Indian academic philosophers the most because in and through him they found the possibility of presenting to the West the indigenous philosophical world-view, especially that of the Advaita Vedānta and, in particular, the conception of Brahman as Absolute. What was needed for this presentation was a similar world-view that was rooted in the Western philosophical tradition. Hegelian absolute idealism was such a world-view.

The Hegelian influence is explicitly acknowledged by philosophers such as Brajendra Nath Seal, Hiralal Haldar, and S.K. Maitra. G.R. Malkani, without explicitly mentioning Hegel, addresses the problem of the Absolute in almost all his writings. In fact, one finds the term 'Absolute' becoming almost a *cliché* in the writings of most modern Indian academic philosophers. It would not be an exaggeration to say that the singular question that occupied these philosophers in the early part of the 20th century was as follows: 'What is the nature of the Absolute?' Almost every one of them proposed 'his own answer to it and in doing so clarifying his own philosophical position' in the context of the Indian and the Western traditions of philosophy (Deshpande 2010: 97). But while appropriating Hegel, Brajendra Nath Seal, Haldar, Maitra, and others are also frank enough to admit that in the course of their philosophical maturation they consciously tried to overcome the Hegelian influence. Haldar departs from Hegel's notion of the Absolute on the question of the relationship between thought and reality. Brajendra Nath Seal who, like Hiralal Haldar, has had the reputation of being 'one of the greatest Hegelians in India' was initially said to be inspired by the Hegelian philosophy of the linearity of history from East to West. But later he rejects it as it imposes uneven conditions for a two way dialogue between East and West. In repudiating Hegel's eurocentricism, Seal has participated, "perhaps unknowingly, in the global debate on Hegel's philosophy of history" (Deshpande 2010: 97). But, barring his exception, most of the modern Indian philosophers of the colonial period were apparently not interested in reacting to Hegel's Eurocentric approach to Indian civilization, nor to his "specific arguments concerning Indian philosophy and religion" (Halbfass 1988: 99). As noted above, they almost entirely restricted themselves to Hegel's metaphysics of the Absolute. The exclusive reference to the Hegelian notion of the Absolute in presenting the Vedāntic notion of Brahman is to be interpreted both hermeneutically and historically. K.C. Bhattacharyya, who is considered to be the most articulate among his contemporaries, responded more to Kant than to Hegel. But his engagement with Kant was not of 'uncritical superimposition' of one tradition of thought upon another, nor was it 'a naïve identification of concepts belonging to' the Indian and the Western traditions (Mehta 1974: 62).

Because of the very nature and historicity of its context, philosophy in colonial India was bound to evoke mixed sensitivities. During the colonial period, Indian philosophers wrote in Sanskrit, in the regional languages and in English. Works in Sanskrit, produced mainly by the traditional *paṇḍits* and *āchāryas*, were and are still treated as exercise in historical scholarship or as Indological. On the other hand, writings in English, produced by the new class of professional philosophers teaching in Indian universities, either received no attention abroad and thereby suffered exclusion from the hegemonic mainstream Western philosophy or were castigated as second-rate historical expositions of Western philosophy or even as 'mimicry' of Western models. But the philosophy that emerged in Indian university system during the colonial period merits a careful re-reading. It is likely that modern Indian philosophers might have pursued philosophy with a certain degree of originality by engaging creatively with both the Western and the Indian traditions of philosophy. Infusing what is distinctively Indian with Western modes of thinking, modern Indian philosophers belonging to the university system of the colonial era might have pursued philosophy in a creative manner to render it both accessible and acceptable to the English-speaking world abroad, as well as to the educated Indian populace at home. Today much of the academic philosophical work of this period stands largely ignored, not only abroad, but also even in India. The reasons for this neglect are political, sociological, and also related to the shift in the very conception of philosophy and of philosophical activity. It is hoped that this anthology will be a step towards overcoming the disconnect between the modern Indian philosophers and the texts they produced during the colonial era and present-day philosophical activity in the academic set-up of Indian universities.

1.7 About This Volume

It is true that there cannot be just one perspective on the dialectics of colonialism. However, the general sentiment manifested in most of the essays in this anthology is that the colonial era in which modern Indian philosophers conducted their philosophical activity marked a period of intense creativity, criticality, and self-reflexivity; yet, it is acknowledged that this period also marks 'a sense of rupture, homelessness, and lack of spirit' which is open to different interpretations and explanations. It is also customary to assume that colonialism was an oppressive condition under which those who philosophized at that historical juncture were forced to live and think. But to make sense of this rupture, we need to raise certain theoretical issues.

Accordingly, Sanil in his *Thought and Context on the 'Eve of Colonialism'* (Chap. 2) focuses on the fundamental question of the relationship between history, thought, and freedom and its centrality to any meaningful discourse on colonialism. Unless one is clear about this relationship, one might end up treating colonialism as a mere historical marker and accordingly discuss the works of philosophers belonging to that period. From the latter perspective, it is often held that colonialism either destroyed the existing traditions of philosophy or inaugurated philosophy proper. This sums up the whole array of our nationalist narratives of philosophy under the colonial period ranging from the destruction stories to those of welcome. But if we wish to take colonialism seriously, as Sanil argues, we need to affirm political freedom as a condition of thought and acknowledge the historical dimension of thought. Having stated this, Sanil then explores some contemporary approaches to the issue of colonialism and its impact on the very conception of philosophy and the nature of philosophizing as an activity. The larger story Sanil wants to tell concerns the way philosophy as a discipline of thought confronts colonialism. According to the Anglo-American analytic tradition, since philosophy is concerned with perennial problems, it does not and it need not register its historical context. By implication, philosophy can treat colonialism only as a historical accident that cannot affect the internal history of philosophy as a discipline of thought. The Anglo-American tradition distinguishes between philosophy proper and the history of philosophy, whereas the Continental tradition grants the historicity of philosophy but neutralizes colonialism as a non-event. Hegel and Husserl either treat colonialism as a moment in the historical unfolding of ideality or treat it as a mere fallout of the crisis of European culture. Sanil observes that the radical questioning of the idea of history in the Continental tradition derives from literature and theology rather than philosophy.

Within the context of philosophy in colonial India, the Anglo-American analytical tradition and the 'modern' Indian philosophy modelled on this tradition, Sanil observes, have no sense of history and 'have nothing much to say on the relationship between historical conditions of thought and freedom.' On the other hand, and despite the fact that the Continental tradition is sensitive to those issues, the masters of this tradition—Hegel and Husserl—were undoubtedly Eurocentric and denied Indian thought the status of philosophy. Having outlined this larger story, Sanil raises such questions as the following: how can philosophy bear the mark of a historical event? Who is the bearer of this historical event—the proposition or the text? How can the internal history of thought register an external event like colonialism? These questions provide a conceptual framework to interrogate the complex relation between colonialism, tradition and modernity. In the light of this framework, Sanil then examines various attempts on the part of the practitioners of Indian philosophy; both in India and abroad, and during and after colonial period, to bring Indian philosophy in face-to-face conversation with colonialism. This survey runs through a project called *Saṁvād*,[23] which was led by Daya Krishna and M.P. Rege, the archival writings of Indian philosophers such as P.T. Raju, S.N. Dasgupta, and K.C. Bhattacharyya during the colonial period, the Sheldon Pollock-led project called *The Sanskrit Knowledge Systems on the Eve of Colonialism* and also his review of *Textures of Time*, and Jonardon Ganeri's article titled *Contextualism in the Study of Indian Intellectual Cultures*. Through this lengthy but fast-paced survey, Sanil has highlighted a number of issues in this discourse keeping intact the basic demand of understanding the historicity of thought in general and of Indian thought under colonial conditions in particular. While interpreting K.C. Bhattacharyya's project of Svarāj in Ideas, he links the historicity of thought with the sense of 'we' that Bhattacharyya is rigorously articulating. On Sanil's reading, the 'we' under the colonial condition lacked 'historical and cultural affectivity.' Within Sanil's framework, Bhattacharyya would say that historicity of thought cannot be assumed by evoking any authentic 'we', a return to the past, to revitalize the colonial 'we.' Instead, as Sanil notes, Bhattacharyya demanded that we bring powers of a new vitality to all that is 'we.' The culturally paralysed intellectual consciousness on 'the eve of colonialism' is likewise interpreted by Sheldon Pollock and Jonardon Ganeri to which Sanil responds extensively.

The reception of the West under colonial conditions comprises three principal reactions to the alien rule: (i) as power which completely decimated both the social body and the cultural self of India, (ii) a force which destroyed the social body but left the cultural self intact, and (iii) a perspective that colonialism could destroy neither the body nor the self though both were damaged. S.G. Kulkarni in his essay *Philosophy in Colonial India: The Science Question* (Chap. 3) underlines the three broad responses of Indian thinkers towards modern science and technology and the two major approaches to science that emerged in the post-Independence scenario. As Kulkarni rightly points out, these responses, as also the philosophy that emerged during the colonial period, was an integral part of a vibrant ethos that structured Indian national consciousness. This ethos consisted of three broad responses—in terms of the theory of total subjugation, the theory of the cultural-self, and the theory of revitalization of the colonial reality—having a clear bearing on the Indian response of modern science during the colonial period.

The introduction of modern science in the educational curriculum itself marks a shift in the Macaulay-led educational policy for Indians. As Kulkarni documents, the introduction of modern science was viewed by the colonial administration as a strategy to reinforce the myth of pre-colonial barbarism, to perpetuate the belief in the absence of scientific outlook in pre-colonial India, and more importantly, to break the self-confidence of the natives and undermine their self-esteem. Indian thinkers were well aware of this project. The issue therefore was 'how to undo or at least mitigate the effects of this project.' In this context, Kulkarni classifies

---

[23] The project brought together Sanskrit-based traditional *paṇḍits* and those trained in Western philosophy to dialogue on certain key concepts in philosophy via interlocutors. See Krishna et al. (1991).

what he calls major and minor responses to modern science. Two such minor, but not insignificant, responses are in terms of the assertion that India had a vibrant tradition of science and in terms of the attempts to establish institutions to promote modern science. Kulkarni cites Prafulla Chandra Sen's *History of Indian Chemistry* and Brajendranath Seal's *History of Positive Sciences in India* as examples of the first kind, whereas Mahendra Lal Sarkar's efforts to establish the Indian Association for the Cultivation of Science are invoked as an example of the latter kind. The three major responses that Kulkarni lists range from the unqualified acceptance of modern science to its qualified acceptance and finally to its qualified rejection. In his highly perceptive account of these responses, Kulkarni shows how our social, political, and religious reformers responded to the science question.

Kulkarni attributes the *first* major response of unqualified acceptance of modern science to the militant nationalists who took modern biology, particularly Darwin's theory of evolution and its philosophical justification by Herbert Spencer as the paradigm of modern science. Kulkarni's account of the nationalist appropriation of Darwin and Spencer exposes the myth of the neutrality of science in general and of the Darwinian kind in particular and demonstrates that such theories may not be free from political intent. The *second* response that of qualified acceptance of modern science is more intricate than the first. In this respect, modern science was dissociated from its essential mark of being Western and was related to the tradition of Vedānta. Kulkarni observes that Vivekananda and Aurobindo responded to modern science with these qualifications. The underlying assumption for this qualification is that science is universal and is not unique to modern Western civilization. Thus, on this qualified acceptance of modern science, neither the social context of its origin nor its *episteme* was thought to be essentially related to the core of modern science. The second feature Kulkarni attributes to the qualified acceptance of modern science is its attempt to separate science from materialism, or more specifically, to denounce what was known in the 19th century as scientific materialism. The separation of science from materialism is again a complex issue that requires a closer examination. Quoting Aurobindo, as perhaps, representing all such attempts to denounce scientific materialism and asserting that the conflict between religion and science never arose in India because the two things were kept on separate but not opposing lines, Kulkarni argues that once science was so dissociated from materialism, just one more step was needed to 'spiritualize' science and domesticate it within the Indian spiritual world-view that was believed to be best represented by Advaita Vedānta. Kulkarni reads this as an effort on the part of modern Indian philosophers 'to own up modern science without falling into the trap of destroying self-confidence of natives.' The *third* response that of qualified rejection of modern science comes from Gandhi and Coomaraswamy. Central to this response, Kulkarni argues, is the belief that modern science is the content of modern technology and thereby of industrialism. John Ruskin, who influenced Gandhi, and William Morris, who influenced Coomaraswamy, stood against industrialism in the West. To Kulkarni, these influences lend a unique character to this qualified rejection of science as being ethical and aesthetical. This characterization distinguishes it from the responses of Vivekananda and Aurobindo which were epistemic in nature. However, it should also be noted, as Kulkarni points out, that though Ruskin was opposed to industrialism, he was not anti-imperialist; while Morris was not an imperialist, but he did not want the British to quit India.

The problem of self-knowledge is a perennial problem in philosophy; but in the colonial context of receiving Kant, it assumed a special significance for modern Indian philosophers, especially against Kant's agnosticism about the knowledge of the Self. Nirmalya Narayan Chakraborty's essay The Self and its Knowledge: *The Legacy of Rasvihary Das* (Chap. 4), is situated in this context. But Chakraborty goes beyond the colonial context and makes available Rasvihary's theory of self-knowledge from the contemporary perspective of analytical philosophy. Chakraborty alludes to the contemporary debates on this issue in the Anglo-American analytic philosophy of language, which holds that since self-knowledge is manifested linguistically in the form of avowals, a philosophy of self-knowledge would involve an account of avowals. Against the background of Rasvihary's treatment of self-knowledge, Chakraborty argues that it is necessary to explain why and how the avowals exhibit the features they have, what is their subject matter and what is the special relation that the subject has to the avowals. For Rasvihary, the way we know ourselves is different from the way we know others. And this comment leads Chakraborty to undertake an analysis of avowals. Chakraborty distinguishes 'phenomenal avowals' from 'attitudinal avowals' and argues that in spite of the differences that these two kinds of avowals have, both exhibit a common feature called 'immunity to error through mis-identification.' It seems impossible to mis-identify oneself. And this lends support to Rasvihary's claim that the way one knows oneself is different from the way one knows other minds.

Amita Chatterjee's essay *Brajendranath Seal: A Disenchanted Hegelian* (Chap. 5) richly introduces the works and thoughts of a forgotten genius who was acclaimed as the greatest savant of the 19th century India. Among the philosophical circles he has had the reputation of being one of the greatest Hegelians in India. But as the title of the essay indicates, Amita Chatterjee takes a closer look at the Hegelian influence that shaped Brajendranath Seal's philosophical outlook in his formative stage, but also his differences with Hegel that Seal began to articulate at the later stage of his philosophical career. Seal's 'disenchantment' is documented by himself (Seal 1899: iii–iv) and by others elsewhere (Das 1968: 139). But Chatterjee probes into this disenchantment in greater detail, acquainting the reader with the intellectual journey and accomplishments of Brajendranath Seal. This journey begins with Seal's assimilation of the positivism of Comte, the Kantian notion of Reason, the gift of the French revolution—the ideals of liberty, equality, and fraternity—and of course, Hegel's concept of the Absolute and its manifestation through different stages of human history as well as Hegelian dialectics, without losing the track of Śaṃkara's Advaita Vedānta. In imbibing these influences, Seal stands out as a representative of most modern Indian philosophers and of educated modern Indians generally. As noted above, the Hegelian notion of philosophy as the science of the Absolute appealed to most modern

Indian philosophers because they found in it a resonance of the Indian notion of *Brahmavidyā*, the science of the highest reality. Seal was also attracted towards the idea of an all-embracing structure of thought in which every phenomenon of natural and spiritual life can be placed. However, no mind which is intellectually alert can hold on to influences if they clash with the quest for truth and the ability to seek it differently. Seal's, or for that matter any modern Indian philosophers' 'disenchantment' with the ideas and ideals that influenced them highlight the fact that the reception of the West was not blind, that those who were influenced were also intellectually able and free to overcome the influences. Seal's dissatisfaction with Hegel's ideas that history is linear and progresses from the East to the West and that Absolute reason has reached its point of culmination in the West, could not have been accepted by a mind capable of seeing things differently. Likewise, the difference in understanding the nature of the State which Seal inherited from Indian sources set him apart from Hegel. Among those differences, the important but somewhat neglected and hardly researched difference was between Hegel's logic of triads—thesis, antithesis, and synthesis—and the *Pāñcarātra* thesis of *Caturvyūhavāda*—the tetradic theory of four grades of divine manifestation held by the *Vaiṣṇavas*, which Seal upheld.

Besides discussing Seal's advocacy of comparative method and his role as an educationist, Chatterjee draws the reader's attention to the fact that he was an architect of the first-ever syllabus of Indian philosophy as we follow it today in almost all Indian universities. Chatterjee observes that the importance of this syllabus is manifold. There was a tendency among the Indologists to construe 'Indian philosophy' as synonymous with the great Vedic tradition. She stresses that it goes to the credit of Seal that he placed an equal emphasis on the great tradition as well as the little traditions including non-Vedic *āgamas* and the philosophy underlying the folk religions. But the most striking and controversial feature of this syllabus is that it employs the modern Western categories of metaphysics, epistemology, ethics, psychology, social and political theories to organize the elements of thought in the traditional 'systems' of Indian philosophy. Whether traditional Indian thought can ever be presented in these categories is a matter of ongoing debate; but the fact remains that after the publication of this syllabus, all the subsequent works on Indian philosophy, as also the teaching of Indian philosophy in the university departments and colleges have, so to say, internalized these categories.

Like Brajendra Nath Seal, Hiralal Haldar too was acknowledged as a profound scholar of Hegel and of neo-Hegelianism.[24] The parallel life histories of these two

---

[24] Haldar's contribution to neo-Hegelianism is acknowledged as very significant even in Cambridge and Oxford during his time. Like Seal, Haldar also thinks that absolute idealism is the only plausible theory to explain the multitude of ordinary experience and science because things make sense only in reference to the 'totality of a system.' Like Seal, Haldar was also a Brahmo Samajist and was described as a Brahmo neo-Hegelian philosopher who opposed the militant nationalism and pleaded for 'healthy nationalism' that would welcome the 'splendid virtues of the west.' Besides these intellectual affinities, both Seal and Haldar have held King George V Professorship of philosophy in Calcutta University. Seal held this position during 1913–1921, while Haldar held it during 1931–1933.

great philosophers makes it all the more necessary to think of them in terms of their respective understandings of Hegel and of Indian tradition. Quoting Hiralal Haldar's famous statement that 'Absolute idealism, whatever may be its merits or demerits, is one of the recognized modes of thinking in the civilized world at the present day', Tathagata Biswas in his *The Notion of Absolute: Hegel and Hiralal Haldar* (Chap. 6) traces how Hiralal Haldar explicates the notion of the Absolute in his engagement with Hegel. Biswas highlights several formulations of the notion of the Absolute as given by Haldar in response to Hegel and the British neo-Hegelians. According to Haldar, the Absolute is Thought, a concrete universal, a synthetic unity of thought and being, of subject and object, and of real and ideal. It is ultimate integration and reconciliation of all contradictions. Having outlined these formulations, Tathagata Biswas then elaborates each one of them in detail and shows that how each successive formulation that Haldar proposes highlights a deeper layer of meaning of the notion of Absolute. The central thesis that emerges out of these formulations, and which is held to be Haldar's distinctive contribution to the philosophy of Absolute, is his *Realistic Idealism*, a synthesis of realism and idealism on the premise that there is no difference between the real and the ideal (Haldar 1936, 1952: 323). According to Haldar, idealism and realism are compatible and not antagonistic to each other. This thesis emerges in the context of the distinction between reality and appearance or between noumena or phenomena and thus goes back to Plato and Kant in the Western tradition and to the doctrine of reality (*Brahman*) and appearance (*māyā*) in the Advaitic tradition. In the colonial context, these distinctions had to be measured against the realism of science, and hence, the reality of experience had to be conceived not as appearance but as manifestation of ultimate reality. Haldar's realist idealism aptly summarizes this reconciliation saying 'the material world is inwardised in mind and mind is externalized in matter. They are the correlated phases of the one all-inclusive spirit.' Biswas rightly observes that in such formulation two senses of mind are at play, one, mind as all-inclusive Spirit, the presupposed ultimate unity of mind and matter, subject and object; and the other is that mind being finite knowing subject. Tathagata Biswas also observes that this realist–idealist position was not only subscribed to by academic philosophers such as Haldar. Even the so-called non-academic philosophers such as Sri Aurobindo subscribed to it. Sri Aurobindo thought that matter and spirit are not of two radically different kinds.

Sharad Deshpande's exposition of G.R. Malkani's 'free and independent rendering' of the classical Advaita Vedānta for those 'who are imbued with the spirit of Western thought' (Chap. 7) places Malkani in the overall context of the emergence of the new form of Vedānta in the academic set-up of colonial India. In this new form, classical Vedānta was claimed to be freed from the compulsions of Sanskrit and also from the traditional text-based erudition. In a sense, this was a liberating move to come out of the insulation that the traditional form of learning in the *pāthaśālas* has imposed upon itself. But at the same time, this way of opening up to the West was not free of the risks involved in articulating a metaphysical world-view which can be projected as the Indian world-view to the West and finding out the appropriate philosophical idiom to make that world-view intelligible to the West. Malkani's free and independent rendering of Advaita Vedānta is located at the threshold of this opening up to the West. Like many of his contemporaries, he took Advaita Vedānta as the only Indian metaphysical world-view to be projected to the West and also to his Indian audience in the philosophical idiom in which the Idealistic thought of Hegel and Bradley found its expression.

The vast corpus of Malkani's writings includes the themes that have determined the philosophical discourse in India during the colonial period. These include, with variations in their verbal expression, such themes as 'Intuition of the Self', 'Creation or Illusion', 'The Absolute', 'Freedom through Knowledge', and 'Reality and Value', among others. One can easily see these themes expressing the problems in Vedāntic philosophy. As Deshpande notes, the arguments in these essays are thematically grounded in Malkani's reflections on the 'intuition of self.' For Malkani, the self is aware of itself, but the analysis of this intuition cannot transgress the limit of 'I'-ness which is the ultimate ground. Malkani dwells upon this theme in further details saying that dualism of the subject and object is the ground of the separation between knowledge and reality. It is only in reflective consciousness that knowledge becomes reality itself. For Malkani, the Hegelian Absolute or the Brahman of the Vedāntin is the self-evident ground of the identity of reality and experience. The Absolute or the Brahman elude dualistic epistemology but can be grasped in mystical experience. Malkani consistently asserts that the Absolute or the Brahman as revealed in mystic consciousness is not to be identified with the reflective consciousness since it admits the revealed content as distinct from itself. Malkani maintains that if the distinction between consciousness and its content is made explicit then object term can sustain no relation and would simply be nothing. In keeping with his Advaitic conviction, Malkani maintains that the explicit distinction between the subject and the object generates the dialectic which cannot be overcome. His main contention is that the terms 'subject' and 'object' gain validity only in their unity. According to him, this unity is possible in four alternate ways: (a) a de facto unity between consciousness and its content, (b) unity through an asymmetric relation, i.e. either the consciousness or the content having primacy, (c) unity in a more fundamental sense which is, as it were, neutral to both the consciousness and the content, and (d) one of the two being real and the other not.

K.C. Bhattacharyya occupies a pre-eminent place in the history of modern Indian philosophy as it flourished in the academic set-up of Indian universities during the 19th century. As a philosopher in the colonial epoch, he turned the colonial infliction of alien ideas and ideals into an 'instrument of lucid vision' comprising the 'truth of his own tradition' and at the same time remaining 'open to the call of the modern' (Mehta 1974: 62). In her essay *K.C. Bhattacharyya and Spivak on Kant: Colonial and Post-colonial Perspectives, Lessons and Prospects* (Chap. 8), Kanchana Mahadevan highlights both these moments in K.C. Bhattacharyya and presents two differing understandings of Kant, namely that of K.C. Bhattacharyya during the colonial period and that of Gayatri Chakravarti Spivak at the turn of 20th century. For Bhattacharyya, as Mahadevan argues,

Kant is a collaborator; while for Spivak, he is an alien. But Mahadevan wonders whether one can read Kant in a way where he is 'neither a friend nor a foe' avoiding particularities and easy categorization and becomes a determining ground for a balanced mode of reception of the 'other.' Mahadevan focuses on the following questions: is Kant's notion of human being vis-à-vis his assumptions against non-European races can be read alongside potentially democratic and pluralistic philosophies of India that shaped Bhattacharyya's life-world? What is the significance of Bhattacharyya's qualified appropriation of the Kantian human subject through a synthesis with Vedānta? Does this synthesis delimit both Kant and Vedānta? How does this synthesis lead to Bhattacharyya's view that philosophy is symbolic, non-literal thought that prepares the human subject with the discipline requisite for spiritual awakening? Thus, the domain of philosophy is a counterpoint to the literality of an object-centered science that neglects the subject. Mahadevan argues that Bhattacharyya's discovery of Vedāntic humanism, inspired by his interpretation of Kant, is an instance of his *Svarāj in Ideas*, where the foreign and the indigenous are assimilated.

Turning to Gayatri Chakravarti Spivak's critical reading of Kant, which indicts his conception of the human being as tacitly endorsing colonialism, Mahadevan argues that Spivak's post-colonial reading examines the limits of Kantian thought. The Kantian subject-position that Bhattacharyya discerns as a complement to independent thinking is seen through the opposite lens by Spivak as an instance of colonial suppression. Spivak argues that the German Orientalists' glorification of Vedānta and Brāhmānism is reflected in Indian attempts to resurrect Vedānta. From this perspective, Bhattacharyya's humanism is problematic precisely because of its assimilation of Vedānta with Kant. This is especially because the ideals of both have diverse social, scientific, and cultural frameworks. Despite being well aware of such differences, Bhattacharyya does not discuss their implications for thinking critically and independently. He suggests a 'comparative struggle' between the philosophies of the colonizer and colonized so that new philosophies emerge. This in turn requires a critical approach that synthesizes alien ideas in the light of indigenous ones. Mahadevan observes that Spivak's post-colonial and Bhattacharyya's colonial readings of Kant do share a common ground, despite their differences. Mahadevan concludes by arguing that despite its comparative dimension, Bhattacharyya's *Svarāj in Ideas* is valuable. Such *Svarāj* consists in independent critical thinking that repudiates the glorification of the Indian past and the imitation of Western thought. It anticipates Spivak's 'planet thought', which overcomes the fixed domains of comparing two cultures and discerns heterogeneity of traditions as central to the philosophical enterprise. Thus, both Bhattacharyya and Spivak redefine the notion of Indian philosophy and create richer possibilities through their interventions in the academic context from their respective colonial and post-colonial perspectives.

In his *The Road Not Taken: G.N. Mathrani's Wittgensteinian Transformation of Philosophy* (Chap. 9), P.G. Jung highlights the waning influence of Kant, Hegel, and Bradley and the beginning of the new occupations of modern Indian philosophers that was to change the subsequent course of the nature of philosophizing in the post-colonial India. As many of Mathrani's contemporaries were still pursuing philosophical issues concerning the nature of ultimate reality under the shadow of British idealism, Mathrani was enthused by G.E. Moore, John Wisdom, and Ludwig Wittgenstein in their rejection of idealism. With that rejection, philosophy of language began to engage modern Indian philosophers. As Jung points out, given that the philosophy of language (especially the works of Wittgenstein), has steadily acquired a prominent place in the Indian philosophical community, G.N. Mathrani deserves more than a passing mention, while one talks of philosophy during the late colonial period.[25] Though Mathrani's philosophical career begins towards the end of the British Raj, his philosophical contributions are significant given the fact that he was amongst the first few philosophers in India to philosophize outside the 'East–West' paradigm during the colonial period. The phrase 'linguistic turn' signifying the adoption of analysis of language as a philosophical tool to resolve philosophical problems was made popular by Rorty's 1967 anthology, *The Linguistic Turn: Essays in Philosophical Method,* where he claimed the said *turn* marked a 'philosophical revolution.' But many philosophers had already begun to use this revolutionary method by then. In India, it is in Mathrani's works that we find for the first time its most explicit appropriation.

Mathrani's steering clear of the comparative East–West paradigm and his emphasis on linguistic analysis leads him to the view that the meaningfulness of a philosophical question cannot be assumed and that a quest to resolve or dissolve a philosophical question must not begin with the search for the solution but rather with ascertaining the meaning of the question itself. Like all linguistic philosophers, Mathrani wants to break away from the view that language is a medium of expression with homogenous symbols and logical structures that execute different functions through distinct and explicitly recognizable structures of grammar. He holds that the symbols of language are of two kinds constituting the two distinct categories of *hard* and *soft* language. The symbols constituting the domain of the former are self-sufficient in their representational meaning, thereby never demanding anything other than themselves in the production of meanings through their use. The symbols constituting the latter domain of language are dependent upon some *facts* such that their meaning production required these symbols to be, so to speak, in touch with a another domain. Hence, these symbols were apt to express *facts* which are themselves not linguistic symbols. Further, the possibility of there being more than one variety of *facts* entailed the possibility of different modes in which these symbols of fluid language could affix and relate themselves with these different facts. Mathrani categorizes the facts with which the symbols of fluid language can relate into three non-exclusive categories of *descriptive, emotive,* and *symbolic* and thereby argues for three possible modes in which the symbols of fluid language relate with facts.

---

[25] In fact, G.N. Mathrani is globally the first philosopher ever to have written a book on Wittgenstein, titled *Wittgensteinian Philosophy or Studies in the New Cambridge-Philosophy* (Mathrani 1940).

Mangesh Kulkarni's *Radical Translation: S.R. Rajwade's Encounter with F.W. Nietzsche* (Chap. 10) presents a well-researched account of the way Nietzsche's ideas were received and interpreted by S.R. Rajwade, a notable philosopher based in Pune (Maharashtra). He focuses on Rajwade's book which contains a Marathi translation of *The Antichrist* as also a commentary on Nietzsche. Like Muhammad Iqbal (1877–1938) and Aurobindo (1872–1950), Rajwade serves as a unique example of the reception of Nietzsche in a colonial milieu where British political philosophy and German idealism were the most appealing sources of inspiration for modern Indian thinkers. Both Rajwade and Iqbal responded to Nietzsche's idea of the 'super man' from the standpoint of their respective religious faith. Iqbal's notion of the 'perfect man', as against Nietzsche's 'super man' is consistent with his Islamic faith, while Rajwade invokes the Vedic concept of '*deva*' as a dynamic radiant (*tejasvi*) trans-human being and argues that the latter truly brings out the Nietzschean ideal. As Kulkarni argues, Rajwade's intellectual endeavours were informed by his keen desire to defend and shore up the traditional Hindu social order in the face of reformist attacks, and to reclaim, what he saw as, the principle of oneness, or *nirdvandva* contained in the Vedas and the Gītā from its later contamination by Buddhism and Śaṁkarācharya's doctrine of non-dualism, i.e. *advaita*. Rajwade drew on Nietzsche's philosophy to bolster this twofold project, for he found in it an affirmation of *nirdvandva* as also reverence for the *Manusmṛti* and the disciplined Hindu social system based on *varṇāśramadharma* as against the Bible and the permissive democratic order anchored in a Christian ethos. It remains an open question as to whether such encounters with European thinkers substantiate Halbfass's contention that 'modern Indian thought finds itself in a historical context created by Europe, and it has difficulties speaking for itself. Even in its self-representation and self-assertion, it speaks to a large extent in a European idiom' (Halbfass 1990: 375).

Rajwade's translation of *The Antichrist* aimed at the deployment of Nietzsche's radical critique of Christianity as a lever to overthrow Western hegemony and to reinstate the pristine Hindu world-view and social order. It shows the translator's uncanny ability to inhabit and appropriate the source text, as also his immersion in the language and lore of the Indic Great Tradition. Kulkarni argues that the Marathi version can be seen as an example of 'radical translation' in two senses: it goes to the root of Nietzsche's philosophical argument, and more importantly, it reinvents the German thinker's 'aristocratic radicalism' in an indigenous context. The phrase 'aristocratic radicalism' was used by Georg Brandes to signal Nietzsche's complete rejection of both ascetic ideals and democratic mediocrity. Arguably, Rajwade translated it into a homologous position that may be characterized as 'brāhmānical radicalism.' This is evident in Rajwade's consistent critique targeting Hindu asceticism on the one hand, and modern egalitarianism on the other. By way of an antidote to such supposed evils, he stridently advocated a rejuvenation of the Hindu philosophical and social ideals contained in the Vedic tradition, which he found consistent with a fascist political vision. By assimilating Nietzsche's philosophy to the supposed message of the Vedas, Rajwade seems to have committed the fallacy of anachronism. But in the process, he foregrounded the fascist potential of the Nietzschean legacy, thereby demonstrating the transformative nature of philosophical translation.

The theme of philosophy in colonial India or more generally the Indian reception of the West cannot be dealt with meaningfully without referring to Rabindranath Tagore. Shefali Moitra reiterates this in her essay *Tagore's Perception of the West* (Chap. 11). She argues that Tagore's reception of the West was not a helpless colonial compulsion that often results into unthoughtful imitation. Tagore responded to the West on his own terms as developed by his self-cultivated understanding of the tradition and of the depths of human life. His philosophy of education stresses that education is not only empowering but emancipating; to use a Bergsonian term, it is a vital force (*élan vita*). This is important because reception of the West is generally associated with the modern, i.e. Western system of education that was being imparted through the newly established institutions of formal learning. Though Tagore himself was not a product of this system, he was constantly preoccupied with its effects. In this respect, Tagore stands out as the lone but perhaps the most illustrious example that problematizes the standard binaries such as academic/non-academic and formal/non-formal.

At a philosophical level, as Moitra argues, Tagore's preoccupation with education was in terms of human identity, i.e. the role of education as a liberating life force in constituting the human identity. As against the system of formal education introduced by the British, his concern was in terms of developing an alternate indigenous educational system, its course content, its medium of instruction; and so on. But Tagore did not look at these issues as mere pedagogic strategies. He insisted on the seminal cause, a *kāraṇ beeja*, a clear vision of purpose. Tagore's second preoccupation with education, connected with the first, actually determines the agenda for *re*-defining the colonized India's relationship with its colonizer in the most vital region of its social and cultural life. Should India reject or accept the Western system of education is the core issue. But Tagore does not perceive it as a local issue; for him the acceptance or rejection of the British educational system is at a deeper level an issue of one's own distinctive cultural and spiritual identity and its opening up to the formation of international relationships. Shefali Moitra rightly notes that Tagore never discusses the East or the West in isolation. Human perfection as engulfed in cultural specificities has to be seen as an instance of the perfection of humanity which is above all such specificities. Thus, the two essential marks of the perfection of humanity are, for Tagore, freedom and creativity. However, freedom is embedded in human relationships, not in the pursuit of the standard paradigms of freedom, namely, 'freedom from' or 'freedom to.' Tagore's Santiniketan experiment was to demonstrate precisely this. In this experiment, every student is initiated into 'forming some bond of relation with fellow beings and with nature.' Thus, as Moitra notes, 'Bonding with nature, and bonding with fellow beings from within and outside the country was essential historical background within which freedom has to be achieved and creativity given expression.' No wonder, the motto of Santiniketan was *yatra viśva bhavati eka nidam*, 'where the world is transformed into a single net.'

Unlike most of his contemporaries, Tagore boldly asserted that both the oppressor and the oppressed are equally responsible for the colonial condition saying that 'India also has her lapses. India has lost touch with her culture.' But more than this, 'India has lost the great honour of being able to contribute to the civilization of Humanity.' Tagore was concerned with this more profound loss which let India allow herself to 'become easy prey to exploitation.' This shows that Tagore was not ready to accord a 'mere victim-status' to India. India is a victim, but she must also take 'the onus of her degradation.' Tagore attributes India's degradation to her blind acceptance of utilitarianism and mechanized lifestyle. Tagore's critique of utilitarianism becomes all the more important since it was a popular philosophy propagated by Mill and Bentham whom many Western educated Indians had assimilated.

In his *Bankimchandra on Morality* (Chap. 12), Proyash Sarkar traces, with special reference to the principles of equality and justice, how Bankimchandra deviated from Rousseau and also the utilitarian ethics of Bentham and Mill, and upheld the traditional *Dharmaśāstras* which he himself had critiqued at the beginning of his engagement with the newly acquired Western ideas and ideals. To trace this deviation, Proyash Sarkar takes up two of Bankimchandra's monographs, namely *Sāmya* (Equality) published in 1879 and *Dharmatattva* (Ethico-Religious Theory) published in 1888.

What is known as the Indian Renaissance, especially in the colonial context, was centered round the principles of equality and justice, which had special significance and appeal for the social and religious reformers of the late 18th and early 19th century India. These principles were deployed against the insidious cast system that had introduced social discrimination among people from the Vedic times. Due to their underlying philosophy, the traditional Hindu law and social ethics as codified and regulated in various *Smṛtis*, *Dharmaśāstras* and even in texts, such as the *Bhagavad-Gītā*, could not provide a definitive articulation of equality and justice, except sometimes symbolically. Rousseau and other egalitarian European thinkers became relevant and the notions of equality and justice got prominence in the renaissance discourse. Most of the social and religious reformers in the colonial period were pre-occupied with giving an adequate account of the latter notions. The discourse thus revolved round such issues as the natural versus artificial and also gender difference. Following John Stuart Mill, not only Bankimchandra but also most social reformers in colonial India held that discrimination based on gender difference is artificial rather than natural. In the tradition-bound Hindu society, these thoughts and the reform movements based on them were radical.

Acceptance of the principles of equality and personal liberty led Bankimchandra to critique the *Dharmaśāstras* and defend widow remarriage; but as Proyash Sarkar notes, Bankimchandra's radical stance is nonetheless ambivalent as is evident from such remarks of his as '…widow remarriage is neither good nor bad' In fact, Bankimchandra's ambivalence later turns into a total acceptance of what the *Dharmaśāstras* say about women. What Bankimchandra says in his *Dharmatattva* amounts to affirming that the only duty of women is to serve men.

Proyash Sarkar is in conformity with the established view that as a defender of the *Dharmaśāstras* Bankimchandra was a Hindu revivalist; but as the author of *Dharmatattva*, he is a religious reformist since he holds that Hinduism, in particular, Vaishnavism expresses eternal truths which have to be interpreted in every era according to the needs and the forms of life of the people of respective age. Bankimchandra's ambivalence is to be interpreted in terms of the reformist and a revivalist role that he was playing simultaneously. Sarkar wonders as to how and why the revivalist Bankimchandra wins over the reformist Bankimchandra. Proyash Sarkar argues that in both these phases, Bankimchandra deviates from the utilitarian principles without giving up them altogether. This deviation is to be interpreted in the light of Bankimchandra's own theory of what he calls *dharmatattva*, i.e. an ethico-religious theory. In the light of this theory, Bankimchandra is in a position to critique the utilitarian morality which consists in arguing that an action or a rule for an action is morally right if it promotes the greatest happiness of the greatest number. Bankimchandra agrees with this but with a qualification. For him 'an action is morally good *not because* it promotes the greatest happiness but *because* it is conducive to the *development of human character*.' Central to Bankimchandra's idea of the development of human character is the notion of balance (*sāmañjasya*) in the context of human life which, according to him has meaning, though no intrinsic value. This enables Bankimchandra to adopt the 'top-down' model to negotiate with the principle of utility as Mill propounds it.

In her essay *Colonialism and Traditional Forms of Knowledge: Now and Then* (Chap. 13), Mohini Mullick addresses the issue of the interaction between the colonial powers and the practitioners of traditional knowledge in 19th and early 20th century India. This interaction calls for the explanation of a number of issues, some of which she brings to the fore. Mullick interrogates the very notion of colonialism and argues that this term cannot be taken as referring to any historically closed period. That colonialism is a state of mind is not an unfamiliar view and Mullick too holds this view and says that with this stipulation we can freely refer to philosophers who may have worked in the first half of the last century, but worked well beyond into the latter half; some indeed are very much still at work. She connects the theoretical works of these philosophers and the language in which they were carried out. Hence, she asks, which language do the *śāstras* now speak? Not only in the colonial period, but also in the post-colonial period, the *śāstras* speak in the 'forked language'; one for the non-English-speaking populace and another for the English-speaking populace and this practice continues even beyond the colonial period and despite every kind of critique and deconstruction in the land of its origin.

The question that emerges in this context pertains to the complex relationship between 'the colonial state of mind' and the language that the colonial mind uses for self-expression. This relationship is sometimes described in terms of the 'movement of harmonization', though this characterization is not only external and superficial; it is also very deceptive. Mullick confirms this by saying that nothing much has changed in this respect even today and asks why this is so. Mullick also confirms the genesis of the East–West binary with its emphasis on the superiority of Eastern spirituality over the material advancement of the West. But for her, this was more an anguished cry of a deeply wounded civilization. But then this construct of the East's superiority can also be seen in comparison with the West's own need to draw normative boundaries between itself and its colonies where it was performing a civilizing mission. Edward Said's *Orientalism* and Ronald Inden's *Imagining India* articulate this view by alluding to the construction of purely masculine, transcendental Reason which the West ascribed to itself. This imagination was translated in the policies of dissemination of Western ideas of reason and progress of civilization. Western discursive dominance thus became a reality. The conquest of language and of epistemic space underlined the conquest of the territorial space. The programme of the translation of Sanskrit texts, the repository of traditional knowledge, was thus symptomatic of the conquest of the epistemic space. The result of this conquest was the turning of the *paṇḍits* and the *pāthaśālās*—the traditional forms of scholarship and institutional learning—into anachronisms.

With the institutionalization of Western knowledge, the traditional knowledge and Sanskrit as its vehicle were pushed to the margins from where no dialogue between the newly defined centre and its margin was possible. Mullick sees this failure as due to the structured incommensurability between the two worlds. She argues that we are the inheritors of this total incommensurability, of a total epistemological break. But with the burden of this inheritance, the Indian philosophers of the latter part of the 20th century tried to 'dispel the image of difference' between the West and the East as an 'Orientalist myth' by bringing into focus classical India's unique contributions in the areas of philosophy of language, logic, grammar, and so on. But Mullick contends that with the newer colonial languages in place, new distortions have crept into the educated Indian's account of Indian thought. These distortions, Mullick observes, have occurred in the very process of making desired corrections. This calls for a thorough philosophical scrutiny of the entire translation programme carried out by the literary theorists and the critics.

1.8 A Plea for Retrieval

The 1950s marked the closure of the colonial era in the political history of modern India. Around this time, academic Indian philosophy underwent yet another change. The first change was the adoption of Hegelian idealism as it was reinvented by the British idealists and its idiom to ground Vedāntic metaphysics, the second change consisted in assimilating what Gustav Bergmann has termed as the 'linguistic turn' (Bergmann 1964) that Western philosophy took after the First World War through the works of the British and the American philosophers. This turn problematized some of the chief presuppositions of idealism that had dominated the British philosophy. However, we need to distinguish between the demise of idealism on the British soil and its abandonment by the post-colonial Indian philosophers. The former was inevitable due to theoretical difficulties logicians, mathematicians, and philosophers had with idealistic metaphysics of F.H. Bradley (1846–1924) who was its most articulate exponent in Britain. For instance, Russell had problems with the idealist doctrine of internal relations that culminates into the idea of the Absolute, G.E. Moore had difficulties with the famous *esse est percipii* doctrine that makes the reality of external material objects dependent on human mind, and A.J. Ayer had difficulties with idealist claims which were not, even in principle, open to verification principle. Apart from such internal difficulties, the change was also due to the fact that the "population of intellectuals, and particularly of academic intellectuals in the British Isles had changed from being a predominantly clerical to an almost entirely lay population" (Ryle 1963: 2).

> "In Bradley's youth … a big proportion of the undergraduates came from, and were destined to go to, the vicarage or the manse…. The burning theoretical issues were between theologians and theologians or else between theologians and anti-theologians…. By the 1920s all of this had gone. Almost all university teachers were laymen; almost all undergraduates came from lay homes and looked forward to secular careers." (Ryle 1963: 2)

But in India, there was no such change in the composition of the class of students seeking graduation or post-graduation in colleges and universities nor was there any change in the composition of the class of teachers teaching at these institutions. In fact, the educational system as well as the educational institutions remained completely insulated from and unaffected by the social and political upheaval that the Indian society was undergoing in its struggle for Independence through freedom movement and the growing atmosphere of the Second World War which was bound to affect India. But barring a few notable exceptions, the trend continued to work under the shadow of neo-Hegelianism and neo-Vedānta to address such issues as *māyā* and illusion, The Definite and the Indefinite, Brahman and Advaita, the Real, the Actual, and the Possible.[26] But at the same time, professional philosophical writings during the late 1920s and the late 1950s published in *The Philosophical Quarterly* (*PQ*) provide a large and fairly representative sample which shows a growing response to the many pronged critique of idealism initiated by the pioneers of what later came to be known as analytic philosophy, namely Bertrand Russell,[27] G.E. Moore,[28] Ludwig Wittgenstein,[29] and Ryle[30] and to the developments in early logical

---

[26] Though planned in 1945 and 1949, the *Krishna Chandra Bhattacharyya Memorial Volume* (Amalner) which finally appeared in 1958, confirms this fact. However, excepting Pravas Jivan Chaudhuri (1916–1961)—a physicist by training and a pioneering figure in philosophy of science during 1940s–1950s—the contributors to the volume like S.K. Maitra, P.T. Raju, and G.R. Malkani were still holding on to neo-idealism.

[27] *See* (i) Sen, N.C., *PQ* Vol. 1, No. 4, January 1926, (ii) Kar, K.N., *PQ* Vol. 24, No. 1, April 1951, also Vol. 25, No. 2, July 1952.

[28] *See* (i) Chatterjee, G.C., *PQ* Vol. 33, No. 2, July 1960, (ii) Nikam, N.A., *PQ* Vol. 33, No. 2, July 1960, (iii) Mathrani, G.N., *PQ* Vol. 33, No. 2, July 1960, (iv) Kaul, B.N., *PQ* Vol. 31, No. 3, October 1958, (v) Banerjee, K.K., *PQ* Vol. 33, No. 2, July 1960, (vi) Misra, N., *PQ* Vol. 34, No. 2, July 1961.

[29] *See* (i) Mathrani, G.N., *PQ* Vol, 16, No. 2, July 1940, also *PQ* Vol. 20, No. 3, October 1946, (ii) Das, R., *PQ* Vol. 17, No. 3, October 1941, (iii) Chandra, S., *PQ* Vol. 33, No. 3, October 1960 and also *PQ* Vol. 34, No. 3, October 1961 (iv) Lal, B., *PQ* Vol. 34, No. 3, October 1961, (v) Srivastava, J.S., *PQ* Vol. 38, No. 2, July 1965.

[30] *See* Ray, B.G., *PQ* Vol. 31, No. 3, October 1958; also *PQ* Vol. 35, No. 2, July 1962.

positivism.[31] Philosophers such as G.N. Mathrani were already responding to Wittgenstein in a sustained manner from the early 1940s. Some were attracted to various methodological issues in philosophy of science,[32] some to Husserl and phenomenology,[33] and some to Sartre, Kierkegaard, and existentialism.[34] Similarly, there are such symposia as 'Is Philosophy Linguistic Analysis?' and discussions on themes such as 'Moore's Refutation of Sidgwick's Pleasure Theory: A Critical Examination.'[35] In addition to this a number of books were reviewed, which were so to say 'against the current.'[36] To add to all this, there were also reviews of other philosophical journals published from Briton like *The Monist*, *Journal of Philosophical Studies*, *Mind*, and *The Hibbert Journal* (Krishna and Bhatnagar 1986: 66). This shows that fresh approaches to problems in metaphysics, ontology, logic, and ethics had already begun registering their presence in the philosophical thinking of a large number of individuals. That these approaches and a set of new issues, even the change in the very conception of philosophy, attracted the new generation of modern Indian academic philosophers is evident in such writings. Unlike their predecessors, this new generation of philosophers was not under pressure to reinvent Indian philosophy in the mould of neo-idealism or any other metaphysical world-view from the west. As a result they could directly relate themselves to, or participate in, current debates over the new set of issues and problems by setting aside what their preceding generation of Seal and Haldar, Radhakrishnan and Ranade, Datta and Malkani, or Das and Raju did. This was due to various factors. Idealism itself had lost its significance in the world of British philosophy. Hence, there was no need to engage with it

---

[31] *See* (i) Datta, D.M., *PQ* Vol. 12, No. 4, January 1937, (ii) Gajendragadkar, V., *PQ* Vol. 25, No. 1, April 1952, (iii) Sastri, P.S., *PQ* Vol. 28, No. 3, October 1955, (iv) Rao, A.L., *PQ* Vol. 34, No. 1, April 1961, (v) Moorty, N., *PQ* Vol. 35, No. 3, October 1963, (vi) Choudhuri, P.J., *PQ* Vol. 29, No. 4, January 1957, (vii) Prasad, K., *PQ* Vol. 13, No. 1, April 1937; also *PQ* Vol. 16, No. 4, January 1941.

[32] *See* Naidu, P.S., *PQ* Vol. 12, No. 1 April 1936, also *PQ* Vol. 19, No. 1 April 1943, (ii) Choudhuri, P.J., *PQ* Vol. 21, No. 1 April 1947, also *PQ* Vol. 21, No. 3, October 1948, also *PQ* Vol. 22, No. 2 July 1949, also *PQ* Vol. 25, No. 3, October 1952, also *PQ* Vol. 30, No. 4, January 1958, also *PQ* Vol. 32, No. 3 October 1959, (iii) Chari, C.T.K., *PQ* Vol. 25, No. 2, July 1952, also *PQ* Vol. 26, No. 3, October 1953, also *PQ* Vol. 37, No. 4, January 1965, (iv) Sastri, P.S., *PQ* Vol. 26, No. 4, January 1954, (v) Kaul, R.N., *PQ* Vol. 27, No. 3, October 1954, (vi) Chandra, S., *PQ* Vol. 29, No. 3, October 1956, (vii) Chakravarti, M., *PQ* Vol. 33, No. 3, April 1960.

[33] *See* Sinha, D., *PQ* Vol. 29, No. 2, July 1956, also *PQ* Vol. 37, No. 2, July 1964 also *PQ* Vol. 37, No. 4, January 1965, (ii) Ramanathan P.S., *PQ* Vol. 21, No. 1, April 1947, (iii) Puligandla, R., *PQ* Vol. 38, No. 3, October 1965, (iv) Mohanty, J.N., *PQ* Vol. 25, No. 2, July 1952.

[34] See Sahu, S., *PQ* Vol. 28, No. 3 October 1955, (ii) Lal, B.K., *PQ* Vol. 38, No. 3, October 1965, (iii) Sinari, R., *PQ* Vol. 36, No. 3, October 1963.

[35] See *PQ* Vol. 30, No. 1, April 1957 and *PQ* Vol. 32, No. 2 July 1959. The symposiasts in the former were Kalidas Bhattacharyya, Daya Krishna and N.K. Devaraja, whereas for the latter it was S.K. Nandy.

[36] For example, a review of G.N. Mathrani's *Studies in Wittgensteinian Philosophy*, H.H. Price's *Hume's Theory of External World*, Ernest Nagel's *Logic without Metaphysics and Other Essays in Philosophy of Science* and A.J. Ayer's *Logical Positivism* appear in 1941, 1942, 1958, and 1960.

the way Hiralal Haldar did. The challenges Frege, Russell, Moore, Wittgenstein, and others had thrown open were far more exciting to engage with than the doctrines of idealism which had become over familiar. New tools of logic and reasoning had become available to address the age-old metaphysical problems. Appropriation of Idealist doctrines in reinventing Advaita Vedānta seemed to have reached a point of saturation and had become repetitious, sterile, and nothing exciting was happening intellectually on the front of the neo-Vedāntins—at least it seemed to be so, as in the case of many neo-Vedāntins. The 'spiritualist turn' that the generation of Radhakrishnan, Malkani and others gave to Indian philosophy had lost its appeal and was no more acceptable. No more it was necessary to stick to the difference between Indian and Western philosophy in terms of such binaries as materialism and spiritualism. All these factors have played a major role in abandoning neo-idealism and neo-Vedānta by the prominent Indian philosophers such as D.Y. Deshpande (1917–2005),[37] S.S. Barlingay (1919–1997), K.J. Shah (1920–1994), Daya Krishna (1924–2007), M.P. Rege (1924–2000), Rajendra Prasad (1926–), and others. But apart from these factors, there is no substantial and sustained *internal* critique of the works of Seal, Haldar, Rasvihary Das, K.C. Bhattacharyya, Malkani and others. More than the inwardly felt theoretical dissatisfaction with what these philosophers have produced during the colonial period, the fascination for the new doctrines and philosophical positions that were emerging in Britain and America as reactions to idealism seems to have motivated this later group of philosophers to push the whole corpus of philosophical writings of their philosophical forebears into oblivion. It is hoped that this volume will initiate a critical engagement with that corpus rather than serving mere archival curiosities and retrieve the insights that might have gone unnoticed which modern Indian philosophers have tried to offer.

References

Bergmann, G. (1964). *Logic and Reality*. Madison: University of Wisconsin Press.

Bhandarkar, R. G. (1919). *The Sāṁkhya Philosophy*. In Indian philosophical Review, Jan. 1919 (Vol II) No.3, 193–199 included in Utgikar, N.B. and Paranjpe, V.G. (1993) (Eds) *Collected Works of Sir R.G. Bhandarkar* (Vol. I) Poona: Bhandarkar Oriental Research Institute.

Bhandarkar, R. G. (1920). Presidental Address. In *Proceedings and Transactions of the First Oriental Conference*, Nov. 1919 (Vol. I) Poona: Bhandarkar Oriental Research Institute.

Bhattacharyya, R. S. (1982). A new approach to Indian philosophy. In S.S. Rama Rao Pappu & R. Puligandla (Eds.), *Indian philosophy: Past and future*. South Asia Books.

---

[37] The founder member and secretary of the Indian Philosophical Association established in 1949 and also the Editor of the *Journal of Philosophical Association*. The formation of association and the publication of the journal were perceived as expression of dissenting voice within the Philosophical Congress demanding critical attitude towards Indian philosophy and receptivity to emerging philosophical movements led by Russell, Moore, and Wittgenstein. Most of the articles and symposia published in the *Journal of Philosophical Association* focus almost exclusively on several issues in early analytical philosophy and philosophers of that period.

Bhattacharyya, K. (Ed.). (1963). *Recent indian philosophy. Papers selected from the proceedings of the Indian Philosophical Congress* 1925–1934 (Vol. 1). Calcutta: Progressive Publishers Calcutta.

Bhushan, N., & Garfield, J. L. (Eds.). (2011). *Indian philosophy in English: From renaissance to independence*. New York: Oxford University Press.

Bowes, P. (1982). What is Indian about Indian philosophy? In S.S. Rama Rao Pappu & R. Puligandla (Eds.), *Indian philosophy: Past and future*. South Asia Books.

Das, R. (1968). *My Teacher As I Saw Him*. In Phanibhushan Chatterjee (Ed) Acharya Brajendranath Seal Birth Centenary Commemoration Volume (ABNSBCCV) Acharya Brajendranath Seal Birth Centenary Commemoration Committee, Calcutta.

Datta, D. M. (1956). India's debt to the West in philosophy. *Philosophy East and West, 6*(3), 195–212.

de Sousa Santos, B. (2007). Beyond abyssal thinking: From global lines to ecology of knowledges. *Review, 30*(1), 45–89.

Deshpande, S. (Ed.). (1997). *Philosophy of G.R. Malkani*. New Delhi: Indian Council of Philosophical Research.

Deshpande, S. (2010). Hegel in India. In H. Casper-Hehen & N. Gupte (Eds.), *Kommunikation über Grenzen*. Gottingen: University of Gottingen.

Devraja, N. K. (Ed.). (1975). *Indian Philosophy Today*. Delhi: Macmillan.

Ganeri, J. (2014). *The lost age of reason: Philosophy in early modern India 1450–1700*. Oxford: Oxford University Press.

Gokhale, P. (2012). Identifying philosophy in Indian tradition. In A.D. Sharma, J. Shankar, & R. C. Sinha (Eds.), *Dimensions of philosophy*. New Delhi: New Bharati Book Corporation.

Halbfass, W. (1990). *India and Europe, an essay in philosophical understanding* (1st Indian ed.). Delhi: Motilal Banarasidass.

Haldar, H. (1927). *Neo-Hegelianism*. London: Heath and Crantor.

Haldar, H. (1936). Realistic idealism. In S. Radhakrishnan & J. Muirhead (Eds.), *Contemporary Indian philosophy*. London (Indian Edition 1952).

Inden, R. (1986). Orientalist construction of India. *Modern Asian Studies, 20*(3).

Inge, W. R., Jacks, L. P., Hiriyanna, M., Burtt, E. A., & Raju, P. T. (Eds.). (1951). *Radhakrishnan: Comparative studies in philosophy presented in honour of his sixtieth birthday*. London: George Allen and Unwin.

Krishna, D. (Ed.), Bhatnagar, R. S. (Comp.). (1986). *Author and subject index of the Philosophical Quarterly*, Volumes I–XXXVIII (1925–1966). New Delhi: Indian Council of Philosophical Research.

Krishna, D., Rege, M. P., Dwivedi, R. C., & Lath, M. (Eds.). (1991). *Saṁvād: A dialogue between two philosophical traditions*. New Delhi: Indian Council of Philosophical Research.

Maitra, S. K. (1936). Outlines of an emergent theory of values. In S. Radhakrishnan, & J. Muirhead (Eds.), *Contemporary Indian philosophy*. London (Indian Edition 1952).

Maitra, S. K., Malkani, G. R., Murti, T. R. V., & Bhattacharyya, K. (Eds.). (1958). *Krishna Chandra Bhattacharyya memorial volume*. Amalner: Indian Institute of Philosophy.

Mathrani, G. N. (1940). *Wittgensteinian Philosophy or Studies in the New Cambridge Philosophy*, Sind: Prabhat Printing Press. (1990) Reprint Darshana Peeth, Allahabad.

Mehta, J. L. (1974). The problem of philosophical reconception in the thought of K.C. Bhattacharyya. *Philosophy East and West, 24*(1), 59–70.

Müller, M. (1879–1910). *The Sacred Books of the East*. Oxford University Press.

Murti, K. S. (1965). *The Indian spirit*. Waltair: Andhra University Press.

Murty, K. S. and Rao, K. B. (1972). (Eds) *Current Trends in Indian Philosophy*. Waltair: Andhra University.

Nurullah, S., & Naik, J. P. (1933). *History of education during the British period*. Bombay: Macmillan.

Patankar, R. B. (1999). *Apurṇa Krānti (in Marathi: Incomplete revolution)*. Mumbai: Mauj Prakashan.

Patankar, R. B. (2014). Indo-British encounter. In A. Joshi & A. Tikekar (Eds.). Pune: Rohan Prakashan.

Prasad, R. (1982). Tradition, freedom and philosophical creativity. In S. S. Rama Rao Pappu & R. Puligandla (Eds.), *Indian philosophy: Past and future*. South Asia Books.

Radhakrishnan, S. & Muirhead, J. (Eds.). (1936). *Contemporary Indian philosophy*. London (Indian Edition 1952).

Raju, P. T. (1936). The inward absolute and the activism of the finite self. In S. Radhakrishnan & and J. Muirhead (Eds.), *Contemporary Indian philosophy*. London (Indian Edition 1952).

Rao, K. B. R. (1982). The quest of Indianness of Indian philosophy. In S. S. Rama Rao Pappu & R. Puligandla (Eds.), *Indian philosophy: Past and future*. South Asia Books.

Ryle, G. (1963). *Introduction to the revolution in philosophy* by A. J. Ayer, W. C. Kneale et al. Macmillan & Co. Ltd.

Seal, B. N. (1899). *Comparative studies in Vaishnavism and Christianity*. Calcutta.

Seth, S. (2008). *Subject lessons: The Western education of colonial India*. Delhi: Oxford University Press.

Shukla, H. (1989). *Sanskrit ka samajshastra: Svanantrata sangram aur Sanskrit sahitya (in Hindi)*. Delhi, Varanasi: Bharatiya Vidya Prakashan.

Tilak, B. G. (1894). Moksha Müller Bhattānchā Vedānta. Editorial in Kesari, 4 September 1894. Reproduced in (1976) Samagra Lokmanya Tilak Vol. 5. Pune: Kesari Prakashan.

Wallerstein, I., et al. (1997). *Open the social sciences*. Stanford: Stanford University Press.

Chapter 2
Thought and Context: *Philosophy on the Eve of Colonialism*

V. Sanil

Abstract Unlike other disciplines in humanities and social sciences, philosophy has been hesitant in taking its colonial and post-colonial contexts seriously. Colonialism belongs to the external history of philosophy. Hence, it is often seen as a temporary disruption in a living tradition of thought or as a harbinger of philosophy proper. Such an external perspective does not help us in understanding the work of Indian philosophers who while living under colonialism actively engaged with both Eastern and Western thought but felt that philosophy of their time had lost its vitality and soul. This essay argues that to study philosophy under colonialism, we need to clarify the relationship between philosophy and its historical context. We discuss Sheldon Pollock's idea of the death of Sanskrit to formulate the temporality of a tradition that can live through multiple deaths. We defend Quentin Skinner's use of speech act theory to study philosophy and deepen Jonardon Ganeri's idea of intellectual context of intellectual traditions in India. Using the insights of historians such as Sanjay Subramanian et al. and philosophers such as Roland Barthes, we argue that the bearer of the marks of context is neither the proposition nor the text, but the texture of discourse for which the photograph is an exemplary instance.

Keywords Pollock · Ganeri · Skinner · Speech act · Swaraj · Context · Time

2.1 Philosophy and Its Historical Context

Colonialism has been a significant historical rupture for the self-understanding of most disciplines in humanities and social sciences. Reflection on colonialism has had the effect of transforming the very nature of these disciplines. Today, the 'post-colonial condition' defines research practices. Interdisciplinary in-disciplines such

V. Sanil (✉)
Department of Humanities and Social Sciences,
Indian Institute of Technology Delhi, Delhi, India
e-mail: mesanil@yahoo.com

© Indian Institute of Advanced Study 2015   41
S. Deshpande (ed.), *Philosophy in Colonial India*, Sophia Studies in Cross-cultural
Philosophy of Traditions and Cultures 11, DOI 10.1007/978-81-322-2223-1_2

as cultural studies and research programmes such as subaltern historiography have emerged from the post-colonial criticism of the epistemological and ontological foundations of traditional disciplines. Philosophy, while contributing to the critical resources of post-colonialism, has kept itself out of that critique. Philosophy sees itself as being concerned about eternal conceptual problems and so acknowledges colonialism only as a historical accident. Such accidents belong to the external history of the discipline and have no significance for the ongoing practice of problem solving. It is often claimed that philosophy does not and need not register its historical context. Here, philosophy would like to see itself in philosophy's own image of natural sciences.

One might object that this characterization of philosophy is only valid for certain ahistorical traditions such as the Anglo-American analytical philosophy. This tradition distinguishes between philosophy proper and history of philosophy and assigns only a pedagogical status to the latter. However, it may be claimed that the European continental philosophy does not work with such a hierarchy and acknowledges the historicity of philosophical reflection. This is only partially true. As we shall see soon, the concept of history or historicity that this tradition grants presupposes the neutralization of colonialism as a nonevent. The unabashed Eurocentrism of the masters of historically sensitive thought like Hegel and Husserl either makes colonialism a moment in the historical unfolding of ideality or a mere consequence of the crisis of European culture. In any case, the radical questioning of the idea of history and the historical ideality in this tradition has found its home in disciplines outside philosophy—such as comparative literature or even theology.

Often, our nationalist narratives of philosophy assume that colonialism was an oppressive condition under which those who philosophized at a particular historical juncture were forced to live and think. It caused the death and destruction of the ongoing tradition of classical philosophy and the advent of Western ways of thought and life (Coomaraswamy 1981: 1–6). Various strands of nationalism differ on evaluating the effect of these changes. Some see this as the destruction of our own glorious and continuous traditions and the imposition of an alien culture and thought. There are others who welcome this destruction. For them, the intrusion of Western philosophy brought out a necessary and fortunate transformation of the philosophy-like practice which existed in classical India to the modern philosophy proper (Mukherji 2002: 931–936). Colonialism as modernity challenged the authority of tradition and made philosophy a rational discourse that responded to the developments in modern science, politics, and art. Here, we can also expect a modern revivalist who locates all the features of modernity back in the very tradition destroyed by colonialism. We can make these claims about colonialism, tradition, and modernity only if we have some hold on the relationship between history, thought, and freedom. Otherwise, we shall end up treating colonialism as a mere historical marker for a period and discuss the works of philosophers who happened to live during that period. From this perspective, colonialism was an external accident that either destroyed existing traditions of philosophy and imposed an alien thought on us, or inaugurated philosophy proper. If we wish to take colonialism seriously, we need to explore the link between political freedom and philosophy and acknowledge the historical dimension of thought. The latter is the task this essay has set for itself.

The two contemporary participants in this debate—Anglo-American analytical philosophy and the Indian philosophy that is reconstructed in the 'Anglo-American style'—seem to be free from any sense of history and have nothing much to say on the relationship between the historical conditions of thought and freedom. The so-called continental philosophy takes both freedom and history seriously. However, the epochal masters of this tradition—Hegel and Husserl—were undoubtedly Eurocentric and denied Indian thought the status of philosophy. For Hegel, the only historical context that matters is the culmination of Philosophy in the West. For Husserl, the only moment of significance is the birth of philosophy in Greece. It is doubtful if we can explain away this Eurocentrism as a personal aberration of individual thinkers and carry on with their philosophy. A concept such as 'tradition' is symptomatic of this muddled state of affairs.

There have been several attempts in post-independence India to bring the traditional scholars and modern academic philosophers to a dialog. The *Saṁvād*, a project initiated by Daya Krishna et al. (1991), is an example. These attempts have failed miserably. The incommensurability of the participants' world-views has often been cited as the cause of this failure. However, as we know, incommensurability does not entail non-translatability. In fact, translation of traditional Indian philosophy into the modern idiom is continuing successfully. The works of B.K. Matilal and J.N. Mohanty are exemplary of this trend. However, such efforts do not seem to inspire either of the parties—modern Western philosophy or traditional Indian scholars. Is it possible to write the history of this indifferent silence and intellectual exhaustion?

Indian academic philosophy was active during the colonial rule. Philosophers who worked in Indian universities did have a presence in international journals. We find occasional review articles on philosophy in India. A review article by Schrader (1937: 335–341) published in *Philosophy* predictably makes patronizing comments on the nascent presence of philosophical impulses in India. Another review article by P.T. Raju in 1949 identifies six kinds of philosophical engagements taking place since the introduction of English education in India (Raju 1949: 342–347). Of these, the first two, namely a collection of manuscripts and translation of manuscripts primarily into English are not philosophy proper. The third kind involves the exposition of Indian thought in English, for example, S.N. Dasgupta, in his famous five volumes on *The History of Indian Philosophy*, and the fourth is the interpretation and evaluation of Indian thought often undertaken by missionaries. Comparative philosophy practiced by the likes of Radhakrishnan comes as the next kind. The sixth one practised by K.C. Bhattacharyya starts from a Western line of thinking but develop it in such way that to reach a result achieved by Indian thought. Those such as Hiralal Haldar, G.R. Malkani, and G.N. Mathrani took the seventh mode; they were proficient in Western philosophy but claimed no acquaintance with Indian philosophy.

All this shows that the colonial era was a period of intense activity which cannot be reduced to the invasion of traditional thought by Western philosophy and its thought habits. However, it was widely felt that this fervent activity did not announce the birth of a new possibility of thought. Even those who were proficient in both the classical Indian traditions and modern philosophy felt a sense of rupture, homelessness, and lack of spirit. A yawning gap seems to have opened up between the demands of philosophy and the clamor for a historical life. This listlessness finds its rigorous articulation in Bhattacharyya's (1984: 385) *Swaraj in Ideas*, a significant text which we shall discuss in the next section.

Serious talk about philosophy under colonialism makes sense only in so far as philosophy registers the event of colonialism. How can philosophy bear the mark of a historical event? Where do we locate this mark? Who/what is the bearer of this mark?—proposition, text or act? Do we expect that, to register the effect of colonialism, philosophers should speak explicitly about colonialism? Or should we try to study the causal influence of colonialism? How do we reconstruct the colonial against a paradoxical demand—the demand for an internal history of thought which could register an external event such as colonialism?

The project under the leadership of Sheldon Pollock titled *The Sanskrit Knowledge Systems on the Eve of Colonialism*[1] is perhaps the first concerted and self conscious attempt to address the significance of the historical context of colonialism for the study of Indian thought. This project focuses on the period between 1550 and 1750. According to Pollock, this period just before the consolidation of colonialism witnessed a sudden spurt of intellectual activity in many areas of classical Indian intellectual life. However, these vibrant traditions yielded to Western intellectual dominance without any resistance or serious engagement. This project demands an internal history of Sanskrit intellectual systems as a necessary condition for studying their encounter with colonialism. It speaks about an internal historical condition that rendered these traditions at once productive and speechless. What concept of historicity does this project propose? Does it have a notion of internal history which is sensitive enough to register an event such as colonialism? These are the questions I shall pursue in this essay. These questions should be important for anyone who accesses *our* traditional philosophical texts and practices without presupposing any strong sense of a *we*.

2.2 Philosophy: Twice Dead?

In K.C. Bhattacharyya, we hear a philosopher who lived and thought under colonialism speaking about his present. His *Swaraj in Ideas* takes his present as an explicit object for reflection. His main concern was not the subjugation of his own living tradition. He argues that such subjection when recognized loses its hold on the subjugated. What worried him was a sense of indifference or lack of vitality that had affected the philosophers and also the whole culture.

---

[1] http://www.columbia.edu/itc/mealac/pollock/sks.

That Indian Mind has simply lapsed in most cases for our educated men, and has subsided below the conscious level of our culture. It operates still in the persisting routine of their family life. And in some of their social religious practices which have no longer any meaning for them. It neither welcomes nor resists the ideas through the new education. It dares not exert itself in the cultural sphere. (Bhattacharyya 1984: 384)

According to Bhattacharyya, under colonialism, the Indian mind was in a state of paralysis. We either imitated the west or impotently resented them. We had failed to have estimates of our own, wrung from an internal perception of the realities of our position. What is 'our position'? Who is this 'we'? What is the mode of access to this reality? Ideas such as tradition and culture cannot provide answers. As Bhattacharyya says, the 'we' of those times was a 'we' who/which did not exert itself in the cultural sphere—a 'we' which lacked historical and cultural effectiveness. We had a soulless thinking which appeared like real thinking. Western ideas that sprang from the rich life elsewhere induced in us a shadow mind. It is important that Bhattacharyya did not appeal for a return to our blood and soil or any authentic 'we' to revitalize ourselves. Instead, he demanded that we bring the powers of a new vitality to all that is 'we.' He did not ask us to go back to our ancient texts. Instead, he wanted us to produce Indian appreciations of Western texts.

Pollock (2001) too attests to this general intellectual paralysis on the eve of colonialism. Even in the 19th century, there was no dearth of intellectual production in Sanskrit in the areas of literature, logic, etc. However, they were lifeless repetitions and not renewals. The Sanskrit scholars were busy "wasting their learning and powers in weaving complicated alliterations, recompounding absurd and vicious fictions, and revolving in perpetual circles of abstractions never ending still beginning" (Pollock 2001: 414).

Pollock gives a novel account of the temporality of this culturally paralyzed intellectual consciousness. First of all, this paralysis is not a consequence of any external invasion. It was also not the case that by the time the British arrived, the classical Indian tradition had died due to internal ailments and Indian intellectual consciousness was eagerly waiting for the new spirit. The degenerate Indian consciousness caught up in endless repetitions without renewal had no life left to wait and anticipate a new life. It simply absorbed the Western ideas into its repetitive grind.

The Indian tradition on the eve of colonialism was not a living one. It was dead in a sense more radical than what phenomenology can ever bring to life. That it was dead, seriously, and severely dead, is no negative judgment. No rational creature endowed with memory allows the dead to rot and disappear. The dead does return in ghostly and spectral apparitions. The dead does not cease to surprise us. The dead can be directly efficacious in the creation of the new. The creation of the new in the present establishes its link not with the dead old but with the 'old new' which the mnemonic practices preserve. How do we understand this mode of persistence of a dead tradition? How many times did Indian philosophy die?

Pollock's history of Indian knowledge systems indicates the complex nature of the historicity of Indian thought. Thought in India died twice. By 12th century AD, the centers of Sanskrit culture collapsed abruptly. This decline can be distinguished from the slowing down of creative process that had happened in earlier centuries. "In the 12th century, by contrast, a decline set in from which there was to be no recovery, contingent on new extremes of royal dissolution and criminality for which it is hard to find precedents" (Pollock 2001: 398–399). Between mid-15th century and the advent of colonialism in 1750, we find a spurt of creativity in Sanskrit intellectual traditions. This period witnessed new formulations of old problems in new genres. Here, we also see scholars who called themselves new (*Navya*). The second death is the death of these 'new' intellectual formations under colonialism. From this perspective, Indian philosophy is not a philosophy of the twice born, but a philosophy that is twice dead. Any attempt to think again with Indian philosophy should first of all recognize and affirm these deaths. How does time unfold through this double death? How can contemporary thinking take hold of this archive of the twice dead? A step in the direction of an answer is to question the very idea of a living tradition. What is it that continues to live in the dead? Freud had an answer—death drive! This survives beyond life and death. In fact, death drive was Freud's concept for immortality. Is there anything like that behind the insistence and persistence of a dead tradition?

2.3 Thought and Context

The valley of death called colonialism is often understood as a rupture. What is the mode of subjectivity that is a correlate of this rupture? To talk about philosophy under colonialism is to explain the works of this thinking subject in the context of a rupture or of a ruptured context. Ganeri (2008: 551–562) in a recent article addresses the significance of context in studying India's intellectual cultures. He brings out the complexity of the context in a discussion of Quentin Skinner's attempts to take the context seriously as part of the theory and method of studying intellectual history. Skinner (2002) uses Austin's speech act theory to study texts, including philosophical texts as performative utterances. To understand a text is not merely to understand its literal meaning but to understand what the text as a performative utterance intended to do. To understand a text means to follow its illocutionary force. To produce an utterance is to make an intervention. Skinner opposes the attempt to abstract particular arguments of thinkers from their context and constructing them as contributions to the perennial debates on eternal philosophical ideas.

According to Ganeri, Skinner's study of the intellectual cultures is based on the following assumptions. It is possible to recover the illocutionary force of past utterances. The illocutionary force is an evidence for what sort of thing the author was up to. We recover the illocutionary force by situating the act in a context. In other words, the context supplies the evidence for the illocutionary force. Ganeri finds many problems with using the Skinnerian contextualism in studying Indian intellectual texts. First of all, not much information is available about the socio-political contexts of pre-colonial Indian texts. However, there is a superabundance of literary or textual material. The primary context of Indian writers was a literary/intellectual context. These are inter-textual contexts. In fact, 'not to be distracted by physical contexts' could be part of the intentions of the illocutionary act. Definition is one such inter-textual illocutionary act. A definition could be an act of consolidation. However, Ganeri wants only a modest contextualism. He wants the contexts to supply some extra but minimum information and leave the philosopher free to deal with the definitions. Ganeri, in my view, wrongly thinks that the Skinnerian context is a physical–socio-political one. In fact, Skinner would readily agree with Ganeri on the importance of the intellectual context to the study of intellectual utterances. However, as we shall see later, contexts whether physical or intellectual do not stand toward speech-acts in the way Ganeri expects them to stand.

Ganeri finds that the Skinnerian context is too poor to account for the illocutionary act where the philosopher makes an utterance to make an intra-systemic intervention. Here, the philosopher tries to anticipate future critics and sympathetic interpreters. The actual intention in writing a text is to be interpreted creatively by future interpreters whose nature he does not know. Ganeri thinks that Skinner has failed to take notice of these 'intentionally proleptic illocutionary acts.' Skinner rejects two mythologies of historical interpretation—mythology of prolepsis and mythology of the doctrines. Prolepsis interprets a text more in terms of the retrospective significance of a given episode than in its meaning for the agent at the time. The mythology of the doctrine involves the presumption that there is a set of doctrines that constitutes a field that then tempts the historian into trying to find out what each classical author had to say or has failed to say about them.

Rejection of these mythologies will be a disaster for the approach of Matilal, Ganeri, and other contemporary interpreters of classical Indian philosophy. So Ganeri tries to defend these mythologies. According to him, both prolepsis and anticipation were part of the intentions of the Indian writers. The Indian writer intended his work for the unknown future readers. The mythology of the doctrine too is part of Indian intellectual reality. Philosophers encountered *śāstras* from the past not as historical documents but as current statements of philosophical knowledge. Each interlocutor regarded his interpretation as anticipated by the early writings. This would allow Ganeri to treat classical Indian texts as if they anticipate his Anglo-American interpretations. Ganeri realizes that Skinner's rejection of prolepsis and anticipation, if accepted, will undercut his access to the classical Indian thought. He finds a way out by making both these as part of the intentions of the illocutionary act. Here, Ganeri ignores a distinction Skinner has always insisted upon—between the intention of the agent *in the* illocutionary act and the plan the agent had while undertaking the act. One may say something with the intention of warning someone. This intention has to be recovered. However, my objective in warning someone is not part of the illocutionary intention. When I make an ironical utterance, I do not mean what I say. However, detecting irony works not at the level of meaning but at the level of the illocutionary act. The potential prolepsis of the classical Indian writers is not to be located at the level of meaning but at the level of the illocutionary act. In other words, the prolepsis as part of the speaker's intention does not escape the present of the utterance. Ganeri's defends the typical hermeneutical strategies of prolepsis and anticipation hoping that they will enable him to maintain a gap between the socio-political and intellectual contexts.

He hopes to recover speaker's intentions in uttering a statement from its context-transcending meaning. Skinner's criticism of these hermeneutical strategies is aimed at such a hope. We need to know a lot more about the context even to recover the context-bursting intention of the speaker.

Ganeri finds the Skinnerian context too narrow in another sense. He thinks that Skinner's appeal to context is merely evidential. The context provides the historian with the evidence for the kinds of illocutionary acts being performed. According to Ganeri, the context has another function—reference fixing. 'Tomorrow will be sunny' 'refers out' to tomorrow when the truth-value of this utterance will be decided. According to Ganeri, Skinner misses the distinction between the context of utterance and the context of evaluation. Indexical utterances may refer out of their context of use to another context with respect to which they will be evaluated. Our most normative expressions are cultural indexicals which refer out. Proleptic illocutionary acts are a special case of these references fixing illocutions. They may refer to future or to broad features of a culture.

Ganeri discusses Matilal's *Perception* as an example of studying intellectual culture. Matilal's context of utterance is contemporary Anglo-American analytical philosophy and his context of evaluation is the intellectual culture of classical India. It is that culture with respect to which the truth and falsity of specific utterances will be made. For Ganeri, these illocutionary acts show that Matilal was immersed in the classical culture of India. How is this possible? Ganeri (2008: 560) emphatically says "Matilal was responding to the obvious fact of colonialism." In other words, language or speech act already contains enough resources to jump over the mere fact of colonialism. The latter accounts for the fact that Matilal wrote in English and taught in the West instead of writing in Sanskrit and teaching in a traditional *pāthaśālā* in India. The colonial context of his utterance does not affect the truth of what he says. The context of evaluation that matters for the truth is the intellectual context of classical Indian philosophical discussions. Through this distinction, Ganeri hopes that he can get rid of the socio-political context from evaluating philosophical utterance. However, he misses the fact that for Skinner and also Austin the radical nature of speech act theory lies in the very idea of context and not in any specific kind of context such as socio-cultural one.

How is it possible for a post-colonial intellectual to jump across the rupture of colonialism and get in touch with the pre-colonial Indian intellectual culture in terms of categories of a post-rupture context? For Ganeri, this pole vaulting is not a new or serious problem. The pre-colonial Indian culture was full of such ruptures. Jumping across the rupture while continuing to be indelibly marked by it, reconceptualising the pre-rupture past in the categories of a post-rupture present—these are among the most characteristic mark of Indian intellectual practice. Matilal can jump across contexts because what awaits him on the other side is nothing but such ruptures and jumps. Quoting J.L. Mehta, Ganeri (2008: 561) argues that the distance introduced by these ruptures is an enabling condition for accessing 'the what' that is on the other side. Hermeneutic patience demands that we see their things in their way and our things in our way while jumping across the rupture of colonialism. But the colonialism has created a rupture between our thing and our way. Journeys in their world would eventually allow us to close the gap between our things and our ways. If colonialism created a distance, it also gave us fast trains to cover that distance faster than ever!

Let us notice that Ganeri is endorsing a modern concept of tradition and the idea of a productive distance from past acts as the very opening for our access to that tradition. Tradition as a hermeneutical idea captures the essential historicity of modern consciousness. It is a relationship with an origin which at once approaches and retreats. Like horizon, it sets the backdrop of our approaching but recedes as we gets closer. This concept of tradition is available only to an effective historical consciousness that affirms the essential historicity of thought. This affirmation demands more than the fallibilist self-understanding of theory construction, argumentation, and debate. It is one thing to hold that ideas evolve in time. It is another thing to say that the sense of an idea is the history of its sense. A historical consciousness which affirms the latter is already always modern.

Ganeri endorses this radical hermeneutic conception of tradition so that he could limit Skinner's appeal to context to evidential value. In fact, Skinner does not look at context for the kind of evidence which Ganeri thinks he is looking for. Ganeri's expectation about this context can perhaps be traced to a certain picture of speech act theory circulated by P.F. Strawson (1964). According to Austin, for the success of a speech act of warning, the agent should secure the uptake of the act as the act of warning. What does securing the uptake mean here? Strawson demands that to secure the uptake, the agent should make some difference to the existing state of affairs as a result of that action. Skinner disagrees with this analysis. Success of a speech act need not cause any change in the surrounding state of affairs. In some cases such as warning, it may be part of the intention of the speech act that it produces no visible change in the state of affairs. To warn someone, I need to point out to him that he is in danger. To succeed in warning, I need to succeed in adverting to that fact. The uptake involves this event of adverting and not anything new in the state of affairs that can be represented as brought out by the successful performance of that act.[2] In case such as warning and informing, the change brought about by a successful speech act may just be the event or happening of the act. In other words, the context does not play the evidential role Ganeri thinks it does in Skinner's account. Had he been right about Skinner then his hermeneutic notion of context would have been a radical alternative to latter's naïve notion. However, in reality, it is Ganeri who fails to see Skinner's radical use of speech act theory. Skinner reaches his illocutionary act after suspending the claims to truth and also about meaning. The intention in warning is the intention to warn seriously. The context seeking entity is not the correspondence seeking proposition nor the meaning seeking and context-transcending text. Language registers context only at this level beneath the proposition and text. Utterances of intellectual culture at this level are neither arguments nor interpretations. They are acts which are meant to be taken seriously.

---

[2] A student in a classroom wishes to warn his fellows who are busy talking among themselves that the teacher is likely to notice them. To succeed, this warning act must call the attention of the talkers to the act of warning without leaving any evidence in the context that which the teacher could possibly notice.

2.4 Textures of Time

Pollock's review (2007) of *Textures of Time* (Rao 2001) is another occasion where the historian of intellectual culture disavows this context registering element of intellectual creations. *Textures of Time* interprets a score of texts from 15- to 18-century South India to demonstrate the emergence of sense of history. The authors see this as a counter to the Eurocentric claims that Indian did not have a sense of history. What makes these texts bearers of a historical consciousness? According to *Textures of Time*, this historical sense lies in their intention to be historical or in their style of being matter of fact or in their texture which a native speaker can easily identify as history and not story. Pollock is surprised by the naiveté of this claim made by three well-known historians. If the sense of history too is historically constituted, how can the native speaker so easily pickup the texture of history? Can the native have such immediate access to the text? Pollock wonders how the authors could; even in this hermeneutical post-modern times, hold that the historical is a register of language that is simple, direct, unadorned and factual.

Pollock quotes Barthes who allegedly denies any difference between narrative of past events and imaginary narration. He goes on to say that for Barthes, the closer we get to the factual, the closer we get not to the historical but to the effect of the real. This is a serious misunderstanding of Barthes' realism. For Barthes, 'effect of real' means reality as in the effect and not a mere effect of or an illusion of being real. It is the bare real that even the worst simulation or manipulative digital photograph would attest to. For Pollock, events become historical facts only when embedded in a narrative. Factuality is a narrative feature and hence cannot be used to identify a narrative as historical. Pollock thinks that authors of *Textures* hold a naïve notion of factuality that can be overcome with the hermeneutic notion of narrative embeddedness of all facts. However, the historical facticality which *Textures* upholds is neither that of brute facts nor of narrated and embedded facts. It is a 'rubbing with reality' which cannot be understood at the level true propositions or of meaningful narratives.

Pollock seems to worry that *Texture's* claim on direct access to historicality implies an objectivist conception of history as knowledge of facts. Such an objectivism, according to Pollock, would reintroduce the dichotomy between history and myth. Hence, he thinks that the texture surrenders the Indian conceptions of temporality to the Western concept of factual history which is often distinguished from the imaginative narrations of myth. Pollock's worry is unfounded. Textures do not pitch history against myth. It shows how the myth itself can directly register reality. This register is not that of narration. Textures talks about the dent reality can make on the plane of narrative. These dents are not accessible through an interpretation of narratives.

Pollock's reference to Barthes is a fortunate one. Though I disagree with his use of Barthes, the latter offers some vital insights into some of the issues we have been discussing—context, historicity, and also death. In his last work, *Camera Lucida*, Barthes (2000) speaks about the reality effect of photographs. We can follow this text and use the photograph as a picture of how the historical discourse refers to historical reality. Neither resemblance nor representation can account for this 'reality effect' of the photograph. Of course, the photograph follows conventions and codes and offers room for interpretation. Yes, it is the photographer who frames the picture and decides what is going to be inside the frame. Despite all these, the photograph bears the 'effect of the real.' Here, Barthes (2000: 25) introduces a distinction between *Studium* and *Punctum*. Studium[3] is the conventional, encoded, or narrativised aspect of the photograph which enables us to recognize the photograph as the photograph of something. *Punctum* is a mark of the photograph's chance encounter with reality. This is not something conventional, coded, or narrativised. It could be a contingent detail or an accident—a singular accident like death. *Punctum*, in Derrida's words, is a poignant singularity:

> … a point of singularity which punctures the surface of reproduction—and even the production—of analogies, likenesses and codes. It pierces, strikes me, wounds me, bruises me, and, first of all, seems to look only at me. …The singular punctum does not negate the general, the law or the convention. It only arrows it, marks it and signs it. (Derrida 1988: 259–296)

The reality claim of the photograph is not based on the fact that the object photographed was once present in front of the camera and was causally effective in making a mark on the film. Digital photography can do away with any direct encounter between the object and the machine. Still, the reality claim of the photograph would persist. One could say that the reference adheres to the photograph. In the intentional movement of reference, the absent referent comes to haunt the photograph. This haunting or spectrality is the mode in which the 'effect of the real' works in the photograph. This adherence implies the 'having-been-there' of a unique referent and thus, 'the return of the dead.' For Barthes, this is the 'stubbornness of the referent in always being there.' The image develops the have-been-there of the noema into an 'intense immobility' of pose through the clicking of the camera. The having-been-there of the referent is immediately separated and attached to the present of the photograph. This is the unique time of the referent which persists regardless of photographic reproduction, simulation, or composition. "It is as if the photograph always carries its referent with itself, both affected by the same amorous or funeral immobility" (Barthes 2000: 6). This immobility resists further development, mediation, and interpretation. Barthes distinguishes between the what-has-been of the photograph from and the temporality of what is no longer. This distinction explains the evidential value of the photograph. The authenticity of the photograph is not inferential. It is direct and immediate. A photograph can lie about the meaning of an object not about is existence. It is indifferent to fiction and metaphor. In a photograph, the past is as real as the present—the photograph we hold in our hands.

---

[3] It is interesting that Barthes uses the Buddhist concept of *tathatā* (*That, there it is*) to explain the referential claim of the photograph.

Since the referential implication is intentional and noematic; the referent is partly in me and also in front of me. The photograph's testimony bears not on the object but on time. The referent is the irreplaceable other, the one who was and will no longer be, who returns like that which will never come back. Such is the 'return of the dead.' The photograph marks this return of the dead to the reproductive image. The power of this authentication exceeds that of representation and narration.

Every photograph, irrespective of the subject matter, registers the catastrophe of death. The reference persists as a specter that haunts the photograph. The *punctum* is at once unique and other than itself—heterogeneous. This unique singular induces and is drawn into metonymy. As Derrida puts it, "If the photograph bespeaks the unique death, the death of the unique, this death repeats itself immediately, as such, and is itself elsewhere" (Derrida 1988: 260). The photograph draws together the unique death and the death of the unique. Hence, death is always in the plural—deaths.

Thus, Barthes' 'effect of the real' when seen in the context of the photograph gives us a model to think about historicity. It allows us to acknowledge 'the direct uptake' of the historical demanded by *Textures* without regressing below Pollock's hermeneutical vigilance. This also enables us to think the historicity proper to colonialism which is often couched in negative terms—as oppression and destruction. Pollock's misguided reference to Barthes' 'effect of the real' gives us a clue to former's idea of the twin deaths of Indian's intellectual traditions on the eve of colonialism. The photograph combines the singularity of the haunting reference with the plurality of death. This opens up a new level of engagement with our intellectual tradition. On this level, the tradition is not available as a set of propositions or narratives. The radical potential of Austin's speech act theory lies in opening up this new level. Ganeri's context-bursting potential of speech acts and the referencing fixing function of contexts have to be understood within the intentional movement of photographic reference. Thus seen, colonialism will be more serious than a mere break in history which we could easily bridge through the rational reconstruction of ancient intellectual traditions. Nor was it a period of and total destruction and enslavement that cut us off from our past. The past persists as our spiritless pursuits.

Textures of Time, when seen through Barthian lenses, does not put history against myth. In fact, it takes myth on the same level as history. It is one thing to collapse the distinction between myth and history and another to see both myth and history as registering the haunting reality of the event. Here, allow me to mention Giorgio De Santillana's *Hamlet's Mill*, study of a myth which encodes data on the precession of equinoxes (De Santillana and von Dechend 1977). Why does these data take the form of myth? For Santillana myth is neither failed science nor misguided technology. According to Santillana, myth is knowledge about cosmological events. "Myths can be used as a vehicle for handing down solid knowledge independently from the degree of insight of the people who do the actual telling of stories, fables, etc" (De Santillana and von Dechend 1977: 312). This knowledge is generated and transmitted without involving the subjective conditions of the knower. What does it mean to represent an event? For us, it involves bringing it under the subjective conditions of space and time. This makes the event into a historico-geometrical fact. The ancients had a different relationship with the event. It is not that the precession of equinoxes threatened the immature science of the ancients forcing them to invent some escapist explanation. They had a cognitive grid that could register barbaric events. To represent time means to set up a theater in which space and time can emerge as characters. This drama stages the very birth of the subject endowed with a sense of history, culture, and science.

Myth is ambiguous and allows a plurality of narratives. But this does not mean that it anticipates and explores an order in the fictional dimension. It is not the stories themselves that maps time but their affect—being appalling, comforting, and fearful. The native in *Textures* is expected to pick up this affect.

So far we have talked about the level of intellectual discourse which could possibly register its historical context. However, as I said in the beginning, talk about colonialism is possible only if philosophical discourse acknowledges a link between thought and freedom. For Hegel, in the Orient only the despot was free, in Greece some were free and only in Western Europe all were free. Insofar as the ideal of Western liberal democratic freedom guides our struggle against colonialism and modernity, it becomes the inescapable framework to relate thought and freedom. Attempt to show that ancient India too had a sense of democracy, sovereignty, and argumentative freedom only expands this framework. Perhaps, we should question this very fantasy of Oriental despotism. Why did Enlightenment reason and its ideal of freedom need this fantasy of despotism? The idea of Enlightenment freedom cannot work without this phantasmatic kernel. Genuine decolonization demands not debunking but an effort to work through this fantasy. This would be the subject matter for another essay.

References

Barthes, R. (2000). *Camera Lucida: Reflections of photography* (Richard Howard, Trans.). London: Vintage.

Bhattacharyya, K. C. (1984). Swaraj in ideas. *Indian Philosophical Quarterly, XI*(4), 383–393.

Coomaraswamy, A. K. (1981). The deeper meaning of struggle. In *Essays in national idealism*. New Delhi: Munshiram Manoharlal Publishers Pvt. Ltd.

De Santillana, G., & von Dechend, H. (1977). *Hamlet's Mill*. New Hampshire: David R. Godine Publishers, Inc.

Daya Krishna, Rege, M. P., Dwivedi, R. C., & Lath, M. (Eds.). (1991). *Saṁvād: A dialogue between two philosophical traditions*. New Delhi: ICPR.

Derrida, J. (1988). The deaths of Roland Barthes. In H.J. Silverman (Ed.), *Philosophy and non-philosophy since Merleau-Ponty*. New York, London: Routledge.

Ganeri, J. (2008). Contextualism in the study of Indian intellectual cultures. *Journal of Indian Philosophy, 36*, 551–562.

Mukherji, N. (2002). Academic philosophy in India. *Economic and Political Weekly, 37*(10), 931–936.

Pollock, S. (2001). The death of Sanskrit. *Society for Comparative Study of Society and History, 43*(02), 364–381.

Pollock, S. (2007). Pretextures of time. *History and Theory, 46*, 364–381.

Raju, P. T. (1949). The state of philosophical studies in India. *Philosophy*, *24*(91), 335–341.

Rao, V. N., Shulman, D., & Subramanian, S. (2001). *Textures of time: Writing history in South India 1600–1800*. Delhi: Permanent Black.

Schrader, O. (1937). Contemporary Indian philosophy. *Philosophy*, *12*(47), 342–347.

Skinner, Q. (2002). *Visions of politics, volume 1: Regarding method*. Cambridge: Cambridge University Press.

Strawson, P. F. (1964). Intention and convention in speech acts. *The Philosophical Review*, *73*(4), 439–460.

Chapter 3
Philosophy in Colonial India: The Science Question

S.G. Kulkarni

Abstract This essay purports to highlight the creative dimensions of modern Indian philosophy by focusing on the ways it configured colonial reality and came to terms with the question of modern science and technology. The three main perspectives on colonialism can be characterized as (a) a theory of Total Subjugation (b) a theory of Cultural Self; and (c) a theory of Revitalization to which correspond, respectively, three points of view regarding modern science and technology, namely (a) unqualified acceptance, (b) qualified acceptance and (c) qualified rejection. The first and the second responses promoted, with different degrees of vehemence, the project of India as a nation state to be built under the leadership of a scientific and technological elite, whereas the third response made room for the project of India as a civilizational endeavour led by artisans and craftsmen.

Keywords Science · Technology · Colonialism · Cultural self · Vedānta · Modernity · Nationalism

The aim of this essay is to make a case against the received view that Modern Indian philosophy is either not modern or not Indian or not philosophy. From the point of view of this essay, two central themes, among others, of philosophical reflections in colonial India are 'Colonialism' and 'India' themselves. In pursuing its objective, the essay (a) looks at the broad philosophical responses to the colonial reality, (b) considers the positions adopted by Indian thinkers regarding modern science and technology and (c) takes a critical look at the academically influential and intellectually powerful anti-colonial theories associated with Franz Fanon, Aime Césaire, Albert Memmi and Edward Said.

Before we go to each of these three sections, it is necessary to note that philosophy in colonial India was an integral part of a vibrant ethos that shaped

S.G. Kulkarni (✉)
Department of Philosophy, Central University of Hyderabad, Hyderabad, India
e-mail: sgkhcu@gmail.com

© Indian Institute of Advanced Study 2015
S. Deshpande (ed.), *Philosophy in Colonial India*, Sophia Studies in Cross-cultural Philosophy of Traditions and Cultures 11, DOI 10.1007/978-81-322-2223-1_3

the national consciousness.[1] The very fact of such an ethos goes against the conventional wisdom that cultural productivity is a direct function of material prosperity. For, never in the history of India, material deprivation was so devastating, as evidenced by the massive decline in agricultural production and near decimation of native industries so well documented by our economic historians. But at the same time, every field of cultural endeavour witnessed abundant creativity.

3.1 Responding to Colonial Reality

We now come to the three responses to the colonial reality made by the Indian thinkers. The first response came in the form of what we may call 'the theory of total subjugation.' According to this response, imperialism decimated both the social–economic–political body of India and its cultural self once and for all. No doubt, some of those who supported the theory of total subjugation were convinced that the pre-colonial India was a decadent society that had to fall as a result of historical necessity and hence, they had no tears to shed. Others who supported the theory of total subjugation did shed tears. But for both, the task at hand was to violently put an end to the conquest and hegemony by the same means adopted by the conqueror. The result was the birth of a militant nationalism which internalized the conqueror even while seeking to nullify the conquest.

It is immature to consider this theory as self-defeating and as a shallow analysis of colonial experience. The ideas of total conquest and complete hegemony which are central to this theory can be of great value in appreciating the precise nature of the devastating effects of colonialism. But what illuminates the colonial situation at the primary level might start giving diminishing returns in understanding in nuanced terms the possibilities the victim of colonialism envisions in facing the challenge. In short, the theory of total subjugation presents the victim as just a victim rather than an active agent and a cognitive subject who refuses to accept his characterization provided by the conqueror and in turn creates an idiom for understanding himself, his situation and even the conqueror.

What is special about the second response—the theory of cultural self—is that while recognizing that the body, i.e. the social–economic–political system, is irreparably damaged, it maintains that the cultural self stands unscathed. The body has to be rejuvenated rather recreated with the help of the West, including its scientific and

---

[1] This is so for every kind of creative endeavour in colonial India. Both in aesthetic theory and practice, tradition was mobilized as 'an oppositional category in the decolonization process' and as a source of creative possibilities (Kapur 1990: 49–53). In her excellent work, Janaki Bakhle (Bakhle 2005) vividly brings out how, among others, V.N. Bhatkhande and V.D. Paluskar sought to make Hindustani *sangeet* the national music of India by integrating it into cultural nationalism. Their attempt to classicize, categorize and thus 'sanitize' Indian classical music was aimed at making it part of the nationalist project. Their attempt involved, among other things, a radical change in the institutional framework of its practice and pedagogy.

technological resources, preferably once colonialism ends. Obviously, the supporters of this view do not show much concern for the material culture of the colonized. The cultural self which, according to them, finds its expression in our spiritual traditions and art as understood in terms of its spiritual meaning is district from and superior to the cultural self of the modern West. By construing the colonized society in cultural terms and by viewing contemporary reality standing outside history and present predicaments, it blacks out the colonizer himself from its purview. This theory thus seeks to establish the self-esteem of the colonized in transcendental terms. The transformation of non-contemporary into the timeless blinds this theory to the serious problems inherent in the colonial society from pre-colonial times. For instance, the supporters of this view typically overlook the problem of caste. Vivekananda, Aurobindo and Ananda Coomaraswamy are the most vocal espousers of this theory though Ananda Coomaraswamy's subsequent concern with craftsmen and artisans saved him from complete absorption into this view.

The third response, best represented by Gandhi, may be called 'the theory of revitalization' of the body and the self of the colonized. The theory of complete subjugation had a marginal acceptance in India. The theory of cultural self was not widely accepted because it was seen to be too exotic to be of any relevance for the political project of independence. The third view even while admitting the damage done to the social body and the cultural self strongly maintains that both can recover, not by following the colonizer and using his method of conquest in reverse or even imitating him either in material or cultural domain. It is only by mobilizing the badly damaged cultural and material resources that ordinary people have jealously guarded and kept alive that both the cultural self and the social body can be rejuvenated. At the core of this view was the faith that imperialism could not help leaving something untouched. What that something is and what saved it could not be clearly identified. Gandhi sometimes even spoke of caste system as the saviour of this something, but did not elaborate on this thesis. Different supporters of the third view articulated this something in different ways. But, what is important is not what this something is, but the fact that there was something which could not be decimated by imperialism. That something was more in imagination and that imagination saved us from losing our agency and subject-hood, in fact from a complete loss of mental equilibrium. It may have been even a utopia or golden past which, as Fanon says, saves the colonized from a total psychological breakdown. The status and the role of that something can be very well brought out by means of a folktale D.R. Nagaraj mentions in this context[2]:

Ravikirti and Chandrakirti were two kings. Ravikirti was aggressive and cruel. He wanted to invade Chandrakirti's kingdom and imprison him. His plan was successful because Chandrakirti's sister who had fallen in love with Ravikirti after seeing his picture had the doors of the fort opened. Ravikirti imprisoned Chandrakirti, and would daily get Chandrakirti to his court, and humiliate and

---

[2] I am indebted to the late D.R. Nagaraj for the identification and characterization for these three broad responses to colonialism as well as the folktale (Nagaraj 1996: 3–8).

torture him. But, Chandrakirti would come to court every day fresh and smiling. The king wanted to know the secret of Chandrakirti's disposition. He went to the prison at night and came to know that Chandrakirti had a monkey as his companion. The monkey, using colourful rags, was dressed like the king and imitated, rather caricatured, him. Chandrakirti burst into laughter again and again and thus overcome the depression and agony caused by humiliation and torture. Obviously, the king had the monkey killed.

For some time, Chandrakirti was extremely depressed. But soon he recovered and again the king was terribly intrigued. He again went to the prison. Chandrakirti was fast asleep. When the king was about to leave, Chandrakirti began to laugh in his sleep and to communicate with the monkey in his dream. The dream monkey was doing the same things that the real monkey had done. The king was helpless since he could not kill the dream monkey. He released Chandrakirti and returned his kingdom to him.

The dream monkey symbolizes that which the colonial elite thought the colonizer could not kill. As Nagaraj points out, if our theorists of colonialism had realized that a dream monkey cannot be killed, their way of looking at the phenomenon of colonialism would have been radically different (Nagraj 1996: 5).

3.2 Reception of Modern Science

We now consider three major Indian responses to modern science (and technology) which square with the three responses to colonialism briefly discussed above.

When the British introduced modern education in India, science was not part of it. Rather, the new educational curriculum consisted of English language, English literature, English law, public administration, etc. This was consistent with their aim adumbrated in Macaulay's Minute. However, subsequently, modern science and technology came to occupy an important position in the curriculum. The reason behind the shift becomes clear from the letter of Sir Richard Temple, Governor of Bengal, dated February 18 1875 written to the Viceroy Northbrook. In this letter, Temple says:

> No doubt the alumni of our schools and colleges do become as a class discontented. But this arises partly from our higher education being too much in the direction of law, public administration, and prose literature, where they may possibly imagine, however erroneously, that they may approach to competition with us. But we shall do more and more to direct their thoughts towards practical science, where they must inevitably feel their utter inferiority to us. (Quoted in Dharampal 2000: 52)

In response to the opinion such as the above modern science was introduced in a big way. It is evident that the aim of such major policy shift was to use modern science to reinforce the myth of pre-colonial barbarism, to beak the self-confidence of the natives and undermine their self-esteem. The Indian thinkers were very well aware of this project. The question they faced was: What are the possible responses so as to undo or at least mitigate the effects of this project?

The responses can be classified into minor and major ones. This characterization should not be taken literally. The minor responses are not minor in the literal sense. They are significant responses. It is only from the point of view of this essay that they are characterized as minor. There are two such minor responses: (i) an attempt to show that pre-British India had a vibrant scientific tradition—an attempt best exemplified in the work of Prafulla Chandra Ray on the history of Indian chemistry and Brajendranath Seal on the history of positive sciences in ancient India; and (ii) initiating an Indian tradition of modern science, with which aim Mahendra Lal Sarkar and his friends started the Indian Association for the Cultivation of Sciences.

3.3 Militant Nationalists: *The Unqualified Acceptance*

Coming to the major responses to modern science, we can discern three. The first response, which we may call unqualified acceptance of modern science, was that of militant nationalists of India. Their focus was on modern biology, and particularly, the theory of evolution which they called 'Darwinism', ignoring the fact that there was pre-Darwinian theory of evolution from which Darwin departed in important ways. However, they understood biological evolution through the eyes of their hero, Herbert Spencer. In doing so, they shut their eyes to the fact that Spencer sought to provide a biological justification for colonialism. In his *Social Statics* (1850), Spencer says "The forces which are working out the great scheme of perfect happiness, taking no account of incidental suffering, exterminate such sections of mankind as stand their way" (quoted in Mamdani 2005: 262). Even Darwin anticipated, without any pain, the elimination of weaker races in a not-so-distant future. In his *Descent of Man* (1871), he says, "At some future period not very distant as measured in centuries, the civilized races of man will almost certainly exterminate and replace throughout the world the savage races" (quoted in Mamdani 2005: 262). One wonders how the elimination of savage races is a biological necessity *à la* natural selection as natural selection works on a whole species and not on sections of it.

Herbert Spencer's thinking fits very well into the idea of progress as a result of elimination of weaker races—an idea which fascinated the militant nationalists of India. A few words are in order regarding the grip of Spencer on the minds of militant nationalists of India for whom Darwinism was the essence of modern science and Spencer's ideas provide a distilled account of Darwinism. Shyamji Krishnavarma (1857–1930) founded India House at High Gate, London, which became a centre for the militant nationalists of India. He had close links with Abhinav Bharat, a militant organization of Maharashtra, one of whose founders was Vinayak Damodar Savarkar. In fact, on Tilak's recommendation, Krishnavarma took Savarkar under his tutelage. Like any young radical of the time, Krishnavarma came so completely under the influence of Spencer that he endowed an annual lecture in Spencer's honour from 1905. It stopped in 1910 when he was asked to vacate his place. He was suspected to have provoked Madan Lal Dhingra into murdering Curzon-Wyllie, the Aide-de-Camp (ADC) to the Secretary of State for India, on 1 July 1909. During his stay in London and subsequently in Paris, he ran a monthly called *The Indian Sociologist* whose head mast carried two quotations from Spencer. The aim of the monthly was the propagation of Spencer's ideas, which were thought to be essential for the modernization of India. Not surprisingly, Krishnavarma, attacking *Hind Swaraj* in his article of October 1913 issue of his monthly, called Gandhi "an admirer of Jesus Christ, trying to practice the extreme Christian theory of suffering" (quoted in Parel 1997: vii) and condemned his philosophy of non-violence as "utterly subversive of all ethical, political and social ideals" (quoted in Parel 1997: xvi).

Another admirer of Spencer was Taraknath Das, an important militant nationalist and a member of Bengal Secret Society—*Anusheelan Samiti*. Like Krishnavarma, Das also ran a monthly named *Free Hindustan* from various places in USA with the same aim as *The Indian Sociologist*. Both the monthlies carried the same quotations from Spencer on their mast head.

Thus, the first response to modern science was one of unqualified acceptances of science which viewed science as the only way of national liberation and nation-building. Modern science was viewed as centred on what they thought to be Darwinism which itself was understood through the prism of Spencer's ideology.

It is interesting to see what Gandhi's view of Spencer was. There is some indirect evidence to the effect that his opinion about Spencer was negative. While condemning Curzon-Wyllie's murder by Madan Lal Dhingra, Gandhi held that it was Dhingra's mentors who were the culprits. Knowing full well that they were admirers of Spencer's works, he held them guilty of undigested reading of worthless books. Secondly, in Chapter IV of *Hind Swaraj* titled 'What is Swaraj?' the reader who represents the militant nationalists is made to say "If the education we have received be of any use, if the works of Spencer, Mill and others be of any importance … I certainly think that we should copy English people…. It is therefore proper for us to import their institutions" (quoted in Parel 1997: 28). What follows this chapter is Gandhi's attempt to show how the reader's notion of Swaraj amounts to craving for 'tiger's nature without tiger.' Thirdly, to counter Spencerian modernists, Gandhi uses with approval a witty article by G.K. Chesterton in which he says, "They talk about Herbert Spencer's philosophy. What is the good of Indian national spirit if they cannot protect themselves from Herbert Spencer? But Herbert Spencer is no Indian; his philosophy is not Indian philosophy … I often wish it were not English either …" (Parel 1997: 28 fn)

3.4 Vivekananda and Aurobindo: *The Qualified Acceptance*

We now come to the second response to modern science. This response which is one of qualified acceptances is philosophically more significant than the first one. The strategy here was to own up modern science while dissociating it from anything Western and relate it to the indigenous philosophical tradition, namely the

Vedānta. This is very clearly articulated in the works of Vivekananda, Aurobindo and other luminaries. A few points are to be noted in this connection. First of all, modern science was de-historicized in the sense it was sought to be shown that the modern Western civilizational context in which modern science was born and grew was taken to be only incidental to modern science. Thus, neither the social context of its origin nor its *episteme*—to use the expression of Bachelard—was essentially related to the core of modern science. This strategy was directly opposed to the usual anti-imperialist strategy of questioning the universality of Western cultural artefacts and demonstrating their historical specificity. The strategy here was to highlight the universality of science and thus rubbish the claim regarding science as being unique to modern Western civilization. Secondly, modern science was separated from the philosophy of materialism the organic relation with which it was taken for granted, particularly in the 19th century, though not all scientists were committed to materialism. In this connection, Aurobindo says

> ... (my) attempt like that of Jeans and others is a reaction against the illegitimate attempts of some scientific minds in the nineteenth century ... who took advantage of the March of scientific discovery to discredit or abolish as far as possible the religious spirit and to discredit metaphysics as cloudy verbiage, exalting science as the only clue to the truth of the Universe. (quoted in Riepe 1986: 14)

Again,

> I think that attitude is now dead or moribund: I may observe that the conflict between religion and science never arose in India because... the two things were kept on separate but not opposing lines. (quoted in Riepe 1986: 14)

And again,

> They (i.e. scientists of to-day) declare that it is not the business of science nor is it within its means to decide anything about the great questions which concern philosophy and religion. This is the enormous change which the latest development of science has brought about.... The rock on which materialism was built and which in the 19th century seemed unshakeable has now been shattered (quoted in Riepe 1986: 18)

Similarly,

> This change can be felt by one like myself who grew up in the heyday of absolute rule of scientific materialism in the 19th century. The way which had been almost entirely barred except by rebellion now lays wide open to spiritual truths, spiritual ideas. (quoted in Riepe 1986: 18)

Once science was de-materialized, just one more step was needed to spiritualize it. The then recent scientific breakthroughs were taken to be consistent with, close to and even support the spiritual world-view and particularly, the Indian spiritualistic world-view best exemplified by Vedānta.

The idea that the extant theories of science facilitate the construction of a metaphysical and even a spiritualist theory of reality was quite palpably present even in the West in the early 20th century. In fact, in the second stage of modern western philosophy of science which ranges over the first three decades of the 20th century philosophy of science was construed as metaphysical edifice-construction on science—just as it was construed as methodological base-construction for science in the first stage during the 17th–19th centuries and logical reconstruction of science and existential deconstruction of science in the third and the fourth stages of modern Western philosophy of science. Mostly, such science-based metaphysical theories were spiritualistic. Many practising scientists from Schrödinger to Wigner indulged in such an endeavour, apart from Jeans, with whom Aurobindo concurs. However, it must be noted that no professional philosopher of science participated in such an exercise. In fact, this stage has been blacked out in the official histories of philosophy of science.

It must be noted that for the scientists reading a spiritual world-view in the extant theories of physics was an avocational endeavour and even a metaphysical luxury. For the post-independent Indian philosophers of science such as Pravas Jeevan Chaudhury and Ruth Reyna, it was an academic exercise. But for the philosophers of colonial India who sought to de-historicize and de-materialize and thus spiritualize modern science, it was an endeavour with a clear-cut political agenda of owning modern science without falling into the trap with which its introduction was linked. The task was to internalize modern science without the painful feeling of imbibing something alien which might continue to exist as a foreign body and, more importantly, to neutralize the imperialist effort to use science as an instrument of hegemony that could ensure capitulation of the colonized.

There was also a religious angle to the whole enterprise of domesticating science by treating it as an extension of Vedānta. It was to neutralize the effort of the Christian missionaries who sought to use science to debunk the native religious traditions. They considered science education as the first major step towards Christian emancipation of heathens. For instance, Alexander Duff started the journal *Calcutta Review* to propagate the idea of secular education as 'a species of religious education.' In fact, according to him,

> … if in India you only import useful knowledge, you thereby demolish what by its people is regarded as sacred. A course of instruction that professes to convey truth of any kind thus becomes a species of religious education in such a land (quoted in Killingly 1995: 177).

Numerous instances like this convinced the Indian thinkers of the need to show that modern science was more in line with the religious philosophy of India than that of Christianity—the official religion of the West—and Vedānta was the religious philosophy of India.

In the process of its deployment for domesticating science and countering the use of science for belittling the native religion, Vedānta became, unofficially speaking, the national philosophy of India. As a consequence, Vedānta as a *darśana* underwent a radical change in form, content, idiom and even its institutional framework. However, the question remains, 'why was only Vedānta thought to be footing the bill?' Part of the answer to this question is that the British dispensation itself had cleared the ground for transforming Vedānta from a popular *darśana* into a quasi-official philosophy in a manner the leading Indian thinkers received it as core philosophical component of the emerging national ethos. This point is very effectively brought out by Trevor Ling.

The most important figure in this connection was the Viceroy Lord Wellesley. Before he arrived in Calcutta in 1798, he had come to know about the revolts and insurrections in various parts of Bengal. He had realized that his brief was partly administrative and partly ideological. Hence, he began to seek principles of religion and governance from the native traditions that could help in conserving and stabilizing the British Empire which was still in the making. He did not take time to realize that the popular religious cults could not yield such principles. Apart from being unsophisticated, those who had rebelled against the British had owned them and even claimed to have inspired by them in their rebellious acts. Therefore, as Ling points out,

> It was necessary to look elsewhere, to something more politically reliable than the vital religion of the lower classes. He [i.e. Wellesley] was not long in finding the answer. It lay in the scholarly and philosophical tradition of Brahmanism, enshrined in the ancient Sanskrit texts which were still preserved and studied by the pundits of Benaras and Nabadwip. Wellesley decided that in future such learning should be promoted more energetically (Ling 1980: 62)

It is with this intention that he founded in 1800 the College of Fort William in Calcutta. As recorded in the minutes dated 10 July 1800, it aimed to fix sound and correct principles of religion and governance for the best security which could be provided for the stability of British power in India. Further, stimulating the milder and more spiritual aspects of Hinduism can neutralize the various Hindu cults to which the rebellious might take ideological resort.

> The Vedāntic philosophy…was now being revived and given a prominence it had not had for centuries… [If] a view of the world was required which would divert men's attention from material concerns and direct it instead to the pure eternal world of the spirit, or Brahman, then no better choice could possibly be made than the philosophy of Vedānta. (Ling 1980: 64)

Though the British policy took time to fructify fully, "by the end of the nineteenth century it had certainly helped very substantially to secure a new status for the purified Vedantic Hinduism, and also for the idea that Indian culture was at heart deeply spiritual while that of the West was grossly materialistic" (Ling 1980: 65). But, ironically, "the reinstatement of Sanskritic culture and the modernized veneer which Hindu religion received in the nineteenth century became for caste Hindus not only the source of new pride in their native culture but also, by the closing decades of the century, the basis of a growing Hindu nationalism" (Ling 1980: 63) the milder version of which produced the second response to modern science—the response of qualified acceptance—which squared with the second view regarding the very nature of colonialism and what it has done.

3.5 Gandhi and Coomaraswamy: *The Qualified Rejection*

We now come to the third Indian response to modern science. This response is best represented by Gandhi and Ananda Coomaraswamy and can be characterized as one of the qualified rejections. Unlike the second response, it does not believe in the desirability or in the possibility of domesticating science and thereby working out our own alternative modernity that can absorb the best of the tradition. According to the articulators of this response, we must not allow science and modernity more than a peripheral presence. Before modernity which by its very nature is exclusivist marginalizes the mass of people, we must marginalize it and the place of modern science in the cultural matrix be determined by such marginalization of modernity. Modernity should not provide the organizing principles of our collective life. Central to this response is the recognition of modern science as the content of modern technology; and hence, its inseparability from the ideology of industrialism. Just as those who came out with the second response creatively used the ideas of Western thinkers such as James Jeans, Gandhi and Coomaraswamy creatively used the ideas of those Western thinkers who stood against industrialism. Two of such thinkers stand out prominently— John Ruskin who was taken seriously by Gandhi and William Morris whose ideas were highly valued by Coomaraswamy. This explains why the core of the third response was ethical and aesthetic, whereas that of the second response was epistemic. It is true that Gandhi worked out an ethical critique of modernity on the basis of his reading of Ruskin's *Unto This Last*. Ruskin's critique of industrialism was not only ethical but also aesthetic. Gandhi would not have missed Ruskin's dictum given in *Unto This Last*, viz. 'Taste is the only morality.' Yet, there is an irony in the so-called inspiration given by Ruskin and Morris. The thinkers with whom the third response is associated were more critical of imperialism than those with whom the second response is associated. Yet, Ruskin was in no way anti-imperialist. In fact, he was a typical Tory imperialist and his attitude towards Indians was anything but positive. No doubt, he acknowledged that unlike the 'puritanical Scots' and 'Brutish Swiss', Indians were artful. In fact, unlike the British who, according to him, were inept at design due to their 'advanced civilization' savage races like Indians excelled in decorative art. However, he was deeply intrigued by the fact that the Indians who were lovers of art could display most despicable bestiality in the first war of Indian independence of 1857. This gave Ruskin sufficient reason for the British imperialism to continue. According to him, England like a kind Christian mother must reform the unruly and spoiled children like Indians (Brantlinger 1996: 467–472). Yet, all these anti-Indian platitudes did not come in the way of Gandhi's admiration for Ruskin's anti-industrialism.

William Morris who is held high by Coomaraswamy was not an imperialist crony. In fact, he was emphatic in saying that the British held India "by force and fraud for the advantage of the robber class in England" (quoted in Brantlinger 1996: 473 fn). Yet, he did not want Britain to quit India. The same is true of Sir George Birdwood, the author of the classic *The Industrial Art of India* (1880) which provided the theoretical basis of the arts and crafts movement that was very close to Coomaraswamy's heart.

All this shows that the Indian thinkers such as Gandhi and Coomaraswamy blacked out the pro-imperialist views, hard or soft, of these thinkers to get from them what they needed, namely an idea regarding how to reject the trappings of industrialism and how not to be overawed by the achievements of modern science and technology. They read in the writings of those Western thinkers the broad contours of a post-industrial vision. In fact, it is Coomaraswamy to whom we owe the concept of the post-industrial. Central to the conception of post-industrial society was the knowledge and practice of artisans and craftsmen.

3.6 Conclusion

We round up our discussion by briefly pointing out the overall philosophical significance of these three responses to modern science which square with the three broad views regarding the nature of colonialism.

Firstly, the three responses to modern science embodied in an embryonic form the two distinct projects of India to be pursued after independence. The first two responses, in different degrees and different ways, shaped the Indian project as one of the nation-building with modern science and technology playing the central role and those trained in them as agents of that transformation. The third response had the consequence of envisaging the project of India as that of a social endeavour in which artisans and craftsmen are the leading participants. In fact, the two projects are the two ends of the spectrum with many possibilities between them. The opening of such pluralistic possibilities rather than a monolithic view of future speaks immensely of the philosophical creativity displayed by the nationalist thinkers. It may be that the project of India as a nation state has overtaken the project of India as a civilizational endeavour and also it may be that at least in sober moments the project of building nation state is closer to the second response than to the first one which rejects anything Indian even at a theoretical level. Yet, the latter project, i.e. the project of India as a civilizational endeavour, exists as a subtext in our national consciousness haunting even those who vouch for the project of India as one of the building nation state as evidenced by the ideas of its most sensitive votary such as Jawaharlal Nehru. This is precisely because that subtext has a pedigree in the philosophically productive phase of our anti-colonial struggle.

Secondly, as mentioned in the beginning, philosophical thinking in colonial India shows how off the mark are the received theories of colonialism. The most sophisticated among those theories undoubtedly capture very well how Orientalism as a profession worked out the strategies to ensure that the colonized internalizes his representation as constructed by the colonizer. Yet, they fail to recognize the creativity in domesticating what is made out of him and what is offered to him and accepting them in his own terms. Philosophy in colonial India is highly significant because it amply brings out the fact that the victim even while being a victim, can transcend the victimhood at least at a cognitive level and thus affirm that victim is not just a victim.

References

Bakhle, J. (2005). *Two men and music: Nationalism in the making of an Indian classical tradition.* New York: Oxford University Press (Permanent Black, Ranikhet 2006).

Brantlinger, P. (1996). A postindustrial prelude to post colonialism: John Ruskin, William Morris and Gandhism. *Critical Inquiry, 32.*

Dharampal. (2000). *Collected writings* (Vol. 5). Mapusa, Goa: Other India Press.

Kapur, G. (1990). Contemporary cultural practice: Some polemical categories. *Social Scientist, 18.*

Killingly, D. (1995). Hinduism, darwinism and, evolution in late nineteenth century India. In D. Amigoni & J. Wallace (Eds.), *Charles Darwin's the origin of the species: New interdisciplinary essays.* Manchester: Manchester University Press.

Ling, T. (1980). Karl Marx and religion. In Europe and India. London: Macmillan.

Mamdani, M. (2005). *Good Muslim, bad Muslim.* Delhi: Permanent Black.

Nagaraj, D. R. (1996). *Sahitya Kathana (in Kannada).* Heggodu, Karnataka: Akshara Prakashana.

Parel, A. J. (1997). A note on the history of the text. In A.J. Parel (Ed.), *Gandhi: Hind swaraj and other writings.* New Delhi: Cambridge University Press.

Riepe, D. (1986). *Objectivity and subjectivism in the philosophy of science with special reference to India.* Calcutta: K.P. Bagchi and Company.

Chapter 4
The Self and Its Knowledge: *The Legacy of Rasvihary Das*

Nirmalya Narayan Chakraborty

Abstract This essay explores Rasvihary Das's idea of self-knowledge and tries to situate his thoughts in contemporary perspective. This essay begins with a description of the source and nature of the philosophical problem that one confronts when one talks about self-knowledge. Contrary to Rasvihary, a non-objectual view of self-knowledge has been shown to be worth considering. In the latter half of the essay, an account of different kinds of avowals has been taken up for scrutiny against the background of Rasvihary's ascription of immediacy to self-knowledge.

Keywords Elusiveness thesis · Non-conceptual information · Inner-sense model · Self-ascription · Misidentification · Avowal

4.1 The Problem of Self-knowledge

The Upaniṣadic seer urges us to know our own selves. The temple of the Delphic oracle carries the inscription 'Know thy self.' Since the dawn of civilization humans started asking about the nature of self. Self-knowledge as commonly understood is a common phenomenon. Every one of us quite effortlessly knows

Rasvihary Das (1894–1973) was born in district Sylhet, now in Bangladesh. He received his higher education in Kolkata. He was deeply influenced by two of his teachers, viz. B.N. Seal and K.C. Bhattacharyya, both very distinguished philosophers of early 20th century India. After completing his postgraduate studies at University of Calcutta, he joined Indian Institute of Philosophy, Amalner where he stayed for more than two decades, first as a senior fellow and then as Professor of Logic and Metaphysics. Here in Amalner he received training in Indian philosophy from some of the best traditional pandits. Later, he joined as a faculty in philosophy department of University of Calcutta where he was till his retirement. He was also visiting professor at the Universities of Harvard and Gottingen. He was the founder of Indian Academy of Philosophy, Calcutta that still fosters research and various other programmes in philosophy.

N.N. Chakraborty (✉)
Department of Philosophy, Rabindra Bharati University, Kolkata, India
e-mail: nirmalyanarayan@gmail.com

© Indian Institute of Advanced Study 2015
S. Deshpande (ed.), *Philosophy in Colonial India*, Sophia Studies in Cross-cultural Philosophy of Traditions and Cultures 11, DOI 10.1007/978-81-322-2223-1_4

a lot of things about our own selves: our beliefs, hopes, desires, fears, etc. We are unhesitatingly sure of our own intentional states, sensations and emotions. Any normal individual would claim a command over all these knowledge.

Even from the ordinary use of the word 'I', it seems that we all know the self. 'I' normally stands for the speaker or the knower. So to know the self is to know it as either the speaker or the knower. The relation between speech and knowledge (thought) has been highlighted in contemporary times by Donald Davidson. Davidson urges that ascription of thought requires ascription of the ability to interpret. Unless one can interpret speech, we cannot give an account of such a creature possessing thought. Ascription of thought and ascription of speech are contemporaneous. This line of thinking gives credence to Rasvihary's comment that to know the self is either to know it as a speaker or as a knower. Since speaking in a significant sense depends on knowing, we can consider the self as knower. To know anything as a knower is to know it as performing the function of knowing. And where else can one have this knowledge except in the direct experience of knowing that one has? When I have a cognitive experience, I know my own self directly as the knower. And precisely here, the philosopher raises the question: in a knowledge situation, do I know myself as the knower?

One could, of course, argue that there is no problem here, for we do certainly know ourselves as knower in the act of knowing. We cannot think of knowledge without any reference to the knower, the owner of the knowledge. We cannot think of colour without there being any object that possesses the colour. Experience of the colour implies experience of the object that has the colour. Similarly, an epistemic experience requires an acquaintance with the knower, the self. Of course it would be rather naive to deny the possibility of any act of knowing, for then we would not even be able to talk intelligibly about knowing. So the argument goes that not only I know, also I know myself as a knower.

If we all are so familiar with self-knowledge, then why do we find people from across the globe urge us to know our selves? This advice to know one's self sounds like telling us the obvious. The philosopher, of course, could say that although we know the self, we do not know its nature. We are aware of the self in its generality, what we need to know is its specific nature and function. I could very well be acquainted with a flower without being aware of the specificities of that flower of which may be a botanist is aware of. In a certain sense, certainly I am aware of my self, my own existence; but then, I might be unaware of the extent of my ability and power.

Here, let me explain the problem of self-knowledge in greater detail. A theory of self-knowledge is expected to explain two points as follows: *one*, our knowledge of what kind of thing we are; *two*, the nature and extent of our knowledge of particular thoughts, sensations, perceptual experiences, etc. Clearly, these two forms of self-knowledge are related. If one believes in the material nature of self, then an account of thoughts and sensations will have a materialist underpinning. If, on the other hand, one believes in an immaterialist theory of self, one needs to reinterpret the physicalist understanding of particular self-knowledge. Nonetheless, the relation between these two forms of self-knowledge has been questioned many a times in Western philosophical tradition. Without going into an exegesis, let us try to understand the source of this scepticism.

To put the point rather bluntly, following Kant, knowledge can be said to spring from two sources. Sensory input is given in, what Kant calls 'intuition', and those raw materials are conceptualized by the faculty of understanding. Now, if this model of knowledge is applied to self-knowledge, we are tempted to think of introspection, instead of 'outer senses', as the source of our knowledge of what kind of things we ourselves are. In this model, introspection is a form of self-perception, involving the exercise of an inner sense. So, inner sense could be thought of as an appropriate source of self-knowledge. And this is precisely the source of discomfort for many philosophers. Many notable names including Hume and Kant have expressed their inability to get hold of a persisting thing called self in introspection involving inner sense. What inner sense provides us with are discrete individual perceptions. If one pursues this line of thinking, then one is led to what might be called 'Elusiveness of self.' Inner sense does not provide any clue to a self that is fixed and abiding. If introspective awareness, involving the inner sense, is suppose to give us the knowledge of our selves as persisting entity, then Elusiveness thesis implies that knowledge of self as an abiding entity is unavailable to us. We are not in a position to know ourselves. We do not know what kind of things we are. This is the sceptical argument for denying that we know what we are. The argument of the sceptic for Elusiveness thesis could be presented in the following way (Cassam 2004: 4).

1. Knowledge requires intuitions and concepts.
2. Introspection is the source of much of our self-knowledge.
3. Introspective awareness is a form of perceptual awareness involving the exercise of 'inner sense.'
4. For a persisting self to acquire the knowledge of her own nature through introspection, she would need to be aware of herself through inner sense.
5. No persisting self could present itself in inner sense.

There are more than one ways one could confront the sceptical argument. One could deny that introspection is the only source of self-knowledge. Much of our knowledge of our selves is gained through interaction with other people. Knowledge of when I was born or whether I have any psychological problem is a respectable piece of self-knowledge that we acquire through testimony provided by other people. On this view, it would be legitimate to claim that outer senses, along with introspection, are important sources of self-knowledge. One could also argue that in introspection, we are aware of ourselves as flesh and blood creatures contrary to what Elusiveness thesis claims. Introspection does provide us with knowledge of our selves.

A more interesting and subtle way of responding to the sceptical argument could be found in Evans (2004: 204). Evans argues that a subject's internal state cannot properly be an *object* to him, as inner-sense model demands. In perceptual experience, what is received as input is the non-conceptual information of the world as being in a certain way. This non-conceptual informational state of the subject later gives rise to conceptualization of such states by making judgements about the world that rest on earlier non-conceptual states. One's self-knowledge is acquired by reusing these skills of conceptualization. Here, we can imagine three steps. First, there is the non-conceptual informational state of the subject representing the world. Judgements appear at the second level by organizing the non-conceptual states with the help of the conceptual apparatus. If the same model is applied to the knowledge of self, then there should be a non-conceptual informational state of the subject representing the internal state, as that internal state stands in a relation to the world. Unfortunately, no such non-conceptual informational state of the subject is available in case of self-knowledge. So, one cannot claim to have a perception of one's own experience.

If Evans's line of argument is correct, then it follows that since Elusiveness thesis requires the inner-sense model of perception and since inner-sense model is unsatisfactory, then Elusiveness thesis is susceptible to doubt. Here, one must resist the attempt to jump to the conclusion that Evans's argument shows that self-knowledge is possible. What this line of argument shows, at best, is that the Elusiveness thesis involving the inner-sense model of perception is open to doubt. One could very well reject the claim that Elusiveness thesis owes all its legitimacy to inner-sense model of perception.

One could confront the sceptical argument by suggesting that thoughts are acts or properties and no act or property can exist without a substance to which it belongs. So being conscious of a thought is also to be conscious of a subject whose thought it is (*à la* Chisholm).

Now what would happen if one is happy with the idea of introspective self-knowledge but rejects the inner-sense model? Here, one faces a dilemma. Either one has to reject the Kantian claim that knowledge requires the contribution of both intuition and concept, or the inner-sense model has to be stopped from applying to self-knowledge. Rejection of either of them comes with a heavy price. The difficult questions that we now face are as follows: *one*, In what sense can there be introspective self-awareness other than through inner-sense? And *two*, Can the non-perceptual mode of introspective self-awareness (whether this is possible at all) be viewed as the basis of one's self-knowledge?

4.2 Rasvihary's Theory of Self-knowledge

Before getting into a detail analysis of Rasvihary's analysis of self-knowledge, let me very briefly present the general trends in Rasvihary's philosophical trajectory. Against this background, it would be easier to situate Rasvihary's theory of self-knowledge.

For Rasvihary, philosophy is concerned with knowledge. Knowledge, according to Rasvihary, is a mode of consciousness where the object is taken to exist independent of the act of consciousness of which it is an object. The object of knowledge must be an existent one and one could think of two aspects of this object, viz. the thing and its character. The former is the *that* part of the object, while the latter is the *what* part of the object. Viewed in this way, knowledge is a form of consciousness of an object having a character. If the character is falsely ascribed to the thing, then the knowledge concerned will turn out to be a false one. The veracity of the character allegedly ascribed to the object cannot be ascertained in the same act of knowledge. Thus, any knowledge remains open to scepticism.

Belief, for Rasvihary, contains two elements: (a) understanding of a proposition and (b) assenting to the proposition. Assenting again consists of two elements: (i) volitional and (ii) emotional. When we assent to a proposition, we decide in favour of it. This is the volitional aspect. Also, when we assent to a proposition, we feel sure of it. This is the emotional aspect. Belief in its volitional and emotional aspects could be strong or weak. Knowledge proper, on the other hand, claims to be objectively valid, and so it does not make sense to talk about strong or weak sense of knowledge.

Philosophy primarily belongs to cognitive realm, as opposed to the domain of action or praxis. Philosophers aim at clarifying the concept of knowledge, its possibility and its nature as it is manifest in the different branches of knowledge. Moreover, philosophical knowledge is communicable or teachable by rational means. It is the onus that a philosopher carries with her for putting forward arguments in favour of her thesis. Philosophical knowledge is out there in an open public space for critical scrutiny. A philosopher cannot claim to have knowledge that is incommunicable and hence not open to rational scrutiny. This is where mystical knowledge is different from philosophical knowledge. Mystical knowledge, in its essence, is not teachable and so defies rational scrutiny.

Talking about philosophy this way would immediately give rise to the issue of relation between science and philosophy. Science, like philosophy, also is a cognitive affair. Philosophic knowledge is different from scientific knowledge in that in philosophical analysis of knowledge the role of subject comes into focus. As a result, consciousness and self-consciousness are important elements in philosophy. Science can afford to ignore the role of subject and instead exhausts itself into an understanding of the object ('fact' in a broad sense) concerned. Whenever scepticism raises its head, or we suffer from illusory experience, we become self-conscious and critical of our cognitive experience, giving rise to philosophic analysis. This is where the role of the knower comes into prominence. It is also noteworthy that the assumptions and the theoretical postulates of scientific theories, the fundamental concepts and methodologies of scientific enterprise form important subject matter of philosophy. This is why philosophical knowledge is always more general than scientific knowledge. Rasvihary does not deny scientific knowledge to be reflective, for obviously scientific analysis focuses on our perceptual experience, a conscious process. But nonetheless scientific judgements are expressed in objective judgements, without any reference to knower or the knowledge itself. In short, philosophy, for Rasvihary, is a critical reflection on life, 'life' taken to include all experiences of science, art, morality, etc. (Das, n.d.: 11).

Rasvihary calls himself a 'common sense realist.' Common sense beliefs are the natural starting points for any philosophical analysis. Rasvihary thinks that we are naturally inclined to realism that does not need justification. It is the rejection of realism that needs justification. Idealism, while opposing realism, holds that the object of knowledge is either illusory or imaginary. While illusion version of idealism holds that there are no objects (of knowledge) at all, the imagination version of idealism holds that what we claim to know is actually a product of our imagination, implying that knowledge is a form of doing or activity. Rasvihary, in many of his articles, argues against each of these versions of idealism. Rasvihary's version of realism consists in the view that the object of knowledge exists independently of the act knowing and that knowledge cannot arise without some object being given to it (Das, n.d.: 15).

The way Rasvihary formulates the idea of knowledge implies that knowledge could turn out to be false resulting in the possibility of an element of scepticism, always following a cognitive experience. Philosophy, which has been identified with critical reflection, has always been made cautious by a sceptical attitude. For Rasvihary, scepticism is not a positive theory; it is an attitude of mind which is the crux of any genuine critical pursuit (Das, n.d.: 20).

Since Rasvihary is more a methodological sceptic, and not a substantial sceptic, he does not hesitate to call himself 'practical idealist.' Rasvihary believes in certain ultimate values, values that are desirable on their own account. Rasvihary claims to give a rational appreciation of these values, and these values are sought to be realized by us. Rasvihary mentions three such values, viz. truth, freedom and love. These three values correspond to three aspects of human existence such as cognition, feeling and willing, respectively.

When philosophers talk about the problem of self-knowledge, they talk about the logical or epistemological problem of self-knowledge, according to Rasvihary (Das, n.d.: 123). In a knowledge situation, we generally make a distinction between the subject and the object. Now, in a supposedly self-knowledge, the self is both the subject and the object. And so the subject–object distinction collapses. But this is the distinction on which knowledge rests. For knowledge to take place, subject–object distinction is undeniable, but in a self-knowledge, this distinction ceases to exist.

Philosophers in the classical Indian tradition who deny that self can be an object of knowledge follow this line of argument. They (the Prābhākars and Advaitins) hold that the same self cannot be the subject and object due to *karma kartṛ virodha*. It is due to the act of the subject (*kartā*) that another thing called 'object' (*viṣaya*) is produced. Self, who is the subject or knower, always knows something else, something other than itself. They further argue that even if self is manifest in knowledge, the definition of objecthood (*karma*) cannot be applied to self. The definition of objecthood is as follows: an object is that which possesses the result of an act that belongs to someone else (*parasamavetakriyāphalavāgitva*). In the case of so called self-knowledge where the self allegedly becomes its own object, it is the self who is both the initiator of the act and possessor of the result of the act. Even the inflexion of objective case ending is not applicable to the statement expressing cognitive experience such as—*Aham ghatam jānāmi*; 'am' (the objective inflexion) is attached to the object '*ghata*' and not to the self (*aham*). But the problem is that there are linguistic uses where the objective case is applied to self. So the middle path could be to acknowledge that where linguistic uses are prevalent, self can be regarded as object of knowledge, but not always. She can further argue that since we can give an account of perceptual experience and also inferential knowledge of self, in these cases at least there is no *karma kartṛ virodha*. Of course, the relation that self holds to knowledge in self-knowledge and in knowledge of other things is different. When the self is knower, the relation is that of inherence (*samavāya*), and when the self is the object, the relation is that of objecthood (*viṣayatā*).

But can't we say that the self is known in self-knowledge, but it is not known as the *object*. Then, the problem of the collapse of subject–object distinction does not arise and also, self-knowledge can be accepted. For Rasvihary, this line of thinking is non-starter. Whenever we talk about 'object' in epistemological context, we mean that which is known. So to know the self is to treat the self as the object and to deny the self to be the object is to deny the knowledge of the self. To claim that the self is known but not as an object, amounts to claiming that the self is known as not known, which is obviously a contradiction.

Here, one can however find a different line of thinking in another essay of Rasvihary (Das, n.d.: 115). The crux of the problem related to self-knowledge seems to be the fact that the self turns out to be the subject and object as well in self-knowledge, whereas normally in any knowledge, subject–object duality seems to be present. If one argues that I is known as a result of reflection in Me (object) where Me is constructed by I, it remains to be proved that what is constructed is actually a reflection of I. What guarantee there is that the reflection is a reflection of I and not of anything else? Unless we have a direct acquaintance with self at certain point, it would be difficult for us to determine something as a reflection of the self. Knowledge of the reflection of self falls short of a genuine case of self-knowledge. Knowing the reflection of the self is different from knowing the self itself. For a genuine case of self-knowledge to take place, the very same self that is the owner of the knowledge must be present in an act of awareness. It does not pay to claim that in self-knowledge, one-half of self knows the other half, for in that case, the knower part is knowing the known part, which is other than the knower.

The problem compounds for if in self-knowledge the self knows itself and so becomes the object, the self, in its knowing capacity, as a subject, is never known. If in the same epistemic act, the same self can become subject and object, and if this were true of object as well, then instead of saying 'I know the table', one could say 'The table knows me.' This, of course, is absurd.

Thus, Rasvihary's diagnosis is that either we have to show that 'what is known in knowledge is not always an object or that there is no absolute opposition between subject and object' (Das, n.d.: 113). As mentioned earlier, Rasvihary does not think that the place of subject and object are interchangeable. The place and the role of subject and object cannot be substituted by each other. Since we are talking about a relation between subject and object in a knowledge situation, any relation requires the *relata* to be different things. Of course, we do talk about identity relation where the *relata* seem to be the same self-identical object. Knowledge certainly does not involve such an identity relation. 'I know the table' does not mean 'I am identical with the table.'

4.3 Metaphysics of Self-knowledge

Metaphysically speaking, one could think of self so constituted that it can perform the dual function of knower and known. But epistemologically speaking, the knower and the known can hardly be identical. Self-knowledge cannot escape the generally accepted mode of knowledge involving subject–object duality. The problem of self-knowledge, in so far as it is knowledge, should be addressed on an epistemological plain. Thus, if self-knowledge is a fact, and since it is not a usual case of knowledge, then "we must believe that what is given in knowledge need not always be an object" (Das, n.d.: 115). This is a line of argument that I would like to explore little later, although Rasvihary does not seem to be sympathetic to this trend of argument, as we shall see soon.

If the subject is to be known at all, it is to be known in its knowing capacity. And here arises the problem. Although when I know you, I can believe that you have the ability to think, but you as a subject, as knowing something cannot enter my area of knowledge in the form of a definitive content, according to Rasvihary. This, however, is not so evident to me. Imagine that you are engaged in deriving an argument from a set of premises with the help of certain rules of inference. I see you as performing the derivation. You as deducing the theorems becomes the object my knowledge. May be, I try to follow your deduction. So I know you as performing the deduction. My knowledge has a definitive content, viz. you as performing the deduction. I know you in your knowing capacity. The subject, as engaged in an epistemic act, becomes the object of my knowledge.

One could, of course, defend self-knowledge and bypass the sceptical argument by claiming that when one is aware of one's own thoughts, feelings, etc., one does not present oneself as an object (Shoemaker 2004: 82). In self-knowledge, the self is not present as an object of knowledge. If awareness of oneself is modelled after perceptual awareness, then as in perception, things are present as object; so in self-knowledge, the self is present as an object as well. Perceptual awareness of oneself when one's own self is present as an object is quite possible, like when one sees oneself in a mirror. But this involves identifying the presented object as oneself. Identification brings with it the possibility of misidentification. But the unique feature of introspective awareness is that the first person statements based on that awareness are immune to error through misidentification. I cannot misidentify myself as having a particular experience expressed in a first person statement, especially when such a statement is a result of introspection. Misidentification being ruled out, there remains little room for identification and as a consequence perceptual awareness where a thing is identified as an object present to a knower ceases to exist. Thus, awareness of oneself as an *object*, modelled after perceptual awareness, is impossible. Here, we have an argument that defends self-knowledge, but denies that in self-knowledge self is present as an *object*.

Moving to the opposite direction, one could claim that self-knowledge is not only a case of knowledge, but it is also a perfect knowledge. In a perfect knowledge, the object merges into the knower. Here, it must be remembered that in a knowledge situation, it is true that the object must be related to the subject, but the relation must not be that of an identity. The object is known in so far as it is distinguished from the knowing subject. Knowing something means that which is known is different from the knower. Knowledge is always other directed, other than the subject.

Rasvihary, of course, concedes that the way we know ourselves is different from the way we know other things. And this is important. It is true that as we know our own mental states, we also claim to have knowledge of other people's mental states. We claim to have knowledge of other people's sensations and intentional states. But this knowledge of people's mental states require reliance on evidences that one can state independent of the ascription of the mental states. These evidences normally consist of the people's utterances and other actions. Knowing one's own mental states, on the other hand, does not require reliance of this kind of evidence. Self-knowledge is thought to be immediate. And here immediately a question crops up. There are many attributes that a subject has and can be known by that very subject on the grounds that can entitle any other person to know those attributes of that subject. If I want to know my height or date of my wedding, then the kind of investigation that I would carry would be the same kind of investigation that anyone would carry had she been interested in knowing these information about me. But why does not the same thing happen when I want to know my own mental states? I do not know my own mental states on the ground that is articulable independent of my self-ascription. The important question is as follows: Why is self-ascription of mental states different from self-ascription of other attributes?

One, however, could retain the subject–object distinction and still accept self-knowledge. One could argue that what is meant by the claim that the knower and the known are distinct is not that what is knower in one case cannot be known in another case. What is rather meant is that what is known in one case cannot be the knower in the same case. So the knower can be known, but certainly not in the same epistemic situation, it can be known in another epistemic situation. Even though it is notoriously difficult to give an account of the knowledge where the knower is known, nonetheless, our problem was to give an account of the knowledge of self in its knowing capacity. We wanted to know the self while it is engaged in knowing activity. The problem is compounded for the same act of knowing cannot apparently seem to be directed by and upon the same thing.

Viewed in this manner, the problem of self-knowledge can be analysed into three questions (Das, n.d.: 125), viz., (i) whether one can perform two acts of knowledge at the same time; (ii) whether the first act is not already past before the second act takes place; and (iii) whether we can identify the subject in one act with the subject in the other.

Rasvihary's answer to the first question is that it is a common experience to attend to two things at a time (Das, n.d.: 125). Psychologists talk about distribution of attention where, for example, I can attend to a colour and a sound at the same time. Attention does not necessarily have to be discretely linear.

Regarding the second question, Rasvihary argues that our mental states have duration (Das, n.d.: 126). They do not appear and then die after surviving for an instant. So, while a mental state lasts, another mental state can very well appear. Our mental life does not consist of discrete, completely separate states having no connection among each other. It is more appropriate to think of the mental states as having continuity where the previous state is available for observation in the latter state. Also, our mental life seems to have a volume in the sense that mental states appear in an incremental way. They are accumulative in nature. It is not that one mental state cannot appear until the previous mental state vanishes making room for the latter. It is not incompatible for a mental state to cohabit with another. While I am enjoying a good piece of music, I might also have the desire to make the music for a longer time. There is a succession in the mental states, but they may also cohabit in that succession. Succession and contemporaneity does not have to be opposed to each other when we talk of mental states.

Regarding the third question, Rasvihary acknowledges the difficulty in identifying the subject as the same if the epistemic acts are different. For if the acts are different, then the subjects as determined by those acts are also different. But then, Rasvihary argues, that we can very well talk about the same self which is the subject in different acts. Determining the same self in different acts is not a problem once we accept the incremental view of mental states that comprise our mental life.

But Rasvihary goes further and claims that in self-knowledge, there are no two separate acts, one supervening on another. In self-knowledge, it is not the case that first I know the object and then, in a separate act, I know myself. "It seems possible that I may be aware of myself as knower in the very act of knowing, in which I know some object other than myself" (Das, n.d.: 127). My seeing the table and my awareness of myself as seeing the table are not separate acts, according to Rasvihary. My knowledge of the table does not hang in the air, it is owned by me. It is my knowledge. I cannot have a knowledge of the table unless I can appropriate this knowledge to my consciousness, without realizing it is I who is having this bit of knowledge. Thus, when I know an object, I also know myself as performing that act of knowing. This is more evident when I am having the knowledge of the object, if someone asks me 'Do you know what you are doing?' I would unhesitatingly and without looking for any evidence answer 'Yes.' This only shows that I am not only aware of the object, but I am also aware of myself as the knower of that object. And this is where immediacy in self-knowledge comes in. I will return to this point later.

The doubt about our having the knowledge of ourselves while having the knowledge of the object arises only because we do not seem to realize this in our attempt to have the knowledge of the object. And the reason why we cannot realize this is because in having the knowledge of the object, our attention is focused on the object and not on ourselves. But lack of attention does not necessarily imply the absence of those things within the range of consciousness. And since memory is conditioned by attention, we do not seem to have a memory of our knowledge of ourselves that we had in having knowledge of object.

In this context, Rasvihary distinguishes what he calls 'primary knowledge' from 'secondary knowledge' (Das, n.d.: 128). When I know an object, where the object is usually understood as being external to the body and so cannot be identified with the subject, this is a case of primary knowledge. In our common parlance, 'knowledge' is used in this sense. My knowledge of myself as knowing the object is a case of secondary knowledge. Rasvihary, of course, accepts that secondary knowledge is parasitic on the primary knowledge for its occurrence. But then, it is only through the secondary knowledge that we can be aware of something called knowing or cognitive act. Secondary knowledge is not a separate act distinct from the primary knowledge; it is the completion of the primary knowledge. Viewed in this manner the prospect of the collapse of subject–object duality does not arise, and so there does not arise any possibility of turning the subject into object. So, Rasvihary concludes that in knowledge along with the object, the knower is also revealed.

One consequence of this account of self-knowledge, Rasvihary reminds us, is that one can know oneself only as a performer of a mental act. And since all mental acts are object directed, one can know oneself only as it is engaged in a primary knowledge. Thus, it is impossible to know oneself independent of any of its conscious functions. Knowing the self independent of its mental acts referring to objects is impossible. Self bereft of its relation to mental acts eludes our cognitive grasp. So it is only through primary knowledge that self-knowledge is possible, but then self-knowledge is not an act separable from primary knowledge.

4.4 Self-knowledge and Avowal

As I have mentioned little earlier, immediacy is the mark of self-knowledge. Moreover, not only I know differently from others my own mental states, but also I regard myself as the best person to know my mental states. My knowledge of my own mental states implies that I really do have them. I am in an unassailable position regarding my knowledge of my own mental states. Also, it is held that if I have a mental state, I am expected to know it. I cannot be unaware of my own mental states. In other words, mental states are salient to the subject. These three features of self-knowledge, viz. immediacy, authority and salience have given rise to a gamut of issues in contemporary philosophy of mind. My project in the following pages is to characterize this domain against the backdrop of Rasvihary's idea of self-knowledge.

It cannot be denied that people can be wrong in their own assessments. They can be wrong in knowing their own motives, in judging their own strengths or weaknesses. But still for the vast area of the realm of the mental, it is perhaps a truism that we know ourselves best, at least better that others know us.

One simple explanation of this would be to claim that my presence is a constant factor in my having the best knowledge of myself. No one else observes me as much as I do. So I have the best evidence of my own mental states. This explanation is typically true of the knowledge of one's own mental states where one's own and another's knowledge of oneself draws on the same kind of evidence. Take, for example, some dispositions characteristics such as honesty. In this case, there is hardly any self/another asymmetry in so far as the evidence of ascription of such a property is concerned. However, in vast majority of cases, I not only know myself best, I also know myself differently from the way others know me. This authoritative, non-inferential knowledge of oneself is best manifest in the phenomenon of avowal. And one of the basic tasks of philosophy of mind is to explain this phenomenon.

One could distinguish two types of avowals: (i) 'phenomenal avowal' and (ii) 'attitudinal avowal' (Wright 1998: 14). Examples of phenomenal avowals are 'I have a headache', 'I am tired', etc. Three important features of phenomenal avowal are worth noting. First, they are groundless. The demand that somebody produce evidence behind her claim 'I have a headache' is unwarranted. In a way, there is nothing on the basis of which one can make such a claim except her having that very experience. Second, phenomenal avowals are strongly authoritative. Assuming that one understands the meaning of the claim that she makes and she is sincere in making the claim, her making the claim itself is the guarantee of the truth of the claim she makes. When I claim 'I am in pain', my making the claim itself, *ceteris paribus*, is the criterion of the correctness of the corresponding third person claim. My avowal that I am in pain must be accepted by others. Third, phenomenal avowals displays the feature of transparency. If I say 'I am in pain', it is rather absurd to say 'I don't know whether I have a pain.' The subject's ignorance of the truth/falsity regarding her phenomenal avowals is normally not entertained.

Let us now talk about attitudinal avowals. They are content-bearing states in the sense that such states are individuated in terms of the propositional content that they have. Examples of attitudinal avowals are 'I believe that the Pune seminar starts on 21 January', 'I am thinking of my mother', etc. One very interesting feature of attitudinal avowal is that they can be part of self-interpretation in the sense that we can say that we have learned about our attitudes by finding out that certain events cause us pleasure or pain. It is not an uncommon experience to have that a person does not appear much in my thoughts, but things unfolded in such a way that I realize that I have always hated that person. Notice that I do not come to this conclusion immediately after certain events took place. First, I even doubt the truth of my claim and then eventually I come to accept the truth of the avowal.

It is interesting to note that none of the features of phenomenal avowal is present in the self-interpretative case. It is perfectly sensible to ask for the justificatory ground of one's attitudinal avowal. Also, one's attitudinal avowal can be doubted for one's sincerity or understanding does not guarantee the truth of the content of the attitudinal avowal. Moreover, it is not awkward for a subject to profess ignorance about her mental states. But what is important to note here is that avowals involving self-interpretation rest on more basic attitudinal avowals. It is only on the basis of certain avowals constructed out of certain events that I indulge in self-interpretation and then, I arrive at self-interpretative avowal. In a way, basic avowals are the datum for self-interpretation. And these basic avowals constitute attitudinal avowals.

Can we talk about attitudinal avowals having the features such as groundlessness, authority and transparency? Attitudinal avowals are not groundless, for we can very well demand that the subject produces reason for her avowal that 'I believe that the Shimla seminar starts on 9 October.' And the subject can produce some evidence that can be understood independent of her making the avowal. Attitudinal avowals, however, lack strong authority. Even if I understand the meaning of my avowal and also I am sincere in making my avowal that does not guarantee the truth of the content of my avowal, 'I believe that the Shimla seminar starts on 9 October.' I might have misunderstood or misinformed some relevant information. Attitudinal avowals can still be said to have weak authority. This weak authority might be said to consist in the presumptive acceptability of testimony in general. What it means is that comprehensive suspicion of all of my attitudinal avowals by others does not make sense. You might doubt my testimony regarding music, for I might have no sense of musicality. Or because of my bad memory, you might doubt my testimony regarding my biographical details. But if you doubt, in general, all my testimony regarding all the attitudinal avowals, then that would really clash with your thinking of me as an intentional subject and consequently your attempt to interpret my mind or mental states would not make any sense. Attitudinal avowals display transparency in the sense that, except self-interpretation, we think that a subject knows what she believes or desires, etc. In case of attitudinal avowals, subject's professed ignorance of her avowal sounds awkward.

In spite of these differences, however, both the two kinds of avowals exhibit a common feature which might be called 'immunity to error through misidentification.' In a large number of cases where the subject makes a subject-predicate claim, the subject might misidentify the subject in way that is impossible to happen in avowal. When, for example, someone walks down the road from a little distance whom I might take to be a good friend of mine, say Radhika, I say 'Radhika is going to university.' But then, I might find out that it is not Radhika, it is somebody else. So here, I am mistaken about the identity about the subject. I may also be mistaken about the predicate. Radhika may be going to see a film; she is not going to university. This kind of mistake cannot happen in avowal. If I avow my indifference to the forthcoming election, then I may go wrong in the predication part of my avowal. But, it seems, I cannot be mistaken about the subject, about which I am making the predication. Misidentifying myself is an impossibility.

The important point here is that this immunity to error rests on the ground that a speaker has for making the claim. Think of my statement 'Radhika is going to the university.' When my thought is defeated, the basis of my claim still survives as a ground of the corresponding generalized claim 'Someone is going to the university' or more generally 'Someone is walking down the road.' But in case of avowal, even if the statement in question is defeated, the ground of that avowal cannot survive as a basis of the corresponding generalization.

In the above discussion, I have talked about avowals in the form of mental states having linguistically expressed in a particular form known as avowal. One radical line of thinking would be to deny the status of assertion to avowal. Avowals are not statements, true or false. They are expressions of the relevant parts of a subject's mind. As moaning is an expression of pain, smile is an expression of pleasure and clenching of the teeth is an expression of anger, 'I am in pain' is a similar expression of pain. On this view, the avowal of pain is an acquired form of pain behaviour which we have learned to supplant the natural expression of pain.

In the present context, it would be an interesting question to see how far this expressivist account of avowal goes with the features of avowal that we explained earlier. It seems they go quite well. If the avowal is an expression of the pain behaviour itself, then it is inappropriate to ask the subject of the ground of her behaviour (groundless). Similarly, there is no question of the subject's ignorance of the truth-value of her avowal (transparency). And given that the subject is sincere and is aware of the meaning of meaning of the expression and then the subject's claim that she is in pain is authoritative in nature.

But this expressivist stance has some serious repercussions in philosophy of language, especially for people like us who defend a truth conditional theory of meaning. If expressivism is right, then the avowals do not have any truth valuable content. Here, we have to give an account of our understanding of these avowals in a way that does not cash on the idea of truth condition. And this is a way that is worth discovering.

Let us wind up our discussion by saying that we started by analysing Rasvihary's idea of self-knowledge where Rasvihary concedes that we know the self in the very act of knowing the object. Since self-knowledge is manifest linguistically in the form of avowals, a philosophy of self-knowledge would involve an account of avowals. And the present essay is an attempt to charter this domain. Against the background of Rasvihary's treatment of self-knowledge, it is incumbent on us to explain why and how the avowals exhibit the features they have, what is their subject matter and what is the special relation that the subject has to the avowals that they make.

References

Cassam, Q. (2004). 'Introduction.' In Q. Cassam (Ed.), *Self-knowledge*. Oxford: Oxford University Press.

Das, R. (Year of Publication not mentioned) 'Self-Consciousness', 'Self-knowledge.' In R. Das (Ed.), *Philosophical essays*. Calcutta: University of Calcutta.

Evans, G. (2004). 'Self-Identification.' In Q. Cassam (Ed.), *Self-knowledge*. Oxford: Oxford University Press.

Shoemaker, S. (2004). 'Self-reference' and 'Self-awareness.' In Q. Cassam (Ed.), *Self-knowledge*. Oxford: Oxford University Press.

Wright, C. (1998). 'Self-Knowledge: The Wittgensteinian Legacy.' In C. Wright, et al. (Eds.), *Knowing our own minds*. Oxford: Clarendon Press.

Chapter 5
Brajendra Nath Seal: *A Disenchanted Hegelian*

Amita Chatterjee

Abstract Brajendra Nath Seal, one of the greatest savants of the nineteenth/twentieth century Bengal, set on his philosophical journey following in the footprints of Hegel. However, he discovered the flaws and biases in the Hegelian system of thought quite early. Having imbibed the wisdom of the East and the West, he developed his own philosophy characterized by syncretism, internationalism and interdisciplinarity. He drew the attention of the Western world to the scientific temper of the Indian mind garnering evidence from the ancient Indian philosophical treatises. He was the architect of the subject 'Indian philosophy' as we study it today. His philosophy of education and academic administration are still relevant.

Keywords Hegelian · Synthetic · Critico-comparative method · *Pāñcarātra* · Grades of divine manifestation · Education · Syllabus · Indian philosophy

5.1 Brajendra Nath Seal: *A Forgotten Genius*

The main objective of this essay is to explore the thoughts and works of a forgotten genius who was acclaimed as the greatest savant of the nineteenth century India. Edward Thompson told in his obituary tribute to the world, broadcast by BBC, "In my judgment, Brajendra Nath Seal was one of the greatest intellects of his time in India, a man in some ways unsurpassed. The late Sir Patrick Geddes used to say that Seal's was the greatest brain functioning on earth."[1] And what was his time? It is 1864–1938 and who were his contemporaries? Rabindranath

---

[1] Broadcast talk from London: Empire Transmission III, January 26, 1939 at 4.20–4.35 p.m., as mentioned in Chatterjee (1968: 58–62).

A. Chatterjee (✉)
Jadavpur University, Kolkata, India
e-mail: chatterjeeamita@gmail.com

© Indian Institute of Advanced Study 2015   81
S. Deshpande (ed.), *Philosophy in Colonial India*, Sophia Studies in Cross-cultural Philosophy of Traditions and Cultures 11, DOI 10.1007/978-81-322-2223-1_5

Tagore, Narendranath Dutta (Swami Vivekananda), Mohandas Karamchand Gandhi, Jagdish Chandra Bose, Prafulla Chandra Roy, Bipin Chandra Pal, Krishna Chandra Bhattacharyya, Hiralal Haldar, Benoy Kumar Sarkar, Hirendra Nath Dutta and many other luminaries who were the architects of modern India and thought to be the products of the controversial 'Bengal Renaissance.' One may not want to take Thompson's words seriously because obituary tributes are often filled with overstatements. However, long before his death, he was acknowledged as the moving encyclopaedia for the extent and depth of his knowledge. According to Sir Asutosh, the most powerful microscope would be needed to detect any cultural germ which might have successfully escaped his omnivorous intellect. However, his mind was not an uninteresting stockpile of information: "what was unique about Brajendra Nath Seal was the soaring quality of his mind which, rising from its base of knowledge could ascend to great heights and see therefore visions of new vistas open before it; To a view of those visions he called everyone" (Chatterjee 1968). He was a friend, philosopher and guide to all who used to come to him for some advice and the man was considered greater than his works. Long after his death, his two students S.K. Maitra and Rasvihary Das reminisced about him in the following manner which, we think will give the readers an idea of his characteristic qualities.

> Indeed very few people have impressed me so much as the late Dr. Seal by the breadth and depth of his scholarship, his phenomenal memory, his urbanity and above all, by his wonderful conversational powers. His conversational powers were indeed so wonderful that I have always regretted that there was no Boswell to record his talks. One had only to mention a topic and words would flow from him like a torrent for hours. And what words! Many leading men of Bengal of the present and also of the past century—writers, teachers, statesmen, politicians—derived the inspiration of their lives from these talks. I have heard him talk in one of the common rooms of the Lowis Jubilee Sanitarium, Darjeeling, or in his room in his house in Rammohan Shah Lane, Calcutta, for hours, keeping his audience literally spell-bound. (Maitra 1936: 382)

> Rasvihary Das wrote,
> I am particularly indebted to Dr. B.N. Seal and Professor K.C. Bhattacharyya. The wide sweep of Dr. Seal's mind and the breadth of his views impressed me, and it was probably from him that I derived an interest in knowledge of all kinds as well as an interest in free speculative thinking. He was an enthusiast for Indian Philosophy and introduced me to Śankara and Rāmānuja. I easily followed him in his sympathy for the latter's teaching. (Das 1936: 232)
>
> He has powerfully influenced my life and thought, not so much perhaps by his actual teaching as by his example and close association. (Das 1968: 139)

Seal's published works are few and none of them was on what academics considered as philosophy even a few years ago, *The Gita: A synthetic Interpretation* (Seal 1964) being an exception. But he generously wrote introductions to scholarly works of heterogeneous genre, which included *A History of Hindu Chemistry* by Ray (1909), *The Positive Background of Hindu Sociology* by Sarkar (1914) and *Indian Shipping: A History of the Sea-borne Trade and Maritime Activity of the Indians from the Earliest Times* by Mukharji (1910). The only available philosophical work, *The Positive Sciences of the Ancient Hindus* (Seal 1985), on which he was awarded a doctoral degree of the University of Calcutta, was a collection of introductions and appendices of the first two books mentioned above and which was sent to press by Benoy Sarkar without informing Dr. Seal. His writings on education administration, education reform, self-study and pedagogy are relevant even today. His philosophical thoughts too need re-evaluation from the contemporary perspectives, the inspiration for which we have derived from K.C. Bhattacharyya, whom we have learnt to take seriously. Bhattacharyya wrote:

> I found out later in conversation and in listening to his discourses before the Philosophical Society that his scholarship in philosophy, I cannot speak of other subjects, was not only very comprehensive and precise but thoroughly organized and grouped round living thoughts, each with a promise of magnificent growth. (Bhattacharyya 1968: 52)

We cannot and should not ignore such a thinker when we are discussing modern Indian philosophy of the nineteenth and the twentieth centuries.

5.2 The Hegelian Impact

Brajendra Nath Seal in his formative years was strongly influenced by Hegel. However, he soon detected the loopholes of the Hegelian philosophy. His thorough grounding in Indian philosophical traditions and acquaintance with the new developments in the field of natural and social sciences made him weary of Hegel's concept of history, philosophy and logic. However, this account should come much later in our narrative. We need to discuss first how Kant and Hegel became two dominant forces amongst the academic philosophers of the nineteenth century.

Indian thought and culture were open to the West, especially through its traderoutes, since ancient times. However, through Arabic translation Indian theories got quite transformed by the time they reached the European soil. So, when the Europeans came to India, they rediscovered India with all its material and cultural richness. Oriental studies comprising Indology, Sinology, etc., started to flourish from the 17th century. The concern of Indology, like Sinology, was not only philosophy but an entire country—including its history, language, religion, culture and civilization. When the Europeans came in contact with Indian culture and civilization, they were quickly divided into two groups; the first group comprising Indophiles such as Max Müller, Schlegel, Kant, Herder, Schopenhauer and Humboldt and the second group consisted of Indophobes such as Hegel, Schelling and Schleiermacher. These two attitudes can be gleaned clearly from Hegel's two articles on the interpretation of the *Bhagavad-Gītā* by Humboldt. Scholars belonging to the first group were enamoured by the philosophical thoughts of ancient India and viewed India through romantic eyes, while Hegel and other Indophobes shared a distinct animosity towards everything Indian. The latter attitude persisted for a long time. Husserl and Heidegger too thought like Hegel that philosophy is essentially a European phenomenon and hence India couldn't have any philosophy.

Indologists discussed Indian Philosophy from a philological orientation and later from anthropological standpoint with the ultimate end of discovering some cultural universals. To both Indophiles and Indophobes, however, Indian thought was an 'other' of the European thought, the study of which would enable Europe to know herself better. Hegel never read original Indian texts, yet considered himself as competent to examine and evaluate Indian thought. When Humboldt commented on Schlegel's Latin translation of the *Bhagavad-Gītā* meticulously, Hegel wrote his infamous essays. Let me at this point compare briefly Humboldt's and Hegel's approaches to philosophy in general, which were opposed to each other.

Humboldt approached philosophy through language. He was an excellent philologist. Language was, to Humboldt, "as realization of the spirit a dynamic progressive process, the never-ending, perpetual striving after the revelation of what is to be revealed" (Herring 1995: xiii). Humboldt had great interest and respect for Indian life and culture, the knowledge of which he gathered from Sanskrit texts simply because he thought that all civilized languages originated from Sanskrit and therefore a thorough study of Sanskrit would enable one to understand and evaluate the history of development of the Indo-Germanic languages. Humboldt's philological interests merged with his religio-philosophical ones. So when he came across Schlegel's Latin translation of The *Gītā*, he wrote in a letter dated 21 June 1823,

> I cannot deny that while reading I was overwhelmed more than once by the emotional feeling of genuine gratitude towards destiny for granting me the opportunity to listen to this poem in the original language…. Nothing of what I have read so far in Sanskrit has exercised such an impression on me, yet I concede that the one who reads it in a translation only, even the best one, cannot at all have such a feeling. The translation of such a work is like the description of a painting: colours and light are missing…. *Gītā* is the most beautiful, presumably the only real philosophical poem of all known literature. (Herring 1995: xiii)

Humboldt advised the German scholars to understand the book as a whole without comparing it with other known philosophical theses and be aware of 'the dark spots' in Indian mythology and not to confuse the philosophical theses with the Purāṇic myths. But, he found to his horror that Hegel had done exactly the thing he had advised people not to do. However, it will be too simplistic if we consider Humboldt's and Hegel's approaches to the *Gītā* in terms of their affective attitude towards Indian or other non-European culture; rather, these reflect their entirely different and antagonistic ideas of the roles of religion and philosophy in unfolding the world history.

Humboldt was thinking within the Kantian paradigm of Critical Idealism. As he wrote, "The true end of man—not that prescribed by changing inclinations but that prescribed by eternal unchanging reason—is the highest and most balanced shaping of his powers into a unified whole" (Herring 1995: xvii). Unlike Hegel, he did not proclaim the state as the metaphysical and political purpose and aim of individual. Second, Humboldt thought the only way the course of history can be investigated was by empirical means. It is necessary for this purpose to do a subtle and detailed study of various peoples and nations and the performances of their great exemplary individuals. We shall see soon that Seal too considered empirical methods important for understanding society and the individual. Hegel, on the other hand, thought that the course of history was to be derived from an a priori teleological principle. Hegel wrote in the Introduction of his *Lectures on the Philosophy of History*,

> The history of the world is none other than the development of the consciousness of spirit. The result is at which the process of world history has been continually aiming…This is the only aim which sees itself realized and fulfilled, the only pole of repose amid the ceaseless change of events and conditions, and the sole sufficient principle that prevails them… This final aim is God's purpose with the world. (Herring 1995: xviii)

Hegel's idea of freedom was also different from that of Kant. To Kant, 'freedom' was a natural capacity to comply with the Moral Law. Hegel, on the other hand, maintained that the slave obeys because he is afraid of his master's whip; the free man obeys because of his voluntary decision when he realizes himself as a moral being. But this is realizable, thought Hegel, only in a 'reasonable state.' In a reasonable human community only the subjective will of the individual submits to law, and hence, the contradiction between liberty and necessity disappears. It was Hegel's idea that the Orientals—in the childhood of history—lived under the impression that only one single man was free, the despot, the tyrant. The ancient Greeks and Romans—representing the stages of adolescence and early manhood in history—were convinced that a few were free, the adequate form of the state in this conviction being aristocracy or democracy. However, history reached its maturity with the Germanic people coming at the stage which generated freedom of each and all, its form of government being monarchy. That India was never governed by one single monarch and consequently there was no idea of a nation-state was sufficient proof for Hegel of political immaturity and lack of freedom of the caste-ridden Indian societies.

Hegel's thesis might appear utterly confusing because we tend to think that freedom of each individual is guaranteed in a democratic form of government. But according to Hegel, democracy represents the will of single citizens who are ruled by individual or group interests. Monarchs, on the other hand, are the great world-historical individuals who keep the universal purpose of mankind as their personal aim.

The progressive course of history, showed Hegel, is from myth to reason, from the idea of the abstract unqualified spirit to consciousness and conscience of the individual as a moral person. In Indian thought, Hegel did not detect any distinction amongst myth, religion and philosophy (which is an unbounded domain of critical thinking) and no concept of individual as a moral agent on its own account. For, the ultimate aim of Indian philosophy was to merge every individual with one absolute, unqualified, indeterminate substance, thus leaving aside all individual distinctions. Since Hegel was convinced that the autonomy in this human world was finally realized in Germanic thought, Indian thought appeared to him as lower than the Occident's because the former was merely in a preparatory stage. The main deficiencies, according to Hegel, of Indian philosophical systems (heterodox and orthodox alike) are its abstractness manifested through the renunciation of the world and the lack of the concept of the autonomous, free, self-conscious individual. But Hegel did not stop here. He further declared that the whole life and imagination of the Indians

> ... is nothing but superstition.... The annihilation, casting away of all reason; morality and subjectivity can only lead to a positive feeling and consciousness...when exceeding to crude imaginations, therein as a dissolute spirit finding no rest, no coming to oneself, but in such a way only enjoying the pleasures of life. (Herring 1995: xx–xxi)

Halbfass (1990: 98) has denounced the Hegelian arrogance which was manifested in his select objectification of India and his idea of Indian thought being superseded by and contained in modern Western thought. However, in spite of Hegel's denouncement of Indian philosophy, the Hegelian logic and philosophy captured the imagination of thinkers of the colonial India and continued to exert its influence for quite long time. Lectures on Kant and Hegel were regular features in liberal arts courses of the University of Calcutta, even before its department of philosophy came into existence. When in 1913 the department started with Brajendra Nath Seal as George V Professor of Mental and Moral Philosophy, works of Kant and Hegel were immediately included in the philosophy syllabus and stalwarts like Seal, K.C. Bhattacharyya, and Hiralal Haldar were the exponents of these works.

Without delving further in the spread of European influence on the colonial Indian psyche, let us remind ourselves that there were various models of interaction between Europe and India in the nineteenth century. Figure 5.1 provides schematic representations of the ways how India, especially her philosophy, affected the Europeans. The *first* scheme represented by two disjoined circles expresses the famous attitude—*the East is East and the West is West; the twain shall never meet.* This attitude did not necessarily imply disrespect to the other culture; nonetheless, European and Indian forms of life and thought were to run parallel and remain alien

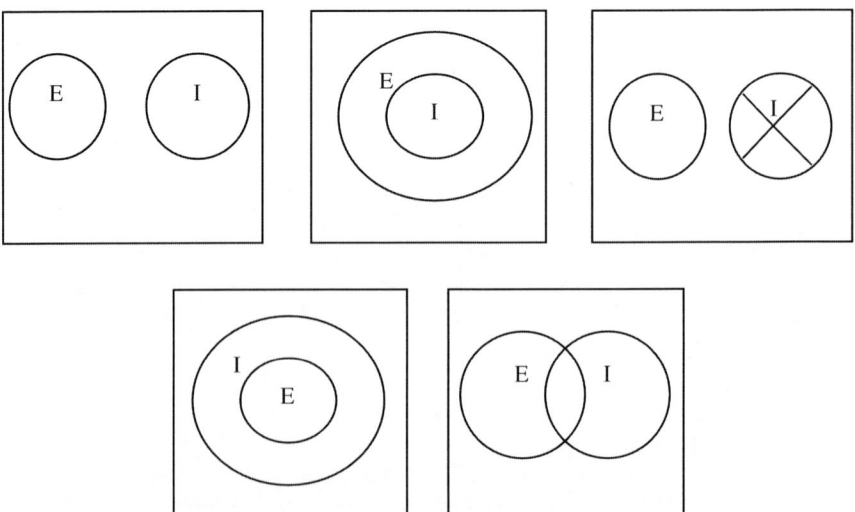

Fig. 5.1 Schematic representations of the ways Indian philosophy affected Europeans

to each other without any prospect of convergence. The *second* scheme represents the Hegelian thought in which Indian civilization was included within the European civilization being its primitive form. The *third* scheme stands for the moments of the European denial of Indian philosophy by Hegel and others. The fifth scheme represents different ways of doing comparative philosophy. The *fourth* scheme shows that ignoring the other tradition of philosophy was not the monopoly of the Western philosophers alone. The same charge can be brought against many Indian scholars who upheld that we need not look at other ways of thinking because the Vedic knowledge system was complete and also against those who wrongly maintained that all brands of philosophizing can be integrated within Vedānta.

5.3 Hegelianism Reviewed

In this backdrop, we shall try to present and understand the philosophical thoughts of Brajendra Nath Seal. Like other thinkers of his time, Seal assimilated the new learning from the West and the social, political and scientific culture embodied in it. During his student days, he was much impressed by positivism of Comte, Kantian notion of Reason, the French Revolution's ideals of liberty, equality and fraternity, as well as Śaṁkara's Advaita Vedānta. He imbibed Hegelian philosophy from Henry Stephen who came to teach mathematics in the General Assembly Institute and Seal accepted whole heartedly Hegel's concept of Absolute Reason, its manifestation through different stages of human history and Hegelian dialectics. What appealed to the polymath Seal most in Hegel was the compactness of his exposition and the applicability of his methods in the most varied disciplines. As has already been pointed out, Hegel started from the basic notion that philosophy as the science of the Absolute, by means of a careful observation of the spontaneous unfolding of Absolute Reason, can deduce the particular from the general, and finally the entire real world by the autonomous shifting of terms. Seal noticed with great fascination that Hegel dealt with every phenomenon of natural and spiritual life and assigned it a place in his all-embracing structure of thoughts. That is why, Hegel discussed in detail the concept of Indianhood in all its forms and in which it has found expression; he had in his own way studied its history, political and social institutions, art, science, religion and philosophy. In 1890, Seal wrote in 'The Neo-romantic Movement in Literature':

> No department of investigation dealing with the mental history of the race promises so much success, if we judge from the magnitude of results already achieved. Hegel's grand generalization concerning the three stages of art, the oriental, the classical and the romantic, is one of the most luminous and fruitful, that the comparative method has given to the world. Indeed it is surpassed in immensity of range only by one or two generalizations of sociology. Comte's law of three stages and Herbert Spencer's classification of types of social structure in the order of their genesis are certainly vaster still, but the one is exploded and the other has been only sketched in outline and waits elaboration. The three stages of Hegel, on the other hand, have been accepted, with whatever modifications, in the highest circle of philosophical criticism. (Seal 1890: 363)

However, the more he read Indian thoughts embodied in different systems, the more he came to understand the shallowness of Hegel's understanding of India and inapplicability of his linear Historical method in explaining the social evolution of the human race and civilization. He became convinced that the civilizations of Egypt and Babylon, Greece and Rome, India, China and Japan could not have emerged from the same root because the multiple bonds of utility that led to the formation of a complex whole called social structure or civilization were distinctive of a particular community in a given age. Moreover, these were not static but evolved like organisms in a biological series. He succinctly expressed his reservations against Hegelian system. "I was convinced", wrote Seal, "that any philosophical system which fails to accept and reconcile the timeless reality and the temporal relativity at once puts itself out of court and is as unscientific as it is unphilosophical" (in Das 1968). Besides, he did not admit that Absolute Reason reached its point of culmination in the European culture. To him East and West were equally valuable and they had equally and independently created culture and cultural values. Though Seal considered reason as the tool of philosophical investigation, yet he did not believe that reason was immutable. He upheld that there was no immutable and infallible means of knowledge in the possession of man. What is called reason and is supposed to be such a means is, like all other capacities of man, dependent on the physiological structure of the brain which may change in course of evolution (Seal 1911). Here, he had deviated from Kant, Hegel and all rationalist philosophers and came closer to neo-Darwinism.

Another point in which Seal diverged from Hegel was his concept of a State. Seal looked upon the nation as a conscious social 'Personality', exercising rational choice as determined by ideal ends and values, and having an organ, the State, for announcing and executing its will. All individuals are integral members of this Composite Personality, but the individual units are themselves Persons, and, therefore, self-determining wills. He was far from transforming the State into a kind of God whom everybody had to obey, or which was above everything in the Hegelian sense. This liberal ideal of State he didn't inherit either from Hegel or from Indian philosophy; it was his own. A compatible marriage between Western knowledge and Indian wisdom gave birth to this offspring. Seal upheld that the best form of State on earth should conform to this ideal. In Indian philosophy, the idea of common good (*loka-śreyas*) was considered more important than individual freedom, though the concept of liberation or *mokṣa* was individualistic. So, social stability (*lokasthiti*), social solidarity (*loka-saṁgraha*), social consensus (*mahājana-prtyaya)* and social continuity (*mahājana-sampradāya*) were taken as the four basic values which were supposedly sufficient for ensuring social progress. However, within Indian tradition, freedom of the individual from the trammels of social custom could be secured in either of the following ways: (a) by accepting *sannyāsa* or *pravrajyā*, i.e., by embracing an ascetic's life, (b) by following the rules of life of a householder who gives up the Vedic values and rites as prescribed in Kulluka's commentary on the *Manusmṛti*, 4/22–24 and (c) by choosing one's own code of conduct (*ācāra*), one's own creed and Guru (the spiritual teacher) and attaching oneself to any of the precepts orthodox (*vedānukūla*) or heterodox (*veda-bāhya*), e.g., Śaiva, Śākta, Bhāgavata, Bauddha, Jaina, Siddha, Nātha, Sahaja or by forming a school by himself (Seal 1924).

Seal also condemned Hegel's logic as defective because of its triadic rhythm scheme. He explained to his student S.K. Maitra, 'The triadic rhythm makes a fine musical appeal, no doubt, but ours is a hard world, too hard to be put under this musical scheme.' He thought that the *Caturvyūhavāda*, the theory of four grades of divine manifestation, as offered in the Pāñcarātra tradition of the Vaiṣṇavas was far superior to the triadic scheme of Hegel. But in the tetradic scheme, reason did not play the leading role; it yielded place to devotion. According to different Pāñcarātra texts, the highest principle, Brahman, voluntarily condescends to emerge in fourfold form out of his compassion for his devotees. The first mode of the highest principle, Vāsudeva, is self-complete and has for his subtle body the total complex of six qualities, three static—knowledge (*jñāna*), sovereignty (*aiśvarya*) and power/capacity (*śakti*), and three dynamic, viz. force (*bala*), valour/creative vibrancy (*vīrya*) and effulgence (*tejas*). Though replete with possibilities, in Vāsudeva all these attributes remain undifferentiated. This subtle body is divided into halves and out of one half emerges the individual soul (*jīva*), named Saṁkarṣana, which combines the attributes of knowledge and force. Saṁkarṣana once again halves himself and there arises the internal organ *manas*, named Pradyumna, possessing the attributes of sovereignty and creative vibrancy, and from one half of Pradyumna emerges the principle of egoity (*ahaṁkāra*), called Aniruddha, having the attributes of power and effulgence. Two important points must be mentioned here. *First*, when one static and one dynamic attribute are combined in a specific mode (*vyūha*), the other four are not absent but only remain dormant. *Second*, as Vāsudeva is successively manifested, none of the modes are incomplete. The process of sequential appearance is compared with the sequential lighting of one lamp from another. *Lakṣmī-tantra* further clarifies this process of the physical and spiritual evolution of beings thus:

> Saṁkarṣana provides the foundation for all the individual souls, Pradyumna enters into the souls, seizes hold of the faculty of awareness and distinguishes between the subjective and objective frames of reference, and Aniruddha projects the world of multiplicity and differentiations.... The four nodes going bottom up are also equated to *jāgrat* (wakefulness), *svapna* (dream), *suṣupti* (deep sleep) and tūrīya (the state beyond it).[2]

This is how the absolute principle manifests itself in the universe through the above-mentioned fourfold modes. When the progressive evolution reaches its culmination, regressive moment starts. In this reverse process, Aniruddha merges with Pradyumna, Pradyumna with Saṁkarṣana and Saṁkarṣana merges with Vāsudeva. So, the entire history of evolution of the universe is nothing but the revelation of these moments. Now we can conjecture how Seal might have assigned logical values to the four modes. If we begin with Aniruddha representing the multiplicity and differentiations of the objective world and assign it the value p, then

---

[2] Sri Pedia Pāñcarātra/modes, downloaded on 4/7/2010. I am indebted to Rupa Bandyopadhyay for providing me with authentic source books on the *Pāñcarātra* philosophy.

Pradyumna can be assigned the value $\sim p$ as the subjective state is opposed to the objective world. Every individual soul contains both the subjective and the objective elements so the appropriate logical valuation of this stage should be p and $\sim p$. As Vāsudeva mode transcends all these stages, it can be assigned the value $\sim(p \vee \sim p)$ from the transcendental point of view.[3] Though Seal highly praised this tetradic scheme, as a mathematician and as a social scientist he believed in the possibility of extending the four-valued scheme to n-valued schemes.

Like Hegel and the Hegelians, Seal did not hold philosophy to be out and out a theoretical discipline. Philosophy, according to him, is a synthetic enterprise which does not place theory and practice in two water-tight compartments. In Indian philosophy, he pointed out that there is no chasm between theory and practice.

When Indians first came in contact with the European culture, there was a wholesale rejection of the tradition in the name of reason and science. In the second stage, however, the pendulum swung to the other extreme and there was a return to the orthodoxy as unassailable. Seal was against both these extreme positions. When Bengal was in deep despondency during the colonial period, aggressive nationalism was being championed by Bankimchandra Chatterjee, Nabinchandra Sen and others in the form of glorification of everything Indian, especially of everything Hindu. Swami Vivekananda was also helping this cause in his own way. An orator called Śaśadhara Tarkachudāmaṇi preached that in the time of the ancient Vedas all the knowledge of modern scientific Europe was known. Seal called this move 'the great sink of national imbecility' (Seal 1903) and warned people not to believe such utter nonsense. Similar note of caution was issued by Sir Asutosh in his Convocation Address of 1911 as the Vice-Chancellor of the University of Calcutta, which was published in Volume XIV of *The Dawn*. All like-minded people condemned this irrational brand of nationalism which betrayed a lack of true historical spirit.

While highlighting the differences amongst different cultures, Seal did not rule out the possibility of comparative study. The early Indologists were engaged in very superficial comparison which neither contributed to intercultural understanding in a significant way nor led to any creative philosophy. There are some methodological problems of pursuing comparative philosophy. One can only manage to offer some external criticism of the other tradition from within one's own tradition. To make a significant comparison of two traditions, one has to take a position beyond both traditions which is not available. It is possible to incorporate ideas from both traditions by internalizing them as had been done by Gandhi, Tagore and Aurobindo. They never took up the programme of bringing the East and the West closer to each other; rather they were immersed in their own tradition. "But life and experience brought them into contact with the West. They responded creatively to that contact" (Mohanty 2001). Seal was aware of this problem and showed us how one can pursue useful comparative philosophy. Seal upheld that any

---

[3] I am grateful to Arindam Chakrabarti for this interpretation of the tetradic scheme.

comparative study, be it philosophy, religion or anthropology has to adopt a critico-comparative method that must emphasize the significant differences between the systems being compared instead of their similarities. Seal said that there are at least two ways of doing philosophy. First, philosophizing is an autonomous activity. The system of thought a philosopher happens to build up is peculiarly his own. In addition to the point of view of the philosopher as a creative thinker, there may be another perspective, namely, that of students of philosophy, where everyone adopts a stance of critical but appreciative spectators of diverse ways of philosophical creation and it is from the latter point of view as distinguished from the former that comparative philosophy is a possibility.

In the Introduction of the essay entitled *Comparative Studies in Vaishnavism and Christianity* (Seal 1899) which was presented at the International Congress of the Orientalists in 1899, Seal made the following observations.

> In the first place, the comparative method of investigating the sciences relating to the history of the Human Mind requires elucidation and correction, for nothing has done greater mischief in the department of research than the ill-conceived and blundering attempts of so many tyroes and "prentice hands" to build ambitious theories and comprehensive systems on the shifting quick-sands of loose analogy and vague generalization in the name of scientific method. Again, historical comparison such as is here proposed implies that the objects compared are of co-ordinate rank and belong more or less to the same stage in the development of human culture. Very few scholars in the West will be prepared to admit that any other religion can bear this relation to humanity.

It is obvious how Seal had already started deviating from Hegel. This becomes more evident from the following excerpt:

> … the Historic method, as reinforced by biology and evolution, requires one more fundamental correction, to fit as an organon for the investigation of social phenomena. As employed by Mr. Herbert Spencer and his school, the historico-genetic method is deviated by an unhistorical and unreal simplicity, a desire to reduce the variety of Life and Nature to a uniform formula. In the result, the method breaks down in its application to the higher stages in each department… The German schools of sociologists following in the wake of Hegel, have a more comprehensive conception of the historico-genetic method, and a super perception of different stages of development; but here also the different races and cults are measured and adjudged by an abstract and arbitrary standard derived from the history of European civilization, and the ethnic varieties are given only a subsidiary and provisional place, as if there were either monstrous or defective forms of life like the monotremata or the marsupialia of a biological laboratory, or only primitive ancestral forms, the earlier steps of the series, that have found their completion in European society and civilization. (Seal 1899: iii–iv)

He suggested that the anthropologists should adopt a synthetic approach while dealing with human civilization. As Radhakumud Mukharji pointed out in his Centenary Lecture,

> With a most remarkable foresight he pleaded in a paper on *Race Origins* (1911), the need of harmonizing the claims of physical anthropology with its permanent anatomical types, cultural anthropology with its geographical zones of ethnic culture and the philosophy of history with its law of three or more stages for a synthetic view of the development of mankind and civilization. (Chatterjee 1968)

Seal thus continued his philosophical pursuits in a truly interdisciplinary spirit, when disciplinary pursuit was the norm.

5.4 Seal's Philosophy of Education

By assimilating the ideas and traditional ideals of education extant in India and combining them with those of the West, Brajendra Nath developed his theory of education which was expressed in his convocation addresses, and in the report of Shimla Commission, set up by Lord Curzon in 1902 and also in the report of the Saddler Commission of 1911. We shall summarize here the most salient points of Seal's theory of education, especially the education in the university system. It will be evident from his thoughts listed below how relevant these are even today.

First, he has said over and over again that a university should not be reduced to a mere examining body and promoter of rote learning. The syllabi should be formed to enhance creativity of the students and not to hinder it. He also fought for giving sufficient autonomy to the university teachers so that they could educate themselves and bring out the best in their students through innovative teaching and research (Chattopadhyaya 1999).

Second, he argued strongly for introducing mother tongue as the medium of instruction, particularly for the students of liberal arts. But he wanted to keep English as a wholesome second language. He wanted English to be taught in three separate lines, depending on the stream of education. He felt that for science teaching and practice English as the medium of instruction should be retained as a matter of necessity. "But English cannot be the language for the masses; so an All-India vernacular has to be found. But while stressing the necessity of solving the problem at an early date, Dr. Seal is not quite sure as to what this vernacular should be..." (Seal 1928–1929).

Third, he pleaded for introduction of social sciences in the curriculum side by side teaching of natural sciences. He was the first person to talk about introducing statistical methods in social sciences including history.

Fourth, he was against creating an educated class engaged in what is known as 'ivory-tower philosophy.' While a university must open the windows to the world, it should also take care of the local needs. In one of his convocation addresses he said:

> It is not merely humanistic culture that a province needs; nor that other type which we love to call "national"; but in addition, that which fits for the land we live in. For this Dr. Seal insists upon the agricultural and industrial characteristics of particular localities being noted in the framing of the curricula of the general school classes no less than in the purely vocational courses. For this, again, he would strictly and mercilessly proportion the output of a University to the demand of the province. (Seal 1928–1929)

Fifth, he addressed the question of adjusting the claims of the arts and science subjects upon the general student. He was for breaking down the artificial barrier between sciences so that new 'border-land' scientific disciplines can be created and students of science can overcome the initial handicap of incipient specialism. However, he was against the burdening of the students of science at the graduate level with an arts subject, however, important it might be to the pure humanist. In arts subject, he was in favour of making compulsory either logic or mathematics, in order to impress on them the virtues of rigorous training which would help overcome looseness in thought and argument. But for all students belonging to any stream he would make a general knowledge of science essential and would also insist upon training in practical use of English as a link language (Seal 1928–1929).

Sixth, Seal insisted that university departments should engage in outreach activities. The academics should try to educate industrial labourers and poor slum-dwellers through films by using 'magic lanterns.'

Seventh, university communities should follow the motto of service to the mankind which according to him was the demand of this age (*yuga-dharma*). This motto, however, does not mean just helping the poor, distressed, disabled and suffering people. The aim of service should be empowerment of the needy and eradication of causes of poverty and suffering. Otherwise, this would be a mockery like allowing the war to go on and at the same time offering services to war victims.

Eighth, the benefits of education should not be ripped by a privileged few; efforts should be made to bring philosophy and culture to the masses through public lectures and public debates. University education should be opened to all eligible persons irrespective of caste or creed.

Last but not the least, great care should be taken in framing the constitutions and syllabi of the Indian Universities. We need not follow exactly the principles adopted in the British or the European Universities. Indian policymakers should scrupulously avoid on the one hand, the aggressive, competitive, heartless, militant culture of the West ensuing from the Malthusian theory of population explosion and the theory of a superior race, and on the other hand, purely mechanical, materialistic system of education built on the utilitarian line. In the traditional education system of India, institutes of higher learning developed norms, which evolved out of indigenous culture, and these should be kept in mind while forming education policy. With his characteristic frankness, Seal drew our attention to the weakness of the traditional system too. He found the system lacking in social equality and justice which needed to be remedied urgently.

All these policy matters were discussed incisively and constantly in the meetings of the National Council of Education, Bengal, of which Seal, Tagore and Satish Chandra Mukherjee were core members amongst others. They dreamed of an education system which would play a significant role in building the character of the Indian nation similar to the role that Harrow and Eton played in building up the character of the British people.

Seal, though a product of the university system of education, did not underestimate the merits of self-study (*svādhyāya*) as enjoined in traditional Indian systems of education. Self-study in the tradition was considered the best means of preservation of our ancient culture through the chanting of the Veda-s and meditation on them. Keeping this spirit intact, Seal offered four most effective principles of self-study which he himself put into practice in his own life right from his childhood days. These principles can be formulated *a la* Seal in the following manner: (a) Educate thyself continuously, (b) pursue only one subject or one interest at a time, (c) discover it or do it if you want to learn a thing and (d) engage in intellectual combat. It goes without saying that there cannot be any better proponent of self-study than Seal who had mastered almost all systems of Indian learning through self-study.

5.5 Seal's Concept of Philosophy

Let us now look at what Seal's idea of philosophy was. According to him, a philosopher is an interpreter of culture, including science, art, religion and morality, and with man as its centre as well as its circumference. N.V. Banerjee elaborated Seal's idea of philosophy thus (Banerjee 1968). Seal divided knowledge broadly into two kinds, scientific and historical. The former is concerned with the nature or the objective world and hence must be free from anthropocentricity which technology is not; the latter deals with the essential features of the human situation in evolution, comprising art and religion and morality. Historical knowledge is essentially anthropocentric. However, it is ultimately concerned with certain types of human behaviour, i.e., with man as objectified instead of with man as he is unto himself and his fellows. So both types of knowledge suffer from some inadequacy which needs to be remedied by philosophical knowledge. The task of philosophy is synthesis, consisting in allocation of an appropriate place to scientific and historical knowledge in the analysis of human situation, based on the idea of man as nonobjective. His insistence on the all-importance of Universal Humanism as a philosophical doctrine seems to lend support to this interpretation of synthetic philosophy.

Because of this synthetic conception of philosophy, Seal was reluctant to write any philosophical treatise. Being endowed with a passion for flawless perfection and knowing that knowledge is ever growing, he recoiled from composing a treatise on philosophy. In one of his speeches he said:

> I had found the scientific discoveries working on special fields, such as the physical, the biological and the social had the advantage of preserving their mental freedom. But a philosopher is denied this privilege. For, a philosopher, who embraces all knowledge for his province and must organize the universe of science as one whole, must build on the widest basis possible or attainable at the time. A philosopher, therefore, must claim all knowledge for his province, but at the same time premature philosophizing will be a real danger and hindrance, if he desires to be a universalist, as a philosopher must be.

In his conversation with D.M. Dutta which was published in *Prabashi* (Bengali year 1338), Seal confessed that when he was on the verge of writing a philosophical work having mastered Einstein's Theory of Relativity, he came to know about the theories of quantum physics. Its implications, he thought, would surely change his world-view. He would be completely inauthentic if he had written his proposed book without considering those implications. So, he could not write his *magnum opus* in philosophy. He was so dependent on the results of scientific enquiry and did not admit any unbridgeable gulf between science and philosophy which lead us to consider him as a 'result-naturalist.'

Seal was totally against any 'heroic' concept of science and philosophy. When many of his students expressed concern that all his valuable thoughts would be lost, if these are not preserved in written form, Seal replied that whatever ideas he had entertained and whatever thoughts he expressed were manifestations of the ideas prevailing at that time; these were not his own. Rather, these thoughts formed part of the Ultimate Whole (*bhūmā*) which he hoped would be manifested by some other individual. When his students argued that he alone had the expanse of knowledge to combine specialized knowledge of different disciplines and synthesize them in the corpus of philosophy, he denied that. He said that India had never been satisfied with the limited perspective of a specialist, so Indian scholars who had internalized its culture had always adopted and would adopt a synthetic world-view. To substantiate his view, he often mentioned Jagadish Chandra Bose who began his career as a physicist but went on to biology and could establish a link between physics, biology and zoology because of his overarching holistic framework of thought. So it is not true that he alone was capable of developing a synthetic philosophy.

S.K. Maitra wrote that Seal became a Vaiṣṇavite when he ceased to be a Hegelian. However, I don't think that Seal's philosophical understanding can be clubbed under Vaiṣṇavism though Rāmānuja's system was more acceptable to him than the world-denying philosophy of Śaṁkara. Even when he discarded Hegelian philosophy and advocated the tetradic logical scheme from the Vaiṣṇava philosophy, he professed a godless humanism, while all Vaiṣṇava systems were theistic in core. He wrote in his unpublished autobiography,

> My creed at that time was a religion without a God or a Godless humanism. I believed in no personal immortality but held fast to a glorious future of the human race which was to me a substitute for personal immortality. This was a new type of humanistic positivism but without the Comtist's borrowed religious paraphernalia. I warred for a long time between atheism and agnosticism on the one hand and theism on the other. But in the end some form of theistic affirmation had my preference.

However, even during this theistic period he upheld a position which a Vaiṣṇavite surely would not hold. First, the God he believed in was a sorrowful God, a concept which he borrowed most probably from Christianity, but God of a Vaiṣṇavite is the Bliss Incarnate. To quote from him, "Suffering humanity impressed me so much that in affirming the reality of the world, I conceived it as an expression of a 'suffering God.' This led me on to an affirmation of *Bhagavan* as *duhkhamaya*—the sorrowful one, who shares in the suffering of the world and thus affirms His own fellowship with his creatures" (Excerpted in *Hindustan Standard* December 4, 1938). This, in a way, was Seal's solution to the problem of evil—God is good but not omnipotent—a view which is in tune with the account of the creator God of Indian philosophical systems. Second, though he believed in the reality of the external world, he could not accommodate it within the transcendent realm because of his own mystical experience in the last phase of his life. A Vaiṣṇavite would have accommodated the empirical within the transcendent. "In the *Bhūmā*, there is no trace of earthly, temporal experience. I do feel that they are totally obliterated or eradicated. I am consequently left fumbling and fidgeting all in vain for a bond of union between the world of daily life and this domain of Life Eternal. As a consequence thereof it appears that the two worlds are discrete and discontinuous out and out" (ibid).

As a historian of culture and civilization, his position was that of a universalist and internationalist, tempered by nationalism as a stepping stone to the coming of humanism. In support of his view, he mentioned the concepts of Brahman and Viśvadevatā which transcend nationalism. At this point, a striking resemblance can be seen between Tagore in his *Religion of Man* and Seal.

As an academic philosopher, he was not interested in building a system of philosophy because he believed that it is possible to defend any philosophical theory with rational justification. Moreover, philosophical systems are temporary in nature, which become extinct after some time. With his exemplary honesty he declared, "the problems of philosophy are of a perennial nature and they are not going to be solved finally by any philosopher, however great. A philosopher is wise, if he does not seek to spread the illusion that he has solved them" (Das 1968). Keeping in mind such a position, K.C. Bhattacharyya wrote in his *Studies in Vedantism*,

> A true philosophic system is not to be looked upon as a soul-less jointing of hypothesis. It is a living fabric which, with all its endeavours to be objective, must have a well-marked individuality. Hence it is not to be regarded as the special property of academic philosophy-mongers, to be hacked up by them into technical view, but it is to be regarded as a form of life and is to be treated as a theme of literature of infinite interest to humanity (Bhattacharyya 1956: 6).

Brajendra Nath championed two complimentary approaches to philosophy—comparative and synthetic. He declared that his account of the positive sciences of the ancient Hindus is intended to serve as a preliminary to his *Studies in Comparative Philosophy*. For,

> Philosophy in its rise and development is necessarily governed by the body of positive knowledge preceding or accompanying it. Hindu philosophy *on its empirical side* was dominated by concepts derived from physiology and philology, just as Greek philosophy was similarly dominated by geometrical concepts and methods. Comparative philosophy, then, in its criticism and estimate of Hindu thought, must take note of the empirical basis on which the speculative superstructure was raised. (Seal 1985: vi)

In this pioneering work on ancient Indian scientific treatises and scientific method, Seal gives a naturalist interpretation of the basic Sāṃkhya-Yoga and Nyāya-Vaiśeṣika tenets, overriding their overtly spiritual interpretations. Within the corpus of approximately 300 pages, he drew our attention to the elements of physics, chemistry, mechanics, acoustics, botany, biology, zoology and physiology, excerpting from ancient Indian treatises which need to be reviewed once again in the light of contemporary developments of science. He considered an intensive study of scientific methodology a necessity because in the absence of a rigorous scientific method Hindu sciences will be construed either as collections of practical recipes or as unverified speculations. In this context, he has provided detailed descriptions of the methods of scientific discovery, rules for establishing causal connection amongst natural phenomena and criteria of theory choice as manifested in their theses of *saṁvāda* (experiential coherence) and *lāghava* (simplicity).

The synthetic strand of his philosophy is well-documented in his short commentary on the *Gītā*, which he named *The Gītā: A Synthetic Interpretation* (Seal 1964). Of all the sacred texts of India, the *Gītā* probably has the largest number of commentaries which have been written in different periods of Indian civilization. During Seal's time, many modern interpretations of the *Gītā* were published and these had a great influence on the nationalist leaders and also on the 'armed revolutionaries' who went to the gallows chanting the verses of the *Gītā*. Most interpreters have written commentaries to support their sectarian view and as a result people are much confused about the real teachings of the *Gītā*. Seal tried to remove those confusions by offering a syncretic reading of the text.

The *Gītā* describes three ways to liberation—knowledge (*jñana*), devotion (*bhakti*) and action (*karma*). Different interpreters have explained the relevance of these three ways to liberation differently relying on their basic philosophico-religious commitments. Some have thought that following any one of the three paths is sufficient for attaining liberation. Others have upheld that one of the three ways is the most effective or the principal way to liberation, the other two are just subsidiary and of secondary importance. Śaṁkara, for example, underscored the significance of the path of knowledge and held that the other two paths are just required for cleansing one's mind which is a necessary prerequisite of liberation, while Rāmānuja and other Vaiṣṇava teachers have highlighted the path of devotion (*bhakti*) as the most effective path, relegating the other two as mere auxiliaries which do not have any significance in the penultimate stage of liberation. Interpreters belonging to a third group, however, upheld that seekers of liberation should choose the most suitable way in accordance with their nature and dispositions. So for some, the path of action may be the most suitable one, while for another having a different nature the path of devotion may be the most effective and so on. This third view indicates towards a fourth one which Seal called 'Electicism.' According to this position, each of the three ways, severally and independently, can yield a combined result—liberation (*mokṣa*). Electicism can be practiced in two different ways. One way enjoins simultaneous practice of knowledge, devotion and action. Depending on the nature of the liberation-seeker, any of these three can be considered primary but that does not make the other two of lesser significance because, on this view, the relation amongst the three paths is organic or internal. Just as in an organism, each organ equally contributes to the survival and benefit of the whole, similarly all three paths have its own significance in bringing about the liberation-seekers' goal. Another brand of electicism advocates sequential combination of these three paths. Usually one starts by following the path of action which enables one to realize the importance of the path of knowledge, which in its turn leads to the path of meditation and devotion.

As a combined result of all these three practices, one attains liberation. Seal further refines electicism and points out that even the so-called internal relation that obtains in the dynamic combination of the paths of action, knowledge and devotion creates a chasm between the knower and the known, the devotee and the devoted. Integration of action, devotion and knowledge in sequence leads to the union of the self with the Brahman which Seal calls '*Ātma-yoga*' or '*Brahma-yoga*' which finally culminates into *jīvanmukti* or the attainment of liberation while living in this world. This, according to Seal, is the essential teaching of The *Gītā*.

5.6 Syllabus on Indian Philosophy

This exploration into Seal's life and intellectual journey will remain incomplete if we do not place it on record that B.N. Seal is the architect of the subject 'Indian philosophy' as we study it today. When Seal joined the University of Calcutta as the George V Professor of Mental and Moral Philosophy in 1913, no Indian system of philosophy was taught there. Seal introduced the courses in Indian philosophy and taught till 1920. Based on his lectures, V. Subrahmanya Iyer published the syllabus on Indian philosophy in 1924 with a view to showing to the world what a rich and inexhaustible mine of philosophical wealth still exists in India for the seeker after truth to quarry. Iyer observed:

> This syllabus at first sight appears to extend over areas placed in Europe, latterly, outside the pale of philosophy. But a little thought will show that philosophy in its wider sense necessarily stretches its roots to every region of Human knowledge and practice, a feature on which the ancient Hindus laid great emphasis. Every Indian system of philosophy attempts at covering the entire field of thought, its ultimate grounds and basic principles, from Physics to Metaphysics, including philology, and a study of social institutions. In using this syllabus for purposes of research or critical evaluation, the student should make a comparative study of both the Indian and Western systems of thought with reference to the entire circle of the philosophical sciences. (Foreword to Seal 1924)

The span of the syllabus is mind-boggling and once again shows the expanse and depth of Seal's knowledge. Starting the philosophical journey from the early Vedic period and progressing to the ages of the systems, a postgraduate student of Indian philosophy is supposed to cover all systems mentioned in Mādhavācārya's *Sarvadarśanasaṁgraha* with special emphasis on Indian attempts at synthesis and critique of all philosophical systems. For the first topic, the teachers need to consult *Ṣaḍ-darśana-samanvaya* and *Sarvāgama-prāmāṇyavāda* and for the critique he prescribed Srīharaṣa's *Khaṇḍana*, Jaina *syādvāda*, Bauddha *śunyavāda*, Dhūrta Cārvāka's *Tattvopaplavasiṃha* and other *sahajamata*-s (non-Vedic folk-systems). All systems are to be discussed keeping in mind the following topics: Ultimate Postulates, theoretical and practical, commonly accepted in systems of Indian philosophy, Principles of Experience, Analysis of Experience, Dialectic of Experience, Dialectic of Nescience, Dialectic of the Self; Philosophical Standpoints—Realism versus Idealism, Mechanism versus Teleology; Epistemology and Logic, i.e., doctrine of *pramā* (valid cognition),

prāmāṇyagraha (means of justification), *pramāṇa* (accredited sources of cognition) and theories of inference from the perspectives of Logic and Scientific
Method; Methodology, general and applied; Various Types of Pragmatism in
Indian Systems—logical (*saṃvāda*), epistemological (*vyāghāta*) as the ultimate
solvent of doubt, linguistic (*bhāvanā, ceṣṭā, vākyārtha*), radical (*arthakriyā*
as constituting *sattvā* or existence), voluntaristic (*vidhi, niṣedha* as forms of
action), absolute (conceptual construct of Nirguṇa Brahman for pragmatic ends);
Categories of Reality, Theory of Being, Ontology and Cosmology; Theory of
Causation, Dialectic of Causation; Dialectic of Relation, Philosophy and Logic
of Language (origin of language, original language, philosophy of grammar, categories of grammar, related to categories of thought, relation of thought to language); Psychology, the Aesthetic Sentiments; Ethics, ethical disciplines and
special problems in Ethics, e.g., Theory of *Karma* and its implications in the
realm of Ethics; Social Philosophy; Political and Juristic Philosophy–Canons
of Interpretation of Codes, Civil or Religious; Theology; Religion (some features of Indian Theism), Krishna cult, Foundations of the Science of Mythology;
Practical Philosophy, Philosophical Disciplines, *Yoga, Mukti, Nirvāṇa*; Psychic
Phenomena, Hypnotism, *Siddhis*; and Stages in Cultural History.

This syllabus is unique in many respects. The time when it was proposed,
Indians had already been somewhat alienated from traditional learning. Besides,
what was going on in the name of educating people about their own heritage was
mostly biased and unscientific. Seal framed the syllabus in such a way that students were compelled to study the original texts and critically evaluate them. The
only drawback of the syllabus was its overambitious character. Only a student with
Seal's acumen can master the whole syllabus. However, assuming the distribution
of labour, it is an excellent syllabus because it is both exhaustive and innovative.

There was a tendency amongst the Indologists to construe 'Indian philosophy' as synonymous with the great Vedic tradition. It goes to the credit of Seal
that he had placed equal emphasis on the great tradition as well as the little traditions including non-Vedic *āgamas* and philosophy underlying folk religions. Most
probably, keeping in mind the Hegelian criticism that Indian philosophy could not
go beyond the mythical stage, Seal tried to show the importance of mythological
stories in later philosophical systems. In Europe, philosophy emerged as a theoretical discipline in *toto*; in India, philosophy was rooted in experience and aimed
at attainment of liberation; hence, theory and practice were never dissociated.
Practical philosophy and philosophical disciplines, therefore, formed an important
part of this syllabus.

Seal imposed contemporary categories to interpret traditional knowledge and
taught us to reinterpret our tradition using contemporary idioms. Thus, we learnt
to differentiate amongst elements of metaphysics, epistemology, ethics, psychology, social and political theories within the integrated systems of Indian philosophy. This was probably the most controversial move. However, after the
publication of this syllabus, all works on Indian philosophy are found to internalize these categories. Of course, there had always been debates on the issues like
whether the *pramāṇa* theories are the same as epistemology or Indian theories

of *anumāna* can be regarded as logic proper; nonetheless, Seal must be given his dues as the trend-setter. Three things probably motivated Seal to re-categorize Indian philosophy. First, many of his associates like Benoy Sarkar requested him to do something so that the British and European academics could appreciate the richness of Indian philosophy. Second, comparative philosophy, of which Seal was a great enthusiast, becomes a nonstarter in absence of a unified set of categories of interpretation and evaluation. Third and most important, it was not possible for the nineteenth century Indian people to set the clock back and travel by time machine to the pre-colonial period; so the only way to integrate traditional Indian values with their contemporary life form and prevent Indian philosophy from obsolescence was by bridging the gap between tradition and modernity, by reinterpreting Indian tradition with the prevalent modernist tools. This way of reinterpreting the tradition by borrowing tools from other traditions have been severely criticised by many. Many are of the opinion that conceptual tools cannot be thus borrowed without warping them because tools are specially designed for solving specific problems. Outside the context of origin, these tools are likely to become ineffective or may distort the significance of the new discourse. These criticisms have some points but should not be taken too seriously. For such a thesis is symptomatic of parochialism like Schopenhauer's, who used to believe that philosophy cannot be done in any language other than German nor can be developed anywhere outside Germany. Moreover, if selected pieces of philosophical tradition are never put to novel uses, the tradition become 'a museum diorama' (Siderits 2003: xii–xvii) to be appreciated from a distance but cut off from the current form of life. Thus, our dream of integrating our philosophical heritage with the contemporary form of life will delude us forever. So by framing the syllabus of Indian philosophy, Seal has made the pursuit of 'fusion philosophy' a feasible enterprise.

Seal's life was synonymous with an eternal quest for knowledge and truth. He took it upon himself to swim in the oceans of world culture and civilization, retrieve treasures from ocean beds like an expert diver and make a gift of them to whoever may care to acquire them. According to the famous historian, Roy Chaudhuri (2009: 150), this was the ideal of nineteenth-century Bengal. Under the influence of the Bengal Renaissance, there emerged a class of people who pursued knowledge for pure enjoyment, not for money or for fame, never considered it a waste of time to pursue theoretical interests without immediate practical gain, never hesitated to share their knowledge with others and never wrote a single line if they did not have anything significant to contribute. Seal was the greatest exponent of this philosophy. Men of this genre are now a rarity, in the market-dominated lifestyle of the 21st century.

References

Banerjee, N. V. (1968). Acharya Brajendranath Seal, the versatile thinker and the passionate humanist. In P. Chatterjee (Ed.), *Acharya Brajendranath Seal birth centenary commemoration volume*. Acharya Brajendranath Seal Birth Centenary Commemoration Committee: Calcutta.

Bhattacharyya, K. C. (1956). Studies in Vedantism. In G. Bhattacharyya (Ed.), *Studies in Philosophy*, Progressive Publishers: Calcutta.

Bhattacharyya, K. C. (1968). Reminiscences. In P. Chatterjee (Ed.), *Acharya Brajendranath Seal birth centenary commemoration volume*. Acharya Brajendranath Seal Birth Centenary Commemoration Committee: Calcutta.

Chatterjee, P. (Ed.). (1968). *Acharya Brajendranath Seal birth centenary commemoration volume*. Calcutta: Acharya Brajendranath Seal Birth Centenary Commemoration Committee.

Chattopadhyaya, A. (1999). *Ananta Eṣaṇā, Brajendranath Seal: Jīvan O Cintā*. Kolkata: Deep Prakashan.

Das, R. (1936). Pursuit of truth through doubt and belief. In S. Radhakrishnan & J. Muirhead (Eds.), *Contemporary Indian philosophy*. London: George Allen & Unwin Limited.

Das, R. (1968). My master as I saw him. In P. Chatterjee (Ed.), *Acharya Brajendranath Seal Birth centenary commemoration volume*. Acharya Brajendranath Seal Birth Centenary Commemoration Committee: Calcutta.

Halbfass, W. (1990). *India and Europe*. Delhi: Motilal Banarsidass.

Herring, H. (Ed. & Trans.). (1995). *G.W.F. Hegel on the episode of the Mahābhārata known by the name Bhagavad-Gītā by Wilhelm von Humboldt*. New Delhi: Indian Council of Philosophical Research.

Maitra, S. K. (1936). Outlines of an emergent theory of values. In S. Radhakrishnan & J.M. Muirhead (Eds.), *Contemporary Indian philosophy*.

Mohanty, J. N. (2001). In B. Gupta (Ed.), *Explorations in philosophy: Indian philosophy*. New Delhi: Oxford University Press.

Mukharji, R. (1910). *Indian shipping: A history of the sea-borne trade and maritime activity of the Indians from the earliest times*. London: Longmans, Green and Co.

Ray, P. C. (1909). *A history of Hindu chemistry*. Calcutta: The Bengal Chemical & Pharmaceutical Works Limited.

Roy Chaudhuri, T. (2009). *Prabandha-samgraha (a collection of essays in Bengali)*. Kolkata: Ananda Publishers Pvt. Ltd.

Sarkar, B. K. (1914). *The positive background of Hindu sociology*. Allahabad: The Pānini Office, Bhuvaneśvarī Āśrama.

Seal, B. N. (1890). The Neo-romantic movement in literature. In The Calcutta review. Kolkata: University of Calcutta.

Seal, B. N. (1899). *Comparative studies in Vaishnavism and Christianity with an examination of the Mahabharata Legend about Nārada's Pilgrimage to Śvetadvīpa and an introduction on the Historico-comparative method*. Calcutta: Hare Press.

Seal, B. N. (1903). *New essays in criticism*. Calcutta: Som Brothers.

Seal, B. N. (1911). *Race origins*. Calcutta: Hare Press.

Seal, B. N. (1924). *Syllabus of Indian philosophy, based on the lectures of Dr. Brajendranath Seal*. Bangalore: University of Mysore.

Seal, B. N. (1928–1929). *Annual report of the University of Mysore, 1928-29*. Mysore: University of Mysore.

Seal, B. N. (1964). *The Gita: A synthetic interpretation*. Calcutta: Sādhārana Brāhmo Samāja (Reprinted) [First published (Kolkata: The Modern Review, July issue, 1930)].

Seal, B. N. (1985). *The positive sciences of the ancient Hindus*. Delhi: Motilal Banarasidass Publishers Pvt. Ltd. (Reprint).

Siderits, M. (2003). *Empty persons*. UK: Ashgate Publishing Company.

Chapter 6
The Notion of Absolute:
Hegel and Hiralal Haldar

Tathagata Biswas

Abstract This essay discusses the notion of Absolute as developed by Hiralal Haldar in response to Hegel and British neo-Hegelians of late 19th and early 20th century. The first section situates Haldar in the broader intellectual context of colonial India. The second and the third sections deal with the complexities of the notion of Absolute and its relation to finite selves. The fourth section addresses the question of the nature of Absolute (God) and its relation to Man (human persons) and whether personality can be ascribed to Absolute. The fifth section discusses the issue of idealism and realism. Haldar develops the notion of Absolute which serves as dynamic principle of spiritual reconciliation between appearance and reality, between real and ideal, between matter and mind, and between science and spirituality. He critiques both subjective idealism and realism and develops what is called 'realist idealism' which is the most favored metaphysical position preva-lent in colonial India both among academic philosophers and public intellectuals.

Keywords Absolute · Spiritual · Concrete universal · God · Hegel · British neo-Hegelianism · Hiralal Haldar · Kant · Divine personality

6.1 Why Hegelian Absolute?

Every nation needs to narrate itself, sustain and direct itself. Thus, it needs a phi-losophy which works as *eye of the mind* (Bhabha 2003: 1). It makes the nation what it is and what it desires to be by providing an ideational ground and theoreti-cal justification. Philosophy as cultural expression is historically related with mak-ing of a nation. The story of Indian nation thus can be looked at through the way how philosophy in its Anglophone (philosophy written in English) variety has

T. Biswas (✉)
School of Education, Azim Premji University, Bengaluru, India
e-mail: biswastathagata@gmail.com

© Indian Institute of Advanced Study 2015
S. Deshpande (ed.), *Philosophy in Colonial India*, Sophia Studies in Cross-cultural Philosophy of Traditions and Cultures 11, DOI 10.1007/978-81-322-2223-1_6

emerged in colonial India during late 19th and early 20th century. Unlike other disciplines, philosophy in India has not only a rich and heterogeneous history of vibrant activities, but also has recent experience of early modernity (Ganeri 2011: 1–3).[1] It emerged, though in new guise, against Western hegemony by producing and circulating counter-universal claims regarding metaphysical and epistemological issues by actively commenting and critiquing both on classical Indian and modern Western philosophical systems. Thus, the intellectual life of 19th century Indian subcontinent has been largely shaped by Indian as well as Western philosophical thought systems. In this engagement, there were conscious efforts on the part of modern Indian philosophers; firstly, to understand the cross-cultural reality of their intellectual endeavor[2] and secondly, to become authentically Indian by maintaining the intellectual and cultural heritage of the classical Indian philosophy. In the context of colonialism and orientalism, modern Indian philosophers wanted to establish continuity between materialism and spiritualism, and also between classical Indian philosophy and modern Western thought.

In the orientalist discourse, India has been depicted as the land of spirituality; and thus, other-worldly. East in general and India in particular has been projected as the 'other' of Europe which is materialist, rational, and this-worldly. This geopolitics enabled colonialism to validate its claim to colonize, to give itself a philosophical ground and ethical justification. In this context, the main concern of modern Indian philosophers was the reconciliation of science and spirituality, matter and mind, and classical India and modern West. In this attempt, they were largely influenced on the one hand by Śaṁkaracharya's *Advaitavāda* (non-dualism) and on the other hand by Hegel's idealism. Both these world-views had played formative role in the formulation of an autonomous subjectivity in the wake of science and colonialism. Thus, *Swaraj* became a desired form of freedom rather than *nihsreyasa*. To forge a positive notion of freedom, modern Indian philosophers felt the need of a dynamic principle. They found this principle in Hegelian notion of concrete universal, a dynamic notion of Absolute. "Hegel's Absolute idealism and in particular his doctrine of the Absolute is a key to determine Hegel's influence on modern Indian philosophers…In fact, the most singular question that has occupied modern Indian philosophers in the early part of the 20th century is: 'What is the nature of the Absolute?' and one finds that almost every modern Indian philosopher is proposing his own answer to it and

---

[1] This is Jonardon Ganeri's claim that there was pre-colonial modernity in Indian philosophy in new research program of *Navya-Nyāya*.

[2] This fact is underlined at the very beginning of *Contemporary Indian Philosophy* edited by Radhakrishnan and Muirhead (1936). The blurb of the volume states: "The most momentous phenomenon of our times is the mingling of East and West. Though it is impossible to foresee the outcome of this process, the contributions to this volume by writers representative of Indian thought as M.K. Gandhi and Rabindranath Tagore, Radhakrishnan and Ananda Coomaraswamy, Dasgupta and Bhagavan Das among others, indicate the direction in which this process is advancing. Apart from its technical value in the field of philosophy, the publication has a certain *political importance*, as India stands to-day both in politics and in philosophy at the opening of a new era in her history. The book, it is hoped, will contribute to a better mutual understanding between the *whole mind* of East and West."

in doing so clarifying his own philosophical position" (Deshpande 2010: 97). Therefore to understand the philosophical concerns of modern Indian philosophers in colonial India, it is important to look at the reception of Hegelian philosophy by modern Indian philosophers, which they have received mainly through British neo-Hegelians, in particular through F.H. Bradley. In this reception of Hegel, Hiralal Haldar[3] (c. 1865–1942) is one of the prominent Indian philosophers who spent most of his life engaging with Hegel's philosophy and with British followers of Hegel since later decades of 19th century. He developed his own philosophy of Absolute Idealism in the light of Hegelian notion of Absolute and in terms of its British appropriation by the neo-Hegelians such as F.H. Bradley, McTaggert, Edward Caird, William Wallace, T.H. Green, Bosanquet, John Watson, Muirhead, Mackenzie, and Haldane. In the following sections, we will discuss Haldar's reception of Hegel and his own conception of Absolute.

6.2 Haldar and Absolute Idealism

> Absolute Idealism, whatever may be its merits or demerits, is one of the recognized modes of thinking in the civilized world at the present day. (Haldar 1899: 261)

Haldar thinks that Absolute idealism is the only plausible theory to explain the multitude of ordinary experience and science; because things make sense only in reference to the 'totality of a system' (Haldar 1899: 262). Haldar gives several formulations of the Absolute in response to Hegel and the British neo-Hegelians.

---

[3] Hiralal Haldar (c. 1865–1942) like Brajendra Nath Seal was a renowned neo-Hegelian of his time though both Seal and Haldar in the later part of their life renounce Hegel and Hegelianism for different reasons. Haldar departs from Hegel's notion of the Absolute on the question of the relationship between thought and reality. He studied (c. 1882) under William Hastie (then principle of General Assembly, now known as The Scottish College, Calcutta). Like B.N. Seal, he was the George V Professor of philosophy at Calcutta University during 1931–1933. He was considered as one of those teachers of Calcutta University who was best liked by their students. He was initiated in studying Hegel by Edward Caird's book, *Hegel* (Blackwood Philosophical Classics Series), William Wallace's Prolegomena to Hegel's *Encyclopedia of Philosophical Sciences* and Bradley's *Ethical Studies*. His *magnum opus* is *Neo-Hegelianism* (1927) wherein he summarizes the British neo-Hegelian movement with his own critical comments on major British neo-Hegelian philosophers such as T.H. Green, Caird, William Wallace, Bradley, Bosanquet, John Watson, Muirhead, Mackenzie, Haldane, and McTaggert. The book is appended with his own independent reading of Hegelianism (see Appendix, "Hegelianism and Human Personality", pp. 438-486). Haldar's contribution to neo-Hegelianism is acknowledged as very significant even in Cambridge and Oxford of his times. Haldar is instrumental in popularizing neo-Hegelian thought among Indian philosophers working in Indian Universities. His Realistic Idealism in *Contemporary Indian Philosophy* (Radhakrishnan and Muirhead) is one of his most important statements of his philosophical position, giving a comprehensive account of realist idealism, which was a dominant metaphysical position of Anglophone philosophers in modern India. Haldar wrote several articles in the journal *Philosophical Review*.

According to Haldar, Absolute is a concrete universal. It is a synthetic unity of thought and being, subject and object, real and ideal. It is truly Infinite, the supreme spiritual personality, eternal tri-union of *sat-chit-ānanda*. It is ultimate integration and reconciliation of all contradictions.

Haldar begins with the assertion that, 'Absolute is Thought' (Haldar 1899: 262). All idealist philosophers agree that thought is the essential nature of Absolute. However, there is disagreement regarding the meaning of the word 'thought.' For Haldar, Absolute cannot be a *mere* thought because it 'hypostatizes (Absolute) as an abstraction' (Haldar 1899: 262). Thus, thought limits the Absolute. Absolute is not *mere* abstraction. It is thought *and* being. This equation between thought and being might seem absurd to one who by 'thought' understands; (a) "psychic process of thinking, or its product and (b) unity of self-consciousness" (Haldar 1896: 264). Haldar is in conformity with Hegel's meaning of 'Thought' which is same as 'Reason' and Reason is the Ultimate Reality. For Hegel and Haldar, "What really exists, the only true Being, is the Absolute Idea, Reason or Thought. The highest Being, the absolutely independent Being, it will thus be seen, is Thought" (Haldar 1896: 264). All content, data, and experience exist *for* Absolute thought. According to Haldar, Absolute thought includes both psychic process of thinking and its product and unity of self-consciousness but it exceeds both psychological and epistemological meaning of 'thought.' Instead of psychological and epistemological explanation of 'thought,' Haldar provides speculative-metaphysical conception of 'Thought as Reason.'

Ultimate reality, Reason or Thought also includes Will. Divine Will is, "that aspect of the Absolute which is expressed in the concrete and differentiated individuality of the world" (Haldar 1899: 264). Therefore, it cannot be said that Absolute is devoid of Will, committing to such position makes any conception of Absolute empty and mere abstraction. But one can argue against this Hegelian proposition and can deny Will to Absolute. The argument against ascribing will to Absolute is based on psychological conception of will which includes attention, desire, choice, effort, and volition. These are mental states and attached to bodily activities. Since Absolute does not have a body, it cannot have Will. To counter this claim, it can be argued that there is richer and higher experience involved in the case of Absolute. It also involves the consciousness of effort[4] which is a necessary aspect of Absolute. As Haldar says, "In the totality of its life, the feelings of resistance and effort, experienced in the parts, are submerged, and transformed into a higher kind of active consciousness, which is an inseparable aspect of the Absolute. Absolute will include within itself feelings of effort and resistance, which are the component factors, though not the whole of will"[5] (Haldar 1899: 266).

---

[4] According to Haldar, consciousness of effort is an essential attribute of Will, and for this reason Will cannot be equated with attention. Haldar is defending the thesis that Absolute or God is also Will (Haldar 1899: 264).

[5] In this context, Haldar criticizes Josiah Royce for reducing will only to attention. Will includes conscious feeling of making effort as an essential element of will. Thus, it cannot be considered only as attention (Haldar 1899: 264).

Absolute is active, "eternally complete consciousness" (Haldar 1899: 266). Absolute has to be eternal or timeless, because any temporal dimension necessarily limits It. If Absolute is timeless or eternal and if it is a concrete universal which involves actual world-process within itself, then how reality of time which is everyday experience of finite individuals can be reconciled with eternity of Absolute? How the world which is in process of becoming be possibly reconciled with the *complete* consciousness? To address these questions, we have to look at the meaning of the term 'eternity' in the context of Absolute as conceived by Haldar. Eternity or 'eternal now' is not the same as 'temporal present' according to Royce (1898: 43–44), whereas in Haldar's philosophy, it is "inclusive of past, present and future" (Haldar 1899: 267). Absolute (God) is omniscient, that is, He knows past and future as well as present. Haldar proposes that even within Absolute consciousness, there is a "real difference between past, present, and future, though they are all together in the vision of the 'eternal now'" (Haldar 1899: 267). But the question that arises regarding this Absolute knowledge of time and eternity is how both are possible in Absolute? Haldar says, unlike human knowledge, Divine or Absolute knowledge is both conceptual and perceptual at the same time. "It is a union of both, which, as we have seen before, is the type of the Absolute consciousness. The criterion of difference, besides that furnished by succession, between past, present, and future seems to lie in the manifestations of will, such as we have seen it really to be, involved in the present, while the representation of past and future implies attention only" (Haldar 1899: 267). Eternity according to Haldar does not cancel succession of time. He says, even in "Eternal Instant," there is a distinction between present on the one hand, and past and future on the other. Will is the sign through which we can demarcate present as distinct instance from past and future which are in turn marked by attention.[6] Thus, Absolute is also inclusive of change in succession of temporal instances; hence, there is scope for novelty. It is like oceans; where there are innumerable waves of events emerging every moment, though the total volume of water remains the same. Likewise, Absolute does not change, but events take place within It, and without these events, we cannot think about the concrete Absolute. As Haldar says, "the world as a whole is not an event at a particular moment of time is not tantamount to affirming that events do not occur and are not comprised within the unity of the Absolute" (Haldar 1918: 389). Eternal order is the presupposition of change in time. Moreover, eternity includes within itself changes in events. Only in this sense, we can call the Absolute as eternal or timeless. Absolute "knows the meaning of the world drama progressively unfolded in time" (Haldar 1918: 389). Here, Haldar talks about Henry Bergson's conception of 'duration' which is the

---

[6] "Professor Royce does not say by what sign the present is to be distinguished from past or future in the eternal instant. This sign, I maintain, is that while the present contains actual expression of force, or, from our point of view, manifestations of the Absolute Will, involving but transcending experiences of resistance and effort, the past and future are only intuited and presuppose attention alone. Unless you make a real distinction between past and present other than that which depends on succession, succession itself loses all its meaning" (Haldar 1899: 268).

"continuous progress of the past which gnaws into the future and which swells as it advances" (Haldar 1918: 389). But Haldar is critical about this view of time because he thinks that it does not take into account discreetness; hence, it is a one-sided view of time. As Haldar puts it, "Time is not simply a continuous flow any more than it is a mere sum of discrete moments" (Haldar 1918: 389). Unlike Bergson, movement of time for Haldar is toward an end. He agrees with Bergson on the point that it is becoming, but with an aim in view. Ultimate Reality or Reason is purposive; it is not a mere flux. Absolute grasps time all at once. But this view raises problem of regress. Even in the case of Absolute, having a complete insight of the whole of time 'all at once' is not possible, because then we have to suppose that temporal series has a beginning and an end, that time has a beginning *in* time and ends at a certain point *in* time. In face of this objection, Haldar took side with Pringle Pattison, according to whom, "The time process is *retained* in the Absolute and *yet transcended*. Retained in some form it must be, if our life experience is not to be deprived of all meaning and value. The temporal process is not simply non-existent from the Absolute point of view" (Pringle-Pattison, 1917: 363). However, exact relation between eternal and temporal order remains elusive to human reason. The aim or the purpose of Absolute is realized through the purposes of constituent individuals. These individuals are "relative wholes within the unity of the Absolute and contribute in various and unique ways to its total purpose" (Haldar 1918: 376).

Absolute as concrete unity is neither *only* the subject nor a *mere* object, neither real nor ideal but unity of both. Following Hegel, Haldar says, "It is not a sum of them but their ideal unity in which their differences are at once preserved and annulled. The Absolute of Hegel is subject–object. It is the all-inclusive unity which is bifurcated into the subject, which is such only as it goes out of itself to the object (the good), and the object, which is real only as it centers itself in the subject (the true). The necessary counterpart of the subject is the object" (Haldar 1917: 389). Objects are elements of world-system, and by virtue of being such elements, they are real. The world-system in turn is "embodiment of a universal mind" (Haldar 1918: 375). Hence, objects are not *mere* objects but "individualized expressions of one ultimate mind" (Haldar 1918: ibid). Objects or things are objects only in their appearance; in their inner being, they are the centers of experience and appreciation of world in which the Absolute reveals itself. Each individual object acquires meaning by virtue of its inclusion within the fold of Absolute; they contribute to 'the life of Absolute' (Haldar 1918: ibid). Objects are not totally foreign to subject. If it were the case, then objects would not have been objects of knowledge for subject. As embodiment of the Absolute, objects are ultimately conscious selves and also possess mind. But objects are not a *mere* impression or subjective ideas. They are *real* in lieu of their participation in the Absolute. Objects not only have both primary qualities of extension and shape and secondary qualities of color and smell but they also have tertiary or esthetic qualities. Here, Haldar is criticizing both rationalists and empiricists for making untenable distinction between primary and secondary qualities, between the objective world and subjective ideas. Haldar endows objects with all kinds of qualities as a realist would do and holds the view that objects are real and they exist independently of ideas or impressions. But his agreement with realists ends here. As an objective idealist, he is extending the realist thesis further by giving the status of *mind* to the objects. According to Haldar, "idealism does not see why the fountain of realism's charity should suddenly run dry as soon as things are vested with diverse qualities. Surely it is intolerable that they should be supposed to have everything except that which alone can make worth having, viz. mind" (Haldar 1918: 379). Haldar makes a stronger claim for idealism by saying that, "things must have mind to understand that they are real" (Haldar 1918: 379). As a highest integration of all objects, the Absolute is Self, as Haldar says, "The Absolute is, no doubt, a self, but it is a self which is manifested in an Infinite number of ways in an Infinite number of things. It is a whole which is completely and indivisibly present in each particular thing, in virtue of which all things are also perfect selves and form a unity of system, and through these selves is bound up with and constitutes the essence of finite selves" (Haldar 1918: 388). Absolute Idea reconciles within itself manifold of evanescent sensations and categories of understanding, it is the true reality. Subject and object are only two aspects of Absolute Idea. Now if Absolute Idea is a higher synthetic unity of subject and object, the relationship between finite beings, i.e., finite subjects on the one hand, and the Absolute Universal becomes an important question. We will dwell upon this issue in the following section.

6.3 The One and the Many

> In his great dialogue, the *Parmenides*, Plato argues that if the one has being, all other things are. The being of the one is not capable of being separated from the others. The existence of the one means the existence of the others which share in its being and are, therefore, whole and *Infinite without prejudice to their plurality*. The others having parts must partake of the whole and be the whole of which they are the parts. *Each part, that is to say, is also an Absolute One*. (Haldar 1918: 374)

For Haldar, the essence of idealism as expressed in Plato's thought is the starting point and of great relevance for modern idealism. The crux of the matter is that there is in reality no separation between the One and many; the Universal and particulars; the Infinite and finite beings. On the contrary, many particular finite beings are One, Universal, and Infinite. Infinite does not exist apart from finites; yet Infinite is not mere aggregate of finite beings. The world constituted by finite individuals is "objective expression of the Absolute mind. Nature as a systematic totality of interrelated things, presupposes a spiritual principle of unity of which it is the necessary manifestation" (Haldar 1918: 374). Nature or the world as a system of interrelated finite things becomes possible because of the fundamental principle of spiritual unity, a unity *not beyond* but *in* difference, that is, not abstract but concrete Infinite. According to Hegel, abstract Absolute is 'false Infinite' because it does not involve finite individuals including human beings, which are the content of Absolute. Without content Absolute is empty, it becomes a 'false Absolute.' An Infinite, which is over and above, that is, outside of finite individuals, can only be another finite. Hence, abstract Infinite is a logical contradiction. Infinite is that which passes over from one finite to another, hence it abides by those finites. Genuine Infinity is, as Hegel says, "what is passed into is quite the same as what passes over, since both have one and the same attribute viz. To be another, it follows that something in its passage into other only joins with itself. To be thus self-related in the passage and in the other is the genuine Infinity" (Hegel 1892: 176). According to Haldar, this is the progress modern idealism has made, that is, to propose a concrete spiritual principle of unity instead of mere abstract unity, which is inclusive of and realized through finite beings. Haldar here reminds us that every finite being is also Infinite. There is no real difference between finite and Infinite. Every finite being is finite in relation to other finite being and in relation to the whole. In virtue of participation in One or Infinite, they are Infinite; being Infinite is their *inalienable property*.[7] Aims and ideals of Infinite are not different from aims and ideals of constituent individuals, but it is also not reducible to aim of any particular individual or group of individuals.[8] This is the distinguishing mark of Hegelian Absolute, which is inclusive of plurality, change, and novelty. Thus, Hegelianism is not monism. The content of Hegelian Absolute is not different from its constituent parts though Absolute is not the same as the sum total of its constituents. The Absolute, "as the synthesis of them, it gives a new value to them but is not other than they. As a *living organism* consists only of its members but is not simply their aggregate, as society is made up of individuals but is not merely a collection of them, so the Absolute self is a complex unity which does not go beyond, and yet reinterprets and gives a higher significance to the experiences of the finite but perfect individuals that compose it. Speculative Idealism, thus interpreted, incorporates pluralism into itself" (Haldar 1918: 377). According to Haldar's interpretation, Hegel's philosophy tends much more toward pluralism than what it is thought of, at least in British neo-Hegelianism. Speculative Idealism, if it wanted to be regarded as plausible theory it has to give account of plurality. Plurality makes Absolute, what the Absolute is that "they are the opposite poles of one *reality*" (Haldar 1899: 270). Professor Howison raises objection against Speculative Idealism, saying that it is solipsistic (Royce et al. 1898: 98–99). But concrete Absolute is not solitary Individual, stands not only for *I*, but also for *We*. Thus, it does not suffer from ego-centricity.

According to Haldar, Hegel's philosophy is different from pan-psychism. Pan-psychism cannot explain the fact of human knowledge. Knowledge is self-transcendence, which pan-psychism cannot explain since according to pan-psychism

---

[7] "...the individuals in which the Absolute is expressed, possessing its nature, are subordinate wholes realized in their own differences which, parts of parts as they are, retain, as integral elements of the Absolute, their inalienable property of being whole and Infinite" (Haldar 1918: 376).

[8] The relation between Absolute, Infinite and particular individual constituent is like the relationship between State and the individuals. "State is other than the aims and ideals of its citizens which are brought into coordination with each other through their sub-ordination to it" (Haldar 1918: ibid).

each object has separate mind of its own.[9] Haldar raises the question about self-transcendence of a knowing subject without which knowledge is not possible, that is, if every object has its own mind, then how is it possible for it to reach out? Pan-psychism cannot provide any satisfactory answer to it. For this reason, it cannot explain combination of individual minds with Absolute Mind, which is the task for any idealist to explain. It cannot explain communication between finite selves; because in pan-psychism, each self is limited by its own respective mind. Ideas of each such finite self will remain contained within its own subjective world. Thus, pan-psychism cannot explain unity of the world. It cannot reconcile individuals with the all-pervading consciousness. Idealism cannot neglect the fact of human cognition. According to Haldar, the fact of human knowledge is the evidence of self-transcendence, it shows that human beings are not mere psycho-physical entities but self-conscious beings and also they are Infinite. Both pan-psychism and Hegelianism talks about unity of differences; but for the former, it is monadic unity, whereas for latter, the unity is portrayed as Self of selves, or the unity-in-difference, as Haldar says, "Pan-psychism is quite right in conceiving of the Absolute as a unity of differences, but it errs in thinking that such a unity arises out of the composition of the fragmentary consciousnesses of which physical objects are the outer aspect. It is not a monadic unity but a self of selves, a one-in-many revealed in the world, the structure and organization of which bears witness to its nature" (Haldar 1918: 381–382).

Hegelianism is also not pantheism since pantheism ignores the differences among finite beings. In the conception of concrete Absolute, "the ultimate unity of self-consciousness is meaningless apart from the plurality of finite objects, and the plurality of finite objects presupposes and has its being in the unity of self-consciousness" (Haldar 1910: 2). For this reason, it cannot be called a revived Spinozism. Another crucial difference between Spinoza and Hegel is that in Spinoza, the Absolute or God is the Infinite *substance*, whereas in Hegel, the Absolute or God is the Infinite *subject*. The problem with projecting Absolute as substance is that the (Spinozist) substance is "omnipotent in swallowing up its modes but impotent to explain their origin" (Haldar 1910: 3). It is for this reason according to Haldar, Absolute is envisaged in Hegel's philosophy as subject and as person. "Absolute is the person, a subject and not mere substance who necessarily reveals Himself in nature and more fully in man" (Haldar 1910: 2). Hence, Absolute as subject is also a person. But attributing personality to the Absolute is not without problems which we will discuss in the following section.

---

[9] "Mind, according to pan-psychism, is the self-appearance of matter and matter in the appearance of one mind to another. A thing, as seen from within, is a conscious being, but in so far as it is the object of knowledge of another conscious being, it is what we call matter. But if each object has a separate mind of its own, a mind which is itself from another point of view, how is it possible for it to go beyond itself so as to bring other things within the fold of its knowledge? How can pan-psychism explain the self-transcendence of a conscious being without which the combination of minds into a larger mind would not be possible?" (Haldar 1918: 380–381).

6.4 The Absolute as Personality

Whether personality can be predicated on to the Infinite Absolute is one of the major debates in idealism. If we do not consider Absolute as personality, it becomes an empty name, a mere abstraction, and we have seen that mere abstraction is not genuine Infinite; thus, Absolute has to be conceived in terms of personality, or following Haldar, we can minimally say that, *"The Absolute cannot be less than personal"* (Haldar 1899: 271). But what we understand by the word 'personality' is a right-bearing, duty-bound finite human being. Hence, Absolute cannot be considered as personality. To address this objection, Haldar reminds us that, "we have to remember that the Absolute consciousness is an *all-embracing, all-reconciling unity*, which perceives all things in space and time and yet transcends them, which includes as component factors of itself all the conflicting items of experience that we have and yet harmonizes them in a perfect synthesis of which we have only an exceedingly obscure knowledge" (Haldar 1899: 271). But in itself, this consideration is not sufficient to prove the necessity of establishing the relation between Absolute and personality. On the contrary, Haldar himself points out the poverty of the category of "personality" to "fathom the depth of Absolute" (Haldar 1899: 271). Hence, Divine personality is also not identical with human personality. Should we then consider Absolute which is a unity of finite persons, as super-personal or impersonal? Philosophers like McTaggert are of the opinion that Absolute itself is impersonal. According to him, Absolute is "unity of persons but it is not person itself" (McTaggert 1901: 58). Other British neo-Hegelian such as Edward Caird and William Wallace holds the opposite view. They hold that, "the Absolute is a person, a subject and not a mere substance, who necessarily reveals Himself in nature and more fully in man" (Haldar 1910: 2). Haldar wants to synthesize both the views. In both of these views, Absolute has been conceived as essentially related with human persons. If we accept that Absolute or God is impersonal, then the problem that arises is the relationship between human persons and the impersonal Absolute, as both of them are qualitatively different from each other. We have already seen that according to Haldar, Absolute as concrete universal is constituted by human persons. Moreover, they are self-differentiation of Absolute. Therefore, we have to accept that there is no qualitative difference between human persons and Absolute. So, the view that Absolute is impersonal has to be abandoned. Impersonal God is only a name, an abstraction, and devoid of any content. Thus, Impersonal God cannot be considered as genuinely Infinite. For these reasons, Haldar says that we have to consider Absolute as a person.

According to Haldar, Absolute in Hegel's philosophy is conceived as "self-conscious unity that comprehends within itself and transcends the relative distinction of subject and object. It is the central unity, the supreme spiritual principle, in which all things have their being and find their ultimate explanation and out of which they proceed. It is the Absolute subject without relation to which no object can exist and whose own existence depends upon its manifestation in the universe of inter-related objects" (Haldar 1910: 2). These objects are not only inert matter but are also selves and as selves they are integral elements that constitute Absolute personality. The relationship between Absolute or Divine personality and human or individual personality is not like the relationship between the whole and its parts. Absolute personality is differentiated in human personality in such a way that each human person in himself is also Absolute personality. This is the implicit truth of human personality, his ideality.[10] Thus, Man needs God for his own self-realization.

Now the question arise in Haldar's words, "Does God need him (man) as he needs God, or is he only a creature of the hour, an essentially ephemeral being, whose existence or non-existence makes no difference whatsoever to the fullness of His life?" (Haldar 1910: 23). There is no one answer to this question in philosophy of religion in general and Hegel's philosophy in particular. According to Haldar, existence of man is necessary in the Divine scheme of things, and "essential to the self-realization of the Absolute" (Haldar 1910: 23). Man is the mediator between Nature and God, rather God returns to Himself from Nature through the mediation of Man; and moreover, "It is in him that nature comes to a consciousness of itself" (Haldar 1910: 24). Thus, "man is the reproduction of God, he can only be the reproduction of one of his differentiations…The self-differentiations are persons, but they exist *in* God as the elements of His being" (Haldar 1910: 24). There is no fundamental separation or division between Man and God. All such self-differentiations of Absolute or God are self-posing: posited to unfold Itself; to be eternally abandoned and done away with.[11] Though there is no real separation of finite from the Infinite, human person from Eternal Personality, there is relative detachment between them in course of self-realization of God. In this process of self-realization, God takes flesh in Man due to relative detachment from the Whole or the Absolute, in His journey unto Himself. In this journey, Man appears as other to God, but this otherness of Man "is a self-differentiation of God, the son of God who is eternally with the Father, but the other, which also comes to have the characteristic of other-being or otherness is man" (Haldar 1910: 24–25). Haldar thus concludes that human beings owe their personhood to God. That is, Man acquires his personhood because he is the manifestation of Absolute or God. By virtue of being a manifestation of God, individual man contains in himself the whole of the Absolute, this is the ideality of Man; in reality, he is a finite being in relation to other finite beingvs. Individual human person has this double feature which is two aspects of the same existence, and hence, there is no scope for dualism here. As ideality, the whole is included in his being, in reality, everything else is being excluded from his finite being. Man potentially reflects God; he is incomplete and finite reproduction of God. The potentiality reflects in his awareness about his incompleteness. As Haldar says, "Man is notoriously conscious of his finitude, he has always made this the burden of his complaint. This is possible because, finite

---

[10] "Man," observes Hegel shrewdly, "if he wishes to be actual, must be there and then, and to this end, he must set a limit to himself. People who are too fastidious towards the finite never reach actuality" (Hegel 1892, 173).

[11] "Eternal Being-in-and-for-itself is something which unfolds itself, determines itself, differentiates itself, posits itself as its own difference, but the difference, again, is at the same time eternally done away with and absorbed ; what has essential Being, Being-in-and-for-itself eternally returns to itself in this, and only in so far as it does this is it spirit" (Hegel 1895, 46).

as he is, he is rooted in the Infinite, wells up from the Infinite. It is the Infinite, in short, that is revealed in him" (Haldar 1918: 383). Now the question is how Man, the incomplete finite self, is being reproduced from the Infinite Absolute or God. Is this reproductive relation direct? That is, is the human soul directly reproduced by Absolute Self? Haldar says that human soul or mind as ideality of his body is related to the Absolute not directly, but through his body. As a partial reproduction of Absolute, Man is a fragmentary expression of differentiations of the Absolute. Human Body as expression of the Absolute is the center of the universe, being such a center, it is the determinate form of Absolute Self through which the Absolute uniquely experiences the world. Man, the fragmentary being "is only a very limited area of this deeper self-detached from it, and it is through it (body) and not directly that he is included in the Absolute" (Haldar 1918: 383). The relationship between Man to his Body according to Haldar is like the relationship between real and ideal aspects of Absolute though with a crucial difference, "body of man is the expression not of the fractional entity we call man, but his true being, viz, a specific determination of Absolute…the body is the objectivity not of the finite man but of his truer self, His subliminal self" (Haldar 1910: 26). In man, his soul and his body in spite of being distinct from each other are united. They can be named independently, yet they live the same life. Moreover, body is the outward embodiment of freedom of the individual self. Individual self-consciousness or "I" become sensible through body (Hegel 1896: 54). Human Body, thus, is an organic unity, as a differentiation of Absolute, a system of selves. Man's real self is ideality of his body, a subordinate society of selves. The fragmentary self finds its being in all-inclusive Absolute transcendental self as Haldar says, "the human self is a fragmentary manifestation of a differentiation of the Absolute, which is itself a system of differentiations, with the aspect of otherness strongly emphasized and in relative detachment from the totality of the Absolute life and consciousness, in which its transcendental self—the self-differentiation of the Absolute, has its being" (Haldar 1910: 27).

Limitation of fragmentary Man, his limited content of mind is being supplemented by Absolute, "before they are allowed to enter the sanctuary of the Absolute" (Haldar 1918: 383). Finite human selves are adumbrations of the Absolute, who is the Individual among individuals. Each individual by virtue of their relationship with each other becomes one with the Absolute Individual. God does not mediate among individual selves; He *dwells* in them. Eternally fulfilled harmonious social life of constituent individuals is the expression of Divine Life. In Divine Life, despite the distinctions various selves are being united. Therefore, no actual difference between appearance and reality, noumena, and phenomena can philosophically be sustained.

6.5 The Real and the Ideal

Absolute Idealism as proposed by Haldar seeks to synthesize realism and idealism on the premise that there is no difference between the real and the ideal. According to Haldar, idealism and realism are compatible and not antagonistic to each other. The former incorporates the latter. Here, one might raise a question about the cognitive status of objective reality. In Western philosophy, Plato has introduced dualism between reality and appearance or between noumena and phenomena. According to Kantian *Analytic*, what we know as external objective world of phenomena is relative to knowing subject. But being of reality does not depend upon mental states of an individual mind. Reality somehow causes phenomena to appear. Understanding constructs the knowledge of manifold of sensation. Forms of sensibility and categories mediate between sense and understanding. But according to Haldar, how sensation is subsumed under schemata of categories remains unexplained here, as he says, "understanding? What mysterious power is there in the understanding to transform the dark chaos of sense into the beautiful cosmos of the world of our experience? If such a power exists, how are we to think of its exercise?" (Haldar 1894: 170). This situation presents a serious difficulty in epistemology, which, according Haldar, is inherited by the British idealists from Kant (Haldar 1894: 171). The gulf between sense and understanding leads one to agnosticism because we can only know sensations, not the reality. However, according to Haldar, this agnosticism is not the only view that is available in Kant. He cites third and fourth antinomies where dualism has been abandoned by Kant. That the phenomena are connected with each other in causal chain suggests that "they are grounded on intelligible principle analogous to self" (Haldar 1918: 385). Haldar concludes from Kant that objects are of double character, empirical or sensible, and real or intelligible. Though these two characters can be grasped as distinct, they are inseparable. Hence, there is no dichotomy, and sensations and categories are not radically foreign to each other. The possibility of their combination is due to the fact that both are elements of same purposive unity of Absolute. For Kant, the correlativity between the subject (unity of apperception) and object of knowledge is possible because of combining principle of self. Self as synthetic unity takes place only through the act of synthesizing the plurality of objective world. This correlativity between self and the world gets sublated in Hegel to a higher principle which is Thought or Being; in "Thought which is Being, Being which is Thought, or, in one word Thinking Being" (Haldar 1896: 265). According to Haldar, such formulation of Kant leads us logically toward Hegelian synthetic unity of Thinking Being. In Haldar's words, "the crowning principle of mind and matter–the Absolute Idea" (Haldar 1896: 267).

6.6 Haldar's Realistic-Idealism

Modern Indian Philosophy is a response of Indian philosophers to Western philosophical traditions. Under the influence of science of the day and the outlook toward the world it generated, modern Indian philosophers were forced to accept the reality of empirical world. This acceptance had to be consistent with the idealistic doctrine of reality (*Brahman*) and appearance (*māyā*) which they have inherited mainly from Advaita philosophy. While accepting the realism of science, they had to conceive the reality of experience not as appearance but as manifestation of ultimate reality. Most of these philosophers had "envisaged the desirability of continuity between matter and spirit, and as a corollary, science, and metaphysics. While conceding the significance of Western thought, they sought to incorporate it within Indian thought" (Raghuramaraju 2006: 93). Reconciliation of idealism and realism is, thus, the major feature of philosophical reasoning of this era. Haldar's 'Realistic-Idealism' aptly summarizes this reconciliation saying "the material world is inwardised in mind and mind is externalized in matter. They are the correlated phases of the one all-inclusive spirit" (Haldar 1952: 323). It will be seen that in such formulation, two senses of mind are at play: one is mind as all-inclusive Spirit, the pre-supposed ultimate unity of mind and matter, subject and object; and the other is that mind being finite knowing subject. Haldar also admits that mind and matter are opposite to each and that without supposing this duality, human knowledge will not be possible. But while admitting this view, Haldar also asserts that "*idealism is in no way inconsistent with realism*. It does not make it its business to deny the reality of the world. On the contrary, it strongly affirms it" (Haldar 1952: 323). Unlike realism, Haldar's Realistic-Idealism does not consider the division between mind and matter as Absolute, nor like subjective idealism does it reduce matter to mental states. It does not dispute the reality of external world outside of perceiving mind; on the contrary, it asserts the determinate experience of external world. This realist–idealist position was not only subscribed to by academic philosophers like Haldar. Even the so-called non-academic philosophers like Sri Aurobindo subscribed to it. Sri Aurobindo thought that matter and spirit are not of two radically different kinds. Spirit is a refined form of matter filtered through various stages of evolution. Matter is a gross spirit, implicit, and unconscious. Thus, there is a synthesis between matter and spirit, science and spiritualism. The evolution from matter to spirit is possible because essentially matter and spirit are made up of the same stuff, that is, consciousness, as he said, "for there seems to be no reason why life should evolve out of material elements or mind out living form, unless we accept the Vedāntic solution that life is already involved in matter and mind in life because in essence matter is a form of veiled life, life is a form of veiled consciousness" (Sri Aurobindo 2005: 5). Thus, science which deals with matter and spiritualism which deals with consciousness are reconcilable. Matter is involved in life, life in mind, and mind through various phases in Supermind and through Supermind to Spirit or *Satchidānanda*. The Spirit or Absolute descends by the process of involution to material world, through evolution, matter journeys back to the divine. Among academic philosophers, A.C. Mukherji is also advocating the continuity between real and ideal, matter and mind. He is pointing at the limitation of realism, as it considers facts only 'at their face value' (Mukherji 2011: 475) and does not enquire about conditions which constitute facts. The main point of contestation between realism and idealism, according to these philosophers, is about the factors that influence our experience. As Mukherji says, "If we are to retain the terms Idealism and Realism, *we must give up the old method of contrasting them*, and define Realism as the habit of accepting the facts as out there unconditioned and Absolute. Idealism, on the contrary, insists on the conditioned nature of the ordinary facts of experience and holds that apart from their conditions, the so-called facts are reduced to non-entities" (Mukherji 2011: ibid).

Whether philosophical writings of professional Indian philosophers teaching in Indian Universities during colonial period are marked by originality and creativity is a debatable issue. But the fact is that barring few exceptions like K.C. Bhattacharyya's revival in the last few decades, no adequate attention has been paid to professional philosophers of this era. The conspicuous absence of most of these philosophers from philosophy curricula in Indian universities bares testimony to this neglect. This lacuna needs to be filled by "undertaking a comprehensive survey of the writings of the modern Indian philosophers which will answer historical questions about various frameworks in which comparisons are made" and by raising "critical questions about the assimilation of western ideas and ideals into the Indian scheme of concepts" (Deshpande 2010: 101). This engagement with Hiralal Haldar is a step in this direction.

References

Bhabha, H. K. (2003). *Nation and narration.* Routledge, 1990.
Deshpande, S. (2010). Hegel in India. In Kommunikation über Grenzen (Eds.), Casper-Hehen, Hiltrud & Gupte Nitin: University of Gottingen.
Ganeri, J. (2011). *The lost age of reason: Philosophy in early modern India 1450-1700.* Oxford.
Haldar, H. (1894). Green and his critics. *The Philosophical Review, 3*(2), 374–391.
Haldar, H. (1896). Some aspects of Hegel's absolute. *The Philosophical Review, 5*(3), 263–277. www.jstor.org/stable/2175612. Accessed: 21-07-2014 07:17 UTC.
Haldar, H. (1899). The conception of the absolute. *The Philosophical Review, 8*(3), 261–272. www.jstor.org/stable/2176242. Accessed: 21-07-2014 07:19 UTC.
Haldar, H. (1910). *Hegelianism and human personality.* Calcutta, India: University of Calcutta.
Haldar, H. (1917). Leibniz and German idealism. *The Philosophical Review, 26*(4), 168–175. www.jstor.org/stable/2178485. Accessed: 21-07-2014 07:21 UTC.
Haldar, H. (1918). The absolute and the finite self. *The Philosophical Review, 27*(4), 374–391. www.jstor.org/stable/2178578. Accessed: 21-07-2014 07:21 UTC.
Haldar, H. (1927). *Neo-hegelianism.* London: Heath Craton Ltd.
Haldar, H. (1952). Realistic Idealism. In S. Radhakrishnan & J. H. Muirhead (Eds.), *Contemporary Indian philosophy.* New York, London: George Allen & Unwin Ltd. (Humanities Press Inc. 1936).
Hegel, G. W. F. (1892). *Logic* (W. Wallace, Trans.). Oxford: Clarendon Press.
Hegel, G. W. F. (1895). *Philosophy of religion.* Vol.III (B. D. Speirs & J. Burdon Sanderson, Trans.). London: Kegan Paul, Trench, Trunker & Co. Ltd.
Hegel, G. W. F. (1896). *Philosophy of right* (S. W. Dyde, Trans.). London: George Bell & Sons.
McTaggert, J. E. (1901). *Studies in hegelian cosmology.* Cambridge: Cambridge University Press.
Mukherji, A. C. (2011). Realist's conception of idealism. In *Allahabad University studies* (Vol. III). (Reprinted in N. Bhushan & J. Garfield, *Indian philosophy in English: From renaissance to independence* (pp. 471–498). Oxford: Oxford University Press).
Pringle-Pattison, A. S. (1917). *The idea of god in the light of recent philosophy: Gilford lectures.* Oxford: Clarendon Press.
Radhakrishnan, S. & Muirhead, J. H. (Eds.). (1936). *Contemporary Indian philosophy* (2nd ed.) (1952). London: George Allen & Unwin Ltd., New York: Humanities Press Inc.

Raghuramaraju, A. (2006). *Debates in Indian philosophy*. Delhi: Oxford University Press.

Royce, J., Leconte, J., Howison, G. H., & Mezes, S. E. (1898). *Conception of god: A philosophical discussion concerning the nature of the divine idea as a demonstrable reality*. London: The Macmillan Company.

Sri Aurobindo (2005). The human aspiration. In *The life divine*. Pondicherry: Aurobindo Ashram Trust (reprint).

Chapter 7
G.R. Malkani: *Reinventing Classical Advaita Vedānta*

Sharad Deshpande

Abstract This essay explores G.R. Malkani's reinvention of Advaita Vedānta in the context of neo-Vedānta in Indian academia during the colonial period. The first section examines why Advaita Vedānta received more attention than Buddhism despite unintelligibility of its central doctrine of the reality of Brahman and the unreality of the world of every day experience and why various forms of Vedānta continued to be vitally relevant to Indian society in its task of reforming itself into a vibrant modern society. The subsequent sections give a detailed account of Malkani's presentation of some key concepts and issues in Advaita Vedānta and the Hegelian influence on his 'free rendering' of classical Advaita Vedānta.

Keywords Neo-Vedānta · Advaita Vedānta · Ajñāna · Hegel · Absolute · Absolute spirit · Reason · Faith · Intuition · Intellect · Revelation · Monism · Ontology · God

7.1 Advaita Vedānta and Modern Indian Philosophers

Modern Indian philosophers' engagement with Advaita Vedānta during the colonial period is a phenomenon in itself. As compared to other schools of classical Indian philosophy, especially Buddhism for its appeal to the masses, Advaita Vedānta received more attention despite the fact that it's central doctrine propagates that Brahman alone is real and the world of everyday experience is *mithyā*: an illusion. Such a doctrine could not have been intelligible to the modern Indian intellectuals whose outlook towards the world around them was being shaped by positivist, empiricist and realist philosophies of the late 18th and the early 19th century European philosophers. But despite this unintelligibility, the philosophy of

Some parts of the exposition of Malkani's thoughts are drawn from my earlier work *The Philosophy of G.R. Malkani* (Ed) Sharad Deshpande, 1997, I.C.P.R. Delhi.

S. Deshpande (✉)
Indian Institute of Advanced Study, Shimla, India
e-mail: sharad.unipune@gmail.com

Advaita Vedānta occupied the intellectual life of most of the newly educated modern Indians who were actively engaged in various reform movements in the public sphere and also in the academic set-up of the newly established university system. Unlike other systems of traditional *darśanaśāstra*, the philosophy of Advaita Vedānta did not remain a matter of antiquarian interest. Its propagation in the wider public sphere and its professional pursuit in the academia was largely determined by diverse considerations such as (a) to assert that science, i.e. scientific knowledge of phenomena (*aparā vidyā*) needs to be complemented by a synoptic vision of reality (*parā vidyā*); (b) to register the national identity as a form of self-assertion; and (c) to negotiate with the dominant Western philosophers and their philosophies; especially, the Bradleyan version of Hegelian Idealism on equal terms. For achieving these objectives, the Advaitic doctrine of Brahman proved to be more promising than any other doctrine from any other school of Indian philosophy. In order to achieve these objectives, reformulation of the classical Vedānta, particularly of Śaṁkara's non-dualistic Advaita Vedānta, seems to have become a major preoccupation of academic and non-academic philosophers during the colonial period. Such nomenclatures as 'contemporary Vedānta', 'neo-Vedānta',[1] '*abhinava* Vedānta' or 'practical Vedānta' as popularized by Swami Vivekananda, and sometimes even such nomenclatures as 'modernist restatement of Vedānta', or 'Vedāntic socialism' (Ramatirtha) or 'political Vedāntism' (Aurobindo) came into vogue to characterize various reformulations of classical Vedānta. In the colonial discourse on the emerging national identity, these nomenclatures were frequently taken as synonyms of 'neo-Hinduism'—the phrase first introduced by Robert Antoine while introducing as a 'pioneer of Neo-Hinduism' (Halbfass 1990: 221). These nomenclatures expressly stress the 'new' or the 'modern' orientation that the classical Advaita Vedānta and Hinduism gained by coming into contact with the West. All these nomenclatures under the rubric of neo-Vedānta "had a significant impact on the public culture of India and the manner in which India has presented itself to the rest of the world" (Halbfass 1991: 377).

However, what is conveyed by these nomenclatures is not inclusive of the age-old heterodox traditions across the country, encompassing the ancient *Cārvākas* who revolted against Vedic authority and Brahmanism; the mediaeval Sant Kabir and Sant Ravidass, and 19th century dissenters like Pandit Iyodhi Thass, Jotiba Phule and Narayaṇa Guru. This exclusion of heterodox traditions is a carry forward from the 14th century *Sarvadarśanasaṁgraha* of Mādhavāchārya. Even Paul Deussen's account of the history of Indian thought in his famous *Allgemeine Geschichte der Philosophie* is based upon *Sarvadarśanasaṁgraha*. Barring the exception of Debi Prasad Chattopadhyaya's *Lokāyata: A Study of Ancient Indian Materialism* (Chattopadhyaya 1959), *Sarvadarśanasaṁgraha* seems to have served as a model for most histories of Indian philosophy written during the colonial period and even after. S.N. Dasgupta's celebrated *A History of Indian Philosophy* which runs into five volumes includes the heterodox Buddhist and Jaina schools but does

---

[1] Neo-Vedānta is usually held to be a reinvention of classical Advaita Vedānta in terms of Kant's transcendental idealism, Hegel's Absolute idealism and British neo-Hegelianism.

not even mention the Cārvāka school of thought. Based on the fundamental distinction between heterodox systems which do not accept the authority of the Vedas and orthodox systems which do so, *Sarvadarśanasaṁgraha* follows a certain order of sequencing these systems. Among the heterodox systems, the Cārvāka, Buddhist and Jaina views are presented as *pūrvapakṣa*, by refuting which the truth and validity of orthodox Brahminical systems of Nyāya-Vaiśeṣika, Sāṁkhya-Yoga and Pūrva and Uttara Mimāmsā, i.e. Vedānta is established. This sequence is so well established that despite its employment of new pedagogic strategies, the first-ever syllabus drafted by B.N. Seal in 1924 for teaching Indian philosophy in Indian universities followed the same *Sarvadarśanasaṁgraha* order of sequencing Indian *darśanas* (Seal 1924). The *Sarvadarśanasaṁgraha* sequencing of 16 systems is taken as suggesting a gradual ascension of all philosophical thought culminating in Advaita Vedānta. The title of R.D. Ranade's book *Vedānta: The Culmination of Indian Thought* (Ranade 1970) most directly expresses this belief. But this belief is not tenable since the heterodox traditions of Cārvaka, Buddhism and Jainism do not, in any sense of the term, 'culminate' into the non-dualist Vedāntic philosophy. This claim must have been made by the followers of Śaṁkara and was reiterated even in the colonial period. Under the spell of the 'culmination theory'; the nomenclatures mentioned above are used almost exclusively for various restatements of the doctrines of traditional Vedānta, and more importantly, for the defence of Hinduism. In order to get a somewhat clearer picture of what is conveyed by these nomenclatures, it is necessary to have a brief background of the tradition of Vedānta.

It is well known that at least for the last two millennia, the tradition of Vedānta has been a living tradition in India and as it happens in the case of every living tradition, it has undergone continuous evolution in terms of its basic doctrines, positions and points of view due to changes initiated from within and outside. As it is well known, Śaṁkara's *Kevalādvaita* (absolute monism), Rāmānuja's *Viśiṣṭādvaita* (qualified monism), Madhava's *dvaita* (dualism), Nimbārka's *bhedābheda* (difference–non-difference) and Vallabha's *śuddhādvaita* (pure monism) indicate the doctrinal changes from within. These changes are centred on the conception of the ultimate reality, i.e. Brahman, *vis-à-vis* the world of experience. For Śaṁkara, the Brahman is without qualification and hence *nirguṇa* and the world of our experience is *māyāsvarūpa*, i.e. of illusory nature. But, this is not so for later Vedāntins like Rāmānuja, Madhva and Nimbārka, and accordingly, different positions are taken within the tradition of Vedānta itself which shows the evolving nature of the Vedānta tradition. In addition, there are innumerable *tikās*, *bhāṣyas* and *vārtikas* which clarify the basic arguments and positions held within the tradition of Advaita Vedānta. As far as the outside influences are concerned, it is well known that Śaṁkara is branded as a '*prachhanna Bauddha*'—a Buddhist in disguise—because of his admission of *ālaya vijñāna*. This is indicative of the Buddhist influence on him and by implication on his brand of Vedānta. But even before him, the Buddhist influence, particularly that of *Vijñānavādins* and the *Mādhyamikas*, is also evident in Gauḍapāda's *Māṇḍūkyakārikās*, since Gauḍapāda talks of *saṁvṛtti* and *ajāti*. All this shows that the tradition of Advaita Vedānta is an ever-evolving tradition. This process continued throughout the Middle Ages until the advent of the

British and even after. During the colonial period, this process assumed the dimension of self-assertion as against the colonial subjugation, but it also involved internal self-criticism of the decadent Hinduism in the light of new ideas and ideals drawn from Christianity and scientific rationality, liberalism and philosophical doctrines coming from the West. Various restatements of the classical Vedānta, particularly that of Śaṁkara Vedānta, were attempted by the (a) *paṇḍits* from the system of *pāthaśālas* who were part and parcel of the living, though fast vanishing, Vedānta tradition, (b) modern Indian philosophers teaching at universities and colleges and (c) social, religious and political reformers during the colonial period. To this, we can also add the teaching of Vedānta by spiritual gurus like Ramakrishna Paramahansa and Śri Ramana Maharshi. Numerous examples can be cited to support this classification. For instance, (i) as part of the living tradition of refuting the rival positions, Kashinathshastri Abhyankar in his *Advaitāmodsiddhi* (Abhyankar 1925) defends the Advaita position against that of Viśiṣṭādvaita, while Pandit Panchānana Tarkaratna's Sanskrit commentary on the *Brahmasūtras* which conceives the ultimate reality as power is yet another example of the restatement and creative interpretation of the Vedāntic position (Chakravarti 2009). But these and numerous other restatements and interpretations were in Sanskrit and therefore remained outside the newly emerging mainstream philosophy of the day whose medium of expression was English. In addition to the corpus of philosophical literature in Sanskrit and Prākrit, there is a vast philosophical literature in regional languages across the country.[2] (ii) Modern Indian academic philosophers like Rasvihary Das, G.R. Malkani, T.R.V. Murti and S. Radhakrishnan also attempted a response to the colonizer in the form of a restatement of Śaṁkara's Advaita Vedānta and projected the uniqueness of Indian philosophy on that bases and (iii) internal self-criticism of Hinduism and through it the reinterpretation or even reformulation of the Vedāntic position by reformers like Ram Mohan Roy, Swami Dayānanda Saraswati and Swami Vivekananda.

7.2 Modernist Restatement of Advaita Vedānta

The restatement and defence of Vedānta and Hinduism by social and religious reformers during the colonial period have been extensively documented and researched. But modern Indian academic philosophers' engagement with classical Vedānta still remains a neglected topic of research. Their attempt to present Indian philosophy as comparable and in certain respect even superior to Western philosophy needs a closer look, particularly on the background of the newly acquired world-views from the West. In the light of those world-views, indigenous traditions of metaphysical thought were proving to be irrelevant for the colonial forms

---

[2] *In philosophy in Fifteen Modern Indian Languages* (Bedekar 1979) gives an exhaustive account of how rich and diverse is the contribution of innumerable thinkers who wrote in regional languages and offered various reformulations of key Vedāntic concepts and also of Hinduism more generally.

of life. The indigenous thought and practices were fast losing their cognitive worth and efficacy to determine the emerging praxis of colonial Indian society. The classical metaphysical systems were getting "exempted from being put to the test of any kind of verification in experience. They thus remained secure but immobile … structures … can never clash with the course of experience, lack the power and responsibility to organize and direct our acting in response to it" (Rege 1996: 195). This description fits well to systems like Nyāya-Vaiśeṣika or Sāṁkhya. But Advaita Vedānta seems to be an exception. The "consensus among Indian thinkers of nineteenth century seems to have been that…the various forms of *Vedānta* continue to be vitally relevant to Indian society in its task of reforming itself into a vibrant modern society" (Rege 1996: 195). The demand of the newly emerging modern Indian society was one of being transformed from hierarchical structure of *varṇas* and *jātis* to an egalitarian social order based on the autonomy of an individual. The 19th and early 20th century reformers in colonial India saw in Advaita Vedānta the possibility of theorizing the notion of an autonomous subject in the domain of philosophy and political theory. Thus, Advaita Vedānta could be conveniently "paralleled and compared with Hegelian metaphysics, and ontology of Bradley, Bosanquet and McTaggert" (Deshpande 1997: xxi).

The nature and mode of this fusion was varied. Some like Radhakrishnan and P.T. Raju followed the comparative method by putting Upaniṣadic philosophy and Advaita Vedānta alongside Western idealism; others like K.C. Bhattacharyya followed the method of assimilation in terms of '*svarāj* in ideas', while philosophers like G.R. Malkani followed the method of a free rendering of both the Indian and the Western traditions of philosophy. The method of comparison and the method of assimilation presented problems of one kind, while the method of a free rendering presented problems of another kind. Within the bounds of methodological requirements, free rendering of texts involved a high risk of being inauthentic, being unfaithful to the tradition of Vedānta, being non-standard and being deviant. Malkani's Vedānta is not presented in the traditional form of commentary on *Brahmasūtrabhāṣya* or any other major or minor text which is integral to the tradition of Vedānta, but in the form of self-contained essays in which philosophical problems are directly raised and answered. This method is typically Western and Malkani, like his contemporaries, finds no difficulty in following it. That he took the risk of following this method is amply evident from the two quotes from his texts mentioned below as well as from his style of writing. Malkani's style of philosophizing was direct; and as commented by Burch, there is 'no evolution' in his thought; "he has never changed his views and he has never doubted their correctness. He has only sought for greater clarity in expressing them" (Burch 1970: 66). As opposed to the obscurity of expression in K.C. Bhattacharyya's writings, Malkani "writes such clear and fluent English that the reader risks being lulled by the simplicity of style into missing the profundity of content" (Burch 1970: 66). Malkani's writings have evoked extreme reactions. The sympathizers of oriental metaphysics appreciate him as a philosopher whose exposition of classical Vedānta is strictly rational and hence "If it is true anywhere and at any time, it is true everywhere and always" (Burch 1970: 70). But he is also critiqued as an ardent exponent of Radhakrishnan's "spiritualist interpretation of the traditional or the classical Indian conception of philosophy" which, according to the critics of this interpretation, suppresses the critical, analytical, and empiricist trends in Indian philosophy and equates it with spiritualism and mysticism (Prasad 1982: 295).

7.3 Delinking Vedānta from Tradition

Among the modern Indian philosophers, G.R. Malkani[3] was perhaps the only one to boldly declare that keeping the spirit of classical Vedānta alive and its free rendering independent of the age-old tradition need not conflict with each other. The prefaces he wrote to three of his books, i.e. *Vedantic Epistemology*, *Metaphysics of Advaita Vedanta* and *Philosophy of the Self* are frank and clear in their statement. In the *Preface* to *Vedantic Epistemology*, he writes:

> … my exposition of the subject is a free and independent rendering which keeps the spirit of Vedānta intact and at the same time adapts the expression to the understanding of those who are imbued with the spirit of Western thought and who are in the habit of thinking on the compartmental lines of western philosophy. It has always been my desire to modernize the form of Vedāntic philosophy so that it can appeal to the wider public and which the modern man can understand easily. (Malkani 1953: v)

In the *Preface* to *Metaphysics of Advaita Vedanta*, he writes:

> … my attitude to the subject is not that of the orientalist who views ancient systems as really ancient and so dead and past. What I want to expound is a *living* system, though ancient. My presentation again will not be scholarly or rooted in the original Sanskrit texts and their commentaries. It will be a presentation of a truth seeker who is more interested in the truth than erudition or scholarship, and who believes what he says. My arguments will be from the books, or they may not be all fours with them. Since I have not taken shelter behind any reputed author of Advaita Vedanta, it will be quite irrelevant to say that my views do not agree with those of any great giant in the field and are therefore to be rejected as not the genuine views of Advaita Vedanta. Many different people can understand this system differently. I claim only a particular interpretation of it, which appeals to me most. (Malkani 1961: vi)

---

[3] Ghanshamdas Ratanmal (G.R.) Malkani (c. 1892–1978) was born at Hyderabad Sind (now in Pakistan). Having obtained his Masters degree in 1916 from the University of Bombay, he became a research fellow in the first batch of the Indian Institute of Philosophy which was situated at Amalner, a small town in the north-western region of India known as East Khandesh in the erstwhile Bombay Presidency. Malkani obtained an M. Litt from Cambridge in 1921 under the supervision of James Ward, a famous psychologist and philosopher of idealist orientation. During his stay, he became acquainted with the philosophies of Kant and Hegel, and also of Bradley, Bosanquet and Bergson. On his return from Cambridge, he was appointed first as the superintendent in1924, as editor of the *Philosophical Quarterly* in 1926, and finally as the Director of the Indian Institute of Philosophy in 1935 succeeding K.C. Bhattacharyya (Deshpande 1997; Burch 1970). Malkani remained the Director of the Institute till its closure in 1966. Besides a large number of articles and monographs, his major publications include *Philosophy of the Self* (1939, Rpt. in U.S in 1966), *A Study of Reality* (1927), *Vedantic Epistemology* (1953) and *Metaphysics of Advaita Vedanta* (1961)—all published from Indian Institute of Philosophy, Amalner.

These quotations reveal how Malkani views his engagement with Advaita Vedānta in particular and philosophy in general. It is a 'free presentation of a truth seeker', and it is primarily for those who have no acquaintance either with Sanskrit or with the classical Indian texts. In fact, some contemporary historians of modern Indian philosophy admire Malkani by saying that by restating Vedānta, Malkani has "freed it from dependence on the Sanskrit language with which it has always been associated" (Burch 1956: 122). By and large, this is true of modern Indian philosophers who wanted to present the doctrine of Vedānta through the philosophical idiom of Western philosophy. That is why they chose to write in English without attending to the problems of translation from Sanskrit into English. By admitting that their works were not necessarily consistent with the traditional *sāmpradāyic* expositions, modern Indian philosophers like Malkani assumed the role of free and independent thinkers than that of Indologists. K.C. Bhattacharyya's most reputed *Studies in Vedāntism* (Bhattacharyya 1907) are "problematic constructions on Vedāntic lines" and are intended to bring out its "relation to modern philosophical systems" (Bhattacharyya 1907: 1). In this exercise, Bhattacharyya claims 'wide latitude of interpretation throughout.' In this interpretative engagement with the classical texts, the more substantial issue that the modern Indian philosophers were addressing to was that of understanding the tradition of thought as living system and not as a historical past. This has helped them define their role as interpreters of ancient systems of thought rather than the narrators of historical texts and traditions. This made Bhattacharyya pronounce, "The attitude of the mere narrator has, in the case of the historian of philosophy, to be exchanged as far as possible, for that of the sympathetic interpreter" (Bhattacharyya 1983: 1).

Malkani's bold assertion that he is delinking the thought couched in the concept of Advaita from the tradition which is built around that thought makes it clear, among other things, that he does not confine himself to the kind of academic scholarship which demands textual validation for the exposition of concepts and doctrines present in the classical texts. He hardly cites textual references to support the views he is expounding. Though he had learnt Śaṁkara's *Brahmasūtrabhāṣya* from Pandit Atmaramshastri Jere, a renowned Vedāntin at the Indian Institute of Philosophy at Amalner (see Chap. 1), Malkani had only a slight knowledge of Sanskrit and hardly had a first-hand acquaintance with Sanskrit texts. But for him, as was the case with most modern Indian philosophers, this was not a handicap, since he was expounding a Vedāntic *point of view*, a hermeneutic reading, and was not engaged in an etymological, philological or historical exercise. This certainly was a step beyond a mere Indological engagement with classical Indian philosophy. Since Malkani was working at the institute which was modelled on the Western system of research, he did not follow the methods of argumentation characteristic of the Indian tradition, which would take other schools of thought as *pūrvapakṣa*. In this respect, he is unlike K.C. Bhattacharyya who takes Kant's notion of self as a point of reference while interpreting the Advaita notion of the subject as freedom. On the other hand, Malkani does not defend the Advaita point of view against any particular philosophical system of the West, except by referring to certain well-known positions, nor does he undertake any sustained textual comparison between Vedānta and its seeming analogues in Western philosophy. This too "sets him apart from some of his contemporaries like P.T. Raju and S. Radhakrishnan, who put Vedānta alongside Western idealism and offer a comparative account of both" (Deshpande 1997: xxiii). Malkani is not doing comparative philosophy, nor is he interested, as are the Indologists, in the history of Advaita Vedānta. What he presents is his *own* understanding of some key concepts and doctrines of classical Vedānta. In all his writings, Malkani seeks to explicate and defend only one thesis, i.e. the non-duality of Brahman. A close textual reading of any one of his writings reveals his overall philosophical position. As Burch writes, "He is not interested in anything except philosophy, and in any philosophy except Vedānta" (Burch 1956: 124). Being a modern Indian philosopher trained at Cambridge, he was well acquainted with the main tenets of Western philosophy, yet he also declared that though the method of exposition he adopted was that of European philosophy, "the ideas are essentially Indian", that "the substance is oriental but the form is very much occidental" (Malkani 1939: v, 1953: v).

Like many of his contemporaries, Malkani draws very heavily from Hegelian idealism as expounded by Bradley and other British idealists. The *Hegelianization* of Advaita Vedānta or the *Vedāntization* of Hegel—both in terms of their terminology and the structure and operation of concepts—is the main feature of Malkani's exposition of Advaitic thought. This is evident when one finds Malkani taking the Hegelian notion of Absolute Spirit which creates the appearance of the world as an act of will. This is a typical rendering of Hegel that finds its fuller exposition in one of Malkani's monographs titled "The Absolute" which was serialized in four consecutive issues of *The Philosophical Quarterly* (Malkani 1934, 1935a, b, c). Not only in this essay, but in most of his writings, it is abundantly clear that Malkani is influenced by the Hegelian idea that the reality of the world of objects is a manifestation of Absolute Spirit and as such has no independent status. What Hegel meant by self-alienation of Absolute Spirit was, for Malkani, the appearance of reality. When this appearance is viewed as self-existent and hence real, it would be an instance of erroneous perception, i.e. *ajñāna*. Malkani employs the Hegelian notions of absolute, substance, quality and spirit in his exposition of Advaita Vedānta which seeks to establish the non-duality thesis. But this in turn initiates new dichotomies such as 'experience *or* reason' and 'revelation *or* reason' which are not present in the tradition of classical Advaita. The introduction of such dichotomies into the traditional mode of indigenous thinking has its own effects which need to be studied in detail (Deshpande 1997: xix).

One can ask the following questions not only to Malkani but to modern Indian philosophers who were negotiating classical Vedānta with Hegel or Kant: (a) Can the Advaitic thesis of non-dual reality be expressed in Hegelian or Kantian interpretative categories? (b) Is the Advaitic thesis of non-dual reality valid? The first question requires an extensive exploration of Hegelian and Advaitic traditions of thought which are labelled as idealistic. But with its interpretative openness, idealism can create many apparent similarities between the Hegelian and the Advaitic world-views. In order to make sense of these similarities, it is necessary to trace the implicit continuities from Śaṃkara to Hegel. But neither Malkani nor most of his contemporaries undertake this task, though their writings do provide a basis for such an exercise. The second question, i.e. whether the Advaitic thesis of non-dual reality is valid, is to be answered in the context of other contesting claims regarding the nature of reality. From within the Indian traditions, Sāṁkhya, Buddhist, Jaina and Lokāyata traditions reflect upon the nature of reality as much as the tradition of Vedānta does; but they do not hold the thesis of non-dual reality. However, this second question and its resolution do not concern Malkani. What concerns him is a restatement of the implicit logic of Advaita as he understands it.

7.4 Reinventing Classical Advaita

A selective reading of some of Malkani's writings in logic, epistemology, metaphysics and ontology reveal the range of issues he addresses to in his books and monographs. In conformity with the prevalent self-image of philosophy, Malkani's major and abiding concern was metaphysics, since that was held to be the innermost core of philosophical reflection on the nature of reality. All other branches of philosophy were thought to be ancillary, though internally and organically related to metaphysics. For instance, in the idealistic framework, whether of Western or of Indian origin, the epistemological issues concerning the relation between intellect and intuition, the nature of philosophical knowledge, the nature of philosophical truth and the validity and invalidity of knowledge become significant only in the context of knowledge in relation to the self. In the context of Advaita, the problem of the authority of *śrūti* or revelation, and the nature of *ajñāna* assume additional significance. It is interesting to note that Rasvihary Das and T.R.V. Murti, two leading philosophers of Malkani's times, wrote along with Malkani, a book titled *Ajñāna* which registers three different perspectives of three different authors on the same issue (Malkani et al. 1933). A theory of knowledge deals with the source, validity and nature of knowledge, and Malkani discusses these issues from a Vedāntic point of view. His point of departure from other positions and his conclusions pertaining to the epistemological issues cited above lie in the firm conviction of the existence of the reality of one undifferentiated universal spirit called Brahman and the possibility of its direct awareness. With this conviction, the autonomy of epistemology, i.e. the possibility of considering epistemological issues in themselves, is reduced to the ontological position that one takes. This reduction is based on the assumption that the appropriateness of the means of knowledge and of the very concept of knowledge is determined by the conception of reality. In Malkani's metaphysics, there is only one kind of knowledge that is true, and that knowledge is the knowledge of the Brahman. Since the ultimate reality, the Brahman, is one without duality of any kind, the appropriateness of knowledge is to be determined by its being able to grasp the non-dual character of reality directly. On this view, only the intuition or the revelation of *śrūti* and no other means of knowledge such as intellect or reason can grasp the non-dual nature of ultimate reality. In the essay "Intellect and Intuition" (Malkani

1930: 262–269), Malkani dwells upon the nature, the function and also the limitation of both intuition and intellect. The intellect is the 'faculty of thought or thinking generally.' The two questions concerning intuition that he addresses are (i) are intuition and the intellect distinct modes of knowledge? And (ii) can the ultimate reality be intuited? For Malkani intuition is 'an immediate non-relational mode of knowledge', a 'direct awareness of anything real that does not involve thought.' As he defines it, intuition is an immediate non-relational knowledge. Hence, for him, knowledge involving the subject–object distinction is not intuitive knowledge. But intuitive knowledge has to have a content which, on the above definition, must be distinctionless, i.e., it must be devoid of subject–object duality. But since intuition presupposes consciousness, the subject has to be present in intuition. So the only alternative is to say that in intuition, the subject knows only itself and nothing else. So the only intuition possible is that of the self. In Malkani's metaphysics, the intuition of the self is the ground of all knowledge. Malkani's reply to the second question, i.e., whether the ultimate reality can be intuited is that there cannot be an intuition of the ultimate reality apart from the intuition of the self. Here, a historian of Vedānta might find a resonance of the controversy between the Advaitin and the Viśiṣṭādvaitin on the mode of knowledge. But as said above, Malkani does not engage himself in the presentation of the philosophical issue involved, i.e. the nature of intuition and the ultimate reality in a historical perspective. His rigid logic terminates in saying that "Either the intuitiveness of our nature is itself the ultimate reality, and there is no need to try to know it in any way other than that in which it is already known to itself, or there is no other ultimate reality that can be intuited..." (Malkani 1930: 269). The intellect, on the other hand, is a "distinct mode of knowledge"; since to be a mode of knowledge is to be a particular way of knowing a certain concept. In Malkani's metaphysics, the duality of the subject and the object constitutes the content of knowledge. But the intuition, qualified as rational intuition, has no content in so far as it transcends the subject–object duality. "The content-less intuition is thus non-relational apprehension of the real; and being non-relational, in the sense of transcending subject–object duality, intuition is 'identical with the reality'" (Deshpande 1997: xxii). "Intuition as an epistemological concept is thus replaced by intuition as the very being, the ontological thing-in-itself that knows itself" (Malkani 1930: 269). 'To know' is thus identical with 'to be.'

This kind of identity thesis is further elaborated in the essay titled *The Self in Relation to Knowledge* by raising two questions, namely (i) Is the self a real substance needed to account for knowledge or is it a formal unity, a unity of apperception and (ii) Is knowledge identical with the self or distinct from it? (Malkani 1932: 430–435) The second question leads him to ask whether knowledge is a quality of the self. These questions have been raised by various philosophers of Vedānta and other traditions. Malkani's treatment of these questions is typically Vedāntic in nature, and he does not depart from it. That the self is a substantial reality and not a theoretical presupposition as it is in Kant is a well-known Vedāntic doctrine. The core of this doctrine consists in recognizing that there is consciousness which is not conscious of anything different from itself. And this is not a theoretical presupposition, but a matter of experience as in the case of a deep or dreamless sleep. In fact, consciousness in its essence transcends the duality of subject and object, which is a mark of forms of consciousness. The traditional exposition of this doctrine consists in the analysis of waking, dreaming and of dreamless experience. Without giving the details of this analysis, Malkani only makes a general statement about the substantiality of the self. For Malkani, if knowledge is not to be "an illusory appearance resting on things that are physical" then such knowledge "must be grounded in a substance that is spiritual" (Malkani 1932: 432–435). This substance is the self and it alone knows. The reality of the self thus implies the reality of knowledge and the two stand to one another in a relation of identity and hence, knowledge is not a quality of the self. As regards the second question, namely 'Is knowledge identical with self or distinct from it?', Malkani's answer is again consistent with the Advaitic position that knowledge constitutes essential intelligence of the self, and hence, any distinction between self and knowledge is relative to objects that are known as constituting empirical reality.

The two essays, *Philosophical Knowledge* (1942) and *Philosophical Truth* (1950)[4] complement each other in defending the Advaitic position on the knowledge of the highest reality. These essays, and also many others on the same issue discussed by Malkani or other modern Indian philosophers, appear to be in response to the growing impact of science, and the legitimacy scientific knowledge was gaining in the colonial era. Therefore, not only Malkani, but also many others undertook the defence of philosophical knowledge and philosophical truth against the scientific knowledge and scientific truth. All these writings address the issue of the ends of philosophy where philosophical knowledge brings forth the philosophical truth which is imminent in experience and the moment of its realization is a kind of mysticism in which reality 'as it is, is presented.' Truth for Malkani is then a 'consummation of all values and its realization brings peace to the will.' Thus, truth is the highest good and a marker of the goals of philosophical vocation.

One of the chief preoccupations of the Indian epistemological tradition is the nature of *prāmaṇya*, that is the validity and invalidity of knowledge. Malkani investigates this question by translating it into the idiom of the correspondence and coherence theory of truth in the Western tradition. Śruti is also examined from this perspective. In the Vedāntic spirit that he has imbibed, Malkani concludes that the truth must be self-evidently true. What he offers is the standard argument that validity is internal and invalidity is due to 'external influence.' This is captured in the familiar Vedāntic distinction between the *svataḥ-prāmāṇya* and the *parataḥ-prāmāṇya* of knowledge. From the Vedāntic point of view, there cannot be any theory of truth unless we know what truth is. On this view, truth is not an empirical discovery but self-certifying revelation. With regards to Śruti, Malkani rejects it in the empirical domain as dogma, but in the domain of the supra-sensible 'revealed word', śruti is the instance of truth. His modernist restatement of Vedānta amounts to a reconciliation of the religious tradition that stresses revelation and the modern Western secular tradition of philosophy that stresses discursive reason.

---

[4] General Presidential Address, Indian Philosophical Congress, XXIV Session, Patna, India, 1949.

7.5 Nature of *Avidyā*

Advaita Vedānta is known to be a system of extreme monism or non-dualism since it recognizes the reality of Brahman alone, and therefore, on this view, the world of veridical experience is an appearance. This appearance is due to *avidyā*, i.e. false knowledge. The two determining notions of the non-dualistic thesis of Advaita are, thus, Brahman and *avidyā*. According to Malkani, these two are therefore, the 'only two important concepts in Advaita', and we may add, in Malkani's own system. However, Advaita does not account for the world of appearance. For Malkani, if appearance is part of reality, the question of *avidyā* or error will not arise; but since appearance and reality are not identical, the knowledge of appearance *as* identical with reality is erroneous. This erroneous knowledge is called *ajñāna*. Malkani's essay titled *Ajñāna* (Malkani 1933) fully and systematically explores the concept of *ajñāna* as expounded in Advaita Vedānta. *Avidyā*, as Malkani emphasizes therein, is a name of the activity of misconstrual or misconception. But this misconstrual or misconception is not psychological, but metaphysical. Unlike many others, Malkani does not attribute any explanatory function to Avidyā, nor does he take it to be any 'mystical entity' which will provide an explanation for the 'illusory appearance of the world.' Malkani does not construe avidyā as a substantial or causal entity like God or *prakriti*. *Avidyā* for Malkani is self-constitutive. But there is also a relation of simultaneity between the illusory appearance of the world and the frame of *avidyā*, i.e. erroneous perception. The world and *avidyā* thus share the relation of implication and are generated from the 'same sort of reality.' It is to be noted that within the Advaitic tradition, there has been a debate over the priority of *avidyā*, i.e. false knowledge *vis-à-vis adhyāsa*, i.e. superimposition. For some Vedāntic writers, *avidyā* is the cause of *adhyāsa*. According to this view, as stated by Malkani, *avidyā* is the material cause of the superimposition and hence objective. Malkani rejects this view. For him, "if there is no illusory appearance of anything there can be no erroneous perception either" (Malkani 1933: 5). Malkani's two-valued approach compels him to avoid the temptation to treat 'the illusory' as an intermediate category between existence and non-existence. According to Malkani, the 'illusory' is non-existent and there is no explanation for it. In fact, *ajñāna* is indescribable, *anirvachanīya*.

What is the locus of *avidyā*? This is one of the central questions in Advaita Vedānta. It cannot be an individual since an individual himself is a product of *avidyā*. Hence, *avidyā* precedes the individual chronologically and also ontologically. This *avidyā* is called *mulāvidya* which appears to reside in the ultimate reality of the Brahman. But *avidyā* cannot reside in Brahman, since it would attribute the Brahman impermanence, illusion and causality, thus subverting its status as the ultimate reality. So Malkani's fundamental question is about the locus of *avidyā*, and his answer, consistent with his Vedāntic spirit, is that it is neither the individual *jīva*, nor the Brahman. This is because *avidyā* or *ajñāna* has no substantial reality, and for the same reason, its removal does not involve any process in time since there is nothing to be negated substantially. Malkani's subtle metaphysics elaborates this timelessness of avidyā and its cancellation, saying that "The end of avidyā may be said to be a timeless and eternal fact; for whatever is brought in time is itself avidyāic" (Malkani 1933: 23). The Advaitic notion of *ajñāna* or *avidyā* problematizes the whole idea of ontology, of 'what there is.'

7.6 Ontological Reflections: The Absolute

Malkani's writings include the themes that determined the philosophical discourse in India during the colonial period. These include, with variations in their verbal expression, such themes as 'Intuition of the Self', 'Creation or Illusion', 'The Absolute', 'Freedom through Knowledge' and 'Reality and Value.' Owing to the limitations of space, it is not possible to summarize Malkani's views on each one of these, except making a few observations to bring out the character of his 'free rendering' of the Advaita doctrine of the reality of the Brahman. From among his other essays, the one titled *Ontological Reflections* (Malkani 1963a, b, 1964a, b) brings out the point made above in relation to his monograph titled *The Absolute* serialized in the issues of *The Philosophical Quarterly* (Malkani 1934, 1935a, b, c). Thematically, the arguments in these essays are grounded in Malkani's reflections on the 'intuition of self.' For Malkani, the self is aware of itself, but the analysis of this intuition cannot transgress the limit of 'I'-ness which is the ultimate ground. Malkani dwells upon this theme further in *The Absolute*, saying that the dualism of the subject and object is the ground of separation between knowledge and reality. It is only in reflective consciousness that knowledge becomes reality itself. "The Absolute is the self-evident ground of the identity of reality and experience." (Deshpande 1997: xxvi) The Absolute eludes dualistic epistemology, but can be grasped in mystical experience. The Absolute as revealed in mystic consciousness is not to be identified with reflective consciousness since it admits the revealed content as distinct from itself. Malkani maintains that if the distinction between consciousness and its content is made explicit then the "object term can sustain no relation and would simply be nothing" (Deshpande 1997: xxvi). In fact, the explicit distinction between the subject and the object generates a dialectic which cannot be overcome. Malkani's main contention is that the terms 'subject' and 'object' gain validity only in the unity. According to him, this unity is possible, in four alternate ways. These are (a) a de facto unity between consciousness and its content, (b) unity through an asymmetric relation, i.e. either the consciousness or the content having primacy, (c) unity in a more fundamental sense which is, as it were, neutral to both the consciousness and the content and (d) one of the two being real and the other not. Here, one is reminded of G.E. Moore who in his famous *Refutation of Idealism* formulated the idealist position in a similar way, way back in 1903 but in order to expose the idealist fallacy (Moore 1903: 433–453). Malkani's formulations are dated 1934. It is surprising that neither Malkani nor most of the idealist modern philosophers seem to have taken cognizance of Moore's refutation despite the fact that it appeared in *Mind*—a very prestigious journal which represented the British philosophy of the day. Perhaps, Moore's refutation of idealism, along with Russell's criticism of the idealist doctrine of internal relations, was just the

beginning of a sustained critique of Bradleyan idealism on the British soil.[5] For
Malkani, the concept of relational consciousness is a misnomer. For him, unitary
consciousness is not the same as 'unity of relation.' If this is realized, 'consciousness is freed from its relatedness to content.' The conclusion of Malkani's reflections is that consciousness freed from relatedness of any kind is the Absolute. The
four alternative modes of the unity of consciousness that Malkani examines point to
a kind of spiritual unity since the spirit is conceived as transcending the subject. But
Malkani also clarifies that if this transcendence is either some kind of higher synthetic experience, the way Bradley conceives of it, or a transcendental presupposition as Kant conceives of it, or a unity of consciousness and content as the Idealists
in general suppose, then these are not acceptable to Malkani.

The essay *Ontological Reflections* addresses four issues in succession, namely
(a) the distinction between being and necessary being, (b) appearance and reality,
(c) being and non-being and (d) the absolute reality or God. It is evident that these
issues are discussed in the mediaeval scholastic tradition of the West. For example,
we find this to be a major preoccupation of St. Thomas Aquinas's famous cosmological proof for the existence of a necessary being, i.e. God. Malkani's reflections
on the distinction between being and necessary being is neither a restatement of
nor a rejoinder to St. Aquinas's position. He takes the notion of being as 'what
is', which is fundamental to all knowledge. But necessity does not characterize
'what is' per se. Malkani makes an interesting claim that 'necessity is external to
being.' "We introduce it into being through extraneous considerations such as illusory appearance and causality" (Malkani 1963a: 88). A necessary being is neither
a pure concept nor a Platonic idea, since they are only conceived and conception
is not "the same thing as direct or intuitive awareness of a self-existing real thing"
(Malkani 1963a: 88). Here, Malkani alludes to the Vedāntic notion that knowledge
is *vastūtantra*, i.e., the character of knowledge is determined by the object. By
invoking this notion, Malkani is then able to critique the idea that the substance
which is conceived as uncaused and thing-in-itself is a necessary substance. But
Malkani argues that "insofar as we are carried to it through the … temporal process, it has a *necessity* in respect of the latter. It is a derived *necessity*" (Malkani
1963a: 90). So, even the uncaused thing-in-itself, conceived as a necessary being,
is not a necessary being. Malkani problematizes this approach and asks "why go to
a transcendent and immutable cause?" He insists that the cause must be essentially
active, dynamic and creative. But then this applies even to the empirical causes,
"every actual entity is a creator of its successor…only it is not a causeless cause,
and it need not be one" (Malkani 1963a: 90). But if we have to look for the first
cause, for example God, under the persuasion of theologians, then Malkani argues,
'we can combine in him mobility with immobility.' Mobility accounts for dynamism of the process. But since the creation must have a goal which cannot be outside the creation, God may be said to be 'immobile or static in nature.' "We can
thus accept a non-empirical first cause that combines the static with the dynamic.

---

[5] But Malkani was aware of these developments such as Logical Positivism (Malkani 1950).

God is permanent and eternal, and at the same time, he is an actor and a creator. "The world is his creation" (Malkani 1963a: 90). Malkani then connects this idea of the being which is both immobile and static with the problem of creation and suggests that the apparent conundrum as to how a being which is static can create anything at all can be resolved by treating the creation which presupposes temporality as false. This obviously echoes the Vedāntic concept of Māyā. In all his elaborations of the concept of the Absolute, Malkani does not depart from his basic position that reality of the self alone is what the transcendental consciousness is, it is what the *ātman* is. The appearance of *ātman* as a knowing subject or the *jiva* is not the ultimate reality. The problem of the certainty of knowledge that engaged Descartes and the phenomenologists also engaged Malkani. But as an Advaitin, he looks at this problem in terms of the adequacy of our knowledge to reality *as such*. It is only from the transcendental standpoint that the certainty of our knowledge can be anchored in the certainty of pure awareness. The certainty of pure awareness is not disclosed in any individual act of consciousness, but it is presupposed in every such act. For Malkani, we are obliged to go from the notion of consciousness as *act* to the notion of consciousness as *actless*. The consciousness as actless in the Vedāntic metaphysics is self-revealing, i.e. *svaprakāśa*.

Like many of his contemporaries, Malkani's exposition of Advaita Vedānta is stressed by the burden of resolving the dichotomy between reason and faith. It is argued that the employment of reason stresses the rational, argumentative and critical side of Advaita Vedānta, while the faith stands for Vedānta as a *way of life*. The rational and the critical side of Advaita Vedānta refute the rival views like the dualism of *Puruṣa* and *Prakriti* and *anātma-vāda* and establish the reality of non-dual Brahman. However, like most of the Vedāntins, Malkani also believes that the rational aspect of Vedānta culminates into faith, thus making Vedānta philosophy as a part of Vedānta religion. The distinction between Advaita Vedānta as philosophy and Advaita Vedānta as religion, i.e., as a way of life, has always been a problem for those who emphasize the analytical and critical aspect of Advaita Vedānta. But for both the traditional Advaitin and for modern Indian philosophers like Malkani, the passage from reason to faith or revelation is not unnatural since as a Vedāntin, Vedāntic philosopher accepts revelation of Vedas and as a philosopher he accepts reason. This is similar to the problem of the relation between reason and revelation as conceived in Christianity, and Malkani's approach towards the resolution of this dichotomy is very much Augustinian.

7.7 Is Doing 'Pure' Philosophy Possible?

While reinventing the classical Advaita Vedānta, Malkani also actively participated in some of the debates of his times. One such debate is about the possibility of doing 'pure' philosophy in the colonial and post-colonial context.[6] The debate

---

[6] This debate is carried out in many ways. One such attempt—to which Malkani is responding—is by P.T. Raju in his *Idealistic Thought of India* (Raju 1953).

assumes that Indian philosophy is, and European philosophy is not, antiquarian. Philosophy, which is not antiquarian and merely interpretative of tradition, or is not mixed up with religion, is 'pure.' But can the 'spirit' of Indian philosophical traditions be revived? Would the methods of European philosophical traditions be of any use? These considerations have led many modern Indian philosophers to propose a synthesis of Indian and Western traditions of philosophy. But Malkani laments these attempts saying "we are alternately Hindu metaphysicians (*tattvajñānis*) and full-fledged European philosophers" the result being that "we are not creative as philosophers" (Malkani 1955). He even goes on to say that we have a choice of doing either Indian or European philosophy, but also cautions saying that "on our decision depends the future of philosophy in India" (Malkani 1955). Malkani not only reflects on the difference between Indian and European methods of doing philosophy but also critically ponders over the difference between the goal and the ideal of Indian and European philosophy. The final answer that he gives to the questions posed by modern European thought is in terms of imbibing the *spirit* of Vedānta which he could never give up.

References

Abhyankar, K. (1925). *Advaitāmodsiddhi*. Pune: Bhandarkar Oriental Research Institute.

Bhattacharyya, K. C. (1907). Studies in Vedantism. In G. Bhattacharyya (1956) (Ed.), *Studies in Philosophy*. Calcutta: Progressive Publishers.

Bedekar, V. M. (Ed.). (1979). *Philosophy in Fifteen modern Indian languages*. Pune: Continental Prakashan for the Council for The Marathi Encyclopaedia of Philosophy.

Burch, G. (1956). Contemporary Vedānta philosophy. *The Review of Metaphysics, 10*(1), 122–157.

Burch, G. (1970). Oriental metaphysics. In R. E. Wood (Ed.), *The future of metaphysics*. Chicago: Quadrangle Books.

Chakravarti, A. (2009). *Looking upon reality as 'power': Reason and philosophical creativity in India during the Colonial Period*. Lecture at the seminar on Philosophy in Colonial India. University of Pune, March (unpublished).

Chattopadhyaya, D. P. (1959). *Lokāyata: A study of ancient Indian materialism*. Peoples' publishing house.

Datta, D. M. (1956). India's debt to the West in philosophy. *Philosophy East and West, 6*(3).

Deshpande, S. (1997). *The philosophy of G.R. Malkani*. New Delhi: Indian Council of Philosophical Research.

Halbfass, W. (1990). *India and Europe: An essay in philosophical understanding* (Indian edition). Motilal Banarsidass.

Halbfass, W. (1991). *Tradition and reflection: Explorations in Indian thought*. Albany: State University of New York Press.

Mādhavāchārya. (1996). *The Sarvadarśanasamgraha: Or, Review of the different systems of Hindu philosophy* (trans.: E. B. Cowel & A. E. Gouch), London (1882, First Indian edition), Motilal Banarsidass.

Malkani, G. R. (1930). Intellect and intuition. *The Philosophical Quarterly, 5*(4).

Malkani, G. R. (1932). The self in relation to knowledge. *The Philosophical Quarterly, 7*(4).

Malkani, G. R. (1934). The Absolute, part I. *The Philosophical Quarterly, 10*(3), 199–224.

Malkani, G. R. (1935a). The Absolute, part II. *The Philosophical Quarterly, 10*(4), 351–364.

Malkani, G. R. (1935b). The Absolute, part III. *The Philosophical Quarterly, 11*(1), 97–104.

Malkani, G. R. (1935c). The Absolute, part IV. *The Philosophical Quarterly, 11*(2), 107–117.

Malkani, G. R. (1939). *Philosophy of the self.* Amalner: Indian Institute of Philosophy.

Malkani, G. R. (1950). Philosophical Truth. *The Philosophical Quarterly* (Reprint in Deshpande, 1977), 20–53.

Malkani, G. R. (1953). *Vedantic epistemology.* Amalner: Indian Institute of Philosophy.

Malkani, G. R. (1955). Two traditions of pure philosophy. *Philosophical Quarterly* (Rpt in Deshpande, 1977), 407–414.

Malkani, G. R. (1961). *Metaphysics of Advaita Vedanta.* Amalner: Indian Institute of Philosophy.

Malkani, G. R. (1963a). Ontological reflections (Being and necessary being), part I. *The Philosophical Quarterly, 36*(2), 85–91.

Malkani, G. R. (1963b). Ontological reflections (From appearance to reality), *36*(3), 171–177.

Malkani, G. R. (1964a). Ontological reflections (From non-being to being), *37*(4), 235–244.

Malkani, G. R. (1964b). Ontological reflections (Absolute reality or God), *38*(1), 21–34.

Malkani G. R., Das, R., & Murti T. R. V. (1933). *Ajñana.* Amalner: Indian Institute of Philosophy.

Moore, G. E. (1903). Refutation of idealism. *Mind, 12.*

Prasad, R. (1982). Tradition, freedom and philosophical creativity. In S. S. Rama Rao Pappu, & R. Puligandla (Eds.), *Indian philosophy: Past and future.* South Asia Books.

Raju, P. T. (1953). *Idealistic thought of India.* Cambridge, MA: The Harvard University Press.

Ranade, R. D. (1970). *Vedanta as culmination of Indian thought,* (Basu-Mullick Lectures, Calcutta University 1929) Bharatiya Vidya Bhavan.

Rege, M. P. (1996). *New Quest,* (Editorial), July–August 1996.

Seal, B. N. (1924). Syllabus of Indian Philosophy Based on the Lectures of Dr. Brajendranath Seal. Bangalore: University of Mysore.

Chapter 8
K.C. Bhattacharyya and Spivak on Kant:
Colonial and Post-colonial Perspectives, Lessons, and Prospects

Kanchana Mahadevan

> *On the negative side then I go much further than Kant. On the positive side, however, I would tone down his agnosticism.*
> Bhattacharyya (1983b: 462)

> *And yet, even here, the native informant is needed and foreclosed.*
> Spivak (1999: 6)

Abstract This essay attempts to understand academic philosophy in colonial India as a harmonization of Indian and Western philosophical traditions. It also contrasts this period with the post-colonial skepticism toward Eurocentric attitudes of Western philosophy. In this endeavor, this essay takes the writings of K.C. Bhattacharyya as its point of departure to examine the Indian philosophical response to its Western counterpart. Bhattacharyya drew upon Kant and Śaṁkarāchārya, to arrive at his neo-Vedāntic philosophy of symbolic non-literal thought that prepares the human subject for spiritual awakening. The essay also examines Spivak's reading of Kant's humanism with respect to Bhattacharyya's assimilation of Vedānta with Kant. By way of conclusion, it is argued that despite some limits, the spirit of Bhattacharyya's '*svarāj* in ideas' is redeemable in his avowal of independent critical thinking beyond the glorification of the Indian past and the imitation of Western thought. Thus, Bhattacharyya anticipates Spivak's 'planet thought,' which overcomes the rigidity of comparative approaches.

Keywords Bhattacharyya · Colonial · Critique · Human subject · Intellect · Kant · Planet-thought · Post-colonial · Scientific · Spivak · *Svarāj* · Vedānta · Transcendental

Segments of this essay were presented at the International Conference, 'India and Germany: Academic and Cultural Linkages and Exchanges' that was jointly organized by the University of Mumbai and Bonn in Mumbai (March 2009).

K. Mahadevan (✉)
Department of Philosophy, Mumbai University, Mumbai, India
e-mail: kanchmaha@yahoo.co.in

© Indian Institute of Advanced Study 2015   137
S. Deshpande (ed.), *Philosophy in Colonial India*, Sophia Studies in Cross-cultural Philosophy of Traditions and Cultures 11, DOI 10.1007/978-81-322-2223-1_8

Almost 32 years since the publication of Said's *Orientalism* (1978), the West's perception of the non-Western world continues to be debated in academic circles. In recent years, the non-Western world's reception of the West is beginning to generate awareness as well. Martin Kampchen, a German writer and activist who has lived in India for several decades, observes that

> ... the West, including Germany, is rather glorified in India. However, it is a very imbalanced view: the high living standards, the relatively high social security, the tourist attractions.... But what about Germany's civilizational achievements like democratic equality, a strong civic sense, a lively cultural life... (Punnamparambil 2007).

Indian's interest in Germany tends to both reflect and belie Kampchen's claims. Though India does veer toward a glorification of its science and technology, it does critically engage with Germany's 'civilizational achievements' (Ibid). This is especially so with respect to philosophy. Consider for instance, the recent attention generated in Immanuel Kant's (1724–1804) philosophy through various seminars and publications in India that have commemorated his impact two hundred years after his death.[1] Many of the articles in these works do a close textual analysis of Kant; some of them translate him to the contemporary context in general and others to Indian specificity.

Yet, the interest in the Kantian corpus is not new. Indian academicians from the colonial period to post-independent India have received Kant in diverse ways. For instance, Krishnachandra Bhattacharyya (1875–1949), during British rule, and Gayatri Chakravorty Spivak, at the turn of the 20th century, have located Kant in the Indian context, in one instance as a collaborator, and in the other as an alien. The colonial phase of philosophy in India brought Indian and Western thought into direct contact and threw up a number of questions. With reference to Bhattacharyya's and Spivak's readings of Kant, some of these questions include the following: Can one read Kant in a way where he is neither a friend nor a foe? Kant's notion of the human being makes disparaging assumptions against non-European races. Consequently, how can Kant be read alongside potentially democratic and pluralistic philosophies in the Indian context?[2] These are some of the issues addressed by this paper which begins by examining Bhattacharyya's qualified appropriation of the Kantian account of the human subject through a synthesis with Vedānta. The second part explores some of the implications of Spivak's critique of Kantian humanism. In conclusion, the paper evokes Bhattacharyya's program of '*svāraj* in ideas'[3] to examine possibilities of reading Western philosophy in the Indian context.

---

[1] See for example Deshpande (2004), Puri and Sievers (2007a, b).

[2] The non-European world does not form a homogeneous group. Hence, the Indian reading cannot be automatically extended to, for example, the Ghanian context.

[3] *Svaraj* or self-determination in thought; this phrase is derived from Bhattacharyya (1984).

8.1 Bhattacharyya's Idealist Appropriation of Kant

In his characterization of philosophy, Bhattacharyya draws upon both Kant and
Śaṁkara to distinguish philosophy as a symbolic way of thought that cannot be
reduced to literal scientific knowledge (Bhattacharyya 1983a: xi-xxxi; Herring
1992: 3).[4] For him, philosophy opens the possibility of knowledge of metaphysical/
spiritual entities such as self/soul, universe, and God. Philosophy, according to him,
is to be experienced personally and culturally, since it as Herring (1992: 3) notes an
elaboration of spiritual concepts. Bhattacharyya's neo-Vedāntic[5] philosophy

> … developed in the favourable cultural environment formed by the struggle for political
> independence, the religious revivals of the Ramakrishna Order and Brahmo-Samaj, and
> the Bengali literary renaissance. Its teachers are university professors writing in English,
> the language of education and scholarship in modern India. (Burch 1967: 612)

In his engagement with Western philosophy; Bhattacharyya, thus "… out-Kants
Kant and out-Hegels Hegel; his favorite western philosophers, in incomprehensi-
bility" (p. 614). During the second phase of his thought, he connects the human
subject with the absolute, following the Upaniṣadic dictum '*Tat Tvam Asi*' or 'That
Thou Art' to affirm an idealism of the autonomy of the subject (p. 623). It is during this phase that one can detect a strong self-acknowledged Kantian influence in
his writings (Bhattacharyya 1983b: 462).

Bhattacharyya incorporates Kantianism as an alternative to empiricism for
which facts are supreme. Kant's second *Critique* in particular is significant for
him because it transcends the empirical through an identification of the self with
free causality (Bhattacharyya 1983b: 462–463, 664–667; Burch 1967: 624). Thus,
he approaches Vedānta through the Kantian structure of the subject or "The psychology of waking, dream and dreamless sleep…" (Bhattacharyya 1983b: 11); he
upholds that such a spiritual approach to subjectivity enriches ordinary psychology, since it views the subject as freedom (pp. 450–454).

8.2 Spiritual Psychology

According to Bhattacharyya, spiritual psychology elaborates the fact of subjective
functions into a system of non-theoretical symbolisms which overcome the attitude of objective knowing (1983b: pp. 5–6). The 'simple teaching of Kant's philosophy' (p. 668) he maintains is that the free self alone is known to be real,
against a phenomenal object (Burch 1967: 624). He observes that Kant's emphasis

---

[4] For Bhattacharyya's discussion of Vedānta see his 'Studies in Vedāntism' (1983b: 1–124); his
engagement with Kant is for instance in his 'Studies in Kant' (pp. 663–722).

[5] The term 'neo-Vedānta' is used following Burch to characterize Bhattacharyya. See Burch (1967).

on the priority of time over space gives his subject an ethical counterbalance as the
cause of moral action at a time of the predominance of value-neutral scientific
fact. Further, Kant's non-dualistic and nonentity approach to the human subject[6] is
for Bhattacharyya captured by the term 'transcendental' (1983b: 664). Thus, for
Bhattacharyya, the Kantian self has practical, theoretical, and aesthetic interests[7];
it enters the object only in a formative way as a thinking form or the logical unity
of the object.

Bhattacharyya turns to Kant's notion of reasoning as transcendental reflection,
which he distinguishes from objective reasoning in that its conclusion is internal
to its premises (1983b: 663–664, 712–713). He argues that ordinarily philosophical reasoning, like science, moves from data to conclusion by taking it as what
must be and not what it is. The content of the conclusion is either perceived or
experienced and is not realized in the process of reasoning itself. Bhattacharyya
notes that hence, the conclusion is independent of the reasoning agent's mind.
He observes that Kant's account of reasoning in his transcendental method differs from such objective scientific reasoning. In Kant, the conclusion is realized
in the very act of reasoning and cannot be separated from the reasoning subject.
According to Bhattacharyya, transcendental investigation links the conclusion
with its premises internally by methodologically deepening its approach to data
through subjective cognition. He remarks that such a subjective level goes beyond
perception to imagination and is an aesthetic intervention because the object is
seen as an expression of the subject's internal dimension. Thus, rather than speculative construction, transcendental reflection is 'aesthetic contemplation' (p. 722),
which is akin to tracing back a poem to the 'formless feeling' (Ibid) that motivated
the poet to write it. For Bhattacharyya, such a stress on inwardness makes it an
ally of Vedānta, which is about an inward process of spiritual awakening.

For Bhattacharyya, spiritual psychology distinguishes the subject and the
object.[8] The 'object' as that which is meant by the subject is known to be distinct
from the subject. Alternatively, the subject is known in itself rather than as related
to the object. Contrarily, it is dissociated from the object and is known with greater
assurance as a unique speaker or 'I.' Bhattacharyya points out that though 'I' is
used as a singular reference, it is understood as general. It differs from a term with
an objective content that can be indicated by 'this' which has the same reference to
the hearer and speaker. The subject is both a known fact and a spoken fact so that
it is not a meant entity, though there is an awareness of the subject. Further, the 'I'
is communicable by speech, and it is not restricted to the literal meaning of a
word. Thus, the word 'I' both expresses and incarnates self-consciousness as an
awareness of the subject between mystical intuition and an epistemological

---

[6] This is Burch's observation. Additionally, Kant's idealism is distinguished from Cartesian dualistic idealism and Berkeley's subjective idealism. In fact, he takes issue with both Descartes and
Berkeley over this. See Kant (1965: 244–247).

[7] See Bhattacharyya (1983b: 662–668) for an account.

[8] The following discussion is derived from Bhattacharyya, 'The Subject as Freedom' (pp. 367–395).

consciousness of meaning. Bhattacharyya remarks that his approach through spiritual or transcendental psychology (i) interprets empirical psychology in terms of the felt and believed freedom of the subject from objectivity and (ii) elaborates modes of freedom that have no reference to the object so that spiritual mysticism is assigned a place.

8.3 The Symbolic and the Philosophical

Bhattacharyya professes to follow Kant in allocating a symbolic role to philosophy (p. 462). Philosophy for Bhattacharyya is an alternative to the informative paradigm of science. In this context, he cites Kant approvingly, "Kant's *Refutation of Idealism* may be taken as founded essentially on the recognition of a form of cognition other than the determinate" (p. 23). For Bhattacharyya, the empirical level of thought employed by science is only one and is beneath the scale of theoretical consciousness or speakability. Its content is factual information, which need not be spelt out in language, as facts need not be spoken for comprehension. A factual object can be sensed or even imagined to be so as its practicality consists in being useful. According to Bhattacharyya, scientific thought is intellectual and has 'an arrogant exploiting attitude' (p. 470), since it aims at mastering the known. He distinguishes between science and philosophy,[9] where philosophical thought's symbolic character is a safeguard against scientific literality and mastery (pp. 469–475).

Bhattacharyya discerns three forms of symbolic judgments in philosophy whose necessary characteristic is speakability (pp. 469–479). These include judgments about the object, the subject, and the truth. Symbolic judgments about pure objective thought whose content is self-subsistent refer to an object, but not to a perceived object (p. 472). The object is no fact, but a self-subsistent form such as a universal concept. This is not science but a philosophy of object, where the object is self-subsistent, rather than an entity to be used. It is the self-evident content of spiritual consciousness. By speculating the object without entering into its use value, philosophy turns out to provide an alternative to the 'predatory outlook of the scientific intellect' (p. 458). Logic and metaphysics are branches of the philosophy of object where it is a self-subsistent form known in contemplation/intuition simply as 'object' (p. 469).

In contrast, a symbolic judgment about spiritual thought whose content is reality has no reference to an object and is the subjective or "'enjoying' consciousness

---

[9] For Bhattacharyya, scientific thought comprises of real judgements wherein the predicate explicates the meaning of the subject that is already believed. While in theoretical thought, the subject is believed to be the self-evident elaboration of the predicate that is already believed to be self-evident. Thus, theoretical judgment that is symbolic is about making the self-evidence of the self-evident.

of content" (p. 464). This is philosophy of subject or epistemology for which introspection is consciousness of the 'I' as what the object is not: as speaking subjectivity. The 'I' or self differs from the mind following Kant. According to Bhattacharyya, for Kant, the mind and the world are both objects that emanate from the self so that the mind in its temporal dimension is not different from the self but transcends it practically (pp. 665–666). He points out that Kant constructs the mental as an image in time that also refers to spatial concepts; it is 'figured cognitively, conatively and affectively' (p. 671) by the self. Bhattacharyya similarly points out that in spiritual introspection, the 'I' is never by itself, but is always unaccountably embodied, whereby the object is the shadow or the symbol of the I and is never by itself. Further, it has personal relations with other selves so that the 'I' and other persons are each not the other and are contradictorily symbols of the other. Moreover, the 'I' has an identity with the over-personal self: This consciousness is always 'nought' and is the center of religious experience. Thus, identity is experienced through difference; it is a concrete identity: It is the felt form of the identity with the 'I.' It is not just consciousness of reality but is reality itself. The 'I' is known in pure enjoyment; hence, 'I am' where 'am' means something that is subjectively enjoyed (p. 458). Thus, the subject is known only through denial of the object; the subject is freedom from the object; in fact, the absolute is 'subject as freedom' (Burch 1967: 631). A transcendental symbolic judgment differs from both the objective and the subjective kind in that it has truth for its content. Transcendental consciousness is neither objective nor subjective hence philosophy of truth that is neither subject nor object. Here, there is a denial of the 'I' because of an absolute that is above it.

The absolute is truth, not as the noun reality, but as in verbs such as self-revealing or speaking. Here, all speaking is regarded as symbolizing so that the transcendental thought is seen as complete only when speaking is dispensed with. By extricating the 'subject as freedom' (Bhattacharyya 1983b: 450–454), Bhattacharyya articulates the task of philosophy in terms of his understanding of Kant. Kant's self-defined transcendental or critical philosophy spells out the conditions or assumptions of knowledge, morality, and art, which are situated in the non-empirical human subject. For Kant, rather than the ampliative task of extending knowledge, philosophy has an explicative or corrective function of investigating the conditions of knowledge by examining its sources (1965: 45–48). Similarly, Bhattacharyya believes that philosophy does not have the function of providing information, but rather one of extricating the subject from its object so that the level of transcendental reflection is reached. However, he goes beyond what he terms as Kant's agnosticism toward the highest form of communication practiced by sages is speechless silence. The latter is not philosophy; it is rather an intuitive experience for which room is made by philosophy through its symbolic communication or theoretical consciousness (Bhattacharyya 1983b: 468). Thus, philosophy is *sādhanā* or discipline whose practice is a preparation for an existential encounter with the absolute. For Bhattacharyya, 'the absolute' spoken of only in symbolic terms, underlies all theoretical consciousness, but transcends them ontologically (Herring 1992: 6).

As Herring notes, one can get its *darśana* or vision in religious or existential experiences of direct awareness; from the religious point of view, advaita is individualistic because it makes one's subjective being inward by deepening the sense of spiritual individuality (*svadharma*) in solitude. But Bhattacharyya maintains that as a philosophy, advaita is universalistic in that it presents a truth for all or a common world, rather than just a vision of a mystic philosopher. It acknowledges that all persons have a sacred *svadharma* and is therefore the most catholic and tolerant among religions. Logic, law, and the revealed word are symbolic in pointing to a reality that is beyond, despite their own unreality (Bhattacharyya 1983b: 119–120). Following Herring, Bhattacharyya is firmly rooted in the Hindu scriptural tradition where intellectual knowledge of the world is not worthwhile (6).[10] Liberation (*mokṣa*) through which there is unification of the self (*ātman*) with the absolute (*Brahman)* from the bondage of the world leads to an experience of the self as the basis or origin of knowledge; such a self is the other side of the cosmic force (*Brahman*).[11]

8.4   Integrating Vedānta and Kant

Bhattacharyya offers a Vedantic reading of Kant, where Kant's self transcends empirical consciousness (pp. 22). He interprets the term transcendental in a Vedāntic way as a spiritual and unifying turn beyond the fact and object-centeredness of science and the intellect. Bhattacharyya, conversely, also offers a Kantian reading of Vedānta. He treats Kant's notion of the subject as that which transcends the empirical domain as a starting point for his own spiritual psychology (pp. 462–463).[12] In a distinction reminiscent of Kant's distinction between the empirical self and the noumenal self, he upholds that the individual self as 'me' is illusory for Advaita Vedānta (p. 113). He observes that for Kant, the need for a transcendental or critical reflection arises because of the need for connecting the certainly of the self in the faith of practical reason and that of the object in theoretical reason (pp. 663–665). Bhattacharyya believes that the problem of the first critique, how is knowledge and its object possible, becomes meaningful only if there is the certainty of a subject; such a spiritual certainty is higher than the object (p. 666).[13]

---

[10] Taking issue with Hegel in offering a single grade of religious experience, Bhattacharyya points out that there is an 'infinite plurality of religious experiences' (Bhattacharyya 1983b).

[11] As Burch puts it, rather than the absolute, *mokṣa* is the goal (617–618).

[12] Bhattacharyya (1983b: 369) upholds Kant's critical philosophy to be a 'disguised form' of spiritual psychology.

[13] Raghuramaraju (2007: 136–137, 139) reads Bhattacharyya as a critic of Kant who offers a Vedāntic solution to Kant's assertion of the unknowability of the subject. However, this paper's reading is an attempt to grapple with the tension in Bhattacharyya's writings, as both Kant's sympathizer and critic.

However, a consideration of Kant's own location and response to the history of philosophy also demonstrates some basic differences between his position and that of Bhattacharyya's. Kant's philosophical project aimed at identifying the foundations of science, rather than seeking a subjective metaphysical domain outside of objective science.[14] According to Kant, knowledge begins with experience but does not arise from it so that accidental observations cannot lead to laws of nature.[15] Thus, experimental sciences arrive at scientific truth under specific conditions. An experiment systematically isolates, combines, and varies some conditions in order to observe and measure the properties that depend on these. Further, it has to be repeated; this in turn requires that the universe is uniform throughout a stable space and time. It is the human subject who supplies concepts for experimentation for Kant. Conversely, Kant also believed that reason has to be supplemented by evidence from sense perception. Kant's correlation between experience and reason is not developed by Bhattacharyya in a direction that would transform science; science remains at the level of the empiricist's value-neutrality for Bhattacharyya. He takes the subject as his starting point to turn to the domain of the spiritual, which leaves scientific data as it is at the level of the literal.

Kant apprehends thought as a wider category, while for Bhattacharyya, it is knowledge (p. 369; Herring 1992: 3). In his famous dictum, Kant reverses the Socratic mantra to one cannot know one self but can only be it (1965: 152–158). Further, unlike Kant, Bhattacharyya believes that the self can be known without thinking about it. Kant's notion of the self as a synthetic unity of apperception differs from that of Vedāntic *ātman* or *caitanya*. The self for Kant is individualized as the underlying source of both theoretical and practical reason. Bhattacharyya, who in the course of discussing this difference, points out that Kant's self aims at knowledge of the thing-in-itself; the 'object in general' is the obverse of this aspiration, the blank canvas on which it wants to have the thing-in-itself pictured. He points out that Kant's self is the agent and form of knowing that is in the process of accomplishing. In contrast, the Vedāntic self is the breath of knowledge or light of consciousness that is eternally accomplished. According to Bhattacharyya, Kant's accomplishing self cannot have triumphed over empiricism or scepticism. He points out that the cohesion between the knowledge of the subject and object demands moving beyond knowledge to the unknowable, which is from both points of view, the object consciousness and subject consciousness. This demand for the unknowable is also for an indeterminate consciousness, which Vedānta can provide as both the thing-in-itself/the unknowable and the self are undifferentiated in its *caitanya* (Bhattacharyya 1983b: 24).

Kant takes epistemology as the starting point to assume the reality of the subject and the subjective function. But unlike Bhattacharyya's Vedāntic approach, Kant does not treat epistemology as a branch of transcendental psychology; it is

---

[14] See Kant (1965: 7–62) from which this discussion is derived.

[15] This 'law' was subsequently corrected by Newtonian mechanics once again by integrating experience and reason.

not just concerned with subjective fact but with the meaning of the preposition 'of' in 'knowledge *of* object.' It does not abandon the objective procedure of the sciences, though it tries to counter its independence (Bhattacharyya p. 392). Consequently, Kant does not believe in the possibility of a spiritual discipline of theoretic reason through which self-knowledge can be attained. Kant also believes in the reality of the thing-in-itself. "… his admission of the unknowable reality appears to be an unwarrantable surrender to realism" (Bhattacharyya p. 393).

Bhattacharyya observes that Vedāntic knowledge differs from intellectual knowing activity in that it leads to *mokṣa* or liberation of the self. Liberatory knowledge becomes possible on hearing scriptural texts, reflecting on them, refuting doubts and contemplation. Liberation thus taken is Brahman itself that is past all strife and illusion. It can only be apprehended as '*neti, neti*' or as the negation of positive determinate characteristics. In doing this, the subject has an activity toward itself through the method of knowing as a cognitive inwardness. The method for such an activity can be articulated through the gradations of subjective functions or modes of freedom from the object as (i) bodily subjectivity, (ii) presentational subjectivity, and (iii) spiritual subjectivity (p. 369).

Bhattacharyya claims to take a cue from Kant's ideas of reason to turn to spiritual knowledge, though he acknowledges that Kant himself confines knowledge to science and moral maxims (pp. 462–463, 471). Kant maintains that the stipulation for spiritual experiences cannot be translated into knowledge; it can only be based on faith. Bhattacharyya differs from Kant in treating ampliative symbolic judgments as cognitive. Thus, according to him, one can acquire knowledge of another domain, namely the metaphysical without thinking literally but symbolically.

Further, unlike Kant, speculative metaphysics is not illusory for Bhattacharyya, who defines transcendental as nonobjective reality akin to Kant's transcendent (Herring 1992: 7, 9; Bhattacharyya 1983b: 663). Bhattacharyya's toning down of Kant's agnosticism gives a non-Kantian meaning to the term transcendental. Yet Kant himself defined metaphysics in an epistemological note as the conditions for the possibility of knowledge.[16] He did so in divergence from empiricists who undermined the metaphysical foundations of science with their sole emphasis on experience. Following the physicists of his times, Kant articulates the need for making room for concepts such as space, time, and causation (1965: 24–25). Each of these plays a role in organizing experience so that knowledge becomes possible; they are all imposed upon perceptual data by the subject, which Kant terms as the Copernican turn.[17] Kant's point regarding the various concepts underlying experience is to engage with and retain the limits of objective knowledge. Bhattacharyya

---

[16] This discussion is derived from Kant (1965: 41, 127).

[17] For Kant (1965: 33) those who renounce concepts and method "… have no other aim than to shake off the fetters of *science* altogether, and to change work into play, certainty into opinion, philosophy into philodoxy."

erases this distinction between metaphysics and speculative metaphysics with his search for a domain beyond the limits of objective knowledge.[18]

Bhattacharyya also differs from Kant in advocating stages of subjective freedom progressing toward the final stage of the self's awareness as one with Brahman. As critics have observed, the notion of a final stage that cannot be described presents Bhattacharyya with a nihilistic dilemma (see Herman 1972). Freedom either admits of no stages, else its stages are endless.[19] It is precisely the possibility of such a dilemma that motivates Kant to disavow the search for the unconditioned seat of the subject as transcendental psychology in his first *Critique* as illusory (1965: 316). Bhattacharyya is well aware of the differences between his own position and that of Kant (1983b: 462). With a Kantian reading of Vedānta and a Vedāntic reading of Kant, Bhattacharyya reinforces philosophical reflection is an instrument through which the human subject arrives at immediate knowledge of identity with the absolute.

8.5 Spivak's Post-colonial Critique of Kant

The Kantian subject position that Bhattacharyya discerns as a complement to independent thinking is seen through the opposite lens by Spivak as an instance of colonial suppression. She argues that nationalist thinkers often did not enter into a debate with the colonizer's science and its claims to material progress to which they had access through class privilege (Spivak 1990: 61). Both colonization and its struggles were carried out in two domains, material and the spiritual.[20] It is through science, technology, economy, and the statecraft that the West colonized the non-Western population. But most nationalist leaders and academics resisted this domination through an emphasis on the East in the field of spiritual culture. There was such a 'selective appropriation of Western modernity' whereby "What was necessary was to cultivate the material techniques of modern Western civilization while retaining and strengthening the distinctive spiritual essence of the national culture."[21]

Bhattacharyya can be partially comprehended through this perspective, though Spivak does not name him. He believes that Western science and rationality are

---

[18] See Herring (1992: 4–5), Burch (1967: 619). In fact, Bhattacharyya has also developed Hegelian dialectic to show how the absolute cannot be affirmatively described. See his 'Some Aspects of Negation' (1983b: 567–579).

[19] Kierkegaard is an instance of understanding 'stages' of freedom as discontinuous options that are simultaneous and overlapping (1991). See Hong and Hong (1991: x). Kierkegaard's aesthetic, ethical, and religious 'stages' of existence are like 'spheres,' overlapping, and nonlinear. Thus, a human being can move toward the ethical and yet slip back into the aesthetic, without moving 'forward' to the religious stage.

[20] Spivak cites Partha Chatterjee for this (1999: 60).

[21] Chatterjee, quoted in Spivak (1999: 61).

universal, while social ideals have a culture specific matrix (Bhattacharyya 1984: 389–391, 392). In his *Svaraj in Ideas*, Bhattacharyya distinguishes between political and cultural subjugation (p. 383). The former controlled external life, while the latter adopted alien ideas without the struggle of comparing or competing with native ones in the spiritual sphere of inner life. Thus, "The question of imposition does not arise in the case of certain branches of learning-mathematics and the natural sciences, for example, which have no nationality and imply no valuation" (p. 392). It is in the spirit of comparing competing ideas that Bhattacharyya translates Kant to the idiom of Vedānta to advocate an approach that fuses the East and the West for the sake of spiritual culture in his response to colonialism. To the extent that Kant is incompatible with the goals of Vedānta, Bhattacharyya is critical of him. In contrast, Spivak critiques Kant's subject position from the domain of post-colonial studies: Her engagement is both a critique of marginal post-colonialism and mainstream German philosophy. She argues that the former tends to propagate the view that colonization is a thing of the past and marks a continuous line from the past to the present. Spivak believes that neo-colonialism with hegemonic aid providing economic institutions shows otherwise (1999: 6). In addition, she maintains that the migrant figure that post-colonialism celebrates has a privileged position in the Western academic world. In this respect, it has no connection with the 'native informant' who occupies an unnamed and underprivileged space in the non-Western world.[22] Spivak implicates mainstream thought, such as that of Kant, as one of 'sanctioned ignorance' in this respect (p. 2).[23]

Spivak professes to read Kant in a 'mistaken' way as a 'bungler' who combines the anthropological with the conceptual (pp. 9–10),[24] to expose the hidden anthropological foundations of his concepts. In this endeavor, she believes for his 'axiomatics of imperialism' (p. 4). The native informant is 'crucially needed' and 'foreclosed' (p. 4). She derives the notion of foreclosure from psychoanalysis: "Here, the ego rejects[*verwirft*] the incompatible idea *together with the affect* and behaves as if the idea had never occurred to the ego at all."[25] The rejection of the affect called the 'native informant' becomes a part of the civilizing mission where there is an initiation into becoming human. The inauguration into humanity takes place through the process of expelling the 'native informant.' Thus, foreclosure contains two complementary operations: (i) introduction into the subject and (ii)

---

[22] Spivak derives the term 'native informant' from Western ethnography, rather than philosophy. She cites the 'poorest *woman* of the South' as paradigmatic of such a 'native informant' in contemporary times. See Spivak (1999: 6) for this point.

[23] She also adds Hegel and Marx as representative of the colonial legacy, which have given a sense of identity to the colonized as well (1999: 9).

[24] The mixing of the empirical and the conceptual is 'bungling,' since there is no necessary relation between the two. It stands in contrast to Kant's account of speculative as a proclivity to remain exclusively in the conceptual domain that is inevitably linked to reasoning. Such speculation he remarks is not one in which '... a bungler' has been trapped due to lack of knowledge. See Kant (1965: 300).

[25] Spivak is quoting from *The Language of Psychoanalysis* by Jean Laplanche and J.-B. Pontalis (1999: 4).

expulsion from the subject. Foreclosure differs from exclusion in that it does not keep an already constituted subject at bay. Rather, it constitutes the subject, upon which the system depends, but simultaneously expels or disavows it.[26]

Spivak argues that the 'native informant' is foreclosed by Kant in his account of the subject. In each of his three *Critiques*, Kant reveals reason to be the subject whose freedom from nature allows for science, morality, and art. In his aesthetic work, the sublime is already framed by the moral imperative. Kant's discussions of the beautiful and the sublime show a connection between aesthetic judgment and theoretical reason. "The sublime in nature, becomes possible because of the respect that human beings have for their own determination 'which, by a certain subreption, we attribute to an object of nature.' It is a dissimulated 'exchange [*Verwechselung*] of respect for the *object* [natural sublime] for respect for the idea of humanity in our *subject*.'"[27] This is the sublime in magnitude. But the dynamically sublime does not hold a dominion over human beings; it is still evoked by the feeling of superiority to nature within and without us (Kant 1790: 119–126). The sublime in nature needs culture, but is not primarily produced by culture; it has its foundations in human nature. Thus, for Kant "Without development of moral ideas, that which we, prepared by culture, call sublime presents itself to man in the raw [*dem rohen Menschen*] merely as terrible."[28] Spivak points out that the term raw or *roh* is often translated as uneducated who for Kant include the child, the poor, and the woman; hence, *der rohe Mensch* or man in the 'raw' stands for everything that is primitive and savage (1999: 13).

With reference to Kant, Spivak points out that the 'raw' man is terrified by what for the cultured, cooked, programmed, tuned, and reasoning man is the sublime (Spivak 1999: 14). He is terrified by nature as chaotic or an abyss with no sense of purpose. Thus, the 'raw' man is not able to cultivate a feeling for the moral because "He is not yet the subject divided and perspectivized among the three critiques" (Spivak 1999: 14). He is a causal object (not subject); he is not an example of the thing or its species as natural product. Kant, according to Spivak, excludes an enormous part of humanity in his account of the human subject (Spivak 1999: 26–27). She cites the following passage from the third *Critique* as evidence:

> Grass is needed for the ox, which again is needful for man as a means of existence, but then, we do not see why it is necessary that men should exist (a question which is not so easy to answer if we cast our thoughts by chance on the New Hollanders or the inhabitants of Tierra del Fuego). Such a thing is then not even a natural purpose… for it (or its entire

---

[26] I thank V. Sanil for bringing to my attention the distinction between foreclosure and exclusion.

[27] Kant quoted in Spivak (1999: 11).

[28] This quote by Kant is from Spivak (1999: 13). In the Pluhar edition, one can discern the following, 'It is a fact that what is called sublime by us, having been prepared through culture, and comes across as merely repellent to a person who is uncultured and lacking in the development of moral ideas' (Kant 1987: 124).

species [*Gattung*—the connotation of 'race' as in 'human race' cannot be disregarded here]) is not to be regarded as a natural product. (Kant quoted by Spivak 1999: 26)[29]

Spivak argues that Kant's naming of the 'raw' or 'uncultured' man is very closely linked to his concept of human being. "We find here the axiomatics of imperialism as a natural argument to indicate the limits of the cognition of (cultural) man" (1999: 27). The subject as such in Kant is geopolitically differentiated. Spivak observes that given the European elements in Kant's human being, it is hardly an elevation but a cultural mastery over the native natural. Nature for Kant is the raw man (*die rohe Menschen*) who he names as the Neuhollanders and inhabitants of Tierra del Fuego. Kant's 'raw' man is not part of his main text and is only mentioned in brackets; Spivak focuses on this neglect of the specificities about Neuhollanders as a corrective measure. Despite her admitted enormity of the task, she dwells on some of the details pertaining to the Neuhollanders.[30] Spivak's apprehensions regarding Kant's views on race can be buttressed by turning to his anthropology (1999: 27–29).[31] As Eze remarks, Kant's work on anthropology is "an exercise in the sympathetic study of European humanity, taken as humanity in itself" (1997: 117).

As Spivak points out, the stress on the idealistic subject makes philosophy a hierarchical mission of civilizing into humanity. For this, she argues there is a move from the fear of the abyss (terror of nature) to appreciation of the sublime through culture, program, the 'cooked.' Spivak upholds that receptivity to ideas is the program of humanity (through culture). In all of this, polytheism is equated with degeneratedness and Christian monotheism is seen as closer to philosophy (Spivak 1999: 31).[32] This puts the 'raw' man, Aboriginal, and other animist or such like cosmologies outside the 'text-civilizational' path. If culture is site of struggle against domination,[33] the violence in the concept of human being celebrated by Kant and Bhattacharyya needs to be acknowledged. Kant himself becomes an ally

---

[29] The quotes in brackets are Spivak's. She also notes that Kant also mentions 'the Greenlander, the Lapp, the Samoyede, the inhabitant of the Yakutsk, etc.' (1999: n. 32). In his 'Grounding,' Kant remarks that the South Sea Islanders have neglected their duty to themselves in spending their lives in indolence (1785: 31). These examples, along with Kant's work on anthropology (1996), go to establish his prejudice against race in several of his key philosophical writings.

[30] Spivak also writes "… I cannot write that other book that bubbles up in the cauldron of Kant's contempt," See Spivak (1999: n. 32, 28). But critics have observed that some of Spivak's details are not entirely accurate. See, Eagleton (1999).

[31] Critics have perceived Kant's third *Critique* as an endorsement of race and gender bias. See Kneller (1994, 1996), Eze (1997), Bernasconi (2002), and Mahadevan (2004) for detailed discussions.

[32] Spivak remarks that Hinduism is dispersed and decentered, and its 'multi-leveled aspect' is 'quite interesting' (1990: 40). However, critics such as Bhatt who accuse her of defending Hinduism (Bhatt 2002: 40–62) ignore her plea that "Any kind of apologetics for Hinduism coming today from Indians such as myself has to take note that one of the most politically pernicious phenomena in India, and also in the United States, is Hindu fundamentalism" (Spivak 1990: 40).

[33] This phrase is borrowed from Agozino (2000). However, Agozino is rightly critical of Spivak for neglecting to take into account discussions by African thinkers in her work.

or a foe depending upon whether one has a colonial or post-colonial perspective. Though the notion of 'nativity' in the native informant has its set of problems, Spivak's call for introducing the dimension of the underprivileged in doing philosophy needs to be heeded. Again, the notion of comparative philosophy initiated by Bhattacharyya through a dialogue between Kant and Śaṁkara needs to be rethought in a post-colonial context.

8.6 *Svaraj* in Ideas

Spivak observes that "India had its own Fuegans, its own Hollanders. The Indian Aboriginal did not flourish in pre-British India ... there is something Eurocentric about assuming that imperialism began with Europe" (1999: 37). Thus, the foreclosure of the indigenous is not confined to Kant; Śankarācārya too has contributed to such a process.[34] He argues against the underprivileged castes, or *śūdras*, as eligible for knowledge of *Brahman*, since such knowledge is the prerogative of the twice-born.[35] In an operation similar to that of Kant with respect to the New Hollanders, Śaṁkara articulates the *śūdra* position only to refute the view that they are twice-born and disqualify them as knowers. He remarks that *śūdras* cannot acquire such knowledge merely by desiring it; rather than a mere temporal capability, spiritual capability of studying the Vedas is needed. Śaṁkara also tries to prove scriptural prohibition against the *śūdras* as ineligible readers and students of the *Vedas*. He argues that this is because they cannot undergo the *upanayana* ceremony, which belongs only to the three upper castes. Śaṁkara maintains that the *śūdras* are declared by the *Vedas* as unfit for knowledge by virtue of being unfit for sacrifice.[36]

In the above context, Bhattacharyya's interpretation of Kant and Śaṁkara would have to address two issues, both of which are at stake with respect to the native informant: lack of privilege and heterogeneity. Bhattacharyya is sensitive to the need for affirming a plurality of religious and spiritual experiences, which he

---

[34] With reference to Hegel, Spivak points out that to follow the foreclosure of the native informant, one needs to "...step into Hegel's Africa, or the *Gitā's* description of the *śūdras*" (1999: n. 64). This discussion follows Spivak's advice in locating the native informant in Śaṁkarācārya's *Brahmasūtra*.

[35] This discussion of Śaṁkara is derived from his commentary on the *Brahmasūtrabhāṣya*. See Śaṁkara (2004: 344–350). I am indebted to Pradeep Gokhale for bringing this passage to my attention.

[36] He also discusses various scriptural references prohibiting the *śūdras* from listening to the *Vedas* and punishment for violating these prohibitions. Śaṁkara also mentions that "*Smṛti*, moreover, declares all the four castes are qualified for acquiring knowledge of the *itihasas* and the *purāṇās*; It remains, however, a settled point that they do not possess any such qualification with respect to the *Veda*" (2004: 350). D.D. Kosambi observes that the underprivileged castes were necessary as audience for the epic *Mahābhārata*; "This made the epic a most convenient vehicle for any doctrine which the Brahmins wanted to insert" (Kosambi quoted in Spivak 1999: 50).

believes Vedānta to propagate unlike Hegelianism.[37] By bringing Kant and Vedānta into contact, he proposes to initiate a philosophical perspective that is aware of global trends and is yet sensitive to ancient Indian thought (Bhattacharyya 1984: 389). The significance of both Kant and *Vedānta* would have to be addressed critically given their respective foreclosures. However, if Bhattacharyya's philosophical perspective has to make room for those who have been traditionally foreclosed by both Kant and *Vedānta*, it would have to dismantle both native hegemony and European imperialism.

A reading of Kant in colonial, and one might add post-colonial, contexts would have to be critical and independent, as Kant himself argues in his essay 'What is Enlightenment?' (Kant 1983c). Such an independent outlook would have to take into account, Kant's move from his earlier problematic claims about nonwhite races to an overt critique of colonialism and commitment to a more egalitarian view of humanity.[38] Independent thinking does not operate in a vacuum, as Bhattacharyya has shown in his analogous essay '*Svaraj* in Ideas'; it takes the cultural perspective into account, since individuals inhabit cultures. Bhattacharyya's colonial perspective has some commonalities with Spivak's post-colonial reading that too pleads for critique. Both are aware of plurality of philosophical systems. Both hanker for the 'native' in the Indian context, against the colonization of Europe over thought. Both search living Indian traditions for the articulation of such a voice.

Spivak herself delineates a kinship in 'global' exploitation processes since the early civilization to globalized times, wherein both ecology and the human community of 'native informants' are injured (1999: 380). She argues that each of the great religions of the world, Hinduism included, is caught up in matrices of the history of such exploitation. Hence, "In the case of Hindu India, a phrase as terrifying to us as 'Christian Europe,' no amount of reinventing the nature poetry of *Rg-Veda* will in this view suffice to undo that history" (p. 383). Instead, Spivak suggests that she has "… no doubt that we must learn from the original practical ecological philosophies of the world" (p. 383). She names the Indian Aboriginals

---

[37] With respect to Hegel, Spivak rightly points out that in his reading of Hinduism, Hegel is not foreclosing the 'native informant' but is rather 'trans valuing cultural texts by appropriating them into a scale' (1999: n. 64). The relationship between Bhattacharyya and Hegel demands separate attention.

[38] He does so in the context of the cosmopolitan right to hospitality. Kant laments that the "inhospitable conduct of civilized nations in our part of the world, especially commercial ones: the injustice that they display towards foreign lands and peoples (which is the same as *conquering* them), is terrifying" (1983c: 119). This shift poses the question of the extent to which Kant's earlier thoughts are implicated in race and whether he did indeed change his position on race. Spivak and Kant's critics on race need to be reread from this perspective. Kleingeld's (2007) discussion on the subject is significant for precisely addressing this complex matter of 'Kant's Second Thoughts on Race.' Yet it is a matter of debate whether Kant really did change his position on race, since no explicit textual evidence is available for the same. See Louden (2011) for a detailed discussion.

as the forest-dwelling tribes of India who were stigmatized by the British as criminal and who were not taken into account by either the British or the Hindus or the Muslim civilizations in India (pp. 384–385). Spivak points out that their culture is closely woven with nature, a weave which can teach one resistance to hegemonies—both within a nation and of the imperialist kind. She also seeks the affirmation of the native informant in non-hegemonic forms of lived polytheistic Hinduism (Bhatt 2002: 59–62). Bhattacharyya similarly finds comfort in the living traditions of native Indian culture where humanity has a quest for infinity, but unlike Spivak, he identifies Śaṁkara Vedāntic high Hinduism as an instance of such indigenousness.

Bhattacharyya proclaims that much of what is attributed to *advaitavāda* "is the most satisfying formulation of the distinctive spirit of Hinduism" (Bhattacharyya 1983b: 122–123). Rather than a rejection, it is for him a realization of concrete religion; the latter becomes a hindrance to advaita Vedānta only when it neglects inwardness. The advaitin would have to join traditional worship and would also bring in the abstract contemplation of self-knowledge as a part of such worship. Bhattacharyya points out that it also influenced the evolution of Hinduism historically in the course of synthesizing other schools of Indian philosophy. It is "... the religion in the simplified and unified form of the realization of subjectivity or self-knowledge ..." (p. 122). However, the problem with this version of 'nativism' is that as Spivak has herself observed, one cannot chart out the lines of the custodianship of a culture, since "... it cannot be denied that such lines are drawn and redrawn" (2004: 8). Bhattacharyya's belief that the native voice can be articulated in first-person experiences relies upon empiricism's appeal to direct experience. However, this can be contested by appealing to Kant's own argument that percepts without concepts do not have a sense of direction. The historical and cultural rootedness of concepts reveals them to be are ridden within foreclosures such as Kant's human being or Śaṁkara's self.

Spivak observes with reference to the German context which initiated the terms of a comparative enterprise that comparison was made in philology, religion, and literature, but not in philosophy (2004). She aptly observes that the relationship of comparison was established through concepts of identity and kinship without taking the distinction between the colonizer and the colonized into account. This was because philosophy in the West, particularly Germany, established itself through "'universal' narratives where the subject is unmistakably European" (Spivak 1999: 8).[39] Against this, Bhattacharyya in his notion of '*svaraj*' or self-determination of

---

[39] It is debatable whether what Spivak terms as 'Marx's socialist homeopathy' was a product of ignoring the relationship between colonizer and the colony as she alleges (Spivak 1999: 8–9). Marx has pondered extensively on the issue of colonialization and nationalism. See Marx and Engels (2001) for a compilation of their contribution to this problem. Further, a comparative study of Marxism and Indian thought has led Chattopadhyaya to a reinterpretation of *Cārvāka* or *Lokāyata* philosophy (2006). Given Spivak's indictment of Radhakrishnan, this reinterpretation questions his hegemonic interpretation of *Cārvāka* thought as endorsing untamed passions and hedonistic. To quote Radhakrishnan, 'The *śāstra* is called *Lokāyata*, for it holds that only this world or *loka* is. The materialists are called *Lokāyatikas*. They are also called *Cārvākas*, after the name of the founder' (1958: 279).

ideas does see the possibility of there being more than one philosophy, which mandates comparison that further takes imperialism into account. He maintains that "it is in philosophy that one could look for an effective contact between Eastern and Western ideas" (Bhattacharyya 1984: 386). Bhattacharyya is well aware that this contact would have to confront the problem of colonization because of which the colonized could mindlessly imitate the colonizer. Further, rather than a 'patchwork of ideas of different cultures' (p. 388), such a comparative philosophy, Bhattacharyya suggests, would assimilate Western ideals with Indian ones; it would also reject those that are alien to Indian thought. For Bhattacharyya, comparative philosophy is a process of 'self-discovery' (p. 384), where one can discover an indigenous form of thought through its process of struggle with an alien form.

Yet as Bhattacharyya's own instance reveals, this search for an Indian paradigm often gives way to the search for an indigenous that is out to discover a uniquely Indian 'identity,' often traditional, religious, or spiritual or even local or lived.[40] As Bhatt observes, such nativism paradoxically resonates with currents of modern German European philosophy's perception of Indian thought.[41] Further, though they did not compare in a formal textual sense, European philosophers did in practice compare themselves to Indian thought to establish their universality. Their comparisons often tended to be random with passing references to Indian thought. Many of the German thinkers during the eighteenth and nineteenth centuries followed an approach similar to that of Bhattacharyya's assimilation the foreign with the indigenous; they rejected the foreign when such assimilation was not possible. As Bhatt argues, many German thinkers thought of ancient *Vedic* thought as the support from whose infancy mature Greek and European thought emerged (pp. 42–45). For instance, Schopenhauer cites knowledge of both Kant and *Upaniṣadic* philosophy as preparation for comprehending his own philosophy.[42] Voltaire located *Vedic* ancient Indian thought as the original impulse for world civilizations. Herder signaled the 'primal seat' (Bhatt 2002: 43) of diverse traditions such as Genesis, Chinese, Tibetans, Arabs, Persians, and Indians in 'a region between the Indian mountains' (p. 43). He derived the image of India as childlike from Kālidāsa's play *Śākuntala*. Kant himself claimed the following about India: "This is the highest country. No doubt it was inhabited before any other and could even have been the site of all creation and all science." (quoted in Bhatt 2002: 45) Yet for Kant, India was in a state of erosion from its original perfection.[43] On both counts, his attitude to India was not as pejorative as it was

---

[40] Bhatt asserts that Spivak's polytheistic and lived Hinduism collides with high German orientalism (pp. 59–62). However, in this equation, he overlooks that Spivak is critical of appropriating elite Sanskrit texts as definitive of Hinduism. Bhatt also does not heed her critique of colonization in her search for the native which is untouched by British, Hindu, and Muslim civilization as she puts it. See for instance, Spivak (1999: 385).

[41] Bhatt's critique of Spivak is extended to Bhattacharyya.

[42] Quote derived from Bhatt (2002: 41). The account of German idealism that follows is based on Bhatt's reading.

[43] See Bhatt (2002: 45–46) for a discussion of Kant's views on India. Also see Said (1978) for Western conceptions of the non-Western world as a non-location.

toward the New Hollanders or the raw man. Hegel did not accord a position to ancient Indian thought in philosophical history, though he does place it in prehistory or general history.[44] This was his response to the historical discovery of his period, namely that Sanskrit has linkages with other European languages. Thus, the primeval condition of perfection in India was for him a matter that fell outside the scope of philosophy.[45] Schelling and Schlegel gave privileged position to India in their philosophies of history unlike Hegel.

Bhattacharyya echoes the eulogistic strain of Indian thought that is equated with Hindu religion in Germanic perceptions of Indian philosophy (Bhattacharyya 1983b: 116–124). He points out that toleration has a religious significance in the sense of mattering to the individual in *advaita*.[46] Since all individual selves are aspects of one self, the individual owes a special allegiance to the religion of the other as well. *Advaita* does not prescribe any mode of enjoyment even an altruistic one 'universal brotherhood' in the sense of promoting the happiness of others like as though it were one's own. Toleration is not an indifferent endurance nor is it a condemnation.[47] The truth itself is cosmically determined and it is also relative (*adhikāri bheda*) to the spiritual status of the knower. Bhattacharyya observes that rather than gradation into higher and lower, which encourages envy, *adhikāra* is an acceptance of the fact of the spiritual sphere. The person discovers his or her external status only so that duties can be performed; it is an inward movement. There is as Bhattacharyya puts it an 'aristocracy in spiritual polity' (1983b: 121), where the spiritual is the achievement of the strong. Further, such merit prevents its becoming a common characteristic of all persons as it is 'sacred.' But Bhattacharyya claims that despite this hierarchy, there is a toleration that prevails in this sphere where those who have attained a 'higher' level of *adhikāra* ought to join with the humblest in worship. Further, every human being has *svadharma* and therefore an opportunity to enter the inwardness of the spiritual.

Bhattacharyya also reveals a disregard for initiating social change from the perspective of society like the German idealists.[48] According to him, *advaita* mandates that all human beings can be graded only in terms of their inward spiritual achievements. A person who is in the process of realizing inwardness can help

---

[44] Spivak also shows how Hegel's reading of Indian art and *Srimadbhagvatagita* from the perspective of the colonizer presupposes "an 'orientalist' semitized, nearly monotheist, homogeneous religion called Hinduism" (1999: n. 51; 37–67). She observes that Hegel packs in 2,500 years of India to demonstrate that India does not have a history (p. 48).

[45] Hegel, however, had a more disparaging attitude. He believed that even though India possessed a true philosophy, it did not have notions of individuality to carry it forward. Bhattacharyya's arguments can be marshaled against this claim to prove that Vedanta does allude to the limits of individuality to move forward to a cosmic notion of the self and Brahman.

[46] This argument is derived from Bhattacharyya (1983b: 109–124).

[47] 'To tolerate them merely in a non-committal or patronizing spirit would be an impiety and to revile them would be diabolical' (Bhattacharyya 1983b: 120).

[48] This discussion is derived from Bhattacharyya (1983b: 121–124).

others expedite their realization through education and prayers. But, according to Bhattacharyya, such a person cannot participate in the others realizing such a level through spirituality; even such a thought would be arrogant. For Vedānta does not undertake the transformation of external phenomena such as a traditionally unequal society as its primary task. Social life and *yajna* are for advaita sacred reflections of the one self. Social duty for Bhattacharyya is only a negative one of abstaining from conscious injustice. Advaita also does not support an iconoclastic intervention in a traditional institution that is held to be sacred. But it does allow for vitalizing an institution that is stagnant. "Spiritual realism would demand both reverence for and dissociation from what is sacred" (122) so that when a sacred symbol becomes redundant, it should be replaced by another. Thus, Bhattacharyya's idealism too fuses with German philosophy in restricting Indian thought to elite ancient schools. As Bhatt puts it, "With some Dionysian exceptions, the European preference was for Sanskritic, *Brāhminic* world views ..." (58).[49] The European imagination did not take the following aspects of Hinduism into account: *bhakti, tantra, dalit, adivāsi,* and even South Indian texts (Ibid). Furthermore, the Indian Muslim is completed erased in this mold of thought. Thus, there is thin ground for simultaneously taking both inequality and cultural pluralism into account in colonial and post-colonial theory.

While inaugurating the possibility of philosophy in the Indian context in the colonial period, Bhattacharyya warns against subservient readings where one unreflectively either submits to a foreign idea or patriotically rejects it (1984). He argues for freedom of thought in way similar to Kant's argument for a public use of reason where one thinks independently without self-imposed immaturity of depending on guidance from others.[50] Kant defines the public use of reason as referring unrestrictedly to the world community, while those in civic posts use it privately or in a restricted way (1983a: 41). Thus, those who live in the system of administrative posts employ reason as a 'drill,' in obedience to 'Rules and formulas ... mechanical aids' (1983a). In contrast, from a philosophical perspective of a world community, Kant upholds that one can argue about the validity of the rules themselves even though one might be obeying them as an officer in a civic post. "The *public* use of one's reason must always be free, and it alone can bring about enlightenment among mankind; the private use of reason may, however, often be very narrowly restricted, without other hindering the process of enlightenment" (p. 42). As Butler argues, this implies a critical identity which refuses to mechanically follow civic authority, which opens up the space for subsequently inventing oneself in non-authoritarian ways (2009).

Bhattacharyya analogously argues that independence in thought comprises of scholarly reasoning before an unrestricted literate community. In the Indian context, the stress on administrative education by the British emphasized on rule bound behavior at the restricted private level of civic posts. As a legislative member in

---

[49] Also see Hsia (2001) for Kant's and Herder's views about the Far East.

[50] See for example, Bhattacharyya (1983b: 41).

the Council of India, Thomas Macaulay in his 1,835 min to the British government argued for standardizing English education in India (Macaulay 1965; Balaram 2001: 733–734). He argued on the grounds of the superiority of English as a perfect medium for creating a class of Indians in administrative posts who would remain loyal to the British by forgoing their own culture (Balaram 2001: 733–734).

Against Macaulay, Bhattacharyya urges philosophers to adopt a 'svaraj in ideas' whereby instead of mindlessly imitating foreign ideas, they are evaluated and assimilated with those native to India. Further, he articulates his critique of subservience in culture and thought in English to demonstrate that it need not be restricted to the administrative regulations of colonial rulers. Rather in so far as it is language, English per se addresses an unrestricted community of actors and can therefore be adapted to critique colonialism. Bhattacharyya also demonstrates that colonization has forcibly brought two cultures into contact—albeit unequally. In such a context, instead of remaining within the compartment of either the culture of colonizer or the colonized, a comparative struggle between the two would allow for critical thought to emerge. Bhattacharyya, thus, advocates a critical attitude for the assimilation of foreign ideas after evaluating them from a native perspective (Bhattacharyya 1984: 392–393). He does this to avoid the two extremes of clash and mindless imitation of ideas. Cultural ideas "… embodied in a foreign language are properly understood only when we can express them in our own way. I plead for a genuine translation of foreign ideas into our native ideas before we accept or reject them." (p. 393). Indeed, in his own working out of a comparative philosophy, he takes the subject as free as the starting point whereby "Its importance will be appreciated by connecting it with kindred Western speculations on the one hand and with Vedantic speculations in metaphysics on the other" (1983b: 11). Bhattacharyya is well aware that comparison will have to be enacted against the backdrop of an unequal relationship between the cultures that are being compared. To quote, "I plead for a genuine translation of foreign ideas into our native ideas before we accept/reject them." (1984: 393). Bhattacharyya upholds that the process of comparison is also a process of discovery where one becomes conscious of one's culture.

Thus, through his reading of Kant, he brings Vedānta into focus as a living tradition. Bhattacharyya's commentaries (bhāsyas) on scriptures such as the Upaniṣadas are not just apologies or compilations. His attitude to commentaries is that of an interpreter who is also a constructor (1983: 4–6). Bhattacharyya's own reading of Kant in affinity with Vedānta is such an attempt at comparative philosophy. Bhattacharyya maintains that a true philosophical perspective would be like a "living fabric which with its entire endeavor to be objective must have a well-marked individuality" (6). He believes that this cannot be achieved in academics alone, but should be entrenched in culture as a theme of literature that is of infinite interest to humanity.

Bhattacharyya distinguishes a philosophical study of 'living' culture from the historical study of the past, echoing Kant once again in maintaining that philosophy forms a normative base for a historical study.[51] He argues that philosophical study

---

[51] This discussion is derived from Bhattacharyya (1983b: 1–6).

is prior to a historical study of any school of thought and should be done by methods that are traditionally accepted as authoritative. Though historical research can be used to correct these later on, Bhattacharyya points out that such a correction mandates that the historian be more than a mere narrator. The historian has to be a sympathetic interpreter who imbibes the school of thought as a way of life so that it can be assessed. Bhattacharyya also cautions against the twin dangers of a philosophic creed that tends to be read into history, and conversely where a philosophic creed is treated as a historical curiosity of explaining it through natural causes rather than studying its philosophical merits. He remarks that Western expositions of Eastern thought tend to veer in this direction. For example, Indian fatalism and pessimism is explained through climatic conditions. Or Indian speculation is denied the status of philosophical speculation because 'the oriental intellect is not sufficiently dry and has not the masculine virility enough to rise to anything higher than grotesque imaginative cosmogonies' (1983b: 2). Citing the example of Thibaut's interpretation of Śaṁkara doctrine of *māyā*, he points out that historical research is prejudiced philosophical appreciation. Bhattacharyya observes that the doctrine of *māyā* cannot be found in the *Upaniṣadas* except in a few passages in an undeveloped form. Yet Thibaut goes on to admit that 'the final absolute identification of the individual self with the universal self is indicated in terms of unmistakable plainness' in the *Upaniṣadas*. According to Bhattacharyya, if Thibaut had focused on philosophical scholarship rather than historical accuracy, he would have seen the doctrine of *māyā* as a corollary of the doctrine of individual being *brahman* in *mokṣa* or absolute liberation. He concludes that it is from the point of view of such identification which is liberation that Śaṁkara sees individuality as appearance, along with distinctions such as subject and object that it generates.

Bhattacharyya's reading, thus, sees Kant as a collaborator and recovers Kantianism as having the resources to challenge the dominance of scientism. However, in assimilating Kant with *Vedānta*, he overlooks the foreclosures that are endemic to both, which have been exposed by Spivak. This reading of Kant and Śaṁkara differs from that of Raghuramraju who is against humanizing Kant's unknowable self and wants to divinize it (2007 p. 145). He wants to perform the latter operation within the Western philosophical tradition so that "… one is sensitive to the cultural differences, and be as cautious as in choosing the blood group for transfusion" (p. 141). Raghuramaraju traces the lack of fit between Kant and Bhattacharyya to a topographic approach of linking disparate cultures to which he suggests a chronological remedy.[52] The latter traces Kant's autonomous self to its theological roots in the Western tradition so that God's omniscience and omnipotence that cannot be known by the human intellect are transferred to the self. This reading explains the unknowability of the self in Kant by linking it diachronically to roots in divinity. However, though the Christian doctrine of God and creation has impacted modern philosophy, one cannot assume that there is a deterministic relationship between God and the autonomous self. Raghuramaraju proclaims that

---

[52] See Raghuramaraju (2007: 142–144) for this discussion.

his turn to Kant's 'disguised theology' wants to 'classize' the self '...unlike Bhattacharyya's attempt that tries to Indianize' it (p. 143). Yet in this, he casts aside Kant's critique of both transcendental psychology and rational theology as exercises in illusion. Further, instead of replacing the human reading with the divine in a quest for cultural consistency, one needs to examine the costs of being human and turn to conditions of foreclosure under which the autonomy of the self in Kant (or that of *mokṣa* in Śaṁkara) becomes possible.[53] Rather than his relationship to the divine, the problem with Kant is that his account of the subject is vitiated by prejudice. Yet Bhattacharyya's comparative enterprise in philosophy across the planet allows for identifying this prejudice. Through the struggle between different cultures of thought, such comparison also leads to a hybridization of thought that dissolves the dichotomy between the East and the West. Bhattacharyya's call for independence in ideas is important, yet his rehabilitation of Kant's subject is problematic.[54] In returning to the problem of foreclosure, one need not renounce Kant, but can rather evoke him in critiquing it. Kant's concepts would thereby become allies in remedying his implicit racism. For instance, one can take recourse to the concept of reciprocity from Kant to connect the human being with its other on the basis of the 'principle of Coexistence, in accordance with the Law of Reciprocity or Community' (Kant 1965: 233). In his first *Critique*, Kant delineates three categories of relation, namely substance/impermanence; causation/dependence, and reciprocity to show how they are the constitutive features of phenomenal events.[55] Human subjects are related to and formed by other phenomenal events in the world. Like all other substances in the world, human beings too are in reciprocal mutual interaction with everything else. Such coexistence consists in mutual influence on each other because of which a community becomes possible. Kant points out that the term 'community' in German can mean either *communio* or *commercium* (1965: 235). The former local community becomes possible because of the latter sense of dynamic community. Such a constant impact of spatial entities on each other shows that they do not have intractable identities, which provides leeway for changing identities that are foreclosed and oppressive. Again, Kant's moral philosophy is not merely about the autonomous will causing an action self-sufficiently as Bhattacharyya maintains. His first thesis in moral philosophy upholds that for an action to qualify as moral, the agent would have to think from the perspective of the other regarding its acceptability or refusal (see Kant 1983b: 1–69). Kant's prescription is therefore to 'Act only

---

[53] Raghuramaraju evokes both Barthes and Althusser in tracing the ancestry of Kant's autonomous subject as replacing the agency of God with that of the human being (p. 141). One also needs to ponder over the inherent historical and temporal discontinuities in the subject position emerging from race, class, caste, or gender.

[54] As Khan notes, "Among contemporary Indian thinkers only Gandhi was least influenced by the age-old Indian tradition. The reason behind this is clear; Gandhi was more a political thinker than a philosopher in the traditional sense" (1998). One might add Jotiba Phule, Savitribai Phule, B.R. Ambedkar, and Pandita Ramabai to this list of political thinkers.

[55] See Kant (1965: 212–236) for a detailed account.

according to that maxim whereby you can at the same time will that it should become a universal law' (1983b: 30). Such a putting of the self in the shoes of the other becomes possible because of the reciprocal interconnectedness among the phenomena in the world.[56] Yet, for Kant, the perspective of the other requires both imagination and acquiescence to difference; one is moral when one dialogues with the other who is different. Thus, even the European subject is frail enough to be a part of a network of relations, so that 'his' moral action will have to incorporate the perspective of the aboriginal. The vice versa holds as well.

In an analogous vein, the Vedantic concept of a non-reductionist and non-determinate oneness can be evoked to critique hierarchy of gender and caste as Avudai Akkal (Natarajan 2013)[57] and Guru (2006: 331–335) have done. However, in doing this, one has to interrogate whether worldly differences would have to be reduced to an illusion (*māyā*). The relationship between exploitation at the empirical level and its absence at the non-empirical level will have to be rethought from an ontological standpoint. Again, the extent to which this notion of oneness can sustain difference would have to be examined as well. Further, turning to social change from a Vedantic perspective need not bind one to making xenophobic claims about Indian superiority.

Despite his limits, instead of rehashing Kant's ideas verbatim, Bhattacharyya has put them to a creative use in the Indian context and endeavored toward the *svaraj* that he himself pleaded for (1984: 386–388). The academic study of Western philosophy in India from a non-scientistic framework emerged through attempts such as that of Bhattacharyya during the colonial period. As Alok Rai observes, in the Indian context, privilege is related to a wholesale endorsement of value-neutral science and technology, rather than seeking an alternative methodology appropriate to the humanities (1994: 316). Bhattacharyya opens up a spiritual path in his quest for an alternative to scientific value-neutrality (1984: 392). Yet this is precisely why unlike Kant, he does not critique the sciences, which he assumes are universal. In its quest for an alternative scheme of understanding and values in spirituality, this approach leaves empiricism as it is; it is also complicit with colonial conceptions of science. To respond to this with a critique of science, one would have to turn to Kant's transcendental method as a scientific one which seeks the conditions of knowledge and discerns an inextricable relation between concepts and scientific facts. However, this method would have to be severed from its relation to Kant's restricted understanding of the human subject. Rather than forgo the domain of science as value-neutral, such a phenomenal (rather than a spiritual) reading of Kant would allow one to exercise *svaraj* with regard to science as well. Kant and Śaṃkara can be read as enabling in a predominantly scientistic academic culture, through their endeavor of linking scientific claims about interdependence

---

[56] This is precisely why Kant's autonomous subject differs from Descartes' pace Raghuramaraju (2007: 143).

[57] I am indebted to Kanchana Natarajan for drawing my attention to this 18th century vedāntin saint whose songs she is translating from Tamil to English for the first time.

and reciprocity with moral action and social change. Both demonstrate that such divisiveness is at the root of a dogmatic worship of empiricism, which can be overcome by acknowledging the concept-ladenness of scientific facts. Consequently, philosophy will have an explicative rather than an ampliative role.[58]

Bhattacharyya's process of humanistic self-discovery in comparison would have to be taken in the direction of critiquing the humanistic legacy in both indigenous culture, as well as alien thought, without which his ideal of '*svaraj* in ideas' would be vitiated. Kant's textual and Śaṁkara's scriptural presence in Indian universities depends upon and yet represses Aboriginals, tribals, and underprivileged castes in their affirmation of the subject position. As Spivak argues in her assessment of comparative literature, while looking at the other in the course of comparison, one might reinforce the prejudices of accepted matrices (Spivak 2004: 1–23).[59] To avert such an eventuality, one needs to introduce the notion of defamiliarization as the ethics of comparative study, "Otherwise who crawls into the place of the 'human' of 'humanism' at the end of the day, even in the name of diversity?" (2004: 23). To answer this, one needs to examine familiar texts, both Vedantic and Kantian, in unfamiliar ways and locate their foreclosures to explore the extent to which these foreclosures support these texts. Doing this would confront Western elite's domination and its complicity with non-Western elite. Spivak terms 'planet thought' or planetarity as having the task of opening up difference (p. 72). She distinguishes it from globalization which imposes uniformity. Further, Spivak points out that the globe can be discerned at a distance like an object on the computer screen and it is not the space of habitation. While the planet is another system of alterity, which is inhabited temporarily 'on loan' (p. 72). Planet thought cannot "transmute the literatures of the global South to an undifferentiated space of English rather than a differentiated political space …" (p. 72) as Spivak argues "To be human is to be intended toward the other" (p. 73). The concept of human being is established by distinguishing it from that which differs from it. These differences include underprivileged castes, tribes, women, nature, and the like. Spivak maintains that if one imagines oneself to be a planetary subject rather than a global agent, or a planetary creature rather than a global entity, one is in a position to comprehend difference as inextricably linked to one's identity. From the perspective of planetarity that which differs from the human being "… contains us as much as it flings us away" (p. 73). Planet thought opens up an inexhaustible list of 'otherness'; it goes beyond humanism to claim that the subject is never all by itself but rather the other translates and 'infects' the self. Thus, planet thought makes the

---

[58] As Khan notes, "Bhattacharyya, though he was influenced by Kant's distinction between *phenomena* and *noumena* in his attempt to defend the *advaita* view of the Vedānta school, yet he did not accept Kant's view of the unknowable." (1998). It is precisely from this point of view that Radhakrishnan's characterization of Bhattacharyya as someone who follows Kant "… and follows the *Upanisads* which declare Brahman [i.e. the Absolute] to be beyond speech and thought and yet not unknowable" (quoted in Khan 1998) is problematic. For Kant cannot be reduced to *Upaniṣadic* thought.

[59] She remarks that this is precisely the reason for Western universities making room for multiculturalism and comparative studies (Spivak 2004: 4–9).

familiar home uncanny, unfamiliar, or *unheimlich* (Spivak 2004: 74).[60] The absence of disparaging references to nonwhite races in Kant's text on perpetual peace (1983c) can be as a step toward planet thought. He upholds the 'right to visit ...' (p. 118) any place, due to humanity's 'common ownership of the earth's surface.' (p. 119). It is only a step since Kant did not proclaim racial equality in his work on world peace! Moreover, he argues for the right to visit in the context of the collective human right to property, rather than Spivak's wider ecological frame. Spivak argues that colonialism, decolonization, and post-coloniality all involve exchanges between humans and people who are their 'other.' Such thinking prompts a rethink of both colonial and post-colonial perspectives in philosophy founded on first-person experience of the indigenous. It 'de-transcendentalizes' cultural origins (p. 102).[61]

Bhattacharyya and Spivak are both urban Indian academics who critique cultural imperialism by mostly writing in English. In their search for the indigenous, both turn to alternate readings of Kant during alternate periods. In Bhattacharyya's colonial appropriation, Kant is a friend of Vedānta, while in Spivak's post-colonial view Kant is a foe who has wiped out the native informant. Despite this difference, both approach Indian thought through a reading of Western philosophers such as Kant and abandon an insulated notion of the indigenous to acknowledge that given cultural pluralism and inequality, independent thought lies in between cultures. However, Bhattacharyya's assimilative globalized reading of Western thought cannot realize his '*svaraj* in ideas' without Spivak's planetarity.

References

Agozino, B. (2000). Z is for Zero and N is for Nigger: Postcolonial theory or theory of recolonization? *West Africa Review*. ISSN: 1525-4488.

Balaram, P. (2001). Macaulay's children. *Current Science, 81*(7), 733–734.

Bernasconi, R. (2002). Kant as an unfamiliar source of racism. In J. K. Ward & T. L. Lott (Eds.), *Philosophers on race*. Oxford: Blackwell Publishers.

Bhatt, C. (2002). Enlightenment and the Indian subject of postcolonial theory. In P. Osborne & S. Stanford (Eds.), *Philosophies of race and ethnicity*. London and New York: Continuum.

Bhattacharyya, G. (1956) 1983a. Editor's introduction. In G. Bhattacharyya (Ed.), *Studies in philosophy*. Delhi, Varanasi: Motilal Banarasidass.

Bhattacharyya, K. (1956) 1983b. In G. Bhattacharyya (Ed.), *Studies in philosophy*. Delhi, Varanasi: Motilal Banarasidass.

---

[60] Spivak also notes that 'The *Heimlich/Unheimlich* relationship is indeed, formally, the defamiliarization of familiar space' (2004: 77).

[61] Eagleton derides Spivak as a purveyor of 'gaudy supermarket' in postcolonial theory which could slip into 'anything goes-ism' (1999). This charge is endorsed by Agoze given Spivak's neglect of African thinkers (Agozino 2000). However, though Agoze is on track, he overlooks that racism can be a part of selling African culture as examples from the media demonstrate. Eagleton's critique on the other hand overlooks Spivak's apprehensions regarding post-colonialism, rigor in textual analysis and practice of interdisciplinarity.

Bhattacharyya, K. (1984). Svaraj in ideas. *Indian Philosophical Quarterly, XI*(4), 383–393.

Burch, G. B. (1967). Search for the absolute in Neo-Vedānta: The philosophy of K.C. Bhattacharyya. *International Philosophical Quaterly, VII*(4), 611–667.

Butler, J. (2009). Critique, dissent, disciplinarity. *Critical Inquiry, 35*, 773–795.

Chattopadhyaya, D. P. 2006 (1959). *Lokāyata: A study in ancient Indian materialism.* New Delhi: People's Publishing House.

Deshpande, S. (2004). *200 years of Kant: Indian Philosophical Quarterly* (Special Number, Vol. 31, pp. 1–4).

Eagleton, T. (1999). In the gaudy supermarket. *London Review of Books, 21*(10), 3–6.

Eze, E. C. (1997). The color of reason: The idea of "race" in kant's anthropology. In E. C. Eze (Ed.), *Postcolonial african philosophy.* Cambridge, Mass & Oxford: Blackwell.

Guru, N. 2006 (1928). *The complete works.* New Delhi: National Book Trust of India.

Herman, A. L. (1972). The doctrine of stages in Indian thought: With special reference to K. C. Bhattacharyya. *Philosophy East and West, 22*(1), 97–104.

Herring, H. (1992). Krishna Chandra Bhattacharyya's concept of philosophy. *Journal of Indian Council of Philosophical Research, X*(1), 1–12.

Hong, H. V., & Hong, E. H. (1991). *Historical introduction in stages on life's way by Soren Kierkegaard.* Princeton: Princeton University Press.

Hsia, A. (2001). The far east as the philosophers' ‹‹other››: Immanuel Kant and Johann Gottfried Herder. *Revue de Littérature Compare*, 13–29 http://www.cairn.info/article.php?IDREVUE=RLC&IDNUMPUBLIE=RLC297&IDARTICLE=RLC2970013.

Kant, I. (1781A, 1787B) 1965. *Critique of pure reason* (N. K. Smith, Trans.). New York: St. Martin's Press.

Kant, I. (1784) 1983a. An answer to the question: What is enlightenment? In his *Perpetual peace and other essays on politics, history and morals* (T. Humphrey, Trans.). Indianapolis: Hackett.

Kant, I. (1785) 1983b. Grounding for the metaphysics of morals. In *Kant's ethical philosophy* (J. W. Ellington & W. A. Wick, Trans.). Indianapolis: Hackett Publishing Company.

Kant, I. (1795) 1983c. To perpetual peace: A philosophical sketch. In his *Perpetual peace and other essays on politics, history and morals* (T. Humphrey, Trans.). Indianapolis: Hackett.

Kant, I. (1790) 1987. *Critique of judgment* (W. Pluhar, Trans.). Indianapolis: Hackett.

Kant, I. (1798a, 1800b) 1996. *Anthropology from a pragmatic point of view* (V. L. Dowdell, Trans.). Carbondale & Eadwardsville: Southern Illinois University Press.

Khan, G. (1998). Philosophy in the South Asian subcontinent: A unity in maladjustment. *Twentieth World Congress of Philosophy* (Boston). www.bu.edu/wcp/Papers/AsiaKhan.htm.

Kierkegaard, S. (1991). *Stages on life's way.* Princeton: Princeton University Press.

Kleingeld, P. (2007). Kant's second thoughts on race. *The Philosophical Quarterly, 57*(229), 573–592.

Kneller, J. (1994). Kant's immature imagination. In B.-A. B. On (Ed.), *Modern engendering: Critical feminist readings in modern western philosophy.* New York: State University of New York Press.

Kneller, J. (1996). Feminism and Kantian aesthetics. In M. Kelly (Ed.), *Encyclopedia of aesthetics* (Vol. 3). Oxford: Oxford University Press.

Louden, R. (2011). *Kant's human being: Essays on his theory of human nature.* Oxford: Oxford University Press.

Macaulay, T. B. (1965). Minute by the Hon'ble T. B. Macaulay, dated the 2nd February 1835. In *National Archives of India, Delhi.* http://www.mssu.edu/projectsouthasia/history/primarydocs/education/Macaulay001.htm.

Mahadevan, K. (2004). Revisiting Kant's reflective judgments. In S. Deshpande (Ed.), *200 years of Kant: Indian Philosophical Quarterly* (Special Number, Vol. 31, pp. 1–4).

Marx, K., & Engels, F. (2001). In A. Ahmad (Ed.), *On the national and colonial questions.* New Delhi: Left Word.

Natarajan, K. (2013). *Transgressing boundaries.* New Delhi: Zubaan Books.

Punnamparambil, J. (2007). Understanding India. *The Hindu.* http://www.thehindu.com/thehindu/mag/2007/03/18/stories/2007031800070500Htm.

Puri, B., & Sievers, H. (Eds.). (2007a). *Reason, morality and beauty: essays on the philosophy of Immanuel Kant.* Oxford: Oxford University Press.

Puri, B., & Sievers, H. (2007b). *Terror, peace and universalism: Essays on the philosophy of Immanuel Kant.* Oxford: Oxford University Press.

Radhakrishnan, S. 1958 (1923). *Indian philosophy.* London & New York: The Macmillan Company, George Allen and Unwin Ltd.

Raghuramaraju, A. (2006). *Debates in Indian philosophy: Classical, colonial and contemporary new.* Delhi: Oxford University Press.

Raghuramaraju, A. (2007). Krishnachandra Bhattacharyya on the unknowability of self in Kant: Problematizing the programme of Indian remedies to western problems. In B. Puri & H. Sievers (Eds.), *Reason, morality and beauty: Essays on the philosophy of Immanuel Kant.* Oxford: Oxford University Press.

Rai, A. (1994). Out there: An English teacher in the provinces. In S. Joshi (Ed.), *Rethinking English: Essays in literature, language, history.* Oxford: Oxford University Press.

Said, E. (1978). *Orientalism.* London: Routledge and Kegan Paul.

Śaṁkarāchārya. (2004). *Brahma-Sūtras.* Delhi: Bharatiya Kala Prakashan.

Spivak, G. C. (1990). *The post-colonial critic.* New York & London: Routledge.

Spivak, G. C. (1999). *A critique of postcolonial reason: Toward a history of the vanishing present.* Calcutta: Seagull.

Spivak, G. C. 2004 (2003). *Death of a discipline.* Calcutta: Seagull.

Chapter 9
The Road Not Taken: *G.N. Mathrani's Wittgensteinian Transformation of Philosophy*

P.G. Jung

Abstract This essay discusses the philosophical engagements of Ghanshyam Nevandram Mathrani, who aberrated from the dominant trends of philosophizing in India then, and began his philosophical career under the influence of the Wittgensteinian approach to philosophy. The essay is thus about the first Anglophone Indian philosopher to operate exclusively with the Wittgensteinian *spirit* of scepticism towards the philosopher's understanding, and her misuse, of language. The first and the second sections of this essay contextualize Mathrani's philosophical engagement within the philosophical environment of his times. The third and fourth sections present Mathrani's view on language and his stand on the nature of metaphysical propositions and consequently his qualified rejection of them. The concluding section then presents Mathrani's reconciliation of metaphysical propositions within the Wittgensteinian folds through his thesis of *logical emergent*.

Keywords Philosophy of language · Nature of metaphysical propositions · Mathrani · Wittgenstein · Colonial · Wisdom · Logical emergent

I am thankful to Ms. Malati Krishnakumar, a former colleague and a close friend of G.N. Mathrani for sharing details about the person that Mathrani was, and to Mr. More, Ms. S.C. Dube, and Ms. S. Phadke of Ismail Yusuf College, Mumbai, for helping me locate various writings of Mathrani, and to J. Garfield for motivating me to explore the nature of philosophy in India during colonial times.

P.G. Jung (✉)
Department of Humanities and Social Sciences, Indian Institute of Technology Bombay,
Mumbai, India
e-mail: pgjung@iitb.ac.in

P.G. Jung
IIAS, Shimla, India

© Indian Institute of Advanced Study 2015   165
S. Deshpande (ed.), *Philosophy in Colonial India*, Sophia Studies in Cross-cultural
Philosophy of Traditions and Cultures 11, DOI 10.1007/978-81-322-2223-1_9

9.1 The Horizon of the 'East–West' Paradigm

The colonizing of India also brought along with it, apart from the railways and the postal systems, the introduction of Western schema of university education, as opposed to the traditional *pāthaśālas* and *madarasās*, thus fostering the introduction of English language and literature, Western philosophical thoughts, occidental sciences, and consequently, Western culture itself.[1] By the first half of the 19th century itself, a large number of educational institutes had been established as mediums to realize this 'introduction.'[2] These institutionalized introductions, apart from bringing about a gradual embracing of change in the spheres of the social, economic and cultural milieu,[3] also brought about pertinent changes that were not merely confined to the sphere of the applied science such as medicine[4] but more importantly, though sparsely discussed, it brought about an unprecedented change in the directionality and flow within the sphere of academic philosophizing in India.

---

[1] This, of course, was firmly ensured by the well-known *Macaulay's Minute on Education* (1835) that was approved by the then Governor General of India, William Bentinck on the 7th March, 1835. The Governor General's approval entailed the British India Government would henceforth spend the money authorized by the British Parliament for the education of her *Indian subjects* on the dissemination of Western sciences, English Literature and Western Philosophies apart from the teaching of English language rather than the prevalent mode of supporting the study of Sanskrit, Persian and Arabic in the *pāthaśālas* and *madarasās*. For details of the thoughts behind Macaulay's *Minute,* see the sixth chapter of George Otto Trevelyan's (1876/1881), *The life and letters of Lord Macaulay.* One can also refer to *Lord Macaulay: The man who started it all,* at www.languageinindia.com/april2013/macaulay.html for an online access to Macaulay's *Minute on Education* with a brief bio-sketch of Macaulay.

[2] For instance, Calcutta Hindu College/Presidency College (1817), Serampore College (1818), Bishop's College (1820), Deccan College at Pune (1821), Hoogly College (1836), Elphinston College (1834), Duff's college/Wilson College (1832), Madras University (1841), Madras Christian College (1837), Nagpur Hislop College (1845), St. John's College, Agra (1850) to name just a few institutions that function till this day.

[3] For detailed exposition of such changes refer; *The new Cambridge History of India* series, especially in this context: Kenneth W. Jones, *Socio-religious reform movements in British India* (1989).

[4] For a detailed and varied exposition of the nature, changes and effects that triggered off in the field of Natural sciences, and the applied science such as medicine see, S. Irfan Habib, Dhruv Raina (eds.), *Social History of Science in Colonial India* (2007); D.M. Bose, S.N. Sen, and B.V. Subbarayappa (eds.), *A Concise History of Science in India* (1971); Mel Gorman, *Introduction of Western Science into Colonial India: Role of the Calcutta Medical College* (1988), H.J.C. Larwood, *Science in India before 1850* (1958), K.C. Sarbadhikari, *Western Medical Education in India during the Early Days of British Occupation* (1961); Aparajito Basu, *Chemical research in India during 19th Century* (1989), Satpal Sangwan, *Indian Response to European Science and Technology: 1757–1857* (1988). For a critical exploration of the significance of the introduction of science in relation to Indian modernity see, Gyan Prakash, *Another Reason: Science and Imagination of Modern India* (1999).

   Also see; *The new Cambridge History of India* series, especially in this context see: Thomas R. Metcalf, *Ideologies of the Raj* (1995), David Arnold, *Technology and Medicine in Colonial India* (2004).

It is in this *change* that almost all of the present academic philosophy fraternity in India can trace their ancestry to. Looking back, the first, and perhaps the most important, change that the introduction of Western philosophers and their philosophies in colonial India brought about was the change in the perspective in which one perceived one's own traditional thinkers and the traditional systems of world views. This change in perspective unfolded and manifested itself in the identification of traditional thinkers and *darśana*-s as 'philosophers' and as 'philosophies', respectively, thus giving rise to a new categorization of traditional Indian thinkers and systems of thought or world views as 'Indian philosophers' and 'Indian philosophies.' This was an important change because it not merely generated the dichotomy between Indian and Western philosophies, but more importantly, it imbibed us with a sense of awareness of the ownership of a vast resource of our own *philosophies* and *philosophers* and managed to unify the various traditions of Indian systems by bringing them under a single banner called 'Indian philosophy.'

The play of this dichotomy was, however, not without its struggle and its shades of grey. The upholding of this dichotomy between 'Indian' and 'Western' philosophies presupposed, at the least, that both the epithets, 'Indian' and 'Western', be treated as legitimate *distinguishers* such that one could act as a differentiating horizon against which the other could be marked and identified. While the Indian philosophical academia was, and has been, by and large, quick to not merely accept but also acknowledge this distinction as legitimate, it was not so the other way around. This could perhaps be placed in the light of the fact that this distinction saw its birth under the colonial regime and thus one can represent this one-sided acceptance of the dichotomy itself as an unfortunate instance of intellectual subjugation by the colonizers. The view that this act of acknowledgement and acceptance was not performed within the nexus of equal power play could be supported, for instance, by pointing to the fact that no voices of doubt pertaining to what this 'Western philosophy' was, or is, is recorded in the annals of history. History suddenly appears to have legitimized the question, 'What is Indian philosophy', but appears to peculiarly bar the legitimacy of the question 'What is Western philosophy?' The non-availability of this question could be legitimized if we speculatively diagnose the interrogative term 'what' to be a marker of a *qualification* rather than a demand for a *description*. This brings to light the possible reading that the prefix 'Western', for the philosophical community in the West then, did not merely highlight certain *differences* among the predication of certain predicates to the term 'philosophy.' That is to say that the prefix 'Western' was not taken to be a mere marker of *difference* but rather functioned as a *qualifier* for

---

Footnote 4 (continued)

For a critical thematic enquiry into the introduction of Western education and its effects in education and the educational institutes see, Sanjay Seth, *Subject Lessons: The Western Education of Colonial India* (2007). Further, B. Narasingaraja Naidu's work *Intellectual History of Colonial India* (1996) attempts to concretely sketch the transformation of education and educational institutes in the case of Mysore during 1831–1920. The initial section of D.M. Datta's *India's Debt to the West in Philosophy* (1956) also sheds interesting light on curriculum of Philosophy graduates during the first half of the 20th century and the impact of Western philosophy upon students in the Indian Universities.

something to *be* 'philosophy.' Hence, while the term 'Western philosophy', for the Anglophone Indian intellectuals, by and large, marked a horizon of differentiation, for the philosophical community in the West, it operated as a horizon of legitimacy, such that only that could be philosophy that was 'Western.' This view is explicitly instantiated in the reviews received in various journals after the publication of Radhakrishnan's *Indian Philosophy* (1923) or Radhakrishnan's and Muirhead's jointly edited anthology *Contemporary Indian Philosophy* (1936)[5] which were amongst the first to explicitly operate within the categorization of 'Indian Philosophy', though Max Müller had worked with the category in his much earlier work *The Six Systems of Indian Philosophy* (Longmans, Green and Co., London, 1899) and had also managed to garnish similar dismissive reviews.[6] Though, this view cannot be taken to be unanimously held in the west given that there were scattered voices of acknowledgement of Indian philosophy as a legitimate and a distinct brand of philosophy in the voices of the likes of Dewey and Santayana[7]; nevertheless, the sceptical view, remained the dominant one.

The politics of reception that came into play by virtue of the distinction raised by the epithets 'Indian' and 'Western' was further made denser by the fact that, by and large, the Anglophone Indian intellectuals started a large-scale restructuring of Indian traditional thought systems into the philosophical concepts and categories that were operative and well recognized in the West. This resulted in the generation of introductions to Indian philosophy that implicitly brought to light the rich philosophical systems available in the traditional Indian thought systems and in a way highlighted the availability of parallel thoughts in traditional Indian thought systems. Though this move was meant to legitimize the epithet 'Indian' as a possible *distinguisher*, the efforts made in this direction too had to, nevertheless, look westwards for its own legitimacy. Hence, in a sense it was a move that implicitly put the West in a position of legitimizers of the very works of the then contemporary Indian intellectuals, thereby further deepening the notion of the 'Western' being a *qualifier* rather than a bearer of mere *differentiation*. This is not to hold that philosophizing in India got reduced to the writing of the history of Indian thought systems but it was, as can be

---

[5] Amongst others, see; Edward J. Thomas' dismissive reviews in *Mind* (New Series), 36: 144 (1927): 490–496, despite S. Radhakrishnan's (1928) explicatory comment on the book already published as "'Indian Philosophy': Some Problems", *Mind* (New Series), 35: 138 (1926); and F. Otto Schrader's review in *Philosophy*, 12: 47 (1937): 335–341. For a much later work reflecting upon the claim of impossibility of 'Indian philosophy' see A.R. Wadia's "Can Indian and Western Philosophy be Synthesized" (1955). Also see, the first part of Rajendra Prasad's "Tradition, Progress, and Contemporary Indian Philosophy" (1965) for an attempt to answer what 'Indian philosophy' had begun to mean for Indian Anglophone intellectuals by the 1960s. Also, Halbfass', *India and Europe: An Essay in Philosophical Understanding* (1990).

[6] See for instance the review of this work by H.D. Griswold, in *The Philosophical Review*, 9: 4 (1900): 432–435.

[7] See for instance John Dewey's (1951) and George Santayana's "On Philosophical Synthesis" (1951). Books introducing 'Indian philosophy' like those by M. Hiriyanna, Radhakrishnan, and Surendra Nath Dasgupta also received a fair share of critical appraisal, for instance see; Nathaniel Schmidt's review in *The Philosophical Review* (1925).

seen in the corpus of writings during that period, entangled and engaged in what I call the drawings of *critical-parallels* between the east and the west and was largely confined to what I call philosophizing within the 'East–West' paradigm.[8]

Very few Indian Anglophone philosophers steered clear of this paradigm, and those who did almost appeared in the Indian philosophical scenario after the 1930s when logical positivism and philosophy of language had secured itself a respectable place in the philosophy circles in Oxford and Cambridge, casting their shadows on the dominant trend of Idealism that ruled prior to them there. Amongst the first few of these philosophers was Ghanshyam Nevandram Mathrani.[9] In fact,

---

[8] For a selected representative corpus of writings of Indian intellectuals during the colonial period, see Bhushan and Garfield (2011). The book provides a good selection from some of the major Anglophone Indian thinkers during the colonial period. For a quick representation of the various views on the fruitfulness of the East–West encounter, one can read perspectives offered on the matter by some of the leading philosophers of both the 'East and West' in the journal *Philosophy East and West* under a common title, 'On Philosophical Synthesis.' As a representative of the seriousness with which such 'East–West' comparative studies were undertaken, see, Raju and Shastri (1937).

[9] Ghanshyam Nevandram Mathrani [1914–1994(?)] did his schooling in Shikarpur and Sukkur, (now in Pakistan) and his Higher Secondary College at Karachi. In 1934, he joined Fergusson College (Pune) for his Honours in Philosophy. He then joined Cambridge for the Moral Sciences Tripos (Metaphysics and Ethics) in 1936 with John Wisdom as his personal supervisor and on completion of the course; he spent a year at Leeds University pursuing a post-graduate course in Education before returning to India in 1939. Apart from John Wisdom, he was a direct student of G.E. Moore, C.D. Broad and A.C. Ewing. Wittgenstein permitted Mathrani to attend the series of private lectures delivered by him in Cambridge during 1937 (this lecture series was not open to all). Mathrani who was familiar with both the *Blue Book* and the *Brown-Book*, apart from the *Tractatus Logico Philosophicus*, was also instructed by Wittgenstein himself to that extent. In fact, as Mathrani has disclosed, he had a copy of the *Brown-Book* typed for himself through a typing firm at Cambridge (This can be testified from the fact that he has provided quotes from the *Brown-Book* in his book on Wittgenstein published in 1940, though the *Blue* and the *Brown Books* were still unpublished then).

On his return in 1939, after having 'met Professors of Philosophy of Alighar, Allahabad, Benaras and Dacca Universities' and also having attended the annual session of the Indian Philosophical Congress (December 1939, Hyderabad), he 'formed the general opinion that the new Cambridge-Philosophy or the Vienna School of Philosophy was hardly known in India [and that] many of the Philosophy teachers had not even heard the name of Wittgenstein.' Thus, to introduce Wittgensteinian philosophy, Mathrani wrote and published, perhaps the first book to be ever written on Wittgenstein, in 1940, titled *Wittgensteinian Philosophy or Studies in the New Cambridge-Philosophy*. We can, however, be assured that the date of its publication could not be later than 1940 from the fact that during the annual session of the Indian Philosophical Congress in 1940 held at Madras, both A.R. Wadia the then Chairman of the Executive Committee of the Indian Philosophical Congress and Surya Narayan Shastri, the then General Secretary of the Indian Philosophical Congress, had a copy of the book with them, based on which Surya Narayan Shastri, requested Mathrani (1948), who was then teaching Philosophy and Logic at Chellasing and Sitadas College at Shikarpur, to lead the Symposium on 'Is the Unverifiable Meaningless' during the next Indian Philosophical Congress session at Aligarh in December 1941, a theme which had been addressed by Mathrani in his book. Apart from the above-mentioned book, he wrote a number of essays that were published in 1991 as an anthology titled, *Philosophy of Wittgenstein*. He also wrote a book titled *Studies in Inductive Logic*. These, to the best of my knowledge, constitute the corpus of his works. Though he mentions in his essay *Wittgenstein and Wisdom* (1968) about a book of his published in 1944, no such work came up during my search and I have begun to conclude that he perhaps meant to refer to his 1940 book.

when one speaks of the introduction of the Cambridge tradition of 'linguistic philosophy' in general, and Wittgenstein and logical positivism in particular, in the context of the Indian philosophy academia, the name of Ghanshyam Nevandram Mathrani would be the first that should come to our mind.[10] Apart from the fact that he was the first individual to put a conscious effort to systematically introduce the Wittgensteinian approach to philosophy to the philosophy academia in India, he consistently, and in fact almost exclusively, wrote on themes pertaining to Wittgensteinian philosophy and the positivist's approach to language, right from the beginning of his professional career in 1940, when most of his academic contemporaries were dominantly philosophizing within the East–West paradigm.

9.2 The Road not Taken: The Spirit of Scepticism

What makes Mathrani's philosophical journey striking is his unwavering philosophical alignment with Wittgensteinian approach to philosophical problems, which in a sense, could not have been at home with the kind of philosophical approach and the philosophical engagements that were prevalent in India then. The framework of idealism in general and the themes pertaining to 'consciousness' dominated the philosophical thoughts of the Anglophone Indian intellectuals in the first half of the 20th century in India. By and large, the period can be characterized in terms of its philosophical engagement with issues within the framework of the East ('Indian Philosophy' in general and Vedānta in particular)—West (Kant, Hegel, Bergson, Bradley) paradigm,[11] which was, by far, the central preoccupation of the philosophy academia in India during the last 5 or 6 decades of the colonial era.[12] In contrast to this, Mathrani's early writings (1940–1955) are exclusively confined to engagements with the works of philosophers such as Russell, Wittgenstein, Moore, Wisdom, Ayer and Carnap. Further, though his later writings (1955 onwards) are more inclined towards the exposition of his own philosophical convictions on the nature of propositions, values and religion (apart from his works on Descartes and Leibniz), these essays on values and religion depart significantly from the then dominant trend in India in the light of the fact that he manages to stay aloof from philosophizing within the 'East–West' paradigm, and as far as my knowledge goes, Mathrani never aligns himself with a specific thinker or a school of 'Indian Philosophy' as such. His essays are suggestive of the fact that he was not at home with 'comparative philosophy.'

---

[10] Though, this is hardly the case. In fact, his works are hardly in circulation now and despite all attempts, we remain clueless about his exact date of demise. The last refuge that could have thrown light on the matter was his service book, maintained at Ismail Yusuf College where he retired from, which I was informed, has been unfortunately lost in a fire.

[11] The notable digressers here are Sir Muhammad Iqbal and Shankar Ramachandra Rajwade, both of whom engaged with the philosophy of Friedrich Wilhelm Nietzsche.

[12] This preoccupation managed to hold sway for a few more decades post-Independence and firmly established itself into the area of 'comparative philosophy', a domain that saw its birth in India during the colonial period.

Further, unlike most of his contemporaries who engaged in the East–West Paradigm, and for whom the major source of influence stemmed from the philosophies of Kant, Hegel, Bergson and Bradley, Mathrani's philosophical roots, as he himself acknowledges (1991: ix, xvii–viii); were grounded in the works of people such as Moore, Wittgenstein, Wisdom and Broad[13] and well anchored within the early developments in analytic philosophy in Cambridge, revolving around the primacy of language. In particular, Wittgenstein and Wittgensteinian philosophy exercised an immense sway over Mathrani's philosophical insights. The kind of empiricism that echoes throughout the *Tractatus*, as well as its much refined form in the *Philosophical Investigations*, undeniably influenced and resonates in almost all of Mathrani's writings. Given this philosophical alliance of his, one can, without much effort, imagine Mathrani's difficulty in aligning himself to the philosophical debates that much of his contemporaries were engaged in. This difficulty becomes even more pronounced since following the Wittgensteinian mode of analysis, he upholds the philosophical position that *most*[14] of the metaphysical statements are 'meaningless utterances', emerging out of the philosopher's negligence towards language; a stance that will be explicated in the present essay.

A radical position such as the one propounded by Mathrani that declares most of the metaphysical propositions as meaningless, within the ambit of the philosophy academia in India during the first half of the 20th century, was bound not to find many appreciators, nor would it have managed to garnish much attention since idealism, the dominant trend then, and the issues of traditional metaphysics and epistemology were what most of Mathrani's contemporaries philosophized about.[15] Further, Mathrani's specific stance on the nature of metaphysical proposi-

---

[13] C.D. Broad too taught Mathrani, though as Mathrani states, Broad was then seen as someone who 'represented the old type philosopher' (the speculative tradition) as opposed to the then dominant trend of 'analytic philosophy' (1991: ix). It was, however, Broad's distinction between 'object of thought' and 'the act of thinking' that played a central role in Mathrani's formulation of 'logical emergents' in the latter half of his philosophical engagements; a notion, that he believed, took him further than both Wittgenstein and Wisdom, as far as the philosophical position pertaining to the function of philosophy and the status of metaphysical propositions were concerned. It is also important to note that this Broadean distinction played a crucial role in Mathrani's divergence and his declared differences with the philosophical positions advocated by both Wittgenstein and Wisdom as found in his 1955 Address at the Nagpur Session of the Indian Philosophical Congress titled 'A Positivist Approach to Religion.' This philosophical shift in Mathrani's thoughts culminated into his 'Nature of Philosophical Statements' (presented in a Symposium of the Indian Philosophical Association held at Pune in 1959) and 'Wittgenstein and Wisdom' (presidential address delivered at the 17th Annual Session of the Indian Philosophical Association held at Pune in 1968) where the shift and the theory of 'logical emergents' is more explicitly argued out, the details of which we shall consider in Sect. 9.5 of the essay.

[14] This *qualified* rejection of metaphysical statements is of some importance as will be explored and elucidated later in the essay (Sects. 9.3 and 9.4).

[15] In fact, A.C. Ewing in his report on the Indian Philosophical Congress of 1950 (Jubilee IPC) registers his surprise to find philosophers in India still largely under the influence of metaphysical idealism and that 'most students are still brought up on Bradley to a large extent', see A.C. Ewing (1951). That this was the dominant trend is also evident from the proceedings and the Presidential Addresses of the Indian Philosophical Congress. See, for instance, the four volumes of Presidential addresses laboriously compiled by S.P. Dubey and published by the ICPR.

tions was itself based upon a distinct philosophical orientation that he had towards the constitutive function of philosophy, which in retrospection, could have significantly contributed to the difficulty of carving out a noticeable space for the kind of philosophical insights and position that he held and argued for, within the academic space of philosophy in India then. Mathrani's philosophical engagement was embedded within the new trend of philosophizing that had begun to dominate the philosophical arena of Cambridge from the early part of the 20th century, which today, following Gustav Bergmann[16] is characterized as the *linguistic turn* in Philosophy—a new revolution in Philosophy that had, as Mathrani himself concedes, not yet reached India by the 1940s (Mathrani 1940: B, 1). Hence, the *spirit of scepticism*[17] towards the philosopher's use of language, if not towards language as such, was not dominant, if not completely alien, to the Anglophone Indian intellectuals then. Though it was this *spirit* that legitimized his philosophical stance and was central to his works, it was, however, unavailable and unfamiliar to many then in the academic philosophical scene in India.

In fact, Mathrani's first work which was published in 1940 with the title *Studies in Wittgensteinian Philosophy, Or Studies in the New Cambridge-Philosophy*,[18] was

---

[16] Writing in 1964, Gustav Bergmann coined the phrase 'the linguistic turn' in his book *Logic and Reality*, as a label of the brand of philosophy that largely developed in Cambridge during the first half of the 20th century. However, this mode of characterization was made popular by Rorty through his adoption of Bergmann's characterization in his anthology published in 1967 which was itself titled *The Linguistic Turn: Recent Essays in Philosophical Method*.

[17] Both the 'ideal language philosophers' as well as 'ordinary language philosophers' (sometimes also referred to as *Cambridge-Philosophy* and *Oxford Philosophy*, respectively), whatever their disagreements, agree minimally on the thesis that philosophical problems arise by virtue of the manner in which philosophers understand and use language in their discourse. It is this minimal thesis that I am here referring to as the *spirit of scepticism*.

[18] It must be noted here that though the cover of this book only bears the title 'Wittgensteinian Philosophy', the title-page has the above-mentioned elaborate title. Two probable reasons for this discrepancy (that was informed by an old publishing house in Pune) are: a. to reduce the cost of prints, since coloured printing of book covers those days were charged depending upon the number of words appearing on the cover and the number of colours that were to be employed, while the author could take the liberty of more words in the title-page, the page that was always printed in black and white. The modesty in the use of colours (a green background with golden lettering is suggestive of cost reduction measure) is suggestive of such a measure to bring down the overall cost of the book to make it affordable. The book was priced at a modest One Rupee. The other possible reason for the shortened title on the cover of the book could be due to the aesthetic aspect, since the mechanism that were employed in printing those days would have made the cover of the book look clustered or would have compromised on the font size used. Whatever be the reasons, it is certain that the title of the book was *Studies in Wittgensteinian Philosophy Or Studies in the New Cambridge-Philosophy* since Mathrani himself refers to it thus in his other essays. For instance, see his essay 'Wittgensteinian Method' in his *Philosophy of Wittgenstein* (1991: 38). Further, the book when republished in 1990 retains the same title. His *Studies in Wittgensteinian Philosophy Or Studies in the New Cambridge-Philosophy* will however be referred to as *Wittgensteinian Philosophy* from here onwards. As an aside, it is worth mentioning that this is perhaps, as K.T. Fann acknowledges in his letter dated 25.1.72, to Mathrani, the first book to be ever written on Wittgenstein.

intended to 'introduce the new philosophy of Cambridge[19] [that had] not yet sufficiently travelled to [Indian] Universities and Colleges' (1940: 8). However,
Mathrani's text is much more than an introduction to the philosophy of Wittgenstein.
The text is more importantly, as suggested by the title itself, an exposition of a new
way of *doing* philosophy in accordance with Wittgenstein's views on the method and
purpose of philosophy. It was thus not only an introduction to a thinker called
Wittgenstein but also, and in an important way, an introduction to a new method of
philosophizing, namely that of *linguistic analysis*; a method that took centre stage in
the Anglo-American philosophical world for a major part of the 20th century.

In other words, Mathrani's project of introducing Wittgensteinian philosophy
was a prescription couched in an exposition of a philosophy that demanded his contemporaries in the Indian philosophy academia to 'do' philosophy in a mode other
than in ones that they were engaging with. The legitimacy and seriousness of this
demand was undeniably lost without the participation of his contemporaries in the
spirit of scepticism. The demand posed by Mathrani was surely not an easy one to
either shoulder, or commit oneself to, especially for those engaged in philosophizing within the East–West paradigm, because it required an overhauling of one's
entire attitude towards the function of philosophy and consequently threatened to
undermine the very underlying premise of such a paradigm of philosophical
engagement, namely that, the function of philosophy was to uncover ultimate nature
of reality; a premise that, as Mathrani contends, legitimizes all forms of traditional
philosophical engagements (1991: 40). Those engaged within the East–West paradigm, irrespective of the camp they belonged to, would necessarily presuppose the
validity of this premise, and thereby engage, in all sincerity and earnestness, to
argue for the legitimacy of the grounds of these discovered truths in one's philosophical tradition and possibly highlight the similarity or the dissimilarity of the
truths discovered in the tradition of the significant-other; or even argue out the
appropriate method to unravel these truths. Mathrani's demand on the contrary challenges this very premise by persuading his contemporaries to adopt the spirit of
scepticism and tune oneself to the proposed philosophical attitude that understands
the function of philosophy as not engaged in the uncovering of truths but rather to
'analyse the already known truths.' That is, Mathrani's proposed mode of 'doing'

---

[19] One can say from the privileged position of 'today', in retrospect, that what Mathrani speaks
of here as 'the Wittgensteinian Method' or the 'New Method of Cambridge' is the method of
'linguistic analysis.' Mathrani writes "… I shall say something in general about this new school
of thought. But before I proceed I may as well mention something about the important members
of this school. Ludwig Wittgenstein is the founder and the guiding star, Professor G.E. Moore is
more or less a Wittgensteinian philosopher, though he has developed his ideas independently. Mr.
John Wisdom and George Paul are Wittgenstein's direct disciples; and then there are so many
who have been influenced by him directly or indirectly" (1940: 1).

Thus, though his book which intends to introduce the philosophy of Wittgenstein, nevethe-
less, discusses at length the writings of philosophers like Wisdom, who he claims, are amongst
those who have completely adopted the Wittgensteinian method or from the writings of Ayer or
Carnap, who he claims, and rightly so, are amongst those who are influenced in the formulation
of their philosophical position by the early work of Wittgenstein.

philosophy upholds the function of philosophy to be *clarification of thoughts*, rather than the discovery of 'comprehensive truths about the universe as a whole'[20] (1991: 40). With the underling spirit of scepticism towards the philosopher's use of language as the driving force, the envisioned task of the philosopher for Mathrani was thus to analyse the truths that are available to her from various quarters, particularly those problematic ones that emerges from the domain of 'traditional speculative' metaphysics (1991: 40), in order to show that the genesis of the problematic emerges by virtue of the philosopher's misunderstanding of language itself. Mathrani championed in and was perhaps the first in the philosophy academia in India to advocate this method of philosophizing. Thus, very early in the history of Wittgensteinian scholarship, Mathrani seems to be clear that Wittgenstein's contribution to philosophy is not a theory or a set of theories but rather a method (a theme that later managed to generate much debate within the circles of Wittgensteinian studies after the publication of *Philosophical Investigations* in 1953). It is worth highlighting that Mathrani, thus, is amongst the first Indian thinkers, who unlike his contemporaries aligned himself with a *method* of *doing* philosophy rather than aligning himself with a thinker or a 'philosophy' as such. This peculiar alignment of his to a *method* of philosophizing is what enables him to steer clear off the East–West paradigm, since the responsibility shouldered by this envisioned new-age philosophy does not necessitate him to distinguish traditions of philosophies since he brings under the ambit of his concern any claim of 'comprehensive truth', irrespective of the tradition from where it emerges, and undertakes a study of the various traditional problems in an attempt to clarify where 'the philosophers of the old were misled'[21] (1940: 147). Hence, the adoption of the spirit of scepticism towards the philosopher's use of language does not in fact engage with 'truths' per se, but with the more underlying category of *meaning* insofar as it attempts to *clarify* the meaninglessness of certain philosophical theses. In the light of this, Mathrani holds that understanding language becomes the 'sacred duty' and the primary engagement of the philosopher since language is where 'meaning' finds its home.

---

[20] Mathrani contrasts such 'comprehensive truths' with the 'partial truths' of a scientist, whose truths make a claim to uncover only certain aspects of the universe. In fact, Mathrani holds that the 'traditional philosopher assumes the role of a superior scientist' (1991: 40).

[21] Mathrani holds such an undertaking of the study of traditional metaphysical systems to be the constructive aspect of the new-age philosophy, but notes that unfortunately "it is a fashion among Cambridge Wittgensteinians to remain ignorant about the traditional metaphysical schools" (1940: 147) and hence the Wittgensteinian method in its actual practice remains, by and large, 'both empty and blind' (1940: 146) since those who uphold it have no constructive programme as such, by virtue of their ignorance of traditional systems. That Mathrani himself took this constructive programme seriously is suggested by the fact that he undertook an extensive study of the works of Descartes and Leibniz, which led to two critical essays on Descartes, *Descartes' Ontological Argument* and *Descartes Idea of 'God as the cause of his God-Idea': A Critical Analysis*, wherein he argued that the whole of the Cartesian proof suffers from the confusion pertaining to meaning of the term 'idea' followed by a critical essay on Leibniz titled *Leibniz's Concept of Monad*, wherein he argued that Leibniz's philosophy is based on the misuse of the term 'perception.' Mathrani also undertook the analysis of *Advaita Vedānta* which we shall later briefly deal with in this essay (Sect. 9.3).

This essay explores Mathrani's solitary philosophical journey through his works to bring to light the *assimilation*[22] of the tool of linguistic analysis as it was then

---

[22] I am of the opinion that in the context of the introduction of Western thought in India, the complexity involved in the course of introduction and the consequent reception is augmented by the fact that the introduction of a 'new' or 'foreign' concept/tool/tradition is not merely confined to the concept, concept/tool/tradition. What makes a concept 'new' or 'foreign' during their time of its introduction within a 'different environment' is precisely the philosophical climate that the concept owes its genesis to. To receive a concept is thus to receive the whole package, the *form of life* in which it is embedded, the connotation it has, and the function it fulfils within a particular world view. In other words, to receive a concept is thus to receive its rule of engagement in the nexus of its philosophical climate. The very qualification of philosophy as 'Western' or 'Indian', or 'Chinese' or 'African' is highly suggestive of the fact that philosophical concepts are largely interwoven with one's 'world view.' Hence, the reception of a concept involves the reception of not merely the concept but also the world view in which the concept finds a place for itself. Thus, appropriating Wittgenstein here, one could say that *to receive and understand a philosophical concept is to receive and understand its form of life and its rules of engagement therein*. This entails that the degree of variance between the world views consequently informs the mode and the degree of a fruitful reception of a 'new' concept. In the context of the introduction of Western philosophy in India, as can be imagined, the two dominant trends within the 'East–West' paradigm were both related with the orthodox retaining of the dominance of one's own world view. Such retention is enabled primarily by virtue of the fact that philosophy as a discipline is much more accommodative of different, and sometimes even opposing positions, about the same object of enquiry. Thus, some stuck to the world view offered by the west while engaging with ideas from the east, while some stuck to the world view offered by the east while engaging with ideas from the west, and as history informs us, the balance was much tilted towards the former for various reasons that come into operation within the structures of colonialism.

But, there is also a possibility to appropriate the introduced concept/tool/tradition and use it within one's own philosophical climate. This, however, demands the skill of playful engagement with this understanding. It must, so to speak, sink in and percolate the veins of its newfound body. The process of reception thus is also an engagement in the sense that the receiver is not a Lockean *tabula rasa*, but has his/her own philosophical climate in which the new concept is to be received. It, therefore, implies an internal engagement within the folds of the receptor or the receiver too. Hence, it not only implies a politics of recognition, but also a politics of intellectual space and craftsmanship of merging world views too. Thus, the demand of a successful reception of a 'new' concept requires the understanding of both the world views, that is, the one where the concept finds its origins and the other of the receiver. Intellectual such as Krishna Chandra Bhattacharyya (1984) recognizes this demand very early as is evident in his *Svaraj in Ideas,* a lecture he delivered sometime between 1928 and 1930 to the students of Hooghly College, where he stress the importance of understanding one's own tradition as an important aspect of assimilating ideas from the West. It is perhaps the arduous nature of this demand that makes such a reception a rarity and hence lacking. It is this lack that Rajendra Prasad highlights within the Anglophone philosophical community in India in his 1965 essay titled *Tradition Progress and Contemporary India.* [However, I must also note that there have been philosophers who seem to completely deny such a thesis of an umbilical relation between a concept and the world view. I have in mind here S.S. Barlingay who was one of the key figures during the third quarter of the 20th century in the propagation of Analytic philosophy and Logic in Western Maharashtra at the least, and who holds the view that "… Philosophy is philosophizing. It is neither Indian nor non-Indian. It is not determined by geographical Boundaries" (1998: 1). A similar view was expressed by Daya Krishna during a personal interaction I had had with him.]

However, within the ambit of the position of holding an umbilical relation between the concept and a world view, the apparently simple claim of Indian intellectuals during the colonial regime as not merely engaging in 'Western' philosophy but fruitfully so, is to implicitly acknowledge this complex process of reception as a dual engagement—both at the level of an engagement without as well as within to have taken place. Instances of this can be found in Krishna Chandra Bhattacharyya and Ghanshyam Nevandram Mathrani.

developing in the Anglo-American philosophical circles in an attempt to philosophically engage with problems of philosophy irrespective of its geographical origins.

9.3 The Wittgensteinian Turn: Mathrani's Analysis of Language

However, the spirit of scepticism that Mathrani invites his contemporaries to partake in is not in itself a baseless presupposition or a dogmatic faith, but is deeply rooted in the analysis of language as a system of signs and symbols and as it unfolds itself in the modes in which we employ them. Mathrani lucidly explicates the analysis of language in the first half of his *Wittgensteinian Studies* justifying the basis of this spirit of scepticism.

Mathrani argues that on analysis one realizes that language operates through the dual modes of 'hard language' and 'fluid language', a division that is based on the nature of symbols that constitute them. The symbols that constitute the former, "do not refer to anything outside themselves, that is, they do not stand for or signify anything other than themselves" (1940: 18) like the symbols constituting the language of the logician and the mathematician (1940: 18). While on the other hand, the symbols that constitute the latter mode, namely 'fluid language', lay a 'claim to or at least are taken to be claiming to refer to something outside themselves' (1940: 18). Thus, the "language of the common man, of the scientist, of the historian, of the poet, of the philosopher, of the theologian and of the mystic may be said to be fluid languages" (1940: 18) insofar as their use of symbols do not confine themselves in relating a symbol with other symbols within a system of symbols alone, but rather claim to relate to something external to the system of symbols. Further, on the basis of the various *functions of expressions* (use of symbols) suggestive of reference external to the symbol, Mathrani analyses fluid language under the three broad aspects of the *descriptive*, the *emotive* and the *symbolic*. This is not to suggest that for Mathrani, these three aspects or modes are 'separate parts of the fluid language, but are [rather] conjunctive or coexisting functions of it' (1940: 18). Such an analysis allows Mathrani to construe a notion of language that is much more inclusive and accommodative than the Tractarian notion of language[23] which, Mathrani holds, limits the boundaries of language to the assertion of external facts alone (1940: 21, 41–47) by imposing a prior limit to the use of symbols and confining symbols to the first aspect of Mathrani's categorization, namely the *descriptive*.

---

[23] The formulation of such an accommodative view of language was largely informed by Wittgenstein's changed stance of 'same-level analysis' which he had begun to develop in his *Blue and Brown Books* and later concretized in his *Philosophical Investigations*. Though the *Philosophical Investigations* was not yet available to Mathrani, he was well acquainted with the *Blue and Brown Books* and informs us that the new theory of meaning was known as the 'language role theory' then within circles of Wittgensteinians in Cambridge in contrast to the earlier Tractarian thesis of meaning. These are today known to us as the 'use theory' and the 'picture theory' of meaning, respectively.

Elaborating upon these three aspects of 'fluid language', Mathrani places expressions that pertain to descriptions, including questions that seek or assume descriptions, under the descriptive mode of fluid language. Expressions that "involve a representative reference to *reality*, [where the notion of] 'reality' does not merely [imply] external reality [or the physical, but includes] the mental [i.e. pertaining to descriptions of the mind] and the spiritual reality" (1940: 19) are descriptive in their aspect. Thus, both the expressions, 'There is a book on the table' and 'I am in pain', though are different varieties of descriptive expressions (1940: 18), they are nevertheless descriptive in nature insofar as both intend to describe or state a *fact* external to the system of symbols used to state it (1940: 18–19). For Mathrani, the difference between these two expressions is based merely on the kind of fact that they intend to express. While the former expresses a representation of a physical state of affairs, the latter expresses a representation of a mental state of affairs (1940: 19). In addition to these, Mathrani holds that "the mystic can make a descriptive statement which may neither refer to physical reality, nor to mental reality but rather refers to what may be called 'spiritual reality.'"[24] Mathrani thus holds that when a mystic intends to describe an experience she had but is unavailable to others; she too is making a descriptive statement insofar as she, in her use of symbols (language), intends to refer to something that is outside the system of symbols employed by her (1940: 19).

Distinguishing these varieties of descriptive aspect of language from the *emotive aspect* of fluid language, Mathrani elaborates that the latter fulfils the task of expressing 'certain emotive states of mind' (1940: 19). They are distinct from descriptive expressions expressing mental facts by virtue of the fact that the *function* of an emotive expression is to express feelings in contrast to a descriptive expression like 'I love Suzanne' which ascertains (or may deny) a certain mental fact. Exclamations and phrases such as 'go to hell!', 'screw you!' are emotive expressions insofar as they express the feelings of the subject making those expressions (1940: 19). Mathrani, of course would not deny that a careful analysis of emotive expressions would inevitably manifest a relation to a certain state of affairs either pertaining to the external world or pertaining to a state of one's mind. This is what he implies when he holds that these modes of fluid language are 'conjunctive' but the function that an emotive expression fulfils, namely of expressing one's feeling, is nevertheless different from the function that a descriptive expression pertaining to a mental fact fulfils, namely of describing or representing a state of affairs pertaining to one's mind. Thus, for Mathrani, "it should be recognized that though conjunctive, they are distinct" (1940: 20) in the light of the functions that these expressions intend to fulfil.

The third mode of fluid language, namely the *symbolic aspect* that Mathrani elaborates, allows for expressions in fluid language where the purpose of the expression is neither to describe a fact nor to express feelings. What Mathrani intends to account for, through this aspect of fluid language, are all our 'formal expressions.' What distinguishes this aspect of fluid language from the symbols of 'hard language' is the fact that unlike the symbols of 'hard language', the symbols of the symbolic aspect of

---

[24] An elaboration on the notion of descriptive statements pertaining to 'spiritual reality' will be taken up in Sect. 9.4 of this essay.

fluid language *can* however be shown to pertain to some fact or the other (1940: 20). Thus, while 'pure symbols' of hard language such as '+', '2', do not have either a direct referent or a fact outside the system of symbolism of mathematics itself, the symbols of fluid language, in contrast, have mediated representations insofar as "we can point out to something real or existent as a 'cause' and something as 'its effect' in the world of facts" (1940: 20).

The explication of these modes of fluid languages allows Mathrani to therefore draw our attention to the thesis that, by and large, philosophical problems are engagements that revolve around the descriptive aspect of fluid language (1940: 21), and his implied assertion that philosophical problems arise when one confuses the symbolism of one aspect of fluid language to stand for the symbolism of some other aspect of it. Mathrani holds that language can be viewed as being 'imperfect [with] its own defects and ambiguities' (1940: 3), insofar as it does not clearly manifest the mode of the expression. That is, the grammatical structure of an expression does not reveal explicitly its logical structure and thereby, it does not explicitly disclose if the expression is descriptive, emotive, or symbolic. Hence, the grammatical structure of an expression does not clearly indicate the nature of the fact it intends to represent or the purpose it seeks to fulfil. Thus,

> … language conceals many similarities and dissimilarities between various expressions … [And while] there are certain sentences which are alike to each other in their grammatical or syntactical construction, the rules of grammar governing their use are [nevertheless] different. In technical terms, they are syntactically similar and logically dissimilar and their logical dissimilarity is concealed by the syntactical similarity between them (1940: 123).

It is, Mathrani argues, "due to this ambiguous nature of language philosophers have fallen into pitfalls which they think are heavenly springs" (1940: 3). Much in tune with what Wittgenstein holds in his *Tractatus*, and then later in *Philosophical Investigations*[25] too, Mathrani holds that more often than not, philosophical problems are nothing more than *language puzzles*. This implies that if the logic of language can be correctly understood, that is, if we understand the varieties and the corresponding nature of the modes of fluid language, most of the philosophical problems would be *dissolved*, for they, on closer examination, would turn out to be mere pseudo-problems and not really deep perplexities.[26] This augments Mathrani's conviction that the primary and the most fundamental business of philosophers is to understand the nature of language itself and to understand how words in fact gather meaning and substantiates the grounds of legitimacy for upholding the spirit of scepticism towards the philosopher's use of language.

---

[25] Wittgenstein holds in his *Tractatus Logico Philosophicus* that '… the reason why these [philosophical] problems are posed is that the logic of our language is misunderstood' (1922/1974: 3). Maintaining a similar stance in his later work *Philosophical Investigations* he holds that '… Philosophy is a struggle against the bewitchment of our understanding by the resources of our language' (1953/2009: 52e, § 109).

[26] However, it must be borne in mind that Mathrani, unlike Wittgenstein, upholds the nonsense of the philosopher to have a positive function. We shall deal with this stand of Mathrani in Sect. 9.4 of the essay.

Mathrani duly acknowledges the fact that philosophers were not oblivion to the question of meaning hitherto (1940: 4). Though he agrees that they indeed have spoken at great length about language and the way in which words come to bear the meaning that it does, his dissatisfaction with the traditional understanding of the nature of language lies with the way in which the very question about language was itself formulated. He contends that their reflections on language are shrouded in the confusion of equating 'meaning' with any other 'adjectival expression.' They failed, Mathrani argues, to see that the question 'what is the meaning of a proposition?' is not akin to questions such as 'what is the length of this stick?', or 'what is the colour of this pen?' Mathrani holds that the difference between the question concerning 'meaning' and questions concerning 'length' and 'colour' skipped the scrutiny of the traditional philosopher because the words 'meaning', 'length' and 'colour' are similar insofar as they are 'adjectival expressions' too (1940: 21–23). Mathrani thus argues that what the traditional philosopher over-looked in this haze of similarity is that 'adjectival expressions' such as 'length' and 'colour' are parts of the things they describe while *meaning* is not a part, in that sense, of a proposition. The distinction, Mathrani argues, would be evident in the realization that 'length' and 'colour' belong to the category of *sensible* adjectives, whereas 'meaning' is not a sensible adjective at all (1940: 22). Mathrani contends that 'meaning' as opposed to 'colour' and 'length' belong to the distinct logical category of '*value* adjective' along with other value adjectives such as 'beauty', 'goodness', 'truth' and 'reality.' He argues that though we do talk about the beauty of things, and of statements being true, or of things being real, but nevertheless, it must be conceded that 'beauty', 'truth' or 'reality' are not parts of the thing they describe. Mathrani contends that unlike sensible adjectives that can be sensibly apprehended by virtue of they being parts of things they describe, there is nothing to be apprehended for value adjectives since 'they are not names of any *existents*, things or their qualities' but are *just* adjectival words we *attach* to certain things (1940: 22–23).

Thus, Mathrani holds "that the only question we can raise about value adjectives is 'why do we attach these names to the respective things?' [and] why do we say, 'this sentence is meaningful', and 'this sentence is meaningless', [or that] 'this picture is beautiful' and so on?" (1940: 23). For Mathrani, questions pertaining to sensible adjectives are thus 'scientific questions' and thereby legitimately demand a discovery of either a relevant sensible *thing* or a sensible part of an object (1940: 22), while questions pertaining to 'value adjectives' are not 'scientific questions' at all but are rather 'criteria-questions, that is, they are questions about the criteria which determine the use of [a specific] value adjective.' Hence "the question 'what is the meaning of a proposition' is a demand for the criterion of meaning, [a] demand for specifying the conditions which should be satisfied in order to that a proposition may be said to have a meaning." (1940: 23)

Mathrani's emphatic insistence upon the difference between 'sensible adjectives' on the one hand and 'value adjectives' on the other makes it possible for Mathrani to shift the emphasis from the notion of 'meaning' to the notion of 'meaningfulness' and thereby enables him to bring about a shift from the *object* of 'meaning' to the 'criteria of meaningfulness' as an alternate point of view to look at 'meaning.' This very shift is what Wittgenstein manages to highlight through the *Brown-Book* and then later, through his *Philosophical Investigations*. But this shift, both Mathrani and Wittgenstein contend, cannot be brought about through a speculative criterion of meaning which is established arbitrarily in isolation from the language that we in fact use.[27] What this shunning of speculative arbitrary acceptance of criterion of 'meaning' does, is that it brings about the necessity to therefore look at the language we in fact use; to look at how meaningfully "words are employed in a language game (1940: 5) [and] ... to find out what we do mean by 'meaning' in [our] ordinary language." It brings to light the insistence that the *criterion* of meaningfulness of an expression has to be located within the meaningful uses of the expression whose meaning is in question. The criterion of meaning has to be unravelled from a situation or situations in which the expression in question in fact bears meaning. Or as Wittgenstein would suggest in his *Philosophical Investigations*, the criterion of meaning of an expression must essentially be captured through the *language-game* in which it is meaningfully employed,[28] or that the meaning of the word must be traced in its *use* (Wittgenstein: 25[e], § 43). Thus, Mathrani contends that the philosopher ought to restrain himself from prescribing a new criterion of meaning and confine himself to the description of the criterion of meaning that is in fact being employed in the general practice of those using the expression meaningfully (1940: 34).

Thus justifying his spirit of scepticism, Mathrani holds that it is due to this turning of a blind eye towards these practiced criteria of meaningfulness of expressions that leads the philosopher astray and covers him in a haze of confused pseudo-philosophical problems. The philosopher, in his attitude of indifference towards these meaning-criteria of expression, tends to overlook the fact that his use of expressions of fluid language, which is his necessary and the only tool for philosophical engagement, requires much more than mere syntactical correctness and that his expression too must conform to the criteria of meaningful usage of such expressions.

In the light of the above criterion of meaningfulness and given that philosophical discourse is, by and large, confined to the descriptive aspect of fluid language, Mathrani contends that in terms of meaningful descriptive expression, "meaning-giving situation of every [such descriptive expression] should be an 'experiential situation' [though] it may be an 'external situation' or a 'mental situation', either actual or possible" (1940: 28). Negligence towards this demand, Mathrani holds,

---

[27] As Mathrani puts it, if "a person says that the essential criteria for a man to be called 'a man' is that he should be six and half feet tall, then according to this definition, many so called men will cease to be called men by him [but] by doing this he will have done nothing [except] that he refuses to call something 'a man' even though in everybody else's eye that thing is a man" (1940: 23–24).

[28] It is this lack of observational perspective that Wittgenstein himself finds missing in the Augustinian conception or the Platonic view of language as he elaborates it in the first five sections of his *Philosophical Investigations*.

has led to the negligence of observance of the necessary condition that descriptive expressions of fluid language, when used, must be done so "in regard to a particular situation, that is, in a sense it must [essentially] describe a situation ... [and that] there should be an actual or possible situation in which that [expression] may be used" (1940: 34). 'Situation' for Mathrani means 'a group of objects or events or activities and their relations.' Mathrani elucidates that the descriptive expression 'I am writing' refers to a 'situation' which is constituted by myself and the activity of writing, while the descriptive expression 'there are two chairs in my room' refers to another situation that is duly constituted by three objects (two chairs and the room) and a particular relation between the chairs and the room (1940: 27–38).

In tune with his analysis of descriptive expression of fluid language, Mathrani holds that the meaning-giving situation of a descriptive expression may either be an 'external experiential situation' which can either be observed, or has the logical possibility of being observed, or it could be a 'mental experiential situation' which can only be apprehended through introspection. It is also the nature of this specific demand levied by descriptive expressions of fluid language that distinguishes it from the symbols of 'hard language' which are non-representational and hence demand a 'symbolic situation' as a criterion of its meaningfulness as opposed to the demand of 'experiential situations' levied by descriptive expressions of fluid language. Thus, Mathrani contends that when we say '$(x + y) \cdot (x - y) = x^2 - y^2$', the meaningfulness of this mathematical expression is provided by the pure symbolic situation within the abstract system of algebra *where it finds a use* while in contrast to this, descriptive situations must always entail a *logically possible experiential situation* (1940: 28). For Mathrani, the idea of a 'logically possible experiential situation' is intrinsically related with the notion of 'describability' through the notion of 'conceivability.' As Mathrani puts it, much akin to Wittgenstein's 'facts in logical space' of the *Tractatus*, 'logical possibility' has no reference to the possibility of its realization but is rather defined in terms of its *conceivability* (1940: 29). Explicating the term 'conceivability', Mathrani states that to conceive *a logically possible situation* is to conceive a situation "whose constituent objects and the mode of inter-relation between them is translatable in terms of familiar experiences" (1991: 145). Thus, when one states that meaning-giving situation of a descriptive expression is a 'logically possible experiential situation', it implies that the situation that the expression must describe a situation, which even if not actual, must be describable in terms of some *actual* situations or situations akin to it. Thus, 'conceivability' for Mathrani is identical to 'description that is actual or, at least, is based on situations that are actual' (1940: 30). Some sense expressions such as 'equations attend meetings' are inconceivable and, hence meaningless.

One can easily uncover the influence of British empiricism upon Mathrani, specially the empiricism of the *Tractatus*, in his formulation of the describability criterion of meaningfulness (1940: 43–44) since the criterion of describability, in a sense, raises the question of the form 'what is it like for the sentence [under consideration] to be true', [were it to be true]? (1940: 31). This is, what was, as is generally accepted in the History of Ideas, appropriated by the logical empiricists like

Moritz Schlick and A.J. Ayer as the central pillar of their thesis of *verifiability* as an alternative criterion of meaningfulness of a proposition. Mathrani, however, admonishes us of the possible danger of equating the *describability criterion* with the *verifiability criterion*. He argues that the former is distinct from the latter insofar as the latter entails an explicit engagement with the notion of temporality while the former does not. In other words, Mathrani clarifies that the verifiability theory implies a demand for the temporal possibility of verification while the thesis of describability only demands the describability of the meaning-giving situation without any demand for its temporal realization (1940: 56). Thus, Mathrani holds that "verifiability is an empirical concept [while] describability is a logical concept"[29] (1940: 56). The pivotal difference, Mathrani holds, is the fine distinction between '*reducing* a concept or idea into experience' and '*analysing* or *translating* a concept into experience', and that while the logical positivists uphold that every meaningful proposition must be reducible to 'experience-born ideas', for the Wittgensteinians it is enough that a meaningful proposition be analysable into 'experiential categories' (1991: 59).

Further, Mathrani argues that the criterion of verifiability confuses 'truth-condition' with 'meaning condition' since meaning and truth stimulate each other. Mathrani argues that in the verification theory, though meaning precedes truth, this precedence is merely chronological since 'logically, in the principle of verification, the criteria of meaning as well as truth are one and the same' (1940: 57–58). However, the describability thesis makes a logical distinction between the two and recognizes the logical priority of the question of *meaning*. The thesis of describability is only a criterion of meaningfulness of an expression, whose truth would be adjudged on the basis of its correspondence with the situation it intends to present (1940: 58).

The novelty of the describability criterion of meaningfulness of an expression, Mathrani holds, lies in the fact *that it is not* a prescriptive theory of meaning but

---

[29] Mathrani puts in tremendous effort to delineate the Wittgensteinian position from the one held by logical positivists like by Ayer and Carnap. In fact, in his first address to the Indian Philosophical Congress at Aligarh in 1941, he emphatically clarifies that while the logical positivists' rejection of metaphysical statements emerge from their thesis that the 'unverifiable is meaningless', for the Wittgensteinians, on the other hand, the criterion of meaninglessness is 'non-describability.' That is to say that though a proposition may be unverifiable, it may nevertheless be analysable in terms of empirical experiences that are describable, and hence could be meaningful (Mathrani 1991: 22). In fact, it is important to note that though Mathrani, as stated earlier, was influenced by the empiricism of the Tractarian kind, his early exposure and knowledge of Wittgenstein's developed position of the *Blue Book* and *the Brown-Book* enables him to look a step ahead of the logical positivists who, Mathrani contends, are trapped within the confines of the *Tractatus*. In fact, he equates his version of Wittgensteinian philosophy (along with Wisdom's) as 'neo-positivism' (1991: 50). Thus, though Mathrani acknowledges that "whatever be the domestic differences between the two schools of positivism, in their foreign policy they are in agreement. They both declare metaphysics to be meaningless" (1991: 51), he nevertheless intends to make it clear that the Wittgensteinians do not confuse, as does the logical positivists, between the criteria of *meaningfulness* and the criteria of *truth*- an emphasis that is central to Mathrani's philosophical pursuit.

rather an explicit formulation of the criterion of meaningfulness that is in fact employed by the everyday language users (1940: 24). The describability criterion viewed in the nexus of Mathrani's elaborate schema of the functions of language that accommodates the 'hard' as well as the various forms of 'fluid' aspects in our use of language, and the movement away from the kind of empiricism upheld by the logical positivists, allows Mathrani to seamlessly move to the view of language in terms of the role it perform in accordance with the criterion of its use. That is to say that the meaningfulness of a proposition is dependent upon the condition of its adherence to a criterion of meaningful employment within a language-game (1991: vii).

The profoundness of philosophical problems, Mathrani claims, are thus, more often than not, pseudo ones arising out of the complete negligence on the part of philosophers to abide by this criterion (1940: 2–3) coupled with the confusion amongst various aspects of expressions in fluid languages.

9.4 The Qualified Rejection of Metaphysics

Mathrani would have surely found it difficult with these philosophical convictions of his to fit into the then prevalent philosophical circles in India, which as noted earlier, was deeply entrenched in engagements that either hinged on, or entailed, certain metaphysical positions. Mathrani's philosophical convictions, on the other hand, led him to emphatically hold that metaphysical statements were products of linguistic confusion (1940: 138) and that even if they were, in some cases, 'penetrative nonsense', they were nonsense nevertheless. Elaborating upon the peculiarity of nonsense produced by philosophers, Mathrani classifies three varieties of 'nonsense' (1940: 8–9).

The first variety is constituted by groups of 'nonsense syllables', such as 'ka' or 'ba' which though are words insofar as they are 'pronounceable groups of letters', yet they have no prevalent *use in language* to describe any possible situation and hence cannot occur as a part of any meaningful expression. The second variety of nonsense, notes Mathrani, is groups of 'nonsense words', such as 'cat up with' or 'hide table things.' Here, though the words can be used in separate contexts to describe certain situations and can be a part of a meaningful expression, nonetheless, when combined together in a certain way, they fail to describe any possible situation and are thereby rendered nonsensical. The third variety, Mathrani notes, is that of *frames without pictures* such as 'Fractions attacked me in the bath room' or 'Equations do not attend race meetings', or 'space and time take tea with sugar.' It is this variety of nonsense, Mathrani contends, that philosophers are prone to produce. This variety of nonsense is peculiar insofar as they are syntactically similar to meaningful expression such as 'Ram attacked me in the bathroom', or 'Smith takes tea with sugar' but they are nonsensical insofar as there are no actual or possible situations when these sentences could be uttered or *used* meaningfully. In other words, Mathrani points out that though they are correct in their grammatical formulation, they do not describe any conceivable situation at all, and hence fail to satisfy the describability criterion of meaningfulness. By virtue of their syntactical similarity with meaningful expressions, the third variety is not explicitly nonsensical as the other two varieties, and has an appearance of a significant expression, and therefore, is the most misleading of all. For Mathrani, these nonsensical expressions are analogous to 'frames without pictures' because unlike a framed picture (the frame symbolically standing for the syntax that encloses the sense or the situation just as the picture is enclosed within the frame), these nonsensical expressions possess mere frames without a picture enclosed within it.

Mathrani contends that when the 'describability criterion of meaning [is applied to], the statements written or made by the so-called metaphysicians of the past and the present, [they turn out to be] meaningless' (1940: 81). These metaphysical statements, Mathrani argues, which in their syntax come across as descriptive expressions, and 'have an empirical air about them', turn out on analysis, to describe no conceivable situations all. Thus, Mathrani contends, that metaphysical statements such as, 'Time is an image of eternity', 'All things are nothing but shadows of eternal ideas which themselves are in spaceless and timeless sphere', 'This world of perception is really an appearance and not a reality' "… both syntactically and intentionally (meaning that those who make such statements claim to state significant truths) resemble ordinary descriptive sentences" without describing anything at all (1940: 81). The metaphysician, and his metaphysical statements, Mathrani holds, is a result of a linguistic confusion that is grounded in the philosopher's ignorance towards the criterion of meaningfulness. Mathrani contends that it is this ignorance or negligence towards the criterion of meaningfulness that leads the metaphysician to wrongly construe and believe that his problems and the solutions to them as being akin to 'scientific' ones thus leading him further to believe that the expressions expressing these discoveries are genuine descriptive expressions about the nature of the world, reality, mind and the like (1940: 82, 102–103).

However, Mathrani's rejection of metaphysics is not as absolute as the one that is entailed by Wittgenstein's standards and does not entail the stance that metaphysical propositions are nonsense best ignored. Mathrani claims, and quite strongly too, that the value of such pseudo-descriptive metaphysical statements lie in the fact that they 'suggest or draw our attention to likeness and differences concealed by ordinary language'[30] (1940: 85). In other words, Mathrani holds that the

---

[30] Mathrani's position of assigning this positive role to metaphysical propositions, as he acknowledges, was largely influenced by Wisdom. Wisdom intended to portray the Wittgensteinian rejection of metaphysics in a positive light through his notion of 'verbal recommendations' and 'linguistic penetration' as argued in his article *Philosophical Perplexity* (1936) wherein he upholds the position that metaphysical blunders made by philosophers due to their misuse of language and their belief in these being descriptive are also essential insofar as these blunders point out various uses and misuses of a word that is concealed by our language. Thus, in a sense, it is precisely the metaphysician's blunder that enables us to *penetrate* into those aspects of language that is concealed by the structures of language enabling recommendations to not fall in the pitfalls that the *concealedness* opens up, thereby recommending us to correct them or, to be careful, at the least.

value of these metaphysical statements, even if nonsense, is that they not only illuminate the fact that language traps us sometimes within its grammatical structure and misleads us into generating nonsense in the garb of illuminating descriptive expressions (1940: 9, 85) but also positively opens up the possibility of a rectification of the symbols of language or the criterion of their usage. Mathrani argues that the linguistic confusions of philosophers engaged in metaphysics by virtue of the syntactical similarities between 'sensible adjectives' and 'value adjectives' in terms of their syntactical appearance *as* adjectival expressions are akin to the confusion amidst which theorists of meaning find themselves, thereby leading them to overlook the logical difference between these terms. On a similar note, Mathrani holds that metaphysicians get trapped in the syntactical similarities between nouns or noun phrases since their logical difference is concealed by the structure of language. For instance, Mathrani argues that the similar syntactical form between existential expressions and predicative expressions gives rise to illegitimate metaphysical formulations pertaining to 'Being.' Mathrani argues, that

> … the sentences 'martyrs exist' and 'Martyrs suffer' both consist of a noun followed by an intransitive verb [thus] the philosopher assumes [that since] the sentence 'Martyrs suffer' implies that suffering is an attribute of martyrs, [likewise, the expression 'martyrs exist' too indicates that existence is an] attribute of martyrs. [This leads the metaphysician] to inquire into the nature of existence as he would inquire into the nature of suffering (1940: 126–127)

without realizing that the words 'suffering' and 'existence', though may occur in the same syntactical place, nevertheless have different usage to describe logically distinct situations. On a grander scale, this confusion is a product of the metaphysician's "superstitious belief that all noun-words functions alike, like generic or proper names [which are] names of certain things or persons, [and] in general may be called entity-names" (1940: 127).[31] Apart from the fact that this superstition has led to the formulation of pseudo-scientific 'what-are questions' pertaining to universals, time, goodness, instinct, sentiment and so on (1940: 127), Mathrani holds that it has also bewitched Indian philosophers to contemplate and make nonsensical statements about 'moon-ness existing in the moon and not in the jar' or have troubled them regarding the question of 'where does the *whole* exist?' or for that matter 'where does many-ness exist?' However, Mathrani contends that these logical blunders of the philosophers, though nonsense, nevertheless point towards the deeper structure of language.

However, the metaphysician, Mathrani claims, is not merely ignorant of the *dissimilar* in symbols of our language. For instance, it is this over emphasis on similarity in symbols of our language, Mathrani argues, that gives rise to the metaphysical problems of 'matter' and 'mind.' Mathrani contends that since "all the objects in the external world are called by one name, 'material objects', even though there are so many differences among them, this induces the philosopher to think that all

---

[31] Mathrani claims that yet another manifestation of this is in the metaphysician's innocent insistence that 'the subject word [of an expression] stands for an entity … [and that] all subject words are entity names' (1940: 128).

the objects are different appearances or forms of one and the same thing" (1940: 129). Similarly, the use of the personal pronoun 'I' in a variety of different purposes in expressions such as 'I am walking', 'I am thinking', 'I am mortal' leads the metaphysician to ignore the fact that the 'I' in the above expressions refers to a body, something other than the body and a yet different thing than the body, respectively. Mathrani contends that its similar occurrence in all these distinct expressions induces the metaphysician to invent a 'transcendental ego' (1940: 130).

In other words, Mathrani's central thrust in the qualified rejection of the metaphysician's claims lies in the fact that the metaphysician fails to distinguish between 'sensible adjectives' and 'value adjectives.' Consequently, the metaphysician, Mathrani argues, fails to recognize that a question pertaining to 'meaning' cannot be formulated and dealt with as one would deal with sensible adjectives, where the 'what is' question is legitimate. The metaphysician, Mathrani contends, fails to realize that questions pertaining to meaning are value-questions that permits only criteria-questions or the 'when is' questions as legitimate ones. Thus, the metaphysician illegitimately raises the question, "What is the meaning of the 'I'?" when he can only be legitimately raising the question "When can I use the word 'I' meaningfully?" Mathrani holds that criteria-questions would invariably lead us to describe a conceivable situation when the word can be used as a symbol to describe a conceivable situation. He holds that the metaphysicians overlook this fact about 'meaning-questions' and are led astray by language in a quest for entities referred to by the word 'I.' Thus, Mathrani insists that majority of the so-called central questions of the metaphysicians are linguistic confusion arising out of their complete ignorance about the nature of language but it is precisely because of their blunders that we come to understand the concealedness of language.

Mathrani argues that it is this ignorance when coupled with the central preoccupation of the metaphysician, namely their engagement with the 'discovery' of 'comprehensive truths about nature of reality', that leads the metaphysician to conjure up entities when there exists none. Mathrani holds that the metaphysician mistakenly believes that his quest for truth is akin to the scientific quest and therefore, a quest for discovery of entities and their nature leading him to generate descriptive statements, which in fact describe no conceivable situation at all (1940: 102).[32]

---

[32] To highlight this highly confused state of affairs of the metaphysician, Mathrani draws our attention to the metaphysician's engagement with the notion of 'reality.' Mathrani contends that the "one thing common between all systems of metaphysics ... is [that] the object of all is to determine the real as distinct from the apparent or unreal" (1940: 103). The root of the metaphysician's confusion, Mathrani holds, is that the metaphysician takes the terms 'the real' and the 'the apparent' as noun-expressions of either generic or proper noun which leads the metaphysician to talk about reality 'as if it were the name of a thing' (1940: 104). Thus, the metaphysician treats 'the real' and the 'the apparent' as sensible adjectives like 'blue', 'yellow', 'tall' or 'short.' He fails to realize that adjectival expressions like 'the real' and the 'the apparent', though adjectival expressions are value adjectives and not sensible adjectives, for "the reality of a real thing [is not] a part of the thing as the blue of the blue thing is part of the blue thing ... one can see the blue of a blue thing, but one cannot see the reality of a real thing" (1940: 104). A failure to recognize this distinction also leads to the failure to realize that 'all the value adjectives are external

Vedānta as a philosophical system too, Mathrani argues, gets entangled in the same linguistic confusion as any metaphysical system does. Mathrani contends[33] that the Vedāntins too treat 'reality' as a sensible adjective and thus think "… as if the unreality of the world is like the colour of my table; as by looking at my table I can see the unreality of the world" (1940: 112). For Mathrani, "this sort of talk is symptomatic of linguistic confusion" (1940: 112). Mathrani argues that the Vedāntic stance that their claims about reality are genuine descriptive expressions about the nature of reality is based on the mistaken belief that their entire metaphysical system is based on the analysis of experience (1940: 113). Mathrani claims that this is a mistaken belief insofar as the analysis of the experience in the metaphysical system of the Vedānta is itself set rolling, and directed, by the acceptance of a certain criteria of 'reality' with which the Vedāntin-s operate (though, Mathrani claims that they are obviously unaware of it) (1940: 112). Mathrani holds that the moment one is aware about this operational criteria of reality with which the Vedāntic philosophy operates, then the expressions pertaining to the nature of reality made by the Vedāntin can no longer claim to be descriptive statements about the nature of reality but rather a criterion providing a recommendation of how the word 'reality' ought to be used. Explicating his point further, Mathrani writes that though the claim of the Vedāntin is right insofar as he claims that his beliefs about the nature of reality is indeed based on the "many qualitative similarities between dream experience and waking experience" (1940: 113)

Footnote 32 (continued)

designations of the designated' (1940: 104) that is, we have to have a definition or criteria of employment of these designations before we can in fact use them meaningfully in our expressions. As mentioned earlier, for Mathrani, value adjectives raise issues of usage-criteria rather than referents to stand for these expressions as in the case of the term "'meaning', 'goodness', 'truth', 'beauty', 'Holiness', etc." (1940: 104). Thus, Mathrani argues that 'no philosopher can talk about the reality or unreality of things unless he has a criterion of reality or unreality. [He further argues that] whether anything is real or apparent, whether the world is real or unreal, whether material objects are real or otherwise, whether other minds are real or not, whether Time is real or not, all this can be deduced from the criterion of reality [that the metaphysician first] accepts' (1940: 104). Mathrani's point is of importance here, for he argues that the overlooking of the fact not only leads to metaphysician to wrongly construe his question about 'reality' but also misguides him about the method he is to employ in generating a solution to his ill-constructed question about reality. Given the fact, that his enquiry into 'reality' can be nothing more than a criteria question, his method too cannot be scientific for the quest in a scientific quest relates to sensible adjectives and not value adjectives. The metaphysician is primarily engaged in a deductive reasoning with his initial premise as the criterion of 'reality' which he misconstrues as observational statements about reality. Thus, what the metaphysician overlooks, according to Mathrani is that all metaphysics cannot help but be a deductive system and are not really descriptive expressions based on observation of the world. At best they are inferences based on a particular criterion of the usage of the value adjectives 'real' and 'apparent.'

[33] Mathrani acknowledges that these arguments are based on his understanding of Vedānta through G.R. Malkani's lectures which Malkani had delivered at the Indian Institute of Philosophy, Amalner, (now in Maharashtra, then in East Khandesh) between January and March, 1940 (1940: 112).

provided to him when "reason analyses experience into its 'logical types'", he is nevertheless mistaken insofar as he holds that this analysis alone provides him the needed premises to reach the conclusion about the unreality of the world. The Vedāntin is mistaken insofar as he fails to realize that he has already accepted 'the real is that which cannot be cancelled' as the criterion of reality (1940: 113). It is the acceptance of this criterion that allows the Vedāntin to argue, through his analysis of experience, that "[since] dream is cancelled by waking life ... therefore dream is unreal and since both waking life is of the same logical type as the dream ... therefore, waking life is also unreal" (1940: 113). The Vedāntin, Mathrani holds, fails to realize that his arguments about the unreality of the world, about illusory argument and genuine experience are all based on a criterion of reality without which nobody can make any expressions about reality or unreality of anything (1940: 113).[34]

Mathrani thus holds that unless the metaphysician considers his metaphysical statements, which are merely garbed in a descriptive form, as 'verbal criterion engagements', or a mode to show us or provide us, or to recommend (1940: 12) a criterion of when to, or not to, employ terms like 'real', 'apparent', 'know' or 'self' in our expressions (1940: 98), they would be reduced to sheer nonsense (1940: 95–100).

9.5 Beyond Wittgenstein: Mathrani's 'Logical Emergents'

In fact, Mathrani's *qualified* rejection of metaphysics receives two distinct ramifications, after 1955 when Mathrani begins to focus on the explication and elucidation of the nature of descriptive statements pertaining to 'spiritual reality' and

---

[34] In fact, Mathrani claims that the ignorance about the question of criteria of value adjective words and its treatment as a sensible adjective is in fact responsible for the prevalent use of argument from illusion. The philosopher, Mathrani contends, pays no heed to the criterion of the criterion of the value adjective 'illusion' and thus violates the "rules of grammar which govern the use of 'illusion'", consequently leading him to generate meaningless arguments (1940: 91). Mathrani holds the criterion of 'illusion' is that "in all cases of illusion, there is a possibility of immediate cancellation of the illusory knowledge" (1940: 92). To substantiate his argument, Mathrani writes that "we may recognize three kinds of illusion [as per criterion of the word as used in our language], (i) where the illusory knowledge is cancelled by the knowledge obtained through the same sense organ, at the next moment, or when we go near the object of perception, e.g. mirage. (ii) When the illusory knowledge is cancelled by the knowledge obtained through some other sense-organ. Snake-rope illusion is an instance of this sort. We seem to see a snake in the dark, but when we touch it or try to hear its sound, we find it is not a snake but a rope. (iii) Where only one man or a group of men under special circumstances suffer from illusions. Drunken men sometimes seeing 'pink rats'; this illusory knowledge is cancelled by the knowledge of other men ... But the philosopher so uses the 'illusion argument' that all the sense-organs of all men are always under illusion" (1940: 92). Of course in the process, the philosopher is completely unaware of his violation of the criterion of the usage of the term 'Illusion' as now there is no possibility of its cancellation. Mathrani argues that the same holds for the dream argument as well (1940: 93).

'religious propositions' steadily drawing him away from the strict confines of the Wittgensteinian frame. The first divarication is constituted by his explicit move in his 1955 essay titled *A Positivist Approach to Religion*[35] where Mathrani argues for the possibility of accommodating religious propositions, though *as nonsense*, but nevertheless as a unique variety insofar as they do not function as indicators of any penetrative 'criterion-engagements' of the terms employed therein, but rather through their 'repeated and rhymical' recitations serve as a tool to induce an "experience of feeling of 'piety'" (1991: xii). Hence, Mathrani contends that religious propositions, though nonsense, function as a linguistic tool to deepen our faith, though 'the contents of faith remains as obscure as before' (1991: xiii) and hence cannot be viewed under the category of *descriptive* expressions intended to 'convey thought and information' (1991: 63) but rather should be seen as a sort of *performative* expression. Hence, though Mathrani concedes that religious propositions cannot be treated as 'forms of intellectual cognition', its rejection as *nonsense,* however, he holds, emerges from the confined perspective of viewing the 'fluid aspect' of language as merely fulfilling a descriptive function. Hence, he holds the view that religious propositions must rather be seen as *linguistic nonsense* that leads to 'mental silence [peace] and moral transformation' (1991: 64). Mathrani thus argues that the mystic can,

---

[35] This essay was presented at the Indian Philosophical Congress held in Nagpur and Mathrani declares that the essay was a "'landmark' in the evolution of [his] philosophical thinking" (1991: xii) since the essay marks Mathrani's steady 'departure' from the Wittgensteinian position not in the sense of being 'opposed' to the Wittgensteinian spirit, but in the sense of taking Wittgensteinian thought ahead through modifications to explore 'landscapes', not explored by Wittgenstein himself. Towards this end, Mathrani writes in his preface titled *In Retrospect*, "… for 15 years [from 1940] I was a committed Wittgensteinian … I began my work as a committed Wittgensteinian and developed into an independent and non-aligned analytic writer on Empiricist Philosophy of Contemporary times" (1991: xviii). But I hold that the essay is a 'landmark' because, Mathrani through this essay manages to reconcile two aspects—his inclination towards the *spiritual* and his *Wittgensteinianism*. Mathrani was always inclined towards the spiritual from his early days and his interest in philosophy 'initially began with reading Spiritual Literature', and he declares, he found the 'Biography of Ramakrishna Paramahansa and that of Lord Gouranga-Chaitanyadev Mahaprabhu' which were given to him as readings by his school teacher to 'wean [him] away from Politics' and which Mathrani confesses to have found 'satisfying.' He was also a regular member at the discourses given by Swami Sharvanand of the Ramakrishna Order, at Karachi during his college days in 1932 (1991: i). I was also informed by Ms. Malati Krishnakumar, who was his colleague at Ismail Yusuf College in Mumbai, the Institute from where Mathrani retired, and who was also one of the few close friends that Mathrani had, that Mathrani had disclosed to her that he regularly attended discourses by Sadhu Vaswani during his early days. In fact, even while in England, he was in contact with Swami Avyktanand who was the in-charge of the Ramakrishna-Vivekananda Vedanta Centre in London.

However, Mathrani claims that his "fondness for spiritual literature, particularly biographies of spiritual heroes and their teachings, which fondness [he] had developed during [his] adolescence, came in the way of [his] total acceptance of the view that all metaphysical propositions are meaningless." (1991: vii) It was this internal tension between his being a Wittgensteinian and his spiritual drives that finally found a ground of synthesis in his 1955 essay.

through Sādhanā,[36] 'attain moral transformation' though he can never 'know God' (1991: 69). Thus, though the term 'knowledge' "cannot be applied to what the religious man calls the knowledge of God [since it is] not of the nature of conscious cognition" that can be "meaningfully described in terms of propositional language" (1991: 65), such religious nonsense nonetheless function as a linguistic tool to aid moral transformation and thus, constitute a peculiar and distinct variety of nonsense.

The second divarication in his qualified rejection of metaphysics is shaped by his theory of 'logical emergents' that has its origin in his 1959 essay titled *Nature of Philosophical Propositions*—an essay that was presented at the Indian Philosophical Association in Pune and more elaborately argued out in his Presidential Address titled *Wittgenstein and Wisdom* at the 17th Annual Session of Indian Philosophical Association, also held in Pune, in 1968, where Mathrani argues for three varieties of 'significant and meaningful' propositions, namely 'propositions about *logical correspondents*, propositions about *logical constructions* and propositions about *logical emergents*.' The first variety of propositions is populated by those propositions whose propositional contents correspond or can be mapped unto the factual world. That is, this variety pertains to propositions that *picture* a fact or an 'empirical situation.'[37] The second variety of meaningful propositions that Mathrani recognizes as 'significant and meaningful', under the influence of Wisdom,[38] are those propositions that could be *analysed* into propositions about *logical correspondents* (1991: 180). Once again, Mathrani, contends that both these varieties of propositions dogmatically remain confined within the paradigm of the empirical, and that consequently, both Wisdom and Wittgenstein fail to envision the possibility of other forms of propositions within the discourse on metaphysics that are neither nonsense, nor mere 'verbal criterion engagements' or 'verbal recommendations' but are significant and meaningful precisely because they are 'trans-empirical' insofar as they are propositions pertaining to 'logical emergents' (1991: 108, 180–181). Thus, in agreement with Wittgenstein, though Mathrani concedes that philosophers *do* misuse language and end up in philosophical muddles, and in tune with Wisdom, does uphold that some of these blunders could be 'verbal criterion engagements' revealing the logical structures of language as well, but he nevertheless contends that there is a third variety of propositions that are meaningful and significant propositions, namely propositions about 'logical emergent/emergents.' Explicating the notion of 'logical emergents', Mathrani holds that "propositions about logical emergent/emergents is one which postulates something *unmanifest* as the ground or a plausible causal hypothesis to

---

[36] Mathrani uses the term '*Sādhanā*' to mean 'a systematic effort to know God and become god-like' (1991: 64).

[37] Logical Positivism of A.J. Ayer and Carnap, for instance, confines meaningful propositions to this variety.

[38] John Wisdom coined the term 'logical constructions' and explicated the notion in a series of essays titled *Logical Constructions* published in *Mind* (New Series) during 1931a, b, 1932, 1933a, b. 'Logical correspondents' and 'logical emergents' are, however, Mathrani's neologisms.

explain the manifest data under investigation... and logical emergents can be found in philosophy as well as in science" (1919: xvi–xvii).[39] Mathrani points out that Locke's 'substratum', Freud's 'unconscious' as well as Newton's 'gravity' are examples of logical emergents (1991: vii, 183). Thus, for Mathrani, unlike Wisdom's propositions about *logical constructions* that can be analysed into *logical correspondents*, a "*logical emergent* is traceable to and derived from, but not analysable into logical correspondents" (1991: 107). In his essay *Wittgenstein and Wisdom,* clarifying his neologism 'logical emergent', he explains that the term 'logical' intends to highlight that these reflections are "guided by a sort of logical compulsion involving a logical process" (1991: 184) and thus must be distinguished from the literary imaginations of the poets that are based upon reflections on the empirical too. He further clarifies that the term 'emergents' intend to highlight that "they do not denote or refer to the empirical [but] rather emerge from a reflection on the empirical" (1991: 183). In other words, Mathrani contends that philosophical statements are not necessarily nonsensical and meaningless, "nor are they merely verbal recommendations...[and that] many of the alleged metaphysical propositions, condemned as pseudo-propositions about the fictitious 'trans-empirical' could be shown to be statements about and statements consisting of logical emergents" (1991: 108), or propositions that contain terms indicative of a trans-empirical reality by virtue of the force of logical necessity of explaining the empirical. Thus, Mathrani holds that that one cannot, as a rule, equate metaphysical statements as nonsense because they are about the 'trans-empirical' just as one cannot equate scientific statement as being meaningful because they are statements about the empirical and observable. Mathrani argues that such a stance towards metaphysics would be a dogmatic one and holds both Wittgenstein and Wisdom to be trapped in this 'dogma of the empirical' (1991: 106).

Mathrani's journey that begins with the Wittgensteinian spirit of scepticism in the philosopher's use of language, and under a deep influence of empiricism, and thus with no room for metaphysics, therefore comes to full circle with his thesis of 'logical emergents'—a thesis that is a product of Mathrani's analysis of language under the spirit of scepticism, but provides room for metaphysics as well as the 'trans-empirical' as 'para-logical possibilities.' Mathrani thus holds that philosophers acclimatized with the spirit of scepticism now ought to take up the constructive task of examining metaphysical propositions, not with the preconceived dogmatic notion that they are nonsensical, but rather with an openness that they might just

---

[39] Informed by Broad's thesis 'that mental images or pictures are never the object of thought but merely an aid to the mind in its effort to direct its attention on its object of thought' (1991: 182), Mathrani contends that "those philosophers and scientists who postulate some trans-empirical grounds as explanation of some empirical facts do not claim to have any pictorial ideas of the trans-empirical grounds conceived by them. In such cases also reflection on empirical facts compels the mind to direct its attention towards the possible trans-empirical grounds of the observed facts. If the effort is successful, the thinker does not get any vision of it nor does he get a mental picture of it; he gets a verbal expression, a formulation, a name, a concept ... a logical emergent." (1991: 183).

be meaningful and significant by virtue of the *function* they perform or by virtue of being propositions about *logical emergents* (1940: 147).

What Mathrani however remains true to, throughout this journey of his, is his spirit of scepticism towards the philosopher's understanding of language including the understanding of language offered by Wittgenstein and Wisdom, through whom he imbibed the spirit. Thus in a sense, Mathrani was a true Wittgensteinian insofar as he managed to move beyond Wittgenstein and Wisdom themselves, while remaining faithful to the Wittgensteinian spirit of doing philosophy.

References

Arnold, D. (2004). *Technology and medicine in colonial India*. United Kingdom: Cambridge University Press.

Barlingay, S. S. (1998). *Reunderstanding Indian philosophy*. New Delhi: D.K. Print World Pvt. Ltd.

Basu, A. (1989). Chemical research in India during Nineteenth Century. *Indian Journal of History of Science, 24*(4), 318–328.

Bergmann, G. (1964). *Logic and reality*. Madison: University of Wisconsin Press.

Bhattacharyya, K. C. (1984). Svaraj in ideas. *Indian Philosophical Quarterly, XI*(24), 383–393.

Bhushan, N., & Garfield, J. L. (Eds.). (2011). *Indian philosophy in English: From renaissance to independence*. New York: Oxford University Press.

Bose, M. D., Sen, N. S., & Subbarayappa, V. B. (Eds.). (1971). *A concise history of science in India*. Calcutta: Baptist Mission Press.

Dewey, J. (1951). On philosophical synthesis. *Philosophy East and West, 1*(1), 3.

Dutta, D. M. (1956). India's debt to the west in philosophy. *Philosophy East and West, 6*(3), 195–212.

Ewing, A. C. (1951). Philosophy in India: Note on visit to Indian jubilee philosophical congress. *Philosophy, 26*(98), 263–264.

Gorman, M. (1988). Introduction of western science into colonial India: Role of the Calcutta Medical College. *Proceedings of the American Philosophical Society, 132*(3), 276–298.

Halbfass, W. (1990). *India and Europe: An essay in philosophical understanding*. Delhi: Motilal Banarasidass Publishers.

Irfan, H. S., & Raina, D. (Eds.). (2007). *Social history of science in colonial India*. New Delhi: Oxford University Press.

Jones, W. K. (1989). *Socio-religious reform movements in British India*. Cambridge: Cambridge University Press.

Larwood, C. H. J. (1958). Science in India before 1850. *British Journal of Educational Studies, 7*(1), 36–49.

Mathrani, G. N. (1940). Studies in Wittgensteinian philosophy or studies in the new Cambridge-philosophy. Sind: Prabhat Printing Press. (Reprinted in 1990, Allahabad: Darshana Peeth).

Mathrani, G. N. (1948). *Studies in inductive logic*. Mumbai: Continental Publishing House.

Mathrani, G. N. (1991). *Philosophy of Wittgenstein*. New Delhi: Ajanta Publication.

Metcalf, R. T. (1995). *Ideologies of the Raj*. United Kingdom: Cambridge University Press.

Naidu, B. N. (1996). *Intellectual history of colonial India: Mysore 1831–1920*. New Delhi: Rawat.

Prakash, G. (1999). *Another reason: Science and the imagination of modern India*. New Jersey: Princeton University Press.

Prasad, R. (1965). Tradition, progress, and contemporary Indian philosophy. *Philosophy East and West, 15*(3–4), 251–258.

Radhakrishnan, S. (1928). Indian philosophy. *Mind, new series, 37*(145), 130–131.

Raju & Shastri. (1937). *Thought and reality: hegelianism and Advaita*. London: George Allen and Unwin Ltd.

Rorty, R. (1967). *The linguistic turn: Recent essays in philosophical method*. Chicago: University of Chicago Press.

Sangwan, S. (1988). Indian responses to European science and technology 1757–1857. *The British Journal for the History of Science, 21*(2), 211–232.

Santayana, G. (1951). On philosophical synthesis. *Philosophy East and West, 1*(1), 5.

Sarbadhikari, C. K. (1961). Western medical education in India during the early days of British occupation. *Indian Journal of Medical Education, 1*, 27–32.

Schmidt, N. (1925). *The Philosophical Review, 34*(3), 292–297.

Seth, S. (2007). *Subject lessons: The western education of colonial India*. London: Duke University Press.

Trevelyan, O. G. (1876/1881). *The life and letters of Lord Macaulay*. London: Longmans Green and Company.

Wadia, A. R. (1955). Can Indian and western philosophy be synthesized? *Philosophy East and West, 4*(4), 291–293.

Wisdom, J. (1931a). Logical constructions (I.). *Mind, New Series, 40*(158), 188–216.

Wisdom, J. (1931b). Logical constructions, (II). *Mind, New Series, 40*(160), 460–475.

Wisdom, J. (1932). Logical constructions, (III). *Mind, New Series, 41*(164), 441–464.

Wisdom, J. (1933a). Logical constructions, (IV). *Mind, New Series, 42*(166), 43–66.

Wisdom, J. (1933b). Logical constructions, (V). *Mind, New Series, 42*(166), 186–202.

Wisdom, J. (1936–1937). Philosophical perplexity. *Proceedings of the Aristotelian Society, New Series, 37*, 71–88.

Wittgenstein, L. (1922/1974). *Tractatus logico-philosophicus*, (D. F. Pears & B. F. McGuiness, Trans.). London: Routledge and Kegan Paul.

Wittgenstein, L. (1953/2009). *Philosophical investigations* (G. E. M. Anscomb, P. M. S. Hacker & Joachim Schulte, Trans.). United Kingdom: Wiley-Blackwell Publishing.

Chapter 10
Radical Translation: *S.R. Rajwade's Encounter with F.W. Nietzsche*

Mangesh Kulkarni

Arms upraised, I cry out; but no one heeds my cri de coeur!
Why don't you embrace dharma which alone guarantees artha
and kāma? (Ūrdhvabāhurviroumyeṣca na ca kaśchit śhṛuṇoti
mām|Dharmādarthaśca kāmaśca sa dharmaḥ kiṁ na
sevyate||)
- Attributed to Vidura in The Mahabharata; cited in Tilak
(1950: 64)

Vyāsa

The work of the German literati consisted solely in bringing the
new French ideas into harmony with their ancient philosophical
conscience, or rather, in annexing French ideas without
deserting their own philosophic point of view.
This annexation took place in the same way in which a foreign
language is appropriated, namely by translation.
- Karl Marx and Friedrich Engels (1973: 131)

Abstract This essay presents an account of the way F.W. Nietzsche's ideas were received and interpreted by Shankar Ramachandra Rajwade (1879–1952), a notable Indian philosopher based in Pune. The focus is on the latter's book which contains a Marathi translation of and commentary on *The Antichrist*. Rajwade's intellectual project—informed by his keen desire to bolster the traditional Hindu social order and its philosophical foundation—is presented as an example of 'radical translation' in two senses: It goes to the root of Nietzsche's theoretical argument; and more importantly, it reinvents the German thinker's 'aristocratic radicalism'in an indigenous context.

Keywords *Dharma* · Fascism · Nietzsche · *Nirdvandva* · Rajwade · Translation

M. Kulkarni (✉)
Department of Politics and Public Administration,
Savitribai Phule Pune University, Pune, India
e-mail: mangshra@yahoo.co.in

© Indian Institute of Advanced Study 2015
S. Deshpande (ed.), *Philosophy in Colonial India*, Sophia Studies in Cross-cultural
Philosophy of Traditions and Cultures 11, DOI 10.1007/978-81-322-2223-1_10

Wilhelm Halbfass concludes his study of the philosophical interaction between
India and Europe with the following words:

> Modern Indian thought finds itself in a historical context created by Europe, and it has dif-
> ficulties speaking for itself. Even in its self-representation and self-assertion, it speaks to a
> large extent in a European idiom. This does not, however, mean that the … debate between
> India and Europe has been decided in favor of Europe … The power of the Indian tradition
> has not exhausted itself … The dialogue situation is still open (Halbfass 1990: 375).

Taking these observations as a point of departure, the essay presents an account of
the way F.W. Nietzsche's ideas were received and interpreted by S.R. Rajwade—a
notable Indian philosopher of the late colonial era. The first section provides a
thumbnail sketch of Rajwade's life and *oeuvre*. The second discusses the apparent convergence between his world-view and that of Nietzsche. The third focuses
on Rajwade's book which contains a translation of *The Antichrist* (henceforth
TA) along with a commentary on its author. The concluding section considers the
nature and implications of this philosophical encounter.

10.1 The Making of an Ahitāgni

Shankar Ramachandra alias 'Ahitāgni'[1] Rajwade (1879–1952) was born in a
middle-class, orthodox Konkanastha Brahman family in Pune—a city which was
then part of the colonial Bombay province and is now in the state of Maharashtra.
He grew up and settled down in this city which had been for long a stronghold of
brahmanical culture. After completing his school education, Rajwade joined the
reputed Deccan College. He had to interrupt his studies and enter Government service due to the financial crunch caused by the death of his father in 1902.
However, he resigned after a few years and completed his graduation. He then
chose to live as an independent scholar and completely dedicated himself to intellectual pursuits which he saw as a nation-building activity.[2]

---

[1] The sobriquet *Ahitāgni* means "he who maintains the *agnihotra*, the perpetual, sacred fire."
As a champion of the Vedic tradition, Rajwade maintained the *agnihotra* at the Sanātana Vaidika
Dharma Kāryalaya.

[2] There was a strong element of *noblesse oblige* in Rajwade's conception of his vocation, which
was not uncommon among the Brahman intellectuals of the time. A similar position is evident
in the following remarks of Krishnaji Prabhakar Khadilkar (1872–1948)—Rajwade's contemporary and fellow alumnus of the Deccan College—who was an outstanding playwright, political commentator, and also a close associate of the renowned nationalist leader and scholar, Bal
Gangadhar Tilak (1856–1920):

It is the task of the Brahmans to offer sublime ideas and a lofty mind-set to the people. If the
Brahmans themselves give up this noble task and become selfish, the country is bound to degenerate.

It was because our noble thoughts deserted us, and we came under the sway of a vile mentality
that our independence (*svarāj*) was lost. We have no option but to revive those noble thoughts and
that lofty mind-set and disseminate them throughout the nation (quoted in Khadilkar 1949: 34).

Khadilkar expressed these views in a book review which was published when he was still in
his early twenties. Tilak liked the review and invited its author to write for his newspaper, *Kesari*.
I am grateful to Dr. Meera Kosambi for drawing this passage to my attention.

Rajwade was an accomplished orator and toured widely throughout the country to deliver lectures on philosophical and social themes. His audience seems to have comprised a wide cross-section of Marathi-speaking educated classes. In his younger days, Rajwade had been influenced by Tilak's blend of militant nationalism and conservatism and had even had a short-lived association with hotheads such as the Chaphekar brothers who were sentenced to death for the assassination of W.C. Rand[3] in 1897. But eventually, the lecture tours along with a variety of debates he hosted at his residence were to be his chief mode of direct public engagement.

Rajwade knew English well, but chose to write in Marathi—the regional language that could claim a millennium-long, rich literary tradition—and published almost all his books himself. His writings give ample evidence of a sound training in Sanskrit, a lifelong immersion in the canonical texts of classical Hindu thought, as also a close acquaintance with many religions, Western philosophy, and modern science. Following a dominant strand of the Indian philosophical tradition, many of his writings were cast in an exegetical mode. However, this format should not be taken to indicate an absence of original thinking and it certainly did not prevent Rajwade from expressing unconventional ideas.

Almost all of Rajwade's works reveal an idiosyncratic blend of philosophy, science, and sociopolitical thought.[4] Commenting on them, the German scholar–priest Matthew R. Lederle—best known for his pioneering (and so far unsurpassed) account of philosophical currents in modern Maharashtra—has observed that they "approach the category of strictly philosophical works. Not many books of this type exist in the Marathi language today" (Lederle 1976: 296). Yet, Rajwade seems to have fallen through the cracks of Maharashtra's intellectual

---

[3] An English official who had incurred the wrath of the people on account of the draconian measures he introduced to quell the plague epidemic in Pune.

[4] The first of these was *Gitābhāshya* (1916), a commentary on the first three chapters of the *Bhagavad Gitā*, published only one year after the publication of B.G. Tilak's *magnum opus* on the subject, namely *Gitārahasya*. This was followed by *Nāsadiyasūktabhāshya* Part I (1927)— an exegesis of the *Nāsadiyasūkta* which is a celebrated cosmogonic hymn in the Rig Veda. The three volumes of Part II (of which two deal with sexology) were to appear over the next 22 years. Meanwhile, Rajwade published his only full-length book on Western philosophy, *Nietzschechā Khristāntaka āni Khristāntaka Nietzsche* (1931)—a translation of Nietzsche's *The Antichrist* together with a commentary on the philosopher's life and work. The subsequent four works dwelt on various aspects of Vedic thought and the six *darśanas* or systems that are central to classical Indian philosophy: *Vaidikadharma āni Shaddarshane athavā Chāra Vidyā va Sahā Shāstre* (Ravbahadur Kinkhede Lectures published by the University of Nagpur in 1938), *Sanātana Vaidika Dharmapravachana Māla* (1947), *Şadarśanasamanvaya āni Puruşārthamimamsā* (1949), and *Ishāvasyopaniṣadbhāshya* (1949)—an explication of the *Ishāvasyopaniṣad*. His autobiography—*Ahitāgni Rajwade: Ātmavṛitta*—was published posthumously by Shreevidya Prakashan (Pune) in 1980, but several of his writings on sexology, astrology, and Zoroastrianism remain unpublished.

history and (to the best of my knowledge) there is not a single book or a full-length scholarly article focusing exclusively on his philosophical legacy.[5]

The leitmotif informing Rajwade's intellectual endeavors was his keen desire to defend and shore up the traditional Hindu social order in the face of reformist attacks and to reclaim (what he saw as) the essential message of the Vedas and the Gitā from its later contamination by Buddhism and Śaṁkarāchārya's doctrine of *Advaita* (non-dualism). In a seemingly curious move, he drew on the thought of the great German philosopher Friedrich Nietzsche (1844–1900) to bolster his twofold project. The publication of *Nietzschechā Khristāntaka āni Khristāntaka Nietzsche* was an important outcome of this philosophical encounter.

10.2 The Dialectics of Polarity

It is well-known that many Indian intellectuals of the colonial era were greatly influenced by European thinkers such as Bentham, Mill, Hegel, and Marx, and by currents of thought such as utilitarianism, liberalism, idealism, and socialism.[6] But the ideas of Nietzsche remained somewhat peripheral to the indigenous universe of discourse during this period. So Rajwade's engagement with Nietzsche was exceptional. Two of his important contemporaries who did take a serious interest in the latter were Sri Aurobindo (1872–1950)—savant extraordinaire, who constructed a grand metaphysical edifice on Vedic foundations—and Muhammad Iqbal (1877–1938), the foremost Muslim thinker and poet of modern India.

As Margaret Chatterjee points out, both Aurobindo and Nietzsche were Heracliteans and 'philosophers of the dawn.' They sought to infuse their philosophies with dynamism. But Aurobindo found a disquieting strain of Titanism in Nietzsche (Chatterjee 2006: 16–17). This is evident in his following remark: "Any attempt to heighten inordinately the mental or exaggerate inordinately the vital man,—a Nietzschean supermanhood, for example,—can only colossalise the human creature, it cannot transform or divinise him" (Aurobindo 1989: 722). As for Iqbal, Nietzsche exercised a deep influence on him during his stay in Germany where he earned a doctorate circa. 1908. Naravane (1964: 286) informs us that

---

[5] Even the relevant volume of the most comprehensive Marathi encyclopedia has no entry on S.R. Rajwade. It does, however, contain an entry on Vishwanath Kashinath Rajwade (1864–1926)—a great historian and polymath scholar (Athavale 1989: 717–718). Incidentally, S.R. Rajwade held the latter in great esteem as a like-minded intellectual and dedicated the Marathi translation of *The Antichrist* to his memory—"the only scholar worth his salt in Maharashtra, who personified the spirit of Nietzsche," reads the dedication. For an overview of V.K. Rajwade's intellectual achievements, see Kantak (1990).

[6] A comprehensive history of the intellectual encounter is yet to be written. One way of pursuing such a project would be to focus on specific instances of the larger phenomenon. The present essay may be seen as a modest effort of this kind.

Iqbal saw the philosopher as 'the prophet of irrepressible Life.' He was fascinated by the Nietzschean conception of the *Übermensch*, which inspired his own philosophy of *khudi* (will power or self-affirmation). This is evident in his following celebrated verse: "Endow your will with such power/That at every turn of fate it so be/That God Himself asks of His slave/'What is it that pleases thee?'" (Iqbal 2008: 19). Naravane goes on to argue that Iqbal eventually overcame the German philosopher's 'voluntarist excesses' through Sufism.

Rajwade was familiar with and admired the work of Aurobindo. However, he found the sage's mysticism rather nebulous (Lederle 1976: 305). It is not clear whether he knew of Iqbal. In any case, as compared to these two thinkers, Rajwade's engagement with Nietzsche, which originated in a somewhat late and chance encounter, was far more thoroughgoing. He had studied Western philosophy at the Deccan College under the able if eccentric guidance of Professor F.W. Bain and had been influenced by the uniquely conservative blend of philosophical, socioeconomic, and political ideas propagated by his teacher.[7] But he first came across references to Nietzsche in Tilak's *Gitārahasya* (Rajwade 1980: 296).[8] Rajwade subsequently delved deep into Nietzsche's philosophy and was glad to discover its consonance with Bain's way of thinking (Rajwade 1980: 297).[9]

Bain derived inspiration from Aristotle and believed that the spirit of the Greek thinker's philosophy had found embodiment in the practical activity of the English people whose *summum bonum* consisted in the exercise of power, that is, the realization of the possible.[10] Following the Aristotelian metaphysic of actuality and potentiality, Bain saw the interplay of action and counteraction in all things. He considered action to be constitutive of being and claimed to have discovered the

---

[7] Francis William Bain (1863–1940) was a fellow of the All Souls College at Oxford. He served as a Professor of History and then as Principal at the Deccan College (Pune) until his retirement in 1919. His publications included notable theoretical works such as *Body and Soul or the Method of Political Economy* (London: James Parker & Co., 1894) and *On the Realisation of the Possible and the Spirit of Aristotle* (London: James Parker & Co., 1899).

[8] The references to Nietzsche in Tilak (1950) are as follows. In a footnote, Tilak argues that the doctrine of rebirth was not confined to Hinduism, but was also found among the Buddhists; even the atheist Nietzsche had affirmed the doctrine through his theory of eternal recurrence (252–253). Subsequently, he invokes Nietzsche as a champion of *karma* (action) contra advocates of *akarma* (renunciation) such as Schopenhauer (288). The next reference is to Nietzsche's notion of the *Übermensch* who is beyond good and evil; Tilak likens the *Übermensch* to the man who performs his ordained *karma* in a selfless spirit (356). He then approvingly cites Nietzsche's critique (in *The Antichrist*) of the Christian spirit of non-antagonism (*nirvairatva*) as a mark of a slave morality (375). Finally, he contends that Nietzsche's cult of action had triumphed over Schopenhauer's counsel of quietism in contemporary Germany (476).

[9] Lederle (1976) points out that Rajwade possessed *The Complete Works of Friedrich Nietzsche* edited by Oscar Levy (London: George Allen & Unwin, 1909–1913). He observes that pencil marks in the books indicated "that they were read with some animation" (301). In Lederle's opinion, "Rajwade fully understood the spirit of Nietzsche's philosophy" (306).

[10] It is obvious that these views stemmed as much from Bain's philosophical proclivity as from his patriotic pride. It may be noted that he also respected the patriotism of others, hence his sympathy for the nationalist youth in India. This is clearly evident in Rajwade's autobiography.

universal law that 'function makes structure.' Bain was critical of Christianity and also rejected the utilitarian, liberal, Marxist, and feminist ideas of his time. Dismissing both spiritual and secular egalitarianism, he emphasized the need to preserve an appropriately hierarchical sociopolitical order.[11]

Rajwade eagerly assimilated Bain's conservatism and deployed it to attack the ideas of liberal, heterodox advocates of social reform such as Gopal Ganesh Agarkar (1856–1895), and Raghunath Purushottama Paranjpye (1876–1966), as also the thought of British thinkers such as J.S. Mill and Herbert Spencer, which was the fountainhead of reformist opinion in India. He came to see Nietzsche and Bain as kindred spirits since they preferred Aristotle to Socrates and Plato, criticized Christianity and Buddhism, but held the ancient Indian law-giver Manu in high esteem, and found fault with Locke, Kant, Hegel, Schopenhauer, Mill, and Spencer. Rajwade believed that Aristotle, Nietzsche, and Bain alike expounded principles that were congenial to his own *Weltanschauung*.[12]

Rajwade held that the true nature of things could be grasped only through the lens of 'polarity' (*dvandva*).[13] According to Lederle, this key concept is centered on collateral and relative opposites such as 'life and death,' 'warm and cold,' and 'joy and pain.' The duality posited here is such that each part necessarily presupposes the other. Rajwade characterized the most profound philosophical formulations contained in the Vedas and the *Gītā* as *dvandvātita* (beyond opposites) and *nirdvandva* (without opposites), respectively. He held that Śaṁkara distorted the central message of these texts by substituting the term *advaita* (non-dualism) for *nirdvandva*.

Lederle argues that Rajwade saw the Absolute in an evolutionary perspective— it potentially contains its fullness from the beginning and realizes it through the process of evolution. The latter explained this notion of the evolutionary Absolute in terms of biological concepts, even as Nietzsche invoked the cycle of life and death to project his doctrine of Eternal Recurrence. Rajwade's deep philosophical affinity with the German thinker can be discerned most transparently in his following statement (Rajwade 1927: 237):

> In Nietzsche's philosophy there is no place either for Christ's extreme dualism [*ekāngi dvaita*] or for Kant's extreme non-dualism [*ekāngi advaita*]. It has no place whatsoever

---

[11] "Liberals think, by reason of their profound ignorance of the nature of things, to make homogeneous the essentially unhomogeneous members of the State, to identify parts that are complementary, polar opposites, and confound distinctions rooted in the nature of things. They might just as well try to make a horse walk with his mouth and eat with his hoof" (Bain 1899: 220).

[12] Ironically, Bain seems to have held Hindu thought in low esteem. Here is a particularly mordant comment: "No two things could be more opposed to each other than Aristotelian and Hindoo philosophy. The Hindoos are the victims of abstraction: it is the root alike of their religion, their ethics, their theory and practice: abstraction from the world, abstraction from others, and abstraction from self: it is their ideal, their core, and their curse" (Bain 1899: 265). Nietzsche offered a more complex account of the *brahmānical* creed; but in the ultimate analysis, he characterized it as a nihilistic religion offering solace to the afflicted (Hulin 1996: 66).

[13] In *Ishāvāsyopanishadbhāshya*, Rajwade (1949: 609) himself uses the phrase, 'the law of polarity' to explain the concept of '*dvandva*.' For a brief exposition of this law and of the allied notion of the Absolute, see Lederle (1976: 303–304).

for the ultra-pessimistic, life-destroying *dukkhanirvāṇa* or cessation of suffering *a la* Schopenhauer. Rather, being in accord with the principle of *nirdvandva* (oneness) embodied in the Vedas and the Gitā, it contains the bliss of *Brahmanirvāṇa* [the unity of *atman* or the Self and *Brahman* or the ultimate reality].

Rajwade concurred that only such a philosophy affirming the will to happiness, the will to power, and the will to suffer could produce the *Übermensch*. He applauded its reverence for the *Manusmṛti* and the disciplined Hindu social system based on *varṇāshramadharma* as against the Bible and the permissive democratic order anchored in a Christian ethos.

10.3 Leveraging Nietzsche

We can now see why Rajwade chose to translate *TA*—a work that may seem quite marginal to the concerns of his readership which essentially comprised upper caste, middle-class Maharashtrian Hindus. Commenting on the mind-set of the English-educated gentry spawned by colonialism, he observed in his autobiography that these people were by and large not inclined to embrace Christianity, but rather wanted to transform Hinduism along Christian lines in the name of social reform (Rajwade 1980: 331). Quite in keeping with this perception, he deployed Nietzsche's radical critique of Christianity as a lever to overthrow the hegemony of Western modernity and to reinstate the pristine Hindu world-view and social order prefigured in the Vedas.[14]

As we have already noted, Rajwade possessed a well-thumbed copy of *The Complete Works of Friedrich Nietzsche* edited by Oscar Levy. It seems plausible to assume that he translated *TA* from this source. Hence, it is important to place on record what the renowned Nietzsche scholar Walter Kaufman has to say about the texts compiled by Levy: "These translations, none of them by Dr. Levy himself, represent an

---

[14] It would be interesting to contrast Rajwade's position with a different but arguably analogous perception articulated by contemporary cultural critics such as S.N. Balagangadhara and Vivek Dhareshwar. The latter emphasize the centrality of Christianity to the constitution of the modern West as also to the epistemic and sociopolitical (re)fashioning of the colonized societies in the era of Western hegemony. Thus, drawing on Balagangadhara (1994), Dhareshwar offers the following formulations:

Everybody knows that Christianity played a central role in the evolution of this [western] culture; that modernity as a specifically western phenomenon introduced radical changes in the world. But in what way does Christianity constitute the identity of the West? How are the secular/liberal self-descriptions of the West related to Christianity? The otherness of western culture consists precisely in its compulsion to transform the culture it studies into [a] variation of itself. So, Balagangadhara is able to explain not only why the western theories look for religion in other cultures but also why their attempt to explain culture as a 'world-view' is essentially secularization of a religious framework (Dhareshwar 1996: 21).

This is not to suggest that Balagangadhara and Dhareshwar necessarily share Rajwade's revivalist agenda. These two scholars were both initially influenced by Marxism and subsequently seemed to operate in a theoretical space opened up by the later writings of Ludwig Wittgenstein and Edward Said's critique of Orientalism.

immense labor of love but are thoroughly unreliable. None of the translators were phi-losophers, few were scholars. Mistakes abound, and it is impossible to form any notion of Nietzsche's style on the basis of these versions" (Kaufman 1974: 492).

A word about the central argument of *TA* would be in order at this juncture. Though first published in 1895, it was among the last five works that Nietzsche completed in 1888. The other four books included *The Case of Wagner*, *The Twilight of the Idols*, the autobiographical *Ecce Homo*, and *Nietzsche contra Wagner*. In *The Twilight of the Idols*, Nietzsche extolled the Greek conception of *Dionysus*. Interpreting it in terms of his own vision of eternal recurrence, he contrasted it with the Christian *ressentiment* against life. *TA* marked his most thoroughgoing critique of Christianity and also formed part of the larger project signaled in the closing statement of that book: "Revaluation of all values!" (Nietzsche 1977: 187).

In *TA*, Nietzsche made a clear distinction between Jesus, "the bringer of glad tidings," and the institution of Christianity that was largely shaped by the legacy of Paul, "the genius in hatred." He saw Jesus as a 'free spirit,' but considered his teachings to be "both childlike and a decadent avoidance of pain" (Magnus and Higgins 1996: 55). It was Paul and his successors who falsified the message of Jesus by providing an account of his death that was anchored in *ressentiment* and construed 'the kingdom of god' not as 'an experience of the heart' but as a promise of future bliss. The outcome of this degeneration was a faith that Nietzsche ruth-lessly condemned: "I call Christianity the *one* great curse, the *one* great intrinsic depravity, the *one* great instinct for revenge, for which no expedient is sufficiently poisonous, secret, subterranean, *petty*—I call it the *one* immortal blemish of man-kind" (Nietzsche 1977: 186–187).

Let us now turn to Rajwade's *Nietzschechā Khristāntaka āni Khristāntaka Nietzsche* (henceforth *NKN*).[15] This is how he situates the translation in the foreword:

> '*Khristāntaka*' is a book originally written in German by a great modern European sage (*mahāmuni*) of a brahmanic disposition (*brāhmaṇavṛtti*). This Marathi rendition (*roopāntara*) of the book … offers … all that the original author meant to convey as well as his distinctive style. Every true-born Aryan and authentic follower of the Vedic *dharma* and civilization must read and ponder over this book. For he will easily find in it the phil-osophical seedbed of the noble spirit to which he is heir—a spirit that is receding in the face of a hostile environment. Any thinking person who is inclined to read this book with devotion will doubtless discover that it is bound to stem the present-day degeneration of the Aryans and provide them succor as well as food for thought. This book contains the original '*Khristāntaka*' in its entirety along with the first of the three proposed volumes of detailed commentary (Rajwade 1931: 7–8).[16]

Both in word and in spirit, this foreword is truly representative of the subsequent translation and commentary.

NKN reveals a register in which the discourse of the typically Brahman Maharashtrian public intellectuals of the time was conducted, a high-flown diction

---

[15] The translation finds a mention in the comprehensive Nietzsche bibliography at http://ora-web.swkk.de/nie_biblio_online/nietzsche.vollanzeige?p_ident=17495 (accessed on 18th January 2009).

[16] The two remaining volumes of commentary never appeared.

replete with words and phrases borrowed (*tatsama*) or adapted (*tadbhava*) from Sanskrit, and a tone echoing the polemical and hortatory tenor of the source text. Rajwade's uncanny ability to inhabit and appropriate Nietzsche's work creatively, as also his immersion in the language and lore of the indigenous Great Tradition, are evident throughout *NKN*. Thus, he aptly invokes Bhavabhūti's famous disclaimer (without naming the Sanskrit author/source), '*taanpratinaisha yatnaha*' (Rajwade 1931: 4),[17] in the Marathi version of the preface to underscore Nietzsche's statement that his book was not meant for lesser mortals. In a more substantive vein, he displays a knack for coining phrases that felicitously convey the precise import of certain seminal but idiosyncratic Nietzschean formulations. This is best illustrated by his rendering of 'the revaluation of all values' as '*sarva arthānche arthāntarikaraṇ*' (Rajwade 1931: 174)[18]—the clarion call which serves as a coda to the book.

In an article on translation and post-colonial theory, Aniket Jaaware offers the following comment regarding *NKN*: "Raajwade feels the power of Nietzsche's writing, but fails to see, translator in a specific sociohistorical condition that he is, the *modern* irony in the style as such. He measures the Greenblattean resonance between himself and Nietzsche with the tuning fork of classicism, and not modernism" (Jaaware 2002: 739).[19] In this context, it is necessary to recall a limitation of Rajwade's translation that we have already recorded: It seems to have been based on a problematic English translation of *TA*, which does not do justice to Nietzsche's style. Yet, a random comparison of *NKN* with R.J. Hollingdale's subsequent and supposedly competent translation (Nietzsche 1977: 113–187) suggests that the former is a fair approximation of the Nietzschean text. At this juncture, it may be pertinent to explore the precise nature and implications of the *philosophical* translation represented by *NKN*.

10.4 Brahmanical Radicalism

In an insightful essay on comparative philosophy, Raimundo Panikkar considers the option of equating a philosophy with a language and offers the following observations on the interface of different philosophies:

> The great merit of this option…is that it shows the relative autonomy (rather *ontonomy*) of each philosophy and its relative completeness…[It] makes us aware that in order to

---

[17] The phrase can be literally translated as follows: "My endeavour is not for them." Bhavabhūti's allusion is to those who may not be capable of appreciating the niceties of his work. He was a great Sanskrit playwright of the 8th century. Nietzsche's relevant statement is as follows: "These alone are my readers, my rightful readers, my predestined readers: what do the *rest* matter?—The rest are merely mankind" (Nietzsche 1977: 114).

[18] The Marathi phrase literally denotes 'the transmutation of all *arthas*.' The *tatsama* term '*artha*' has a wide range of connotations including 'end' (as in *Puruṣārthas* or the ends of human life), 'means,' 'meaning,' and 'subject-matter' (See Devasthali et al. (1993: 97)).

[19] *NKN* is one of the examples adduced by Jaaware to support his larger argument concerning translation.

understand we do not need properly to compare, for we do not bring the *comparanda* on a neutral scale, but bring one *comparandum* into the field of intelligibility of the other; in other words, we translate. Translation means finding the corresponding equivalences (homeomorphic equivalents) between languages...Each translation transforms both the host language by the new shades of meaning and association of the newly translated word, and the language from which the translation is made (Panikkar 1989: 125–126).

Viewed in this perspective, *NKN* can be seen as an embodiment of 'radical translation' in two senses. It is radical in the literal sense that it goes to the root of Nietzsche's philosophical argument in *TA*. More importantly, it reinvents the German thinker's 'aristocratic radicalism' in an indigenous context.

The phrase 'aristocratic radicalism' was used by the Danish literary critic Georg Brandes (1842–1927) in the title of a pioneering essay on Nietzsche published in 1889. It is not clear whether Rajwade had read the essay, but he does make a passing reference to Brandes in *NKN* and finds the term 'aristocratic radicalism' incapable of capturing Nietzsche's advocacy of a social system akin to the *varṇa* order prescribed by Manu (Rajwade 1931: 384–385). Brandes himself used the term to connote a complete rejection of both ascetic ideals and democratic mediocrity.[20] Arguably, Rajwade translated it into a homologous position that may be characterized as 'brahmanical radicalism.' This is evident in his consistent critique targeting Hindu asceticism (that he traced to the *advaita* doctrine of Śaṁkara) on the one hand and modern democratic politics on the other. By way of an antidote to such supposed evils, he stridently advocated a rejuvenation of the Hindu philosophical and social ideals contained in the Vedic tradition, which he found consistent with a fascist political vision.

Judged from this point of view, Rajwade found the Hindu leadership of his time utterly wanting. To him, even Vinayak Damodar Savarkar (1883–1966)—a prominent leader of the Hindu Mahāsabhā and the ablest champion of Hindutva or Hindu nationalism among his contemporaries—seemed misguided.[21] Savarkar had imbibed the utilitarianism and agnosticism of English thinkers such as Mill and Spencer; consequently, he rejected several traditional Hindu beliefs and practices including the caste system.[22] Moreover, his political activities seemed to lack a

---

[20] For a detailed account of Brandes's interpretation, see Behler (1996: 289–291).

[21] The Hindu Mahāsabhā was a Hindu nationalist political party founded in 1915 as a reaction to the decision of the British government in India to grant separate electorates to the Muslims. It sought to safeguard and promote the Hindu race, culture, civilization, and nation. Under the leadership of Savarkar, who became President of the party in 1937, it cooperated with the British rulers and opposed both the Muslim League and the democratic secularism of the Congress. Savarkar considered India to be primarily a nation of the Hindus. He defined a true 'Hindu' as one who treated the country as the land of his forefathers (*pitrabhu*) and his holy land (*punyabhu*). This definition excluded significant religious minorities such as Christians and Muslims as their holy lands were not located in the country. However, Savarkar was willing to accord juridical and political equality to these communities. What he opposed was granting them preferential treatment. Therefore, as Prabha Dixit rightly points out, in spite of "chauvinistic elements in Savarkar's ideology, it cannot be termed Fascist" (Dixit 1986: 134). Cf. Raghuramaraju (2007: 80–81).

[22] For an overview of Savarkar's philosophical ideas, see Lederle (1976: 278–295).

positive thrust as they were chiefly directed against the Indian National Congress and the Muslim League. Rajwade was equally critical of the orthodox Hindus who had left the Hindu Mahāsabhā to form the ineffectual and short-lived *Varṇāshrama Svarājya Sangha*. He considered them to be devoid of political vision and leadership (Rajwade 1980: 281).

Rajwade had a distinctive understanding of fascism (1980: 259–264). While noting that the term had acquired a negative connotation, he claimed that in fact every person was a fascist by nature. He considered the fascist tendency (*fascist-giri*) to be a purely natural phenomenon—a symbol of the power (*bala*) every individual has and uses to safeguard and pursue one's interests in various domains such as the family, the caste group, the village, the nation or the world at large, and depending upon each person's capacity and ambition. Accordingly, he viewed all other isms—in particular socialism, communism, and bolshevism—as artificial or ersatz ideologies, springing from weakness.

Rajwade's list of fascist heroes included Lord Rama, Alexander the Great, Caesar, Shivaji, Napoleon, and, of course, Hitler. To him, what these *Fuehrers* had in common was a clear understanding of their superior power or strength together with a complete lack of inhibition in displaying it. A born fascist would naturally subscribe to the celebrated affirmation of Louis XIV, *L'état c'est moi*, and consider his authority to be divine, while spontaneously evoking respect and love from the masses. On the other hand, those who were feeble tended to suppress their innate fascist disposition out of cowardice and resorted to various kinds of subterfuge to achieve their objectives.

In characteristic fashion, Rajwade posits a polar relationship of *dvandva* between fascism and socialism. The former is rooted in nature and is an embodiment of self-interest, whereas the latter is a product of art or artifice and is an embodiment of cowardice. In a curious formulation, he then goes on to assert that the true fascist, who transcends this duality, is *dvandvātita*; hence, it is wrong to label him as a fascist. The course of evolution leads human beings from the primitive fascism of animal existence to the socialism of civil society and thence to the higher fascism that culminates in the rule of the *Übermensch*. Rajwade saw the Nazi regime as an approximation to the latter and regretted its collapse: "[Had Hitler] enjoyed the good fortune of emerging victorious in the last World War, the flag of *Ārya Dharma* would have been flying over the world today rather than that of Christianity, and this country [India] would have witnessed the uplift of the Brahmans instead of the uplift of the untouchables" (Rajwade 1980: 264).

Rajwade evidently treated Nietzsche as a proto-fascist. A prominent school of contemporary Nietzsche scholarship considers such an interpretation of the German philosopher to be utterly wrongheaded. Scholars who represent this school point out that he was completely opposed to aggressive nationalism and racism—two key ingredients of fascism. They further argue that it was Nietzsche's sister who perversely projected his philosophy as a pro-Nazi doctrine. Thus, the Nietzschean *Übermensch* who symbolized a Goethe-like genius capable of prodigious creativity came to be cast in the mold of Hitler—a power-mongering maniac of the sort Nietzsche would have detested.

Yet, it can hardly be gainsaid that Nietzsche's unashamed espousal of 'master morality' made him susceptible to a fascist reading. Peter Singer clearly explains this susceptibility as follows:

> Nietzsche left himself wide open to those who wanted his philosophical imprimatur for their crimes against humanity. His belief in the importance of the *Übermensch* made him talk of ordinary people as "the herd," who did not really matter. In *Beyond Good and Evil* (1886), he wrote with approval of "the distinguished type of morality," according to which "one has duties only toward one's equals; toward beings of a lower rank, toward everything foreign to one, one may act as one sees fit, 'as one's heart dictates'"—in any event, beyond good and evil. The point is that the *Übermensch* is above ordinary moral standards (Singer 2011).

In this sense, Nietzsche's thought was available to and was actually appropriated by European fascists. Rajwade's version of Nietzsche may be seen as a cross-cultural instance of such appropriation.

10.5 Concluding Remarks

By assimilating Nietzsche's philosophy to the supposed message of the Vedas, Rajwade seems to have 'translated' it in the manner of the *literati* excoriated by Marx and Engels. But in the process, he foregrounded the fascist potential of the Nietzschean legacy, thereby exemplifying Panikkar's insight into the transformative nature of philosophical translation. It is also important to note that Rajwade did not rest content with a merely adulatory invocation of Nietzsche. He was quite capable of critically interrogating the latter from an indigenous standpoint *à la* Halbfass. Thus, Rajwade found fault with Nietzsche's account of the *Übermensch*. He thought the commonly used English equivalent 'superman' was unhelpful and argued that the Vedic conception of a '*deva*' as a dynamic, effulgent (*tejaswi*), trans-human being truly corresponded to the ideal the German philosopher was trying to formulate (Rajwade 1938: 21).

Rajwade's inquiries into a wide range of texts and traditions show a curious blend of erudition and eccentricity. He addressed Indic, Zoroastrian, and Islamic as well as Western philosophical and scientific thought from an original, critical, and comparative perspective.[23] However, he has received scant posthumous attention. Rajwade had no respect for academic philosophers, and with the odd exception, they in turn have ignored him. Neither the contemporary champions of Hindutva (ostensibly, his 'natural constituency') nor their critics have shown much interest in his ideas. Like Vidura's *cri de coeur* cited at the outset, Rajwade's plea for the primacy of *dharma* has gone unheeded.

---

[23] Rajwade's interest in Islamic thought is exemplified by his comparative exegesis of the *Agni Mantra* in the *Ishāvasyopaniṣad* and the first *sūra* (chapter) of the *Koran* (Rajwade 1949: 671–678). He also expatiated upon certain key ideas drawn from modern Physics and Astronomy (Rajwade 1949: 440–544).

[**Note**: Unless otherwise stated, all translations from the Marathi are mine. I am thankful to Sharad Deshpande, Ram Bapat, Pradeep Gokhale, Abhay Datar, Meera Kosambi, Jatin Wagle, Martin Tamke, Walter Reese-Schaefer, Lars Klein, M.G. Dhadphale, and D.K. Kulkarni for their intellectual support.]

References

Athavale, S. (1989). Rajwade, Vishwanath Kashinath. In *Marathi Vishwakosh* (Vol. 14). Mumbai: Maharashtra Vishwakosh Nirmiti Mandal.

Aurobindo, S. (1989). *The life divine*. Pondicherry: Sri Aurobindo Ashram.

Bain, F. W. (1899). *On the realisation of the possible and the spirit of Aristotle*. London: James Parker & Co.

Balagangadhara, S. N. (1994). *'The heathen in his blindness...': Asia, the west and the dynamics of religion*. Leiden: E. J. Brill.

Behler, E. (1996). Nietzsche in the twentieth century. In B. Magnus & K. M. Higgins (Eds.), *The Cambridge Companion to Nietzsche*. Cambridge: Cambridge University Press.

Chatterjee, M. (2006). The diversity of the Nietzschean heritage. In F. Manjali (Ed.), *Nietzsche: Philologist, philosopher and cultural critic*. New Delhi: Allied Publishers.

Devasthali, G. V., Joshi, Y. B., & Kulkarni, G. R. (1993). *The students' new sanskrit dictionary*. Bombay: Keshav Bhikaji Dhavale.

Dhareshwar, V. (1996). Valorizing the present. In *Seminar 446*, October.

Dixit, P. (1986). The ideology of Hindu nationalism. In T. Pantham & K. Deutsch (Eds.), *Political thought in modern India*. New Delhi: Sage.

Halbfass, W. (1990). *India and Europe: An essay in philosophical understanding*. Delhi: Motilal Banarsidass Publishers.

Hulin, M. (1996). Nietzsche and the suffering of the Indian ascetic. In G. Parkes (Ed.), *Nietzsche and Asian thought*. London: The University of Chicago Press.

Iqbal, M. (2008). *Shikwa and Jawab-i-Shikwa* (Complaint and Answer; Iqbal's Dialogue with Allah), (K. Singh, Trans.). New Delhi: Oxford University Press.

Jaaware, A. (2002). Of demons and angels and historical humans: Some events and questions in translation and post-colonial theory. *The European Legacy, 7*(6), 735–745.

Kantak, M. R. (Ed.). (1990). *Rajwade and his thoughts*. Pune: Bharat Itihās Samshodhak Mandal.

Kaufmann, W. (1974). *Nietzsche: Philosopher, psychologist, antichrist*. Princeton, New Jersey: Princeton University Press.

Khadilkar, K. H. (1949). *Deshabhakta Krishnāji Prabhākar urfa Kakasaheb Khādilkar Yanche Charitra*. Pune: D. T. Joshi.

Lederle, M. R. (1976). *Philosophical trends in modern Maharashtra*. Bombay: Popular.

Magnus, B., & Higgins, K. M. (Eds.). (1996). *The Cambridge companion to Nietzsche*. Cambridge: Cambridge University Press.

Marx, K., & Engels, F. (1973). *Selected Works* (Vol. I). Moscow: Progress Publishers.

Naravane, V. S. (1964). *Modern Indian thought: A philosophical survey*. Bombay: Asia Publishing House.

Nietzsche, F. (1977). *Twilight of the idols and the anti-Christ* (R. J. Hollingdale, Trans.). Harmondsworth: Penguin Books.

Panikkar, R. (1989). What is comparative philosophy comparing? In G. J. Larson & E. Deutsch (Eds.), *Interpreting across boundaries: New essays in comparative philosophy*. Delhi: Motilal Banarasidass.

Raghuramaraju, A. (2007). *Debates in Indian philosophy: classical, colonial and contemporary*. New Delhi: Oxford University Press.

Rajwade, S. R. (1927). *Nāsadiyasūktabhāshya, Part I.* Pune.
Rajwade, S. R. (1931). *Nietzschechā Khristāntaka āni Khristāntaka Nietzsche.* Pune.
Rajwade, S. R. (1938). *Vaidikadharma āni Shaddarshane athavā Chāra Vidyā va Sahā Shastre.* Nagpur Vishvavidyalaya.
Rajwade, S. R. (1949). *Ishāvasyopaniṣadbhāshya.* Pune.
Rajwade, S. R. (1980). *Ahitāgni Rajwade Ātmavṛtta.* Pune: Shreevidya Prakashan.
Singer, P. (2011). Ethics. In *Encyclopedia Britannica Student and Home Edition.* Chicago: Encyclopedia Britannica.
Tilak, B. G. (1950). *Shrimadbhagvadgitārahasya athavā Karmayogashāstra.* Pune: Tilak Bandhu.

Chapter 11
Tagore's Perception of the West

Shefali Moitra

Abstract This essay discusses Tagore's deep concern about the search for identity through education and what should be our response to the science-culture of the West—how could local identities be related to global identities? Tagore believed that the dignity of man was of central importance and any compromise on this account will ultimately lead to disaster. His philosophy of education reflects on the aims of human development and the impediments that might stand in the way. His philosophy of education was founded on the concepts of love, creativity and freedom.

Keywords Creativity · Freedom · Philosophy of man · Education

11.1 Critique of Colonial Education System

When we look at the scenario of philosophy in India during the first half of the 20th century and try to assess the relationship between Indian philosophers and the Western philosophers—of this colonial period—we can clearly identify a divide between the pursuit of philosophy within the confines of university institutions and outside the boundaries of universities. Depending on their location, in relation to academic institutions, the reception of the West by Indian philosophers and the acceptance of Indian philosophers by the West also varied. K.C. Bhattacharyya, Hiralal Haldar, B.N. Seal, Rasvihary Das and others were distinguished professors of philosophy. Their philosophical pursuits were carried on very much within the university system. Outside the university system, there were well-known philosophers, such as Swami Vivekananda, M.K. Gandhi, Lokmanya Tilak and Sri Aurobindo among others. Sri Aurobindo was associated with the National Council of Education, Bengal, for a short period. Arguably thinkers,

S. Moitra (✉)
Formerly Department of Philosophy, Jadavpur University, Kolkata, India
e-mail: smoitra22@rediffmail.com

© Indian Institute of Advanced Study 2015
S. Deshpande (ed.), *Philosophy in Colonial India*, Sophia Studies in Cross-cultural
Philosophy of Traditions and Cultures 11, DOI 10.1007/978-81-322-2223-1_11

who remained outside the university system, had a greater impact both on global culture and on our national culture compared with university teachers of that time or even of today. Vivekananda's 'Practical Vedānta', Aurobindo's 'Integral Yoga' and Gandhi's philosophy of 'non-violence' are well known, in academic circles as well as outside, whereas the works of university teachers of this period are seldom discussed today within the academic circles, not to speak of the community at large. Sarvepalli Radhakrishnan was an exception. He was a university teacher and a renowned exponent of Indian philosophy as well. His *Indian Philosophy,* in two volumes (1923), and his translation of the *Bhagavad-Gitā* (1948) have had a major role in popularizing Indian philosophy in the West. Many, however, have expressed doubts about the originality of Radhakrishnan's philosophy; he is better known as an expositor of philosophy. The division of philosophers into those affiliated to universities, and those outside universities, was never a clear-cut one. There were philosophers who did, and did not, belong to the university system. These individuals were neither fully insiders, nor were they fully outsiders. If we try to keep to the strict dichotomy of university/non-university philosophers then, of course, Rabindranath Tagore's position appears to be enigmatic. Where do we place him *vis-à-vis* the university system—is he an insider, or is he an outsider? Maybe he himself would prefer to be considered an outsider.

On many occasions Tagore has referred to the fact that he did not complete his schooling, he disliked the mode of formal school education imparted by the Indian school system. He writes,

> And this was how I suffered when I was thirteen years old. And then I left school, and in spite of all the efforts of my guardians, I refused to go to school. Since then I have been educating myself, and that process is still being carried on. And whatever I have learned, I have learned outside the classes. And I believe that that was a fortunate event in my life. (1930a/1996b: 931)

The few people, who made a mark as philosophers, during the colonial period, were all self-made scholars. There was no discernible genealogy or *paramparā* of Indian philosophers which they belonged to. None of these philosophers could be neatly fitted into any of the traditional schools of Indian philosophy, such as Nyāya, Vedānta, Sāṁkhya, and Yoga.

Tagore maintained that there is something in the Indian university system that impedes creativity. The philosophers who flourished had done so in spite of the system, or by remaining outside the system altogether. The philosophical heights that they had reached would not have been achieved without favourable circumstances. Tagore is an outstanding example. Without circumstantial support, he would have ended up as an anonymous school dropout. Even though he rejected formal schooling, he was still nourished by a rich cultural ambiance provided by his family. He proudly states, "We in our home sought freedom of power in our language, freedom of imagination in our literature, freedom of soul in our religious creeds, and that of mind in our social environment" (1929/1996b: 611). Pursuing studies independently, i.e. outside the university set-up, could hardly be offered as a universal prescription for all. The common man is not endowed with an environment as rich and pulsating as was that of Tagore. Some kind of institutional education had to be made available to the ordinary man. Tagore also admitted this need.

Even though Tagore was trained outside the formal system of education, he was deeply concerned about the future of our public education system. From his initial engagement with the education problem in India, Tagore was simultaneously addressing two issues—one was the search for identity through education. Connected to this search was his concern about the aim of an indigenous education system, its course-content, its medium of instruction, etc. The second issue he was addressing was the question of India's relationship with the West, more specifically with the British—should we copy the Western system of education or should we reject it? What should be our stance? Both these groups of questions, he felt, were related to deep philosophical questions pertaining to the role of tradition, culture and other local identities on the one hand, and questions relating to global citizenship and man's relation to the universe on the other hand. To his mind, the two questions were integrally related—the question of identity and the question of international relations. That is why we see, he never discusses the East or the West in isolation. Tagore had his own conception of human perfection along with a conception of the perfection of humanity. He also had a sequential notion of the stages through which this perfection could be approximated and sustained. Training and education, naturally, had a central role to play in preparing an individual for the journey towards perfection. His philosophy of education, like his philosophy in general, was founded on two pillars—the concept of freedom and the concept of creativity.

While addressing 'The English Teachers' Association' in Peking, Tagore explained why he took up the cause of education, he says, "The first question you may all ask is: what urged me to take up education. I had spent most of my time in literary pursuits till I was forty or more" (1924/1996a: 658). In this speech, he goes on to explain the principal features of the school he set up at Santiniketan. He chose a location that was conducive to freedom. An atmosphere of freedom was essential for learning. For Tagore, detachment and distancing were not necessary conditions for gaining freedom. Freedom can be enjoyed from within a relationship. Some relationships are oppressive and freedom-denying; others are emancipating and freedom-affirming. Education helps us to recognize and develop liberatory relationships. The relation of love could flourish into a freedom-generating relationship. Tagore tried to create an atmosphere in his school where people from various parts of the world could come and contribute to the culture of the place. Most urgently, every student must be initiated into forming some bond of relation with fellow beings and with nature. People from across the globe display differences, there are contradictions yet we must find ways of bonding with people. Tagore says, "There must be some bond of relation, otherwise they will knock against one another. They will be like an ill-formed and unfinished body whose limbs are disjointed, causing constant internal friction" (1924/1996a: 661). It was also important to be close to nature, to appreciate her beauty and respond creatively through artistic expressions. Bonding with nature and bonding with fellow human beings from within and outside the country was the essential historical background within which freedom has to be achieved and creativity given expression. The motto with which he set up his school at Santiniketan was *yatra visva bhabati eka nidam,* 'where the world is transformed into a single nest.' For him, this was a cherished ideal.

Tagore was protective of his institution. He felt 'the molestation from the prosperous' needed to be guarded against since they were always afraid of idealism that is working for the sake of an ideal. He also felt the threat "from the politically powerful who are always suspicious of men who have the freedom of spirit" (1924/1996a: 661). His philosophy of education reflects the aims of human development and identifies the impediments that may stand in the way. The aim of education was to nurture freedom, creativity and a bonding with nature and with fellow human beings. The hindrance to this kind of learning came from excessive consumerism, and from political interference. In the context of the national/ colonial interface, similar problems are identified by Tagore. Colonial India was oppressed by problems, such as lack of freedom, lack of creativity, alienation from nature, intolerance of difference and a utilitarian approach to life in general. In the colonial context too, the solutions to these problems are forestalled by narrow political agenda and by suspicion of all forms of idealism. Tagore saw a parallel between the colonization of education and the colonization of a country. The two sets of problems were structurally identical. We shall turn to this point later.

11.2 Decolonizing Education

In spite of Tagore's total disenchantment with the formal education system of our country, he was, on many occasions, closely associated with it. The association was at times voluntary and at times solicited. His first essay on education "*Sikshar Herpher*" (in Bangla) was published in 1892 in the Bengali periodical *Sādhanā* (1892/2005: 7–19). Through this essay, he attempted to impress upon the administration of the University of Calcutta the urgent need for introducing Bengali as the medium of instruction. He considered this to be a first step in the direction of de-colonizing education. Tagore's prescription for the introduction of vernacular education led to a heated and prolonged debate both in print as well as at the meetings of the Senate of the University of Calcutta; the debate is well documented. Tagore did not succeed in instituting this change.[1] The concern, however, remained with him till the end of his life. In this instance, Tagore took a voluntary initiative, as an outsider, to bring about a change in the education system of the University of Calcutta.

In 1906, during the formation of the National Council of Education, Bengal, Tagore's guidance was solicited; he was requested to write the foundational paper

---

[1] For a detailed discussion on this debate and on Tagore's position on vernacular education, see Moitra "The Indian Education System and Tagore's Unmitigated Pain" (2011: 157–195).

(*gathan patrikā*) for the school section. As is well known, the National Council of Education, Bengal was instituted as an alternative to the colonial system of education prevalent in the country at that time. Tagore had already founded his school at Santiniketan, but he was not a Nobel laureate till then. This award came in 1913. The invitation to perform the task of formulating the foundational paper for the National Council of Education, Bengal, indicates the fact that Tagore was received by his fellow countrymen not merely as a poet, he was considered to be a visionary, a philosopher and an educationist in his own country even before he was internationally received. He had realized that the formulation of a foundational paper was not to be an easy task. In order to begin writing, he wanted to know what the concept was behind the formation of such an institution, what was the seminal cause (*kāraṇ beej*) of forming this Council? He felt that without a clear vision of purpose, any amount of money, any number of committees, or a proliferation of rules and regulations will be futile. He went on to say, the desire of founding a new school could not simply be the result of rage against a foreign education system. That could only be a negative justification and not a seminal cause. He asked for a positive justification for setting up such a Council of Education and found none as forthcoming. He suggested holding a national debate to decide the purpose of national education, but he received no positive response. Nobody took up this suggestion for a debate in right earnest. Till date, this question remains unanswered: what is the seminal cause or purpose of our education (*kāraṇ beej*)? (1906/2005: 38–55).

Whatever Tagore believed, at that time, in relation to forming a 'national' education system, he reiterated in other contexts as well. He never subscribed to an exclusionary politics, or to an exclusionary philosophy. This was one of the main issues of controversy between Tagore and Gandhi. Tagore never supported the boycott movement and the burning of foreign goods. Unreasoned rejection of a position, or a system, was a mere strategy of denial. Denial for the sake of denial leads to a void. Denial is not the corollary of affirmative action. Affirmative action can only be arrived at as a result of a full-fledged philosophy and not by mindless copying, nor by mindless rejection. What is needed is a critical engagement with the 'other.' This other could be a foreigner; the other could also be a fellow countryman.

On another occasion, in 1919, Tagore was interviewed on the eve of the publication of the report of *The University of Calcutta Commission* (1919/1996b:746-747). He was requested to offer his views on some basic questions relating to the method of selecting professors, selection of men of specialization. There were also questions on the suitable subjects of study, the medium of education, the inclusion of fine arts in the university, Sanskrit education, so on and so forth. Tagore gave a detailed reply to each one of these questions. Sisir Kumar Das remarks, "Since this was the time when Tagore was contemplating to establish a new centre of learning—Visva-Bharati—his opinions expressed here are of great interest to historians of Indian education" (1996b: 981). I would say, his replies were not only of historical interest, many of his insights merit serious consideration even today.

Apart from playing an intervening role in institutional matters relating to education, Tagore also delivered visiting lectures at many universities both in India and abroad. His travels not only took him to the West, he also visited China, and Japan, Soviet Russia and many Middle East countries. Tagore's Visva-Bharati was not affiliated to the University of Calcutta, yet there was a special arrangement by which his students appeared for examinations, conducted by the University of Calcutta. His association with the University of Calcutta grew closer when he acted as Special Professor of Bengali during 1932–1934. Tagore was above 70 years of age at that time. By mentioning some of the major events instantiating Tagore's relation with the formal education system in India, both at the school level and at the university level, I have tried to corroborate my initial comment that Tagore was both an insider and an outsider to the formal education system. His role as an insider was a privileged one, since it did not coincide with his career or primary occupation. He has a no-loss/no-gain relationship; therefore, he could maintain his autonomy and creativity as a thinker and as a poet, while at the same time, he could be directly involved with university teaching and make critical observations where necessary—without fear or prejudice. In no way can it be said that Tagore was a product of the university system, nor was he answerable to the system.

11.3 The Ill-Effects of Utilitarianism

Tagore repeatedly referred to the claustrophobic atmosphere of the universities and to the fact that everything related to literature and philosophy cannot be taught in the classrooms. Institutional learning has a reductionist approach. Institutions attempt to treat all topics as being 'teachable', and the resulting skills as being testable through quantification. Life's experiences are too deep and too wide to be fully captured in a formal syllabus. Moreover, there is the aspect of *rasa* that needs to be encountered personally; it can never be comprehended through a regimented syllabus. Tagore felt, "the candidates for the M.A. degree in the vernaculars should not be compelled to attend classes." He further added "if such freedom be given to the students, the danger of imposing upon their minds the dead uniformity of some artificial standard will be obviated" (1918/1996b: 743–744). The same would be the case with philosophy. The grammar of the subject may be taught in class, but the subject itself needs to be grasped through experience, through contemplation, and through discussion, not through pedantry.

The problem, as perceived by Tagore, was that institutional education in our country failed to educate students in developing a complete life. Our education system aimed and succeeded in inculcating certain negative meaningless utilitarian values. Tagore writes, "Utilitarian education has its value but it is deprived of all significance if in its fragmentary pursuit of narrow immediate ends it fails to arouse in the mind of students the impulse of larger purposes, of aspirations which comprehend the fullness of our personality" (1932/1996b: 944). An exclusively utilitarian approach to education was never a characteristic of Indian culture. Pan utilitarianism has been acquired from the West. Tagore refers to "the wriggling tentacles of a cold-blooded utilitarianism, with which the West has grasped all the easily yielding succulent portions of the East" (1922/1996a: 531). As a result, blind utilitarianism gradually became a cultural mode in the colonized countries. Education, which has a utilitarian aim, succeeds in colonizing the mind into becoming a utility maximizer. The utilitarian ideal of education retards the free creative mind. This was to Tagore's utter dislike. Utilitarian values encourage a consumerist lifestyle. Tagore felt that excessive consumerism dulled an individual's sensitivity to his surroundings. However, he was not thinking about the replacement of utilitarianism by asceticism. He observes, "But the callousness of asceticism pitted against the callousness of luxury is merely fighting one evil with the help of another" (1931/1996b: 160). His prescription was one of moderation; the Buddhist middle path, the golden mean.

Tagore held that the damaging effects of colonialism in India could maximally be attributed to two Western inputs: utilitarianism and mechanization of life. At times, it is difficult to recognize the damage since both utilitarianism and mechanization are dispensed by the West in the guise of welfare for the colonized. In their utilitarian beneficence, the West claims to be helping with commodities that the colonies hardly need and which, as Tagore says, "they vomit forth because they are a great deal more than they can consume themselves" (1925/1996b: 552). Tagore felt that gross utility killed beauty (1933/1996b: 675). He repeatedly referred to the Upaniṣadic saying *ma gridhah*—thou shalt not covet (1913/1996a: 288). The main idea was to be able to love material things without being grossly attached to them. He entreated the youth of Hyderabad "not to be turned away by the call of vulgar strength, of stupendous size, by the spirit of storage, by the multiplication of millions, without meaning and without end" (1933/1996b: 675). The utilitarian education of our country was producing multiplication of millions, without a meaning and without an end.

One wonders if gross utilitarian values are not a part of Indian culture then how did these values take root in our culture. Tagore observes, "the system of education in India remained, and still remains, absurdly un-Indian, making no adequate provision for our own culture" (1935/1996b: 353). It is true that a certain number of people feel that our culture has no value, but Tagore is not engaging with this group. There are also a large number of people, who even if they accept the value of our culture in theory, seldom subscribe to it. They seem to have a very narrow concept of the ideal of Indian culture and are also very protective of this narrow cultural identity. Tagore observes, "so the *dharma* (principle) of life which thinks and doubts, accepts and rejects, progresses, changes and evolves, cannot, according to orthodoxy, be a part of the Hindu Dharma" (1935/1996b: 354). We must not fail to note the distinction Tagore makes between the *dharma* of life and the orthodox Hindu Dharma, the former is critical and progressive, the latter is not. Tagore reminds us that there was a time when Hindu civilization was giving to and taking from the world. We choose not to remember this history. As Tagore says, "man shows his mental feebleness when he loses his faith in life" (1935/1996b: 354).

While addressing the colonial question or any other question of oppression, Tagore always diagnosed the cause as a two-way process—both the oppressor and the oppressed were to be held responsible. He felt that there was no doubt that the West has been disrespectful of the East. Along with disrespect, there has also been a deliberate exclusion of the East. Exclusion is a necessary corollary of ruthless competition, and competition is a part and parcel of every culture primarily based on commerce and colonization. A kind of exclusionary 'form of life' is practiced by the West. Tagore attributes this to the attitude of success. He says, "for the attitude of success is exclusive, it is by nature suspicious and arrogant" (1925/1996b: 552). Tagore observes that even after centuries of contact with the East the Western mind "has not evolved the enthusiasm of a chivalrous ideal which can bring this age to its fulfillment" (1922/1996a: 534). He reminds us,

> ... there was a time when we were fascinated by Europe ... We believed that her chief mission was to preach the gospel of liberty to the world .... But slowly, Asia and Africa have become the main spheres of Europe's secular activities, where her chief preoccupations have been the earning of dividends, the administration of empires, and the extension of commerce. (1935/1996b: 350)

The commerce that took place was substandard and exploitative. Tagore tells us that "through her filter, whatever is finest in Europe cannot pass through to reach us in the East" (1935/1996b: 350). He also said that this is only one side of the story; India also has her lapses. India has lost touch with her culture. She has not only lost touch with whatever was of worth in her own civilization; she has lost "the great honour of being able to contribute to the civilization of Humanity" (1921/1996b: 964). India has lost confidence; therefore, she borrows the culture of others and lives like eternal schoolboys. In this way, she has allowed herself to become easy prey to exploitation.

Thus, the East and the West have both contributed to the subjugation of the East. Tagore was not willing to attribute a mere victim status to India. She is, no doubt, in part a victim but she must also take the onus of her degradation. Tagore was worried by the fact that Asia was astounded by the efficiency of the West and was preparing to imitate the ruthless aspect of the West. He says, "Asia is preparing to imitate the ruthless aspect which slays, which eats raw flesh, which tries to make the swallowing process easier by putting the blame on the victim" (1935/1996b: 350).

11.4 Perils of Mechanization

So far we have briefly discussed Tagore's views on the damaging effects of sheer utilitarianism. Mechanized lifestyle is the second damaging effect of Western colonialism discussed by him. Western countries are founded on a positivistic science paradigm. For Tagore science by itself is value-neutral, it is neither good nor evil. It could, however, be put to good or evil use. He admitted the immense power of science and the advancements made by Western civilization on the basis of their European-science culture. He went to the extent of saying, "it does not hurt my pride to acknowledge that, in the present age, Western humanity has received its mission to be the teacher of the world; that her science, through the mastery of laws of nature, is to liberate human souls from the dark dungeon of matter" (1922/1996a: 532). Of course, there are always negative pressures and allurements that keep distracting Man from his chosen ideal. Tagore believed that science gives us power of reason; it also has the capacity to lead us out of the obscurity of dead habit. In relation to science education in India, he said, "we must turn to the living mind of the West with gratefulness" (1933/1996b: 672).

We all know that power could be put to malevolent purposes as well as to benevolent purposes. It all depends on the ideal by which power is guided, be it scientific power, political power or power of any other form. To believe that science can beget the good independently of a normative regulative principle is to take a mechanistic approach to science. As Tagore said, "the world to-day is offered to the West. She will destroy it, if she does not use it for a great creation of man. The materials for such a creation are in the hands of science; but the creative genius is in Man's spiritual ideal" (1922/1996a: 532). It is to be noticed that Tagore uses the word 'man' in two senses. While referring to the popular connotation of the word, he uses the lower case, and when referring to man in his ideal form, as a free and loving creative being, he uses the upper case 'M.' He asks, "'where shall I find him? Man the Great? The Supreme Man?' Not in the machinery of power and wealth shall I find the humanity of the world. If he is not in the heart of a civilization, where is he?" (1930b/1996b: 632–633). This, no doubt, is a rhetorical question. So, Man is to be found in the heart of a civilization and not in some secluded place away or beyond a civilization.

11.5 Neglect of Creative Genius

When science, utilitarianism and commerce come together, tremendous power is generated, but the role of the creative genius in man is ignored. This is exactly what has happened in the contemporary West. Tagore approvingly refers to the period of Shelly, Byron and Keats when there was an upheaval of idealism in the West. Needless to say the period was short-lived. While identifying streaks of idealism present in Western culture, he also refers to Garibaldi and Mazzini as the worshippers of freedom, freedom of self-expression for all races and all countries. Then, he goes on to characterize the present-day situation and says, "I may tell you what I think is the characteristic difference to-day between the East and the West. We, in the East believe in personality. In the West you have your admiration for power" (1930b/1996b: 631). What he finds missing in the West is the recognition of the constitutive role of personality. The West through its scientific culture is a great worshipper of law and order. Tagore asks, "It has come to the perfection of a mechanical order but what is there to humanize it?" (1930b/1996b: 634).

Science has often been used for dehumanizing purposes. Tagore points to a number of cases where in the West the sanction of science has been invoked to establish all sorts of oppressive theses. He says, "we have also read western authors who, admirably mimicking scientific mannerism, assert, as you [Gilbert Murray] point out, that only the so-called Nordic race has the proper quality and therefore the right to rule the world" (1934/1996b: 349). He, however, made it clear that his "occasional misgivings about the modern pursuit of Science are directed not against Science, for Science itself can be neither good nor evil, but its wrong use" (1934/1996b: 347). Tagore was, however, always against speaking in sweeping generalizations. His comments were primarily addressed to the organizations and institutions, and to the individual members of Western society. He says, "we must again guard our minds from any encroaching distrust of the individuals of a nation. The active love of humanity and the spirit of martyrdom for the cause of justice and truth which I have met with in the Western countries have been a great lesson and inspiration to me" (1922/1996a: 534). He had some very positive things to say about Western culture. He felt that with the progress of Western science, the Western man was losing faith in religion. But that did not necessarily lead to a kind of nihilistic approach to all values. Western man had great faith in humanity. There are many evils in the West; no doubt, side by side there is a vitality that leads the people of the West to address these evils. Tagore remarks, "the bigger thing to remember is, that in Europe these evils are not stagnant" (1934/1996b: 351). This, he felt, was a positive sign. Tagore himself was not a follower of religion in the traditional sense.

He did feel that the Western man, like the men of the East, did have prejudices but his faith in man's personality led him to believe that there cannot be any permanent barrier in the way of the unity of the world. To bring about unity, the acknowledgement of personality was necessary. In the absence of this recognition, all attempts at achieving peace and unity will fail. The notion of personality plays a central role in Tagore's philosophy. He felt that science has tried to do away with personality by taking the perspective of the near and not of the distant. Tagore holds that, "this feeling of the touch of personality has given the centrifugal impulse in man's heart to break out into a ceaseless flow of reaction, in songs and pictures and poems, in images and temples and festivities" (1917/1996a: 374). He also held personality to be "the centripetal force which attracted men into groups and clans and communal organizations" (1917/1996a: 374). It is through personality that man first gains the consciousness of separation and then the consciousness of unity (1917/1996a: 385).

Tagore felt there was an acute insensitivity in the West to the presence of personality, especially among the politicians, not so much among the common man. He remarks, "our task is every day growing harder: for the situation, is solely left in the hands of the politicians, who represent the organization and not the humanity of a people" (1930c/1996b: 788–789). All the attempts at creating international peace treaties through international organizations will lead to nothing, as long as they are made in a heartless manner, or made with purely utilitarian motives. Nations may get together, sign joint agreements and get more and more powerful. They can cause external hurt but they cannot heal from within.

11.6 The Colonizer and the Colonized

Though the colonizers have a proximate relationship with the colonized, the relationship is never personal. It is never the meeting of one personality with the other. Tagore reminds us, "when two different peoples have to deal with each other and yet without forming any true bond of union, it is sure to become a burden, whatever benefit may accrue from it" (1918/1996b: 376). This is exactly what has happened in the case of India and the West. Tagore observes, "it is true that they are not yet showing any real sign of meeting. But the reason is because the West has not sent out its humanity to meet the man in the East, but only its machine" (1922/1996a: 536). There is no creative touch in these relationships. Tagore observes, "But Europe's connection with Asiatic countries has not yet developed that personal character in its organizations" (1925/1996b: 550). Unfortunately, the entire world is being bared to the European powers. According to Tagore, these powers do not have the capacity to unite, they can merely exploit. In his diary entries, in Bangla, made during his visit to Persia, he writes, "Europe has received the weapons of god but has not received the heart of god. It is under such a calamity that the *Brahmāstra* turns back and kills the warrior." (1930d/2001: 1166). In many contexts, Tagore has pointed out that exploitation does not merely harm the exploited it also degrades the exploiter. This is true in all cases of exploitation; in the case of international exploitation, in the case of class exploitation, and also in exploitative relationships of romance. As he says, "humanity is a truth which nobody can mutilate and yet escape its hurt himself" (1918/1996b: 378). Therefore, it is not only India that is being brutalized, Europe is also being dehumanized, and it is thus in the interest of both parties to find a solution to the crisis.

Tagore had no ready-made solutions, nor did he feel the West had any answers. He says, "for there are grave questions that the Western civilization has presented before the world but not completely answered" (1915/1996b: 365). All that Tagore had to offer were some ideals. These ideals could be realized in multiple ways, according to the proclivity of a civilization. In his letter to Murray, he writes, "I must confess at once that I do not see any solution of the intricate evils of disharmonious relationship between nations, nor can I point out any path which may lead us immediately to the levels of sanity" (1934/1996b: 347). Tagore was always against preaching solutions and imposing prescriptions. He had his ideals, he had forceful arguments in support of his ideals, and opinions on what would be the consequences of not following his ideals. He felt it as an insult to Man's personality, to his freedom, to force him in any way, either through foreign pressure or through domestic pressure. Every individual must have the freedom to choose one's own goal. Every choice is welcome as long as it does not display disrespect to others. This was also Tagore's response to the language issue; he felt that there should be an Indian link-language, but Hindi should not be introduced by force.

11.7 Spirituality Without Metaphysics?

Tagore never denied the utilitarian aspect of man. In his *Sādhanā* talks he says, "of course man is useful to man, because his body is a marvelous machine and his mind an organ of wonderful efficiency. But he is a spirit as well, and this spirit is truly known only by love" (1913/1996a: 322). When Tagore refers to the spirit of man, his remarks are endorsed by thick metaphysical underpinnings; it is primarily the metaphysics of the *Upaniṣads*. But there are also very strong strands of *Vaiṣṇava* and *Baul* metaphysics in his works. It may be thought that one cannot go very far with Tagore without subscribing to his metaphysical beliefs and that would detract from a global reception of his philosophy. I would like to argue that almost all of what Tagore says in relation to interpersonal unity and the solution to the oppressive global 'top-down' power structures can be reconstituted from his works without reference to his metaphysics. We could reconstruct a consistent metaphysically neutral version of his philosophy that would resonate with his views on creativity and freedom. True, in his acceptance speech for the Nobel Prize, he says, "It is the East in me which gave to the West. For, is not the East the mother of spiritual Humanity?" (1921/1996b: 963). This remark should not be read as a typical orientalist remark where the East represents spiritualism and the West represents science. By spiritualism, Tagore does not mean some kind of other-worldly orientation. On the contrary he asks, "who so steeped in untruth as to dare to call all this untrue—this great world of men, this civilization of expanding humanity, this eternal effort of man, through depths of sorrow, through heights of gladness, through innumerable impediments within and without, to win victory for his powers?" (1913/1996a: 331). Man's consolidated effort, his *sādhanā* or aim, is to pass from one nature to another nature; he strives to pass from an egocentric nature to an all-embracing nature based on love. The concentric circles of man's unity with the world are ever-widening. According to Tagore, no prior path has been charted for this onward journey and there is no guiding force to help us along. Thus, we find the metaphysical underpinning of Tagore's philosophy does not constitute a regulative principle for this onward journey.

Any suggestion of a non-religious, non-metaphysical reading of Tagore may seem totally unacceptable to many. This reading therefore needs further corroboration. To accept Tagore's position along with his metaphysics is a perfectly legitimate stance. But, in this way, Tagore would be relevant only to those who subscribe to his metaphysics. If Tagore's philosophy of education could be extrapolated without all this metaphysical baggage, he could be acceptable to a much wider audience. A larger number of readers could appreciate his philosophy of education and his philosophy of Man—the artist. Abu Sayeed Ayyub, a renowned Tagore scholar's exposition, is a case in point. He was an ardent follower of Tagore in spite of being an atheist. Many have, however, attempted to project a metaphysical reading of Tagore onto Ayyub. Sankha Ghosh, another famous Tagore scholar, has tried to clear this confusion. Ghosh refers to Ayyub as "the religious man without a religion" (*dharmahin ek dharmik manush*) (Ghosh 2009: 145). Ayyub had no faith in institutional religion. He was a radical humanist, and Tagore's humanism appealed to him. Ghosh argues that Ayyub felt it was not possible to believe in an omnipotent (*sarvashaktimān*), benevolent (*sarvakaruṇāmaya*) god (Ghosh 2009: 147). Ayyub held that Gandhi was a spiritual healer and Nehru a social engineer, he agreed with neither position. He did not believe that the problem was one of the merely changing people's hearts. Ghosh tells us that for Ayyub one sense of the term 'religion' connotes an attitude of mystery (*rahasyabodh*), amazement (*vismaya*), *ānanda* or joy and reverence towards the infinite (Ghosh 2009: 150). There was a central place for this mystery in Ayyub's understanding of Tagore's *dharma*, but there was no place for god or metaphysics, nor was there a place for immortality of the soul and rebirth. For Ayyub, *dharma* meant a journey. Ayyub would agree that the more we knew the external world, the more do we understand ourselves. This becoming is a kind of religiosity, a kind of *dharma* for him. The journey is not a theistic journey nor is it a moral journey; it is a journey through an aesthetic experience. As Ayyub says, if we receive the sensitivity, the expansion and the generosity of a great poet then that will constitute our religion. Ayyub perceives himself as a traveller on this path and he perceives the poet Tagore to be his friend, philosopher and guide (*sakhā*) in this pursuit (Ayyub 1973: 11–18). Ayyub felt that great art brought highest peace and the extreme experience of sorrow expanded our experience of life—the life that includes both the individual and the universe. For Tagore too the avenue for creative expression was art. Ayyub's interpretation of Tagore does not seem to be off the mark. A non-spiritual reading of Tagore's philosophy is consistent with his philosophy of education.

We have already referred to Tagore's disappointment that we have not nurtured our heritage with an open mind. Instead, we have either taken recourse to protectionism that has led to dogmatism, or else we have leaned heavily towards the aggressive utilitarian approach. At the very end of his *The Religion of Man*, Tagore states his dream for the future. He says, "And I had intently wished that the introspective vision of the universal soul, which an Eastern devotee realizes in the solitude of his mind, could be united with this spirit [Western spirit of humanity] of its outward expression in service, the exercise of will in unfolding the wealth of beauty and well-being from its shy obscurity to the light" (1931/1996b: 159).

Obviously, the realization of this dream is going to be a long-drawn process. The change has to be initiated at an interpersonal level, and not through the mediation of policy decisions, or by mechanical measures. As Tagore says, "the cure must be constitutional, not formal" (1925/1996b: 540). A change from within is necessary. A change cannot be initiated without knowledge. Tagore makes a distinction between knowledge that is a mere acquisition of certain skills, as well as certain information, and knowledge as wisdom. He also makes a distinction between pedantry and wisdom. He says, "the primary object of an institution should not be merely to educate one's limbs and mind to be in efficient readiness for all emergencies, but to be in perfect tune in the symphony of response between life and world, to find the balance of their harmony which is wisdom" (1931/1996b: 159). Finding this harmony and balance is not a one-time affair, it is a continuous process. Tagore holds, "love and action are the only intermediaries, through which perfect knowledge can be obtained" (1931/1996b: 159).

For the realization of Tagore's dream of bringing the East and the West together, he says, "the feeling of resentment between the East and the West must be pacified" (1921/1996b: 965). He felt that cultural exchange would go a long way in mitigating the distance and distrust. As a matter of fact, he founded his school at Santiniketan with this mission in mind. For the two cultures to meet there must be mutual understanding and trust. Such a meeting cannot take place without a common field of cooperation. Communication has a major role in facilitating cooperation.

Tagore identifies himself as a poet and an artist and not as a philosopher. Truly he was not a philosopher in the academic sense, specializing in any single branch of philosophy. But very definitely he had a clear philosophy of Man and of Man's place in the universe. It is from this philosophical perspective that he tried to understand the contemporary predicament of man and the future goal that is worthy of man. He believed that the dignity of man was central to his philosophy; any compromise on this account will ultimately lead to disaster. The damage would be in proportion to the indignation caused. The three central notions in Tagore's philosophy are love, freedom and creativity, and the three must work in tandem to bring about a harmony in man's thought and action.[2] While examining the relationship between the East and the West generally, and the relation between the colonizing British and the colonized Indians specifically, he found the problem was directly related to the lack of love, freedom and creativity. The end result of which was disharmony, pain and suffering on both sides.

11.8 Concluding Remarks

I would like to end with a metaphor used by Tagore to further elaborate on the nature of the onward journey to be taken by each individual. He uses the metaphor of the car festival, the *Ratha Yātrā*. Through this metaphor, he tells us that the time has come for mutual commerce. This is the time for interaction at the global level. He says, "the Divinity dwelling within the heart of man cannot be kept immured any longer in the darkness of particular temples" (1934/1996b: 354). We must note the expression 'particular temples.' All of us are familiar with his *Gitānjali* poem where he writes: "Where the world has not been broken up into fragments by narrow domestic walls" (1912/1994: 53). This is not a time for isolationism and seclusion. He could not, however, give the assurance that all the individual voices will be preserved till the very end; the hocus pocus, disharmonious voices will be gradually eliminated through a natural process. Continuing with the 'car festival' metaphor, he says, "each of us must set to work to build such car as we can, to take its place in the grand procession. The material of some may be of value, of others cheap. Some may break down on the way, others last till the end. But the day has come at last when all the cars must set out" (1934/1996b: 354).

---

[2] For a detailed discussion of this point see Moitra (2010: 53–96).

References

(a) In English

Das, S. K. (Ed.) (1996b). *The English writings of Rabindranath Tagore, (EWRT)* (Vol. 3). New Delhi: Sahitya Akademi.

Moitra, S. (2010). Thoughts of Tagore on man, freedom and value. In I. Sanyal & Sashinungla (Eds.), *Ethics and culture: Some Indian reflections.* New Delhi: Decent Books.

Moitra, S. (2011). The Indian education system and Tagore's unmitigated pain. In I. Sanyal & A. Ganguly (Eds.), *Education: Philosophy and practice.* New Delhi: Decent Books.

Radhakrishnan, S. (1923). *Indian philosophy* (Vols. 1 & 2). London: George Allen & Unwin.

Radhakrishnan, S. (1948). *The Bhagvadgita.* London: George Allen & Unwin.

Tagore, R. (1912/1994). Gitānjali. In S. K. Das (Ed.), *The English writings of Rabindranath Tagore, (EWRT)* (Vol. 1). New Delhi: Sahitya Akademi.

Tagore, R. (1913/1996a). Sadhana. In S. K. Das (Ed.), *The English writings of Rabindranath Tagore, (EWRT)* (Vol. 2). New Delhi: Sahitya Akademi.

Tagore, R. (1915/1996b). The spirit of Japan. In S. K. Das (Ed.), *The English writings of Rabindranath Tagore, (EWRT)* (Vol. 3). New Delhi: Sahitya Akademi.

Tagore, R. (1917/1996a). Personality. In S. K. Das (Ed.), *The English writings of Rabindranath Tagore, (EWRT)* (Vol. 2). New Delhi: Sahitya Akademi.

Tagore, R. (1918/1996b). Vernaculars for the M.A. degree. In S. K. Das (Ed.), *The English writings of Rabindranath Tagore, (EWRT)* (Vol. 3). New Delhi: Sahitya Akademi.

Tagore, R. (1919/1996b). On some educational questions. In S. K. Das (Ed.), *The English writings of Rabindranath Tagore, (EWRT)* (Vol. 3). New Delhi: Sahitya Akademi.

Tagore, R. (1921/1996b). The Nobel Prize acceptance speech. In S. K. Das (Ed.), *The English writings of Rabindranath Tagore, (EWRT)* (Vol. 3). New Delhi: Sahitya Akademi.

Tagore, R. (1922/1996a). Creative unity. In S. K. Das (Ed.) *The English Writings of Rabindranath Tagore, (EWRT)* (Vol. 2). New Delhi: Sahitya Akademi.

Tagore, R. (1924/1996a). To the English Teachers' Association Peking. In S. K. Das (Ed.) *The English writings of Rabindranath Tagore, (EWRT)* (Vol. 2). New Delhi: Sahitya Akademi.

Tagore, R. (1925/). Judgment. In S. K. Das (Ed.) *The English writings of Rabindranath Tagore, (EWRT)* (Vol. 3). New Delhi: Sahitya Akademi.

Tagore, R. (1929/1996b). Ideals of education. In S. K. Das (Ed.) *The English writings of Rabindranath Tagore, (EWRT)* (Vol. 3). New Delhi: Sahitya Akademi.

Tagore, R. (1930a/1996b). Conversations in Russia. In S. K. Das (Ed.) *The English writings of Rabindranath Tagore, (EWRT)* (Vol. 3). New Delhi: Sahitya Akademi.

Tagore, R. (1930b/1996b). Meeting of the East and the West. In S. K. Das (Ed.) *The English writings of Rabindranath Tagore, (EWRT)* (Vol. 3). New Delhi: Sahitya Akademi.

Tagore, R. (1930c/1996b). India: An appeal to idealism. In S. K. Das (Ed.) *The English writings of Rabindranath Tagore, (EWRT)* (Vol. 3). New Delhi: Sahitya Akademi.

Tagore, R. (1931/1996b). The religion of man. In S. K. Das (Ed.) *The English writings of Rabindranath Tagore, (EWRT)* (Vol. 3). New Delhi: Sahitya Akademi.

Tagore, R. (1932/1996b). Interviews in Persia. In S. K. Das (Ed.) *The English writings of Rabindranath Tagore, (EWRT)* (Vol. 3). New Delhi: Sahitya Akademi.

Tagore, R. (1933/1996b). To the youth of Hyderabad. In S. K. Das (Ed.) *The English writings of Rabindranath Tagore, (EWRT)* (Vol. 3). New Delhi: Sahitya Akademi.

Tagore, R. (1934/1996b). Letter to Gilbert Murray. In S. K. Das (Ed.) *The English writings of Rabindranath Tagore, (EWRT)* (Vol. 3). New Delhi: Sahitya Akademi.

Tagore, R. (1935/1996b). East and West. In S. K. Das (Ed.), *The English writings of Rabindranath Tagore, (EWRT)* (Vol. 3). New Delhi: Sahitya Akademi.

(b) In Bengali (Unless otherwise stated, all translations from Bengali are mine.)

Ayyub, A. S. (1973). *Panthajaner Sakha*. Kolkata: Dey's Publishing.

Ghosh, S. (2009). *Bhinna Ruchir Adhikar (Bengali)*. Kolkata: Talpata.

Tagore, R. (1892/2005). Sikshar Herpher (in Bengali). In *Shiksha*. Kolkata: Visva-Bharati Granthan Bibhag.

Tagore, R. (1906/2005). Sikshasamasya. In *Shiksha*. Kolkata: Visva-Bharati Granthan Bibhag.

Tagore, R. (1930d/2001). *Parasya-Yatri, in Rabindra-rachanabali (Granthaparichaya), (in Bengali)*, (Vol. 16). Kolkata: Paschimbanga Sarkar.

Chapter 12
Bankimchandra on Morality

Proyash Sarkar

Abstract Bankimchandra's controversial views on morality are closely related to religion. This essay discusses some of the central problems of his theory of ethics, including his views on equality, which went through a significant change in the last years of his philosophical career. Further, his convoluted relationship with utilitarianism has been examined. An attempt has been made at reconciling Bankim's claims that *sukha* (pleasure/happiness) is permanent and that it is produced by virtue.

Keywords Religion · Utilitarianism · Perfectionism · Equality · *Dharma*

12.1 Bankim: The Intellectual Journey

Bankimchandra Chattopadhyaya (1838–1894), one of the greatest thinkers of what is often regarded as 'Bengal renaissance' of 19th century, touched upon almost all aspects of human life and Indian society through his writings. He had keen interest in art and literature, science, philosophy, politics, economics, sociology and religion. He was a satirist of the calibre of Voltaire and Dickens, and in philosophy, he had in-depth scholarship in both the Indian and the Western traditions. Being the most versatile author of 19th century Bengal and having an encyclopaedic wisdom, he ventured in all domains of literary work that could be of interest to his readers. However, he had his own limitations—in some areas, like poetry, he could not achieve success that might suit his talent, and in some other cases, he put up constraints on his own writings as he advised young writers, "write only to create beauty or to promote welfare of human society, writing for any other purpose is a sin" (Chattopadhyay 1983e: 272, translation mine).[1]

---

[1] A citation of Bankim's original Bengali works are from (Chattopadhyay 1983a).

P. Sarkar (✉)
Department of Philosophy, Jadavpur University, Kolkata, India
e-mail: proyash@rediffmail.com

© Indian Institute of Advanced Study 2015
S. Deshpande (ed.), *Philosophy in Colonial India*, Sophia Studies in Cross-cultural Philosophy of Traditions and Cultures 11, DOI 10.1007/978-81-322-2223-1_12

Bankim's philosophy was the confluence of different thoughts, both Indian and Western. In his earlier days, he was deeply influenced by the thoughts of Jean-Jacques Rousseau (1712–1778), Jeremy Bentham (1748–1832), Auguste Comte (1798–1857), John Stuart Mill (1806–1873), Henry Thomas Buckle (1821–1862), Wilham Lacky (1838–1903) and others. If we look at his development as a social thinker, we will notice a sharp difference between the two phases of his philosophical life—the earlier phase, when he wrote *Bangadeśer Kṛṣak* (Chattopadhyay 1983f) and *Sāmya* (Chattopadhyay 1983b), and the later phase when he expressed his matured thoughts in *Dharmatattva* (Chattopadhyay 1983d). His readers never miss out the philosophical rigour and the sharp critical approach that is so typical of his writing style. He was quite conscious of his target readers, who were 'Western' educated middle-class Bengali *bābus*. The enthusiasm with which he received the newly acquired Western education and with it the individualistic utilitarian ethics of the West could hardly be overlooked. He deeply believed in those ideals and meticulously applied them to the Indian context. This was soon to die out as he gradually started appreciating the inner strength of Indian religion (Hinduism), culture and civilization. He never gave up his conviction in utilitarianism, though later on in his life, under the influence of the *Dharmaśāstras*, he denounced it as his guiding philosophy. During this phase of his life, he delved deep into the *Dharmaśāstras* and the *Purāṇas* and wrote two books which were rich in philosophical content. We will track this transition while discussing his views on morality and see how much he could free himself from the influence of Western thought. This essay focuses on Bankim's views on equality and justice as expressed in two of his monographs *Sāmya* (On Equality) (Chattopadhyay 1983c) and *Dharmatattva* (An Ethico-Religious Theory) (Chattopadhyay 1983d).[2]

---

[2] The term *dharma* is often used as a synonym of 'religion.' However, in Indian languages, especially in Sanskrit, it has a wide range of connotation. It originates from the root verb '*dhṛ*', which means to hold or to support. Thus the term *dharma* has a wider application than 'religion.' Whatever supports the human society and life is called *dharma*. Therefore, it is, not correct to translate *Dharmatattva* as 'An Ethico-Religious Theory.' Still, there are two reasons for this translation. First, due to the lack of any other expression that can more accurately express the sense of *dharma*, translating it as 'ethico-religious virtue' comes closest in meaning to '*dharma*.' Secondly, as far as Bankim's philosophy is concerned, *dharma* and 'religion' are intertwined in such a way, that they can hardly be separated from each other. Bankim writes, "If you say that you don't accept God, then our debate ends there. I am ready to discuss religion (*dharma*) as detached from after-life, but not ready to discuss it as detached from God." (Chattopadhyay 1983d: 605, translation mine). He is aware of this fact as he discusses the meaning of '*dharma*' elaborately in the endnotes ('*Kroḍapatra Ka*' and '*Kroḍapatra Kha*') to this essay. In 'endnote A', he mentions six different senses in which this term is used in Bengali, whereas in 'endnote B', he discusses the different senses in which this term is used in different classical Indian traditions starting from *athāto dharma-jigñāsā* of *Jaimini Sūtra*. After a long discussion, he comes to the conclusion that we do not have a single term for religion in any of the Indian languages. The Indians could never separate religion from the other aspects of life. *dharma* is all-encompassing when it comes to human life and society.

12.2 On Equality

Sāmya is an attempt to understand the Indian society and its history in the light of the teachings of Buddha, Jesus, Mill, and Rousseau. The aim of this monograph, i.e. *Sāmya*, is to critique the age-old discrimination that impoverished the Indian society for centuries and also to explore the possible solutions to this problem. Though it reflects one of his boldest reactions against social discrimination, Bankim disowned it in his later life. He reportedly told one of his contemporaries, "There was a time when I was greatly influenced by Mill, now all is over.... The views expressed in *Sāmya* are utterly wrong, though they sell well; I won't print [it] again."[3] It is interesting to explore why Bankim refrained from publishing *Sāmya* again in his lifetime. Just within a span of nine years, he seemed to have undergone a sea change in his thought from the days of *Sāmya* to the days of his matured philosophical thinking expressed in *Dharmatattva*. His commentators express a divided opinion on this issue. Some say that the difference is just superficial, as Bankim claimed that the views that he advocated in *Dharmatattva* had no conflict with his earlier views about equality. Hiranmoy Banerjee seems to subscribe to such a view as he writes, "Bankim remained loyal to his early fascination for utilitarianism, but he considered it to be a part of the highest religion" (Banerjee 1998: 55). Others, like Baridbaran Chakraborty (Chakraborty 1989), hold that the departure from his earlier views is significant and they discuss possible reasons for that. We will try to throw some light on this issue and try to show how far, if at all, Bankim digressed in *Dharmatattva* from his earlier views as expressed in *Sāmya*.

Allegiance to equality was in the intellectual atmosphere of Calcutta at that time. As a leading intellectual, Bankim could not distance himself from this movement. Rousseau said that human beings are born equal. However, we need to qualify this statement in order to render it acceptable. In *Sāmya,* Bankim makes a distinction between differences among human beings that are *natural* and differences which are imposed upon them *artificially*. In contemporary terminology, some differences are natural and others are social constructions. The natural differences are there in the nature, they are not man-made. On the other hand, differences that are social constructions, i.e. artificial differences, are not there in nature. They are human creation and are held by Bankim to be the root cause of social discrimination. All attempts of rationally justifying discrimination stem from and are founded on some sort of artificial difference or other. The question still remains, can difference, be it natural or otherwise, justify discrimination? If it cannot, then any attempt of vindicating a discriminatory system on the premise that there are differences among the concerned parties, would turn out to be futile. The folly of this line of argumentation was not unknown to a scholar like Bankim, as he wrote, "We do not accept the view that difference can justify discrimination. This statement utterly goes against the theory of equality" (Chattopadhyay 1983b: 399, translation mine).

---

[3] Quoted by J.C Bagal (Bagal 1983: xxiii, translation mine).

This statement needs to be further qualified in appropriate ways. Don't we appoint men in the defence forces following certain standards and reject others who fail to pass the tests according to those standards? Do we ever think this to be unjustified? In every society, people possessing certain physical and mental abilities enjoy certain privileges. Those who lack these abilities are considered to be ineligible to enjoy these privileges. This principle, therefore, cannot be accepted even by its supporters in the manner in which it is presented here. Nor can it be rejected in this form as difference is often accepted as the basis for distributing rights and privileges to groups of people. Bankim is quite conscious of this fact, as he claims that this principle cannot be universally true. Arguing against the contention that the *natural* difference between men and women justifies lesser opportunity for women, he writes,

> The type of difference of character existing between men and women does also exist between the English and the Bengali. The English are mighty and the Bengalis are meek, the English are strong and the Bengalis are weak, the English are courageous and the Bengalis are coward, the English are tenacious and the Bengalis are quiescent, and so on.[4] If these natural differences could justify difference in rights, then why do we protest against the difference in rights between the English and the Bengalis? (Chattopadhyay 1983b: 399, translation mine)

What he intends to say is that even if natural difference can sometimes justify lack of equal opportunity, yet it cannot be made a universal principle, as it cannot be applied indiscriminately. The mere presence of natural difference cannot vindicate discrimination. Any discriminatory treatment of different groups within a heterogeneous society requires further justification.

Besides, all discriminatory power-structures in all societies hinge on some artificial difference between people who are discriminated against and people who are privileged. Following John Stuart Mill, Bankim considers gender to be a case of *artificial difference being naturalized for discriminatory purposes*. With regard to women, he says that the differences that are supposed to be the ground for a discriminatory treatment, worse than animal, of women, are all social constructs. Given equal opportunity and being freed from social prohibition women can attain those coveted qualities, which are in the common parlance supposed to be exclusively men's prerogative to acquire.

The point that Bankim makes here is extremely important with respect to the study of the mechanisms operative in social discrimination. He, however, could not realize its entire significance as he made this observation only in passing while discussing gender-related discrimination. If A and B are naturally different in some respect, then they may be subjected to unequal treatment without thereby necessarily implicating discrimination. 'Equality' does not mean equal treatment of all under all circumstances; it means the presence of equal opportunities to all who

---

[4] It is noticeable that the characteristics Bankim associates with the English are generally associated with masculinity and valourized and those he ascribes to Bengalis are pejorative and associated with femininity.

are otherwise equal in all relevant respects. Discrimination, thus, means unequal treatment of, and the lack of equal opportunity to, the people who are equal in all relevant respects with the people enjoying certain privileges. If the differences are natural and relevant to the unequal treatment of groups of people, then it cannot be called discrimination. It is a different question as to what makes a particular feature relevant for some particular purpose. In almost all societies, minors and adults are unequal in their right to freedom. We do not call this unequal treatment 'discrimination.' However, similar difference of rights between two adults may be considered to be discrimination. No minor has the right to vote in the general election of a country, and this can hardly be said to be discrimination. But if an adult, having sound mind and having been not convicted by any trial court of the country, is prohibited from voting in the general election, we call this discrimination. The question of discrimination, therefore, arises only when there is no natural difference between the concerned parties. It implies that any discriminatory power-structure that aims at justifying itself would rely upon a *mechanism of an artificial property being naturalized*. By 'artificial', we mean properties that are results of social construction in the sense that they are neither produced by nature nor are they homogenously present in the group which is thus discriminated against. These properties are pajoratized and are perceived to be characteristic of the target group. Returning to the discussion of gender, human mental properties have always been thought of in terms of binaries, like reason/emotion, objective/subjective, detached/related, etc. The former of each pair is valourized and is considered to be masculine and the latter pajoratized and is associated with femininity. These properties are *considered to be* natural to men and women, respectively, though they are results of social construction and in this sense these artificial properties are *naturalized*.

Another point to be noted here, though Bankim himself did not make it explicit, is that by artificial properties we do not mean all non-natural, *vis-à-vis* cultural or cultured, properties whatsoever. The existence of properties that are produced by nurture or by observance, like wisdom, or skill in a game, may be a valid ground for unequal treatment. Hence, when we use the expression 'an artificial property being naturalized', we mean by 'artificial property' an attribute of a person or a group that is *socially constructed,* and it is 'naturalized' in the sense that it is *considered to be* natural. The difference between natural and artificial properties drawn by Bankim is, therefore, of enormous importance to us in understanding social discrimination. We shall return to this point while discussing his views on *varṇa* and *jāti*. Let us now concentrate on his view about gender.

12.3 On Gender Discrimination

Keeping in mind that Bankim was writing in late 19th century Calcutta, his views on women as expressed in *Sāmya* are equally revolutionary. He claims equal opportunity for women with men in all spheres of life including political, social, economic, and educational. He acknowledges that women should have the right to be members of the legislative assembly and should take part in its proceedings. They should have the right to work and the right to property; they should also have equal right to inherit ancestral property with their male siblings. They should have the right to education. He urges that widows should have the right to remarriage if required. On the last issue, Bankim appears to be in a duel state of mind. When we read *Sāmya*, we readily realize that we are confronted with a highly rational and philosophical mind, which can follow any argument to its logical consequences. We know that at this stage in his life, he was greatly influenced by John Stuart Mill. Acceptance of the principle of equality and also the newly imported Western ideas of personal liberty compelled him to accept widow-remarriage. During this period, he used to believe that the entire ethics is embedded in the two theses of equality and liberty (*svānuvartitā*) (Chattopadhyay 1983b: 403, translation mine). Behind this rationally committed mind, we find another Bankim speaking out his inner self, "… widow-remarriage is neither good nor bad … but it is expected that widows should have the right to remarriage. The loyal (*sādhvī*) wife, who loves her husband, [however,] would never wish to get married again after his demise" (Chattopadhyay 1983b: 401, translation mine).

Manu, the Hindu law-giver, said that women should be protected and kept under constant surveillance by their male counterparts to protect their chastity, which was supposed to be one of the most coveted virtues in women. It was argued that if women were given freedom, they might lose their chastity. Bankim ridicules this argument with an analogy that women's chastity is not water enclosed in cloth (Chattopadhyay 1983b: 403). It is not as fragile and as mutable as has traditionally been thought of. He realized that the cause of the plight of women in India is the orthodox system promoted by the *Dharmaśāstras*. He is so much charged with emotions, and that at places so agitated, that he makes such comments as, "If this is *dharmaśāstra* (a theory of virtue) then what is *adharmaśāstra* (a theory of vice)?" (Chattopadhyay 1983b: 405, translation mine).

He repents that in the entire Hindu literature only one female character, viz. Sītā, who in spite of having numerous good qualities lacked independence and vigour, was eulogized. In sharp contrast to Sītā, Draupadī had vigour (*teja*), and vanity (*darpa*) in her character. It is unfortunate that Draupadi so distinct in her identity failed to become an icon for the Hindu litterateur (Chattopadhyay 1983g: 194–195).

The key to women's emancipation from their predicament lies, according to Bankim, in their education, which can alone eradicate all social evils. If our women folks get proper education, they will become economically independent, which in its turn will help them come out of the miserable condition they live in. He is not ready to accept the view that women in India are unwise. Drawing a distinction between knowledge and wisdom, he urges that our women folks might lack knowledge, but they do not lack wisdom, as traditional wisdom is entrusted upon them through verbal tradition. However, technical education is also important (Chattopadhyay 1983d: 612).

However, contrary to the position that he takes in *Sāmya*, Bankim advocates the exactly opposite view in *Dharmatattva* on the issue of women and virtually accepts everything proposed in the *Dharmaśāstras* of which he was so critical in his earlier life. In *Sāmya,* he leaves no stone unturned to disprove the contention that women are inferior to men; however, in *Dharmatattva,* he admits that women are inferior to men in their physical abilities. So it is a duty (*dharma*) of men to protect women. This duty has a purpose—if women folks are perished from this world, then the human race will also disappear. For him, human life does not bear any significance outside of a society in which alone it can flourish. Considered as such, this statement appears to be almost a truism. The consequences are, however, far-reaching. Since women are unable to protect men and also themselves, their only duty is to serve men, take care of their pleasure and to support them in attaining their divine goal. Thus, the only purpose of life for a woman is to help man attain his goal of this life and the life beyond death.[5] This is a total regression compromising his earlier views on equality and liberty to the system of *Dharmaśāstra* of Manu.

12.4 On *Cāturvarṇya*

During the last few years of his life, Bankim delved deeper in the *Vedas* and *Dharmaśāstras* and found the latter more accurately expressing the Indian ethos,[6] not to say, he accepted them uncritically. He was a Hindu revivalist and argued extensively to prove that Hinduism was the best religion in the world. For him religion, by which he means Hinduism, or *Vaiṣṇavism,* expresses eternal truths, and hence, religious doctrines should be reinterpreted in every era according to the needs and the forms of life of the people of the respective ages. His *Dharmatattva* is an attempt to take up that task for Hinduism. He repeatedly urges that he is not expounding a new religion, but is merely making explicit what is implicit and acceptable in Hinduism as expressed in the *Dharmaśāstras* and *Bhagavad Gītā.* This shows that he was a Hindu revivalist and a religious reformist of Hinduism at the same time. So, it is understandable that he was writing under the pressing need for not digressing much from the doctrines expounded in the *Dharmaśāstras.* Placed in this context, his later views would perhaps invite less criticism than it ordinarily does.

Bankim did not say anything which was novel and also of philosophical importance in *Sāmya.*[7] Being charged with the newly acquired ideas such as liberty and

---

[5] The duties, universally entrusted upon women, of bearing and rearing of children are also only for this purpose, and in this regard, bearing a male child is all the more important than giving birth to a female child, according to the *Dharmaśāstras*. Though both the male offspring and the female offspring have some role to play in the family, as well as in the society, yet the sacrificial rites towards the ancestors can be performed, and the family lineage be maintained, only by a male offspring.

[6] It is worth noting that for other scholars of 'Bengal renaissance', like Tagore and Vivekananda, the *Vedas*, especially the *Upaniṣadas*, rather than the *Dharmaśāstras* were the true representative of the Indian culture. Here lies a huge difference between Bankim's system of thought and those of his contemporaries.

[7] Though for this he can hardly be accused as he writes elsewhere, "Very little can be said in this world, which is at the same time novel." (Chattopadhyay 1983d: 595).

equality, he got a new vision and started reassessing his understanding of the history and culture of Bengal in particular and that of India in general. Most of what he said about Bengal also applied to India. In this essay, his thrust was on the condition of Bengal-peasantry of his time and the condition of women in Bengal. In connection with the former, he also discussed the perils of the system of *varṇa* prevalent in Indian societies. Though it is an important historical document, his discussion of Bengal-peasantry has lost much of its importance. This is one reason why we would not discuss it here. However, his remarks on *varṇa*, though not more than just passing comments, still bear significance in the changed socio-economic context of the 21st century.

In spite of refraining from publishing *Sāmya* again, Bankim published a significant portion of it later on under the title *Baṅgadeśer Kṛṣak* (Bengal-Peasantry). In this article, he argues that the greatest social evil of ancient India was the development of the system of *varṇa*, which in the course of history became hereditary. It was found to be the greatest hindrance to the principle of 'the greatest happiness for the greatest number of people.' Though later on in *Dharmatattva* and in his commentary on the *Bhagavad Gītā*, he became greatly appreciative of this (the *varṇa*) system, he never forgets to express his aversion to its hereditariness. He classifies all human activities, which are directed towards producing commodities and services that human beings enjoy, into five groups: (1) acquisition and dissemination of knowledge for the masses, (2) defence or vigilance, (3) industry or trade, (4) production or agriculture, and (5) service. The first three of the above list were entrusted upon the first three *varṇas*, and the last two were assigned to the *śūdra*. This strict division of labour helped India develop the skills of its people and excel in all walks of life in the ancient times. He did not realize the enormous significance of his distinction between natural and artificial difference in understanding and eradicating the perils of this system, ignoring the fact that an artificial difference was created among the people of India in the name of *varṇa* and that with the help of it a discriminatory system was promoted. Perhaps, his lineage as a *kulīna* Brahmin, an identity of which he became conscious late in his life, along with his apprehension of the internal strength and the beauty of the *Sanātana* tradition prevented him to realize the importance of '*jamming the theoretical machinery itself*, of suspending its pretension to the production of a truth and of a meaning that are excessively univocal', to borrow a concept from Irrigaray (1985: 78, emphasis mine). The gunpowder was prepared by him to be put into the barrel and to be ignited; still something very strange, perhaps his identity, prevented him from taking the final step. Instead of attacking the system of *varṇa* head on, as he apparently did in *Sāmya*, he started whitewashing the dilapidated structure. Granting him his theory of human nature and also the Hindu revivalist's view of the benefits of division of labour with regard to *varṇa*, we still wonder why a critical mind like his preferred keeping mum on the discriminatory aspect of this system. He also did not take up for discussion the issue of *jāti*, which would have drawn him into a discussion of the discrimination existing in his contemporary Indian society among the different classes of people, including those of the conqueror and the conquered. He was quite conscious about it.

Admitting that such discrimination did really exist in India, he went on to say that he did not take it up for discussion because it was much discussed by his fellow Indians (Chattopadhyay 1983b: 406).

Though he was aware of the perils of the British rule in India, and believed in the 'drain-of-wealth doctrine', yet, at the same time, he believed that India had received many things from the British rule, including an improved trade and commerce, and education in return. Hence, he was not in favour of a total rout of it.

12.5 A Utilitarian After All?

We have discussed above some of the most important respects in which we find a significant change in Bankim's thought from his earlier position. This gives us a glimpse of how he deviates from utilitarianism in both the phases. He was a system builder. His quest for the meaning of life led him to build up a religion-based system of ethics that took in its purview all aspects of human life and society. In his later life when his earlier enthusiasm with hedonistic utilitarianism died down considerably, Bankim found utilitarianism to be inadequate and expanded it to a great extent. He never abandoned the doctrine altogether, rather accepted it as a part of his system of ethics. In what follows we will discuss in brief Bankim's theory of the highest religion and in the course of that discussion try to track the development of his thought.

Contrary to what is widely believed, Bankim did not subscribe to utilitarianism with regard to moral norms. Roughly speaking, hedonistic utilitarianism as a theory of ethical standard is the view that a conduct or a rule thereof is ethically right if and only if it promotes, or at least tends to promote the greatest happiness for the greatest number of people. He was a perfectionist in the moral and political, *vis-à-vis* the psychological,[8] sense of the term. He never claimed himself to be a perfectionist but what he says about morality and human nature gives us good reason to characterize his position as perfectionism. He agrees with Mill[9] that a morally good action promotes the greatest happiness for the greatest number of people. However, as a perfectionist he maintains that an action is good *not because* it promotes the greatest happiness but *because* it is conducive to the *development of human character*. As it has already been mentioned, human life, for him, has a meaning, though it does not have any intrinsic value. He had a lifelong quest for this meaning, which he ultimately discovered in his 50s, when he was able to build

---

[8] His claim is not merely that we need to have a perfect state of mind by harmonizing all our psycho-physical dispositions through observance. He rather claims that such a balanced (*sāmañjasyapūrṇa*) development of human character is the very essence of morality, and that it ensures socio-political good for the person as well as the community.

[9] Mill is sometimes called a perfectionist, as for him an action is good not just because it produces the greatest amount of happiness, but because it produces a particular kind of happiness that accords with good life. This is also the main reason why Mill is accused of accepting an extra-hedonistic calculus setting aside his favoured pleasure principle.

a system of ethics in his *Dharmatattva*. Life has a purpose and is worth living as far as it aims at attaining that purpose. It, therefore, has only an instrumental value. An unreflective life devoid of that purpose is comparable to that of an animal. Consistent with the orthodox Indian thought, like that expressed in the *Dharmaśāstras*, he maintains that the purpose of life is the overall well-being of the society. And for the well-being of the society, a holistic and balanced development of character traits (*vṛttis*) of the individuals is required. A human being attains moral standard as far as she succeeds in developing all her character traits in a balanced manner. This concept of balance (*sāmañjasya*) among the character traits/faculties[10] plays an important role in his system of ethics. Considered as such these character traits are neither good nor bad; if they are developed in a balanced manner, they can yield good results—actions that are conducive to the optimal happiness and the well-being for the masses. On the other hand, if any of the faculties is given undue importance and is developed disproportionately, it can produce results that are pernicious to the life concerned and the society at large.

Bankim primarily classifies these abilities into three types, viz. the cognitive abilities, the conative abilities and the aesthetic abilities (Chattopadhyay 1983d: 592). All these are mental abilities. Later on he adds to this list the physical abilities (Chattopadhyay 1983d: 606). Thus for him, human beings have four types of abilities. The difference between the conative and the physical abilities is that the former are mental in nature and comprise dispositions, such as devotion, love, and hatred, that induce us to action. The religion of observance (*anuśīlana dharma*) advices us to act in such a manner that it will promote the optimal development of all these abilities in a balanced manner. Humanity (*manuṣyatva*) is nothing but a balanced development and an optimal expression (*sphūrti*) of these abilities. Even the so-called negative dispositions (emotions) have some positive aspects—they are produced (by God) to serve some purpose for the well-being of the society. Anger is pernicious if developed disproportionately; however, in the absence of it the individual and her society become victims to external onslaught. Thus, for Bankim, all human dispositions are important for life and society, and they must be developed in a balanced manner.

As an empiricist Mill relied upon the bottom-up model, or the composition model, for deriving his altruism:

> No reason can be given why the general happiness is desirable, except that each person, so far as he believes it to be attainable, desires his own happiness. This, however, being a fact, we have not only all the proof which the case admits of, but all which it is possible to require, that happiness is a good: that each person's happiness is a good to that person, and the general happiness, therefore, a good to the aggregate of all persons. (Mill 1863: 52)

Mill is severely criticized for supporting his utilitarianism by this fragile argument. Bankim, on the other hand, accepts a top-down model to support the principle of utility. He accepts holism as an ethico-metaphysical doctrine; a sort of coherence

---

[10] With some reservation, Bankim accepts the word 'faculty' as a translation of '*vṛtti*' (Chattopadhyay 1983d: 588) Any of the terms 'character trait', 'disposition', or 'ability' would have been a better translation. In the present paper, these terms have been used interchangeably.

prevails within this world. Everything is connected with everything else with internal coherence. With the help of this notion, he tries to solve all the problems of ethics including that of evil (Chattopadhyay 1983d: 598). Unlike Mill he derives the principle of utility and his ethical holism from his metaphysical holism. Thus, utilitarianism becomes just a part of a larger system of ethics. He was a believer in an omnipotent personal[11] God,[12] who possesses all the good qualities that we can conceive of. Such a God, who is the creator of this world, could not have created a world inhospitable to the human race. So even if there appears to be some evil in this world, it is also ultimately for the benefit of mankind.

He also parts company with Mill in his understanding of human psychology. Being a psychological hedonist and an empiricist, Mill's conception of a human being is too selfish. The moral agent in Mill's system is psychologically programmed to seek only her own pleasure. Bankim finds no reason whatsoever to suppose human nature in this way. Why do we have to say that the desire for the well-being of others, i.e. the altruistic desire, is not intrinsic to human mind? Devotion, for him, is nothing but altruistic love. Similarly, patriotism, or the love for one's own offspring, is also included in altruistic love and is as natural and original to the mind as is egoistic self-love. The only difference is that some dispositions are consistent with the egoistic self-love, like the love for one's own offspring. They tend to override the others, like the love for one's own neighbours, which are not consistent with egoistic self-love (Chattopadhyay 1983d: 647–661). It is our moral duty to control the former and develop the latter by constant observance.

---

[11] "[A]ll who are personally acquainted with popular Hinduism as professed by the people at large, know that the belief in a Personal God is of the very essence of the creed of the Hindu peoples. The words 'Iśwara,' 'Parameśwara,' 'Jagadiśwara' are on the lips of every Hindu and are used by them to denote not the philosophic conception of a pantheistic God, but a Personal Ruler of the universe, and the Supreme Disposer of all things." (Chatterjee 1969b Quoted from Chatterjee 1969a: 269).

[12] He provides us with no arguments for the existence of such a God. He simply takes it as a primitive. He has an incommensurable difference with the atheist (Chattopadhyay 1983d: 605, see fn. 1). At times when Bankim lacks arguments, he adheres to his own faith dogmatically, or at worst, his strategy is to rebuke his opponent with abusive language. At one place, he claims that the Brahmins of ancient India sacrificed their lives for the benefit of the masses by adopting the life of an ascetic living on alms. Then, he goes on saying, "No nation of the world is as talented, powerful, wise and virtuous as the Brahmins of ancient India. The citizens of Ancient Athens or Rome, medieval Italy, or those of modern Germany or England were not as powerful and as talented. The Roman cleric, the Buddhist monk, or people from any other community were not as wise or as virtuous [as the Brahmins of ancient India]" (Chattopadhyay 1983d: 618). At another place, he claims that he has "proofs" (pramāṇa) in support of rebirth, yet at the same time he admits that it is a highly contentious issue. When asked to produce the 'proof', he, without doing so, prefers to say, "It is only due to the superstition of the modern scientist that this debate is still going on." (Chattopadhyay 1983d: 603).

12.6 Pleasure and Moral Virtues

Bankim's view on *sukha* (pleasure/happiness) is philosophically problematic. He maintains, on the one hand, that *sukha* is produced by virtue (*dharma*) and that it is permanent (*sthāyī*), on the other. The term '*sukha*' is generally translated as pleasure. It is widely held in the orthodox Indian philosophy that a virtuous life gives rise to pleasure. Pleasure is the product of virtue. There is a causal relation holding between the two. It follows that pleasure is impermanent, as nothing which has a cause is permanent. Due to its impermanence, pleasure ultimately leads to pain. Bankim's contention that pleasure is permanent thus appears to be inconsistent with his view that pleasure is caused by virtue.

Bankim is aware of this problem, as he draws a distinction between pleasure that ultimately leads to pain and permanent pleasure. The first type of pleasure, properly speaking, is no pleasure, according to him. It is pain in disguise. The permanent pleasure is the only pleasure we can think of (Chattopadhyay 1983d: 602). What we have translated as 'permanent pleasure' (*sthāyī sukha*) is more akin to happiness in this respect; and something being permanent need not be eternal. Thus what Bankim means when he says that *sukha* is produced by the observance of virtue is that a virtuous life is a happy life—a life full of bliss. This is the state of liberation. Happiness is permanent in the sense that it covers this mundane life (*ihakāla*) as well as the life after death (*parakāla*). This also goes well with the ordinary usage of the term '*sukha*' in Bengali. '*Sukhī parivāra*' means a *happy* family; a 'pleasant family' makes no sense. Though this happiness is a permanent state, as opposed to the fleeing state of pleasure, it is in no way eternal. Similarly, the state of liberation (*mukti*) is necessarily accompanied by permanent pleasure produced by virtue.

A virtuous life consists in self-purification (*citta-śuddhi*), which is the result of the proper development and manifestation of all the dispositions of the individual concerned. The only way to attain such a life is through the development and manifestation of the dispositions already there in a dormant state in human character. Observance (*anuśīlana*) is suggested as the means to attain such a goal. This alone is *dharma*. It is thus called the religion of observance. Some dispositions are self-manifesting, like the sexual urge; they tend to develop themselves to the fullest. The duty of a morally good life is to arrest the development of these dispositions to balance them with others which are not self-manifesting. Bankim repeatedly says that unlike an ascetic he does not advice a complete extirpation of any of our dispositions. "Irrespective of whether it is good or bad, extirpation of any of our dispositions is a vice (*adharma*)" (Chattopadhyay 1983d: 598). On the other hand, the dispositions which are not self-manifesting need to be developed to an optimal proportion. But the question is, how do we know which dispositions are to be developed and which are not? According to Bankim, *pleasure* (*sukha*) is the 'touchstone', with the help of which we decide in case of any particular disposition whether or not it needs to be developed (Chattopadhyay 1983d: 600). The dispositions that can ultimately produce the greatest amount of happiness for the society need to be developed; and those which restrict the optimal happiness should be deterred.

This appears to be going against our earlier contention that Bankim was not a utilitarian with regard to the moral standard. If morality depends upon the optimal development of human dispositions, and if we need to refer to the pleasure principle in order to decide which dispositions are to be developed and which are to be restricted, then morality seems to depend ultimately on the principle of the 'greatest happiness of the greatest number.'

Objections like this arise due to confusion between the moral principle and the principle for judging the moral worth of actions. The moral principle sets the conditions the fulfilment of which is essential for an action or a rule to be morally good/correct. It says nothing about the criterion/criteria with the help of which we can decide in any particular situation whether or not these conditions have been fulfilled. A Kantian, for example, can say that an action is morally right if it is produced by good will. But this Kantian moral principle tells us nothing about the criterion, which enables us to decide, in a given situation, whether the action has been produced by good will.[13] The principle that judges the moral worth of an action, on the other hand, provides us with a criterion (or criteria) that allow/s us to decide in a given situation which actions fulfil the conditions set forth by the moral principle. Theoretically, there is no necessary connection between the moral principle and the principle of judgment. One may propose a moral principle without thereby saying anything about the principle of moral judgement.[14] Utilitarianism accepts the principle of the greatest happiness for the greatest number as the moral principle, yet it may propose a very different principle, or may prefer to remain silent, as it generally does, about the principle of moral judgment. The proponent of utilitarianism may accept intuitionism with regard to the principle of judgment. The crucial question on utilitarianism with regard to the latter is, how do we know which actions produce the greatest happiness for the greatest number of people? Here, our utilitarian may accept an intuitionist position saying that if by rational *intuition* one discovers that an action produces happiness of higher order, then it (the action) can be said to be following the principle of utility, viz. the principle of the greatest happiness for the greatest number. Bankim accepts perfectionism with regard to the moral principle, according to which, an action or a rule of action is morally good if it develops or seeks to develop the dispositions already there in human nature. However, the happiness principle acts as the principle of moral judgment, that is to say we need to endorse those actions, as promoting a balanced development of character, which alone can secure happiness of their agent.

If our reading of Bankim is correct, then he is not a utilitarian in a very important sense of the term. The engagement of Bentham and Mill with the hedonistic

---

[13] In Kant's ethics, being solely produced by good will is the nature of a moral action. He, however, provides us with a different *criterion* with the help of which we can judge the moral worth of an action. For him, the principle of universalizability seems to act as a moral criterion.

[14] However, the principle of moral judgement depends upon the moral principle.

utilitarian principle is much more central than what we find in Bankim, who confines its role as a principle of moral judgment and never uses it as a moral principle. Bankim was never comfortable with the idea that morality be based upon the principle of happiness. In one place, he ridicules utilitarianism as the philosophy of the stomach (Chattopadhayay 1983h). He created a character, Kamalakanta Chakrabarty (Chattopadhayay 1983c), who was addicted to opium. Kamalakanta used to become clairvoyant while in an inebriated state under the spell of opium and could read the thoughts not only of his fellow beings but also thoughts of other creatures like cats. While in such a state, he wrote an article on 'utilitarianism', which sets, as the moral principle, the dictum that we should try to satisfy our appetite. His landlord, Bhishmadev Khoshnavish, who happened to be also the editor of his works did not know English well, asked his son the meaning of 'utility.' This boy had just started learning English. It was only with the help of this boy Bhishmadev could make out the sense of the term. In a footnote to Kamalakanta's article on 'Utility' Bhishmadev writes, "The term 'u' refers to the second person, 'til' refers to cultivation, and 'it' refers to the fulfilment of appetite" (Chattopadhayay 1983h: fn. 54). His son could not make out the meaning of the case ending 'e' pronounced at the end of the term. To his utter surprise and indignation, now Bhishmadev could discover Kamalakanta to have abused us calling all of us peasants, since by using the term 'utility' he advised us to cultivate and eat.[15]

References

Bagal, J. C. (1983). Introduction to Sāhitya Prasaṅga. In Chattopadhyay, 1983a.
Banerjee, H. (1998). Society, morality and culture: Bankim Chandra's response to western thought in Kalyan Sengupta and Tirthanath Bandyopadhyay (Eds.), *19th century thought in Bengal*. New Delhi, Calcutta: Allied Publishers.
Chakraborty, B. (1989). *Sāmya: Bankimbīkṣaṇ*. In K. Gupta (Ed.), *Bankimchandra: Ādhunik Man*. Calcutta: Pustak Bipani.
Chatterjee, B. C. (1969a). In J. C. Bagal (Ed.), *Bankim Rachanavali* (A collection of Bankim's works in English). Calcutta: Sahitya Samsad.
Chatterjee, B. C. (1969b). Letters on Hinduism: Polytheism—first stage. In Chatterjee 1969a.
Chattopadhyay, B. C. (1983a). In Y. C. Bagal (Ed.), *Bankim Racanāvalī* (Vol. II). Calcutta: Sāhitya Saṁsad.
Chattopadhyay, B. C. (1879/1983b). Sāmya. In Chattopadhyay, 1983a.
Chattopadhyay, B. C. (1885/1983c). Kamalākanta. In Chattopadhyay, 1983a.
Chattopadhyay, B. C. (1888/1983d). Dharmatattva. In Chattopadhyay, 1983a.
Chattopadhyay, B. C. (1983e). Bāṅgālār Navya Lekhakdiger Prati Nivedan. In Chattopadhyay, 1983a.
Chattopadhyay, B. C. (1983f). Bāṅgadeśer Kṛṣak. In Chattopadhyay, 1983a.
Chattopadhyay, B. C. (1983g). Draupadī. In Chattopadhyay 1983b.
Chattopadhayay, B. C. (1983h). Utility Ba Udar-Darśan. In Chattopadhayay, 1983d.
Irrigaray, L. (1985). *This sex which is not one* (C. P. & C. Burke, Trans.). Ithaca: Cornell University Press.
Mill, J. S. (1863). *Utilitarianism*. London: Parker, Son and Bourn.

---

[15] I am indebted to Professors Shefali Moitra, Tara Chatterjee and Madhumita Chattopadhyaya for their critical comments on earlier drafts of this chapter.

Chapter 13
Colonialism and Traditional Forms of Knowledge: *Then and Now*

Mohini Mullick

> *The history of the West as the West arises out of an orientation*
> *that understands the Orient as a space of disorientation.*
>
> Spurr (1993: 143)

Abstract By raising the question 'which language do the *śāstra*s now speak?', this essay illuminates the predicament of Indian knowledge systems in the era of colonial hegemony. It grapples with a number of issues including the very notion of colonialism which cannot be taken as referring to any historically closed period. The question that emerges in this context pertains to the complex relationship between 'the colonial state of mind' and the language that the colonial mind uses for self-expression. The essay examines various formulations of this relationship such as 'movement of harmonization,' 'East–West binary' with the alleged superiority of Eastern spirituality, the Anglo-German world-view, the policies of 'dissemination of Western ideas of reason and progress of civilization,' and 'the structured incommensurability between the two worlds' as revealed in the program of the translation of Sanskrit texts. It is argued that we are the inheritors of this incommensurability, of a total epistemological break. This calls for a thorough philosophical scrutiny of the intercultural translation program anchored in colonialism and its repercussions.

Keywords Colonialism · *Sāstra* · Translation · *Dharma* · Rationality

There are two themes that we wish to draw attention to: one, the nature of the interaction between the colonial powers and the purveyors of traditional knowledge in the 19th century and early 20th century; and two, following on the first,

Mohini Mullick has retired from the Indian Institute of Technology Kanpur.

M. Mullick (✉)
Formerly Department of Humanities and Social Sciences, Indian Institute of Technology Kanpur, Kanpur, India
e-mail: mohini.mullick@gmail.com

© Indian Institute of Advanced Study 2015
S. Deshpande (ed.), *Philosophy in Colonial India*, Sophia Studies in Cross-cultural Philosophy of Traditions and Cultures 11, DOI 10.1007/978-81-322-2223-1_13

the relation between the system of knowledge introduced by the British and the system that was in place in the India of this period. *Inter alia*, we will raise the question of when colonialism ended–or did it?

Motivating the following discussion is what one may term 'the Received View' on these questions which could be framed thus: 'Indian philosophers of the colonial period wrote in a context of cultural fusion generated by the British colonial rule. As a consequence, they pursued Indian philosophy in a manner which was both secular and modern (read 'rational') in order to render it both accessible and acceptable in the Anglophone world, as well as the educated Indian populace at home.' The key phrases in this formulation are as follows: one, 'fusion'; two, 'accessible and acceptable'; three, 'educated'; and four 'secular and modern.'

13.1 The Colonial State of Mind

But let us start with key word zero: 'colonialism' itself. When does/did the colonial period end? In 1947 at the stroke of midnight, etc., etc.? Give or take a few years as personnel departed and institutions got dismantled? This essay is partly an effort to answer this question. I begin by plagiarizing an entire paragraph from an historian's work. But as in all plagiarisms, one changes a word here, a phrase there. (Here, 'history' is replaced by 'philosophy.') Thus:

> That Europe works as a silent referent in historical/philosophical knowledge itself becomes obvious in a highly ordinary way. There are at least two everyday symptoms of the subalternity of non-Western third-world histories/philosophies. Third-world historians/philosophers feel a need to refer to works in European history/philosophy: historians/philosophers of Europe do not feel any need to reciprocate…the 'greats' and the models of the historians/philosophical enterprise are always at least culturally 'European.' 'They' produce their work in relative ignorance of non-Western histories/philosophies, and this does not seem to affect the quality of their work. This is a gesture, however, that 'we' cannot return. We cannot even afford an equality or symmetry of ignorance at this level without taking the risk of appearing 'old-fashioned' or 'outdated.' (Chakrabarti 1992: 2)

Although this cannot be argued out at length, or demonstrated by citing chapter and verse, the position that this essay takes following from the above is as follows: The term 'colonial' refers not only to a slice of history, although undoubtedly the end of British imperial rule marked a significant transformation in the sociopolitical sphere in this country, but also it is a state of mind. Part of the present argument is that we in this country have only entered a new phase of colonialism: neo-colonialism, quite misleadingly termed 'post-colonialism.' For our purposes, the term refers primarily to a kind of discourse, both the first-order level in which philosophical writings were produced—and are still produced—and works at the second-order or meta-level used to critically evaluate, i.e., analyze and comment on works of the former kind. As a name of the end of the historical colonial era, 'post-colonialism' is thus a misnomer. As we are well aware, the products of the mind and the spirit are even more resistant to change than governments are. We can therefore freely refer to philosophers who may indeed have started their theoretical work in the first half of the last century, but worked well beyond into the latter half; some indeed are very much still at work. This said, what is of as great interest, is the resistance to these colonial philosophies in the minds and in the practices of ordinary Indians. This resistance is of significance in that it reveals the extent to which 'philosophy' practised in this vein in our centers of higher learning has become irrelevant to the life of the nation.

This story of political oppression and intellectual hegemony is not without its lighter moments. We start with an anecdote which apart from enlivening the discussion also serves to encapsulate some of its major concerns. The celebrated missionary, Alexander Duff addresses a group of natives–heathens all—in 19th century India, in the hope that he will enable them to 'see the light.' Later in his diary, he recounts his frustrating experience thus:

> … tell the people that they must be regenerated or born again, else they can never 'see God.' Before you are aware, they may go away saying, 'Oh there is nothing new or strange here; our own *Shastras* tell us the same thing; we know and believe that we must be born again; it is our fate to be so…you vary your language, and tell them there must be a second birth—that they must be twice-born. Now it so happens that this and all similar phraseology is preoccupied. (Bhabha 1994: 33)

That was in 1839. A hundred years later, Britain had colonized not just the world, but the word as well. So acutely has the loss of language been felt worldwide, that it is a Frenchman–recall that France was only a step behind the British Isles in colonizing the non-Western world—who laments this loss with the words: "I hope to die before hearing only a single language in the world" (Serres 1989: 3).

Which language do the *śāstras* now speak? That is the big question today. If we venture an answer we would say: They speak in 'forked' tongues. To the '(*un*)educated populace at home,' the *śāstras* still speak in the language of tradition: No proof of this is required. But to the 'educated Indian' and (he/she has got to be Anglophone), they have been speaking and still do speak the language of Enlightenment, long after it has been subjected to every kind of critique and deconstruction in the lands of its origin.

The received view suggests that Indian philosophers of the colonial period pursued Indian philosophy in a manner both secular and modern which rendered it both accessible and acceptable to the Anglophone world abroad. Let me cite a specific argument to this effect. It goes thus: "The creative juxtaposition, and often fusion, of Indian and Western philosophy thus served several purposes at once. *First it enabled the legitimization of Indian philosophy as part of a global enterprise* (italics mine). Second, it provided a model for a secular Indian philosophy independent of the *maths*" (Bhushan and Garfield 2009: 144). The argument goes on to suggest that "in virtue of the infusion into India of Western ideas and models of academic life" this period "is enormously philosophically fecund." (Bhushan and Garfield 2009: ibid). Note here the seamless passage from 'fusion' to 'infusion' in the selfsame paragraph! ('Cross-fertilization' is also thrown in for good measure.) Note also how a millennia old gratified civilization found its legitimation at last!

The claims of secularization will be examined below. Let us analyze the claim of the globalization of Indian philosophy, more closely. In this context, we refer to an Anglophone philosopher *par excellence*, working at the turn of the 19th–20th century, Sarvepalli Radhakrishnan. In the introduction to his exegesis of the

Brahma Sūtra, Radhakrishnan conceded that his work "has grown out of vital urges and under the pressure of a concrete historical situation" (Halbfass 1990: 252). He adds: "For us Indians, a study of the Upaniṣads is essential if we are to preserve our national being and character" (Halbfass 1990: 531 fn 22). But in which 'language' was this to be done? Note that the connection Radhakrishnan makes between reading the Upaniṣads and national identity is a political one. However, as Halbfass notes

> ... he [Radhakrishnan] adapted himself to Western premises and expectations, and used Western concepts and terminology for his cross-cultural interpretation and reinterpretation ... he wants to show the concordance of the authoritative texts of Hinduism with exemplary expressions of Western religion and philosophy as well as the achievements of modern science. (Halbfass 1990: 252)

How does one understand this, not unique reaction to 'the pressures of a concrete historical situation'? Does it represent a culture of 'fusion'? Is it not more a sign of the overwhelming compulsions to conform to new norms, to a new sensibility that resulted, however, only in a slowly growing schizophrenia? Schizophrenia all round it would appear, as those who talk of fusion also refer to the 'double existence' of Indian philosophers of this period! (Bhushan and Garfield 2009: 152). Radhakrishnan himself puts a fine dissimulating gloss on his interpretations of various 'Hindu' texts: "Any system of thought should satisfy two basic requirements; it should state the truth and interpret it for each new generation" (Halbfass 1990: 531 fn 24). Tall order that—'accessible and acceptable'! As Nirmal Verma observes: "This movement of Indian intellectuals of the 19th century is usually called a 'movement of harmonization' (*samanvaya kā abhiyān*). It was an external and superficial harmonization, but also a very deceptive one..." (Verma 1976: 67).

13.2 Deceptive Harmonization

Not much has changed in this respect even today. We still operate in a state of near total intellectual dependence, straining to ensure that our own offerings are suffused with the latest theoretical language produced in the West. Thus, it is not a coincidence in the present view that as fashions changed in the European philosophical world, various schools of Indian thought became more visible in the country's academic institutions. In the phase of European Idealism, it was Vedānta that reigned supreme. Later in the time of Russell and Frege, Nyāya 'logic' was rediscovered; even later, during the phase of the 'linguistic turn' that Western philosophy underwent, the study of Pūrva Mimāmsa's rules of interpretation suddenly became very respectable (which hitherto they were emphatically not). With the rise of Marxism, the 'materialist' Carvāka also found his day in the sun. All this reinterpretation was performed in the 'analytic' mode. And although there were parallel explorations of Indian science texts that revived Indian chemistry, metallurgy, and medicine, there was an understandable clamor for the teaching of Western science in the universities.

The new theoretical languages could only be taught in one natural language. Thus, traditional texts were translated into 'acceptable' English. Why is this so? Classical Greek texts were indeed translated into English, but were they ever translated into 'acceptable' English? No one had to learn the Greek. Greek terms abound in Western scholars' writings, often in the original script, precisely where exact translations are not available, even in the writings of those that speak of the 'myth of origins.' Although it may have close to third world status today, Greece was *part* not a colony of Europe. A great deal of translation from the Greek had been undertaken during the European Renaissance; Europe was rediscovering *its* glorious past then. In similar vein, Latin, German, and even French terms were incorporated into the English language. The 'sheer authority ascribed to the origi-nals' has been remarked on by some historians.

This being said, a distinction needs to be made between our contemporary state of intellectual abdication and the compulsions arising from political subjugation under which 19th and early 20th century philosophers were working, conditions of humiliating pressure, the likes of which we do not experience today. They needed every stratagem, every ruse, at their disposal to save, even salvage the dignity of their heritage. They thus sought to make a distinction between the West's scientific and technological progress and hence material advantage which was undeniable and the spiritual progress and advantage of the East. In Vivekananda's words: "It is...fitting that when the Oriental wants to learn about machine making, he should sit at the feet of the Occidental and learn from him. When the Occidental wants to learn about the spirit, about God, about the soul, about the meaning and mystery of this universe, he must sit at the feet of the Orient to learn" (Halbfass 1990: 233). This feeling of superiority in the life of the spirit, no doubt animated by a reverse pride in what the foreigner did not possess, was further fueled by the fires of nationalism, but it was more an anguished cry of a deeply wounded civilization. And the panic is palpable.

Still this construct of the East's superiority in the world of the Spirit makes for interesting comparison with the West's own need to draw normative boundaries between itself and its colonies where (it made itself believe) it was performing a civi-lizing mission. This has been stressed in a number of works, since Said's *Orientalism* which perhaps first gave this thought articulation. In *Imagining India*, Ronald Inden has given this very sentiment voice when, in alluding to the colonial construct of an essence termed the 'Hindu mind', he cautions the (Western) reader, thus:

> Skepticism is especially prudent when we consider that orthodoxy is itself as much the product of the Anglo-German imagination and of its shifting desires in the nineteenth century. Among those was a wish to create a purely masculine, spiritual, transcendent Reason for itself...This construct implied its opposite, a feminine, visceral, immanent Imagination, one that remained ever necessary to Reason, but also always a threat to it. Without India to act upon, without a civilization in which this internal other could be externalized and worked upon, it is hard to see how our ancestors could have convinced themselves they had succeeded to the extent they did. (Inden 1990: 130) India of the Life Divine! India, the land of idolatry and superstition!

Such were the sentiments of the colonizer pitted against those of the colonized; what was the outcome? Clearly, the battle was unevenly joined: The colonizer held all the cards. Not the least important among these were the policies imposed for the dissemination of Western ideas of reason and the progress of civilization itself. After 1857, the doting Orientalist poring over ancient texts in Sanskrit and Persian gave way to the much harsher administrator, the General Committee of Public Instruction, the modernizer. "The age of chivalry had gone; that of sophisters, economists and calculators was to succeed" (Stokes 1989: 13). The colonizer was well aware of what he was up against: Numerous dispatches sent 'home' testify to this. Well thought out investigative strategies were put into play resulting in the decision to make available to the natives through translation, the narratives of modernity.

The age of enumeration, of positivity and of the universal, was finally inaugurated in India. How could this not cast a shadow on the interpretations of Indian theories of *pratyakṣa* (perception), of *anumāna*, of *pramāṇa* itself, (the means of acquiring *jñāna* (knowledge?), of *dharma*, the Waterloo of all translators! Only *śabda* as a *pramāṇa* remained an embarrassment for decades (for language as a means of *knowing*, is neither purely empirical nor truly rational) until it was accommodated in various revisionary moves in the latter half of the 20th century. J.N. Mohanty's interesting claim was that in fact no truths are learnt from it. Thus, "in this sense *śabda* (*śruti*) is not itself a *pramāṇa* but underlies their application. *Apauruṣeyaśrūti* is not the supreme *pramāṇa*, infallible and raised above the rest; it is rather the source of all those concerns and inquiries (not answers) in the solution of which the different *pramāṇa* exhibit their social and philosophical relevance"[1] (Mohanty 1989, 229). Indeed, as Michael Dodson remarks: "…particular strategies of translation can be viewed as a key mechanism through which Western concepts of progress through a civilizational hierarchy, at the top of which stood Britain, were authorized for Indian acceptance" (Dodson 2005: 810). A very good example of this claim is indeed witnessed by the slow, torturous but inevitable transformation of *dharma* into law in colonial India.

13.3 A Hybrid Monstrosity

In fact, a key (if not *the* key) concept that demonstrates the use of such strategies is that of *dharma*. Any attempt to offer an in-depth exposition of the fecundity of meaning that this term invokes would run into volumes. Here, we will touch on the question of *dharma* and its slow, torturous but inevitable transformation into the law that succeeded it, first in the very name of the *Dharmaśāstra* (which the British were desperate to master in the interest of governance) and then as with all other matters, in the name of the law, democracy, secularism, and what else have you. It was decided to extract the major tenets from the texts of 'Hindu Law' and then render them into English.

---

[1] There is a play on the word 'truths' here that permits this ingeniously creative but facile conclusion. The *śrūti* texts teach not 'what is the case' but delineate what 'ought to be done.'

This story has now been ably recounted by specialists in the history of the Indian Legal System. (Significantly, the *Dharmaśāstras* find no place in the numerous law schools of this country, not even as history.) Philosophers have paid less attention to the conceptual revolution that the 'strategies of translation' wrought in the thinking about and the practice of the resolution of disputes in Indian society. This translation took the form of two Digests prepared by *paṇḍits* at the behest of first Warren Hastings and later of William Jones: The *Vivādārṇavasetu* and the *Vivādabhangārṇava* composed by Jagannatha Tarkapancanana which were then translated into English by Colebrook. What had started out as a genuine search for the natives' legal system and the ancient Indian constitution (!) ended up with the imposition of a system built on a conceptual foundation in radical dissonance with the deep but complex grammar of an essentially non-normative *dharma*. It gave rise to a normative legalese that remained incomprehensible to those it was meant to serve and control. The result was a 'hybrid monstrosity' without parallel in the world (Derrett 1968: 298). The authority of localized, hence diverse, customary practices of *vyavahāra* and *ācāra* was sought to be replaced by a uniform case law: As we know, this effort only succeeded in rendering the traditional dharmic dispensation unwritten and informal as it was, more invisible, but not nonexistent, notwithstanding the illusions nurtured by the 'educated' classes. Thus, it is claimed that: "As state consolidation made strides, traditional forms of authority became even more limited in their sway… With traditional authority dropping out of the picture, in practice the sole recourse … was popular mobilization in some guise or other. Only democracy could fill the void" (Mehta 2004: 108).

Have traditional forms of authority 'dropped out of the picture'? Where then shall we place the *khap panchayats* of northern India? In what form was democracy internalized and appropriated? Here, let us also note that the vote bank, a uniquely Indian identitarian institution, is a far cry from the individualism that is the *sine qua non* of (at least) the theory of Western democracy. These are the real questions, they are questions of meaning, and they parallel the questions raised on the subject of the true nature of the *darśanas*.

However, there are important differences as well. Philosophy, as they say, bakes no bread; this cannot be said of the law. In the normative realm—unlike the dharmic dispensation of pre-colonial India—the prevailing notion of the 'right' directly regulates the realm of social action. The ascription of normativity to 'Hindu' law, and an accompanying rigidity in its application, created a situation that was untenable in the exercise of actual power and government. Contrary to Mehta's self-assured pronouncements that suggest that democracy neatly stepped in to fill the vacuum left by 'disappearing traditional authority,' the facts suggest otherwise. The legal system was manipulated, disregarded, and even openly flouted by an uncomprehending public in colonial India when Anglo-Indian Law was finally imposed in the name of the Empire and later drove a deep wedge between the educated elites and the man in the street or village dirt track. That this deep divide has not closed till the present is all too evident. To take just one intractable example, the battle surrounding the meaning of 'secularism' rages unabated to this day.

Although this is not the occasion to attempt an answer, the theme of secularity that accompanies the idea of democracy cannot go unremarked. Thus, when it is claimed that 'a steady respect for the proper autonomy of different spheres of human action' was soon in place, its implication is that, as if by magic, Indian legal practices became 'secular' just as philosophy did (Bhushan and Garfield 2009: 144). On this subject, I will permit myself just one observation. Secularism can only be defined against the backdrop of religion; thus, the primary question to be raised and answered is as follows: Is there such a thing as Hinduism and is it a religion? (*Dharma* figures here again.) Without prejudging the answer, over which now much ink is being spilt, it is still necessary to point to the Judaic–Christian origins of the very word 'religion' which has no counterpart in Sanskrit though it does now in modern Hindi and always had in Urdu. Wilfred Cantwell Smith minces no words when he labels the concept of religion as a clear and bounded historical phenomenon. Far from being a universal and self-evident category, "it is a distinctively western invention which has been exported to the rest of the world" (Smith 1967: 73). How then should we describe the practices of *dharma* in pre-colonial India that would lend any credibility to the claims that Indian philosophy became secular in colonial times as did its polity?

13.4 Discursive Dominance

Western discursive dominance was soon a reality. The conquest of India indeed was the conquest of language and of an epistemic space as much as it was conquest of territory. Some names like that of William Jones at one end and of Macaulay at the other stand out, but perhaps only in the collective memory of the nation's 'educated' classes; it is of utmost salience to stress the limited impact of this epistemic 'revolution' in Indian society as a whole and thus of the conquest itself. For almost no one speaks for the Indian masses.

The first translations carried out in the 19th century were from English into Urdu and only later into Sanskrit as debates among the 'educators' concluded that the way to the hearts of the Indian intelligentsia was through Sanskrit, not a vernacular. Further, the subjects of these translations were of scientific and 'other useful knowledge'; science was after all, the West's greatest gift to India at the time. Let me qualify this: Christianity also, but at another level. It is only much later in the very early part of the 20th century that need was felt—the ascendancy of English now no longer in question—to make available Indian classical texts in the English language. A more telling example of the power/knowledge nexus in representation would be hard to find. Could intervention be far behind?

The strategies that eventually triumphed were part of a process long in the making. They did not succeed straightaway. To brighten this account, here is another hilarious story. It was decided to translate the *First Book of Genesis* into Sanskrit to enlighten the natives. The first verse states that God created Heaven and Earth which were duly translated as *ākāśa* and *prithvi*. As we all know, these are only two of the five elements in the Nyāya-Vaiśeṣika system. So when in the next verse, it was stated that God's face appeared on the surface of the waters, the *paṇḍits* were "staggered by the doubt whether it is to be understood that the waters were *uncreated* or whether the sacred penman had created an oversight." The Bible contained a 'palpable contradiction' (Dodson 2005: 826).

We know the sequel. The resistance of the intelligentsia was finally worn down; the intractable *paṇḍits* were, by the early 20th century totally sidelined, confined to their *Pāthshālās* or the *Gūrūkūlas*, whatever, where to this day they remain. It is claimed that by the time the British began to rule over India, Sanskrit learning had become moribund, and the *paṇḍits* and their learning are now anachronisms. Some never acquired the English language and went into oblivion. Others, notably Pandit Ganganath Jha and Gopinath Kaviraj who translated classical texts into English, "became living symbols of the breadth and comprehensiveness of the Sanskrit tradition" (Halbfass 1990: 258). More pliable and receptive intellectuals were overwhelmed by the ideas of liberal individualism and secular citizenship. It has even been suggested that 'the intellectual class in India rushed to western philosophy as ducks to water' implying a deep elective affinity between such intellectuals and the Western ideals of the British (Mukherji 2002: 933). The circularity in defining the 'intellectual class' notwithstanding, there is a certain depressing truth with regard to 'rushing' in this blithe claim. Historians are less hesitant to call a spade a spade. For instance, Dipesh Chakrabarty minces no words: "… to Indians in the 1830s and 1840s to be a 'modern individual' was to become 'European'" (Chakrabarti 1992: 7). Impossible desires!

The Hindu College was established in Calcutta in January 1817 for the education in law, engineering, and drawing of the scions of the respectable *bhadralok* Hindu families. In a span of four decades, this teaching was expanded into India's first full-fledged university. Western knowledge was thus institutionalized, stamped with the authority of imperial ordinance. Traditional knowledge shrank further into the recesses and by-lanes of Banaras and Madras. Some of us, who have participated in the late Daya Krishna's attempts to restart a dialogue between the professors and the few remaining *paṇḍits* of traditional knowledge, are aware of the sad results. These worthies speak, if at all, from the margins of the philosophy establishment. The analyses of these results are revealing in more ways than one. Here, I would like to add my voice to Raghuramraju's 'call for serious introspection' into the causes of repeated failure in the *Saṁvād* efforts to create conditions conducive to dialogue. M.P. Rege's observation, as reported by Raghuramraju, that "they remain apart. There never was interplay of Western and Indian philosophical ideas" (Raju 2009) is at the heart of the larger thesis that the present essay seeks to underscore. The onus then is on those, who along with Bhushan and Garfield claim that there was cross-fertilization and fusion of ideas *during this period*, to give substance to the narrative that they wish to impose on the uninformed/unsuspecting reader and to explain the abject marginalization of traditional scholarship. (We stress 'this period' because there is a very real sense in which Gandhian thought *has* 'fertilized' if we wish, the notions of resistance, violence and nonviolence in the contemporary world.) Post-colonial talk of hybridity has failed to counter the conclusion that the worlds of which the *paṇḍits* and the philosophers spoke were and are, incommensurable. The rupture when it came had to be in the form of a complete displacement in the academy as it was set up.[2]

13.5 The Other Text

In an article titled *The Sudden Death of Sanskrit Knowledge*, Sudipto Kaviraj finds it remarkable that "… in the colonial setting, advancing systems of modern knowledge rejected traditional conceptions in a large range of cognitive fields without subjecting them to this [verificationist] procedure" (Kaviraj 2005: 133). For instance, "… Āyurvedic medicinal systems … were … rejected wholesale … i.e. ideologically." (Kaviraj 2005: 133). Kaviraj could at this point have taken a leaf out of Kuhn's book that he cites elsewhere to show that at times of radical change, of epistemological break—and this was just that sort of time—no dialogue *can* take place, no methodologies are adequate for the evaluation of systems that do not even share assumptions about what would constitute a refutation! There was literal incomprehension on all sides. There is certain poignancy in the following statement which we must take seriously today. "The Hindu text is unwritten at the moment of its colonial appropriation. Alternatively, there is a founding incommensurability from a European hermeneutical gaze, and hence Hindu writing is always invisible" (Bhatt 2002: 58). We are the inheritors of this epistemically violent course of events. How indeed could it be otherwise? Why would an imperial power seek to explore, beyond the demands of the practical concerns of governance, the strange cults of the heathens whose lands and its riches were now at their disposal? Understandably then, describing the colonial world as it then stabilized in India, the post-colonial critic Bhabha observes: "… the Other text is forever the exegetical horizon of difference, never the active agent of articulation … The Other loses its power to signify, to negate, to initiate its historic desires to establish its own institutions and oppositional discourse" (Bhabha 1994: 31).

Philosophers of the latter half of the 20th century have strained every nerve in their body to dispel the image of difference as an Orientalist myth. There is little doubt that a much needed correction has been made that has brought into focus classical India's unique contributions in the fields of theoretical grammar, philosophy of language, and theory of action, to name a few. But then, one must add that they have selectively mined the ancient texts in search of those elements that might be pertinent to issues that are of interest to Western philosophers. In a

---

[2] More recently, a very telling example of this divide is available in a review of a book by a twentieth century Indian philosopher Bimal Matilal, which is worth reproducing here. Referring to the claim made by Ganeri: "that he sought to bring classical India into the philosophical mainstream … that he attempted to create the means whereby different philosophers of different ages and societies may converse," Taber observes that judged by these standards, "Matilal certainly failed." "Contemporary analytic philosophy … has no reason to concern itself with Indian philosophy; … thank you very much!" (Taber 2005: 405) In all fairness, we must record that the review notes that Matilal's efforts "rescued the study of Indian philosophy from the seeming oblivion of historical-philological research." The question is with what consequences was this effort fraught?

volume published as late as 2009, one scholar in search of the 'nature of Indian philosophy' justifies at the outset, her choice of two major categories of Western philosophical thought: 'the two alternatives empiricism and rationalism [which] have dominated the scene ever since Parmenides,' in light of which she sets out to construct her account. In her words:

> … here as well, in order to determine the nature of Indian philosophy rather than indulging in free play of one's preferred choices, one may look for specific concepts, and in that case, *it would be natural to ask*, in what form or shape important Western concepts figure in Indian thought, which in turn would lead one to search for their Sanskrit equivalents. (Gupta 2009: 8, emphasis mine)

It does not take much imagination to anticipate the conclusions of a work as explicitly derivative as this: The conclusions are foregone. In the Introduction itself, the author stoutly maintains that "although Indian thinkers do not thematize about [sic] 'reason' per se, a conception of reason and a clear understanding of its various kinds is there" (Gupta 2009, 17). Later with a sense of relief, as it were, we are told that "[t]he case of 'experience' is more *promising…*" (Gupta 2009: 18, emphasis mine)—the promise of legitimation no doubt.

Now, the choice of reason and experience is a conservative—one might say— even dated one. One of the arguments of this essay is, however, that with newer colonial languages in place, new distortions have crept into the 'educated' Indian's account of Indian thought. These distortions have occurred, moreover, in the very process of making the desired corrections. The second argument of this essay pertaining to the more serious fallout of this entire way of 'doing Indian philosophy' is, that that which constitutes its unique vision of man, the world and the way out of human suffering, that which is most valuable in traditional Indian thought, being alien to the dominant Western world-view, is in real danger of being irretrievably lost to the intellectuals of this country.

To examine in some depth, the nature and extent of these distortions is a matter of great urgency for reasons I have indicated above. To repeat, we live in a very much more dangerous period of colonization today, for it is our minds that we stand to surrender. Gayatri Spivak was writing of thinkers of the classical colonial period when she said of the decades following Hegel's notorious reading of the *Bhagvad Gītā*: "In fact, a few decades later, the slow epistemic seduction of the culture of imperialism will produce modifications of the *Gītā* that argue for its world historical role in a spirit at least generically though not substantively 'Hegelian.' And these will come from Indian 'nationalists'" (Spivak 1999: 49). A slew of Indian Kantians and later, Hegelians as well, took over the academic culture of this country (to which this very volume bears testimony) before the wave of Marxism displaced them in the academy. The fact is that new epistemic seductions are constantly on the horizon. Alas, these are not the only seductions at work today.

Whereas philosophers of the 19th century were confronted with radically opposed world-views which challenged received wisdom and finally their self-confidence, we of the late 20th and 21st centuries have far less excuse for our undying allegiance to Western theory—which is itself a product of Western crises, intellectual and historical—(think of the depredations of two world wars, of the traumas wrought by the very knowledge of concentration camps in the land of Kant and Hegel, of the collective guilt of developing and then deploying the atomic bomb in a non-Western country). Interest in the sociology of knowledge is rare among philosophers; it is thus only to be expected that our sensitivity to difference has been submerged in our fascination with *différance*.

Now of course there is the entire gamut of theoretical 'posts-' following on post-modernism: post-structuralisms, post-colonialism, some have talked of post-orientalism, each with its own vocabulary and 'registers' of concern. Of these, the post-colonialist critics are at least directly concerned with understanding, interpreting, and representing the discourses of the colonial period and its aftermath. And it would be only just to explore what new vistas they may open up for us, what new horizons of meaning, in our deliberations. That would however become, and is, the subject of another study. Thus, it is only coincidentally that I turn to some remarks offered by Gayatri Spivak on the politics of translation.

13.6 The Politics of Translation

Spivak compares her translation work in Bengali with her well-known translation of Derrida (for which rather than work in Bengali she shot into the intellectual firmament) and observes: "The status of a language in the world is what one must consider when teasing out the politics of translation"[3] (Spivak 1993: 190–191). And because it is so to the point of the present discussion: "If you want to make the translated text accessible—(that word again) try doing it for the person who wrote it" (Spivak 1993: 190–191). Shades of Chomsky's native speaker! In the context of traditional knowledge, this demand becomes an impossible thought experiment with the 19th century native informant. Let us, however, not forget that there are *still* those traditional scholars who, even in the 20th century, when confronted with modern renderings of classical texts in the *Saṁvād* sessions, were at a loss to follow what was going on.

Now a large part of the contemporary work in and on translation has been done by literary theorists and critics (someone has uncharitably labeled them 'the minor philosophers of today')—Spivak belongs to this group—and they are naturally concerned with issues of the rhetoric as opposed to the logic of languages. Philosophers must however delve even deeper and examine the entire network of cognitive structures of a society's collective unconscious that brings language into play—or is it work—in a dialectical construction of meaning. At this level, it is the intimate, by which I mean the lived knowledge of the native speaker of the furniture of her/his

---

[3] Spivak who has herself translated Mahashweta Devi's work, writes of the politics of translation, and says of her own work: "I am able to say to her: I surrender to you in your writing, not to you as intending subject, for there are the *'protocols of the thing in front of me.'*" (italics mine). She gives the example of a translation of Devi's *Stanadāyini*, a story replete with the despair of a woman whose breast milk becomes a commodity in a relentless marketplace. One who cannot feel her helplessness translates the title accurately?—as 'Wet Nurse'; Spivak's own title is 'Breast Giver.'

world, not just any theoretical account of underlying ontological commitments that alone can certify the authenticity of a translated text and its representations.

We, however, address a very special subset of natives. Taking this into account, the example that follows is drawn from recent history of theoretical philosophy. On the vexed question of the importance of reason in classical Indian thought, Sibajiban Bhattacharyya notes: "In Indian philosophy, there does not seem to be any concept of faculty, and hence the concept of reason is not found" (Bhattacharyya 1987: 89). Arindam Chakrabarti, on the other hand, takes this bull by the horns. Some years ago, he began a seminar presentation with the words:

> You cannot say 'thank you' in Sanskrit. From this, it would be ridiculous to deduce that gratefulness as a sentiment was unknown to the ancient Indian people. It is no less ridiculous to argue that rationality as a concept is absent from or marginal to the entire panoply of classical Indian philosophical traditions on the basis of the fact that there is no exact Sanskrit equivalent of that word.[4]

Is it that ridiculous? Were the linguistic resources of Sanskrit so meager, its semiotic base so unstable that it could not, or cared not, to create a word for what in European thought is the central faculty that defines man as man, indeed for some, the teleological goal of human existence itself? More generally, can one accept without further discussion that in any effort to understand and then render the thought of a people in another language, the absence of an equivalent word or even group of words, in either one of these languages is insignificant? Should this fact not even give one pause? What is one claiming when one says for example that Urdu poetry is untranslatable? Certainly, the problems that arise in such contexts do not just 'pertain to the *accuracy* of translation.'

13.7 Conclusion

A word is necessary in conclusion of an essay that possibly comes across as overly, even unnecessarily, polemical. First, we must make clear that in rejecting the thesis of fusion and cross-fertilization, of dialogue and legitimation, the motivation of this essay is emphatically not a revivalist one. The arguments offered here are that such claims are simply (to use the most charitable term), historically

---

[4] Chakrabarti, Arindam, 'Rationality in Indian Philosophy.' This preoccupation with displaying the 'rationality' of Indian thought is demonstrated time and again in the writings of contemporary philosophers. Clearly, this is because its absence in the western sense is perceived as a *lack* of a primal feature of the 'human.' Here are a few examples: Ganeri's subtitle to his book on Classical Indian Philosophy: '*The Proper Work of Reason*'; *Mimāṃsā and the Ritual Roots of Moral Reason* and so on; Mohanty's *Reason and Tradition in Indian Thought*; Matilal's apologetics in an article '*Dharma* and Rationality,' to mention some works at random. This is at a time when the western obsession with rationality has been hauled over the coals in the countries of its origin. I am supporting my contention, by the following statement: "Using one's own reason in religious matters is one thing, and this is what the new philosophers did in India; spreading the lights of Reason is another thing and this was never an issue in India." (Zimmerman, 2008: 648).

inaccurate. Further, we have sought to show that the agenda underpinning this thesis of the universal ideal of 'rational' thought simply seeks to subsume Indian thought traditions under the rubric of mainstream Western philosophy for reasons that are intellectually spurious and unacceptable. It is time to return not only to the major texts of the great traditions but to discover those of the numerous lesser traditions that have remained largely unexplored, first in the Brahmanical and then in the colonial world.

Finally, this essay is motivated by a concern created by the fear of imminent and permanent loss of a world-view which with roots seemingly, otiose and moribund, still sways the lives of millions. To close the gap between contemporary scholarship and an internally differentiated, multi-hued but nevertheless coherent tradition (which for better or for worse, is *one's own*) is becoming a matter of some urgency. What is at stake here is the very survival of many Indian languages in which this thought tradition has been given varied expression down the centuries, an expression which remained largely oral. (One cannot and should not expect greater fixity in an originally oral tradition.) Such understanding alone can illuminate the problems faced by contemporary Indian society, its polity and its intellectual life. True, this can only now be done from the horizons of where we stand, at the beginning of the 21st century. That said, it is this very world-view that has demonstrated time and again, vast renewable energies of its own, and a surprising resilience through an embattled history.

References

Bhabha H. K. (1994). *The location of culture*. London: Routledge.
Bhattacharyya S. (1987). *Doubt, belief and knowledge*. Delhi: Indian Council of Philosophical Research.
Bhushan, N., & Garfield, J. (2009). Pandits and philosophers: The renaissance of secular India. *Journal of Indian Council of Philosophical Research, 26*(1), 141–159.
Chakrabarty, D. (1992). Postcoloniality and the artifice of history: Who speaks for India's pasts? *Representations, 37*, 1–26.
Chetan, B., & Being, P. (2002). Enlightenment and the Indian subject of post-colonial theory. In P. Osborne & S. Sanford (Eds.), *Philosophies of race and ethnicity*. New York.: Continuum Books.
Derrett, J. D. M. (1968). *Religion law and state in India*. London: Faber and Faber.
Dodson, M. (2005). Translating science, translating power. In *Comparative studies in history and society*.
Gupta, B. (2009). *Reason and experience in Indian philosophy*. New Delhi: Indian Council of Philosophical Research.
Halbfass, W. (1990). *India and Europe*. Delhi: Motilal Banarasidass.
Inden, R. (1990). *Imagining India*. Oxford: Basil Blackwell.
Kaviraj, S. (2005). The sudden death of Sanskrit knowledge. *Journal of Indian Philosophy, 33*, 119–142.
Mehta, P. B. (2004). Hinduism and self rule in world religion and democracy. *Journal of Democracy, 15*.
Mohanty, J. N. (1989). Indian philosophical tradition: The theory of Pramāṇa. In S. Biderman & B.A. Scharfstein (Eds.), *Rationality in question*. Leiden: E.J. Brill.
Mukherji, N. (2002). Academic philosophy in India. *Economic and Political Weekly, 37*(10), 931–936.

Raju, R. (2009). *Texts on sabbatical. Paper Presented at the International Conference on Philosophy in Colonial India*. University of Pune (unpublished).

Serres, M. (1989). Literature and the exact sciences. *Substance, 59*, 3–34.

Smith, W. C. (1967). *Questions of religious truth*. London: Victor Gollancz Ltd.

Spivak, G. C. (1993). *Outside in the teaching machine*. Routledge: New York.

Spivak, G. C. (1999). *A critique of post-colonial reason: Towards a history of the vanishing present*. Seagull.: Calcutta.

Spurr, D. (1993). *The rhetoric of empire: Colonial Discourse in Journalism, Travel Writing, and Imperial Administration*, Duke University Press.

Stokes, E. (1989). *The English utilitarians and India*. Delhi: Oxford University Press.

Taber, J. (2005). Review of the collected essays of Bimal Krishna Matilal. *Journal of the American Oriental Society, 125*(3).

Verma, N. (1976). *Śabda aur Smṛti*. Delhi: D.K. Publishers.

Zimmerman, F. (2008). Patterns of truthfulness, *Journal of Indian Philosophy, 36*, 643–650.

Index

A

Abhinav Bharat, 59
Abhinava Vedānta, 120
Abhyankar Kashinathshastri, 122
Absolute (The), 103, 113, 131
   and its relation to finite selves, 103
   as concrete universal, 112
   consciousness, 107
   (God) and its relation to Man, 103
   idea, 109
   idealism, 19, 105, 114, 120
   individual, 114
   mind, 111
   monism, 121
   personality, 112
   reason, 25, 88
   self, 110
   will, 107
Academy of Philosophy, Calcutta, 67
Āchārya-Kula, 14
Action *(karma)*, 97
Adharmaśāstra, 230
Adhikāra, 154
Adhikāri bheda, 154
Adhyātma-vidyā, 1
Adjectival expressions, 179, 186
Advaita, 19, 30, 198, 200
Advaitāmodsiddhi, 122
Advaita Vedānta, 87, 119, 120, 123, 126,
    133, 143
   as philosophy, 133
   as religion, 133
Advaitic world-view, 126
Aesthetic
   contemplation, 140

judgment, 148
   sentiments, 99
Affirmative action, 213
African thinkers, 149
Agarkar, Gopal Ganesh, 10, 200
Age of translation, 9
Agnosticism, 204
Agozino, 149
Ahitāgni, 196
Ajāti, 121
Ajñāna, 126, 127, 130
Ālaya vijñāna, 121
Alexander the Great, 205
Aligarh, 169, 182
Allahabad, 169
Allgemeine Geschichte der Philosophie, 120
All India Oriental Conference, 6
Althusser, Louis, 158
Amalner, 17, 124, 187
Amarkośa, 4
Anachronism, 30, 34, 247
Analytic philosophy, 24, 171, 175
Anātma-vāda, 133
Ancient
   Athens, 235
   Indian Constitution, 245
   Indian thought, 151
Āṅgleya-Chandrikā, 9
Anglo-American analytical philosophy, 42,
    43, 48
Anglo-German
   imagination, 243
   philosophy, 2
   world view, 239

© Indian Institute of Advanced Study 2015
S. Deshpande (ed.), *Philosophy in Colonial India*, Sophia Studies in Cross-cultural
Philosophy of Traditions and Cultures 11, DOI 10.1007/978-81-322-2223-1

Printed by Books on Demand, Germany